DOREEN HODGSON

Clipper®
Programming Guide

The DATA BASED ADVISOR® Series
Lance A. Leventhal, Ph.D., Series Director

Clipper®
Programming Guide

Rick Spence
Co-Developer of Clipper®

Microtrend Books ™

ISBN 0-915391-31-7

Library of Congress Catalog Card Number: 89-60505

Microtrend™ Books
165 Vallecitos de Oro
San Marcos, CA 92069

Cover Design by Lorri Maida
Interior Design by Dave Morgan, Slawson Communications, San Marcos, CA
Edited by Lance A. Leventhal, Ph.D., San Diego, CA

Printed in the United States

10 9 8 7 6 5 4 3

Contents

Foreword

The *Clipper Programming Guide* comes at a key time in Clipper's history. The current release marks Clipper's maturation from a useful tool to a complete development language. Clipper has reached a level of sophistication not found in other PC database systems.

This new level of programming requires an explanation. Rick Spence has taken on the formidable challenge of writing the definitive Clipper text. He takes a complex development language and provides step by step methods that help you build applications that no other database language can handle. He offers valuable programming tools and concepts to both novice and veteran Clipper users.

Rick contributed significantly to several Clipper versions and understands the elegance and complexity behind the language. Working with Rick for several years convinces me that no other author could explain Clipper so succinctly to database developers. He has the precise style and examples required to demonstrate Clipper's strengths: the ability to create sophisticated user interfaces, the database engine, and the unique open architecture through the extend system.

I feel fortunate that Rick joined our development team and through his experiences is able to bring the entire Clipper story to the database community.

Brian Russell
Nantucket Corporation
August 1988

About the Author

Rick Spence was a member of the Nantucket development team for three years and a co-developer of Clipper. He is the author of the monthly "Hardcore Clipper" column in *Data Based Advisor* and a monthly expert columnist in *Reference (Clipper)* magazine. He has worked on many Clipper and dBASE applications with Nantucket, Tom Rettig and Associates, MCI, Teksoft, and Fidelio Software.

Before starting with Nantucket Corporation in 1985, Mr. Spence worked for Burroughs machines (Scotland), and Computer Technology (England), Tycom Corporation (England), and Corona Data Systems. He has extensive experience in C programming, 8086 assembly language programming, I/O device drivers, operating system development, multiuser and multitasking systems, dBASE programming, networked applications, and Xenix. He received a Bachelor of Science degree with Honors in Computer Science from the University of Manchester (England).

Mr. Spence is currently employed by Software Design Consultants in Munich, West Germany. He is also working on an advanced data-based management book which will be announced in the near future.

About the Series Director

Lance A. Leventhal is the author of 25 books, including *80386 Programming Guide*, *68000 Assembly Language Programming*, *6502 Assembly Language Programming*, and *Microcomputer Experimentation with the IBM PC*. His books have sold over 1,000,000 copies and have been translated into many foreign languages. He has also helped develop microprocessor-based systems and has served as a consultant for Disney, Intel, NASA, NCR, and Rockwell.

Dr. Leventhal served as Series Editor on Personal Computing for Prentice-Hall and as Technical Editor for the Society for Computer Simulation. He has lectured throughout the United States on microprocessors for the IEEE, IEEE Computer Society, and other groups.

Dr. Leventhal's background includes affiliations with Linkabit Corporation, Intelcom Rad Tech, Naval Electronics Laboratory Center, and Harry Diamond Laboratories. He received a B.A. degree from Washington University (St. Louis, MO) and M.S. and Ph.D. degrees from University of California, San Diego. He is a member of the AAAI, ACM, ASEE, IEEE, IEEE Computer Society, and SCS.

Preface

This book is about programming in Clipper. Through practical examples, it shows how to use Clipper extensions to the dBASE III language, and how to use the base language more efficiently.

It is aimed at two audiences: those now programming in Clipper who want to use it more efficiently, and those programming in dBASE III PLUS who are considering moving to a compiler. Both will find the book a mine of useful information, full of tips to make your applications excel, usually with little programming effort. Clipper's extensions make producing sophisticated applications simpler than ever.

The Clipper novice will learn how to use arrays, the memoeditor, DBEDIT, and ACHOICE, to name a few features. The advanced user will learn how to interface a mouse to MENU/PROMPT, how to process file structures directly from C, how to write generic code, and how to create robust network applications.

Although it covers basics, the book is an advanced guide. It assumes that the reader has a working knowledge of dBASE III PLUS commands in program mode.

The book does not duplicate the Clipper manual; it is all new material. It is not based on long programs - each chapter covers one subject in depth, and can be read separately.

After mastering this book, you should consider yourself a Clipper expert. You will realise that you can program almost anything in Clipper. We show examples ranging from pulldown menus and database queries to controlling a PBX and interfacing a mouse.

To me, the power of Clipper comes from three main sources:

- The simple and efficient way in which one can program sophisticated user interfaces
- The powerful and flexible database engine
- The open architecture of the extend system

They allow speedy development of sophisticated database applications.

Being a C programmer, my concern about using Clipper to develop serious applications was a fear of reaching the language's limits. The Summer '87 release has extended the limits greatly. If you cannot do something with Clipper, switch to C. You can still use Clipper's poweful user interface and database processing commands, but you now have the flexibility of low level machine code. An example is a system I wrote for controlling a PBX in a hotel. 95 percent of the code is Clipper. C is used only to control the serial port. The C part puts call records into a database; the Clipper part produces the reports and handles the user interface.

Here is a chapter by chapter description of the topics covered in this book.

Chapter 1 covers compilation and linking. It shows several ways to organize programs for efficient compilation. It also shows how to use the make program to streamline the process. It ends with several case studies of installed Clipper applications.

Chapter 2 discusses Clipper's new error handler, similar to that of the Ada language. Programs need no longer die an inelegant death. Better an elegant one with a complete autopsy, don't you think? Chapter 2 also covers parameter passing, defining call by value and reference, variable scope, and evaluation of conditional expressions. An understanding of these subjects, the backbone of any programming language, is essential. Read this chapter first.

Chapter 3 describes arrays. These little understood matrixes act like memory-based data tables that you can create, fill, and use on the fly to speed up programs.

Clipper's context sensitive help is only one use of the generic SET KEY TO command, described in Chapter 4. It allows program execution to be interrupted at any point and directed to another procedure.

New functions and commands make pop-up windowing and bounce-bar menus simple to create. Browsing databases has never been easier. See Chapters 5 and 6 for a comprehensive description of user interfaces.

The extensible MEMOEDIT function provides full featured text processing, activated by just a few lines of Clipper code. See Chapter 7 for details on programming this built-in WordStar-like editor.

Chapter 8 covers database handling, the backbone of Clipper. It discusses multiple relations, alias functions, and query performance analysis. It includes a comprehensive set of examples.

The ability to directly access and process files in any format has long been a request of the serious applications programmer. Those who know C often resorted to it, using Clipper's extend system as an interface. With the Summer '87 release, Nantucket provides a set of functions, almost identical to the C functions, to do the same tasks. Chapter 9 describes them.

Chapter 10 discusses the problems encountered in networking. Although the chapter may seem negative, always pointing out problems, I think this is the best approach. It is relatively simple to adapt a single user system to conform to Clipper's file and record locking rules. But to make it work correctly, on a network with high traffic and the potential for data corruption and loss, you must take the what if approach. This chapter shows you how to use worst case analysis to uncover potential problem areas. It also provides solutions.

Chapter 11, which I think is the highlight of the book, discusses using C with Clipper. This link with the outside world is essential for the advanced programmer. If during the development of an application, you reach one of Clipper's limits, you can use C code to get complete machine control. Choosing the examples for this chapter was difficult, as the potential is so enormous. I included the save and restore state functions because many applications require them. I included the mouse code because of the increased importance of mice - besides, it's fun to program. You can extend the routines in many ways. I included serial communications because it provides access to the outside world. It allows many external devices to be interfaced to your database program. These are just a few examples of what you can do with C. The chapter also shows you how to get data into and out of Clipper, and how to debug ill-behaved routines.

Chapter 12 on file structures presents a byte by byte analysis of all dBASE/Clipper files. I know of no other source of this information. The chapter develops utilities in C to display the contents of the files, and to process them in a variety of ways. Examples include a pack routine for memo files and a database create routine. The chapter also develops Clipper callable routines to change the name and type of any field in the database.

Appendix A discusses using a preprocessor with Clipper. A preprocessor runs before the compiler, processing the program file based on directives.

Appendix B lists the C code for a set of functions that return the status of Clipper's internal SETs (EXACT, CURSOR, etc.). These are described in Chapter 11.

Appendix C shows Clipper code to emulate GET/READ in a way that can be nested. This allows a hot key procedure, or a VALID, to issue another READ, a feature missing from Clipper. By applying one GET at a time, and using the READ command, the code runs as fast as the Clipper GET/READ command.

Using The Book

Read the chapters in any order you want. I strongly suggest starting with Chapter 2. After that, choose the areas that interest you. The chapters are as self-contained as possible, but direct you to material in other chapters when absolutely necessary.

This book contains a lot of code, all high-quality and well-tested. However, the possibility exists of the editor or publisher introducing errors. The author, of course, is faultless and produces perfect code. Fortunately, you can get the author's versions and save hours of typing by buying a disk of the programs. Contact the publisher or see the ordering information elsewhere in the book.

This book should help you create exciting new applications with Clipper. Remember what Samuel Eliot Morison wrote about its namesake (*The Oxford History of the American People*, ch. 36). "These Clipper ships of the early 1850's were built of wood in shipyards from Rockland in Maine to Baltimore. These architects, like poets who transmute nature's message into song, obeyed what wind and wave had taught them, to create the noblest of all sailing vessels, and the most beautiful creations of man in America."

Acknowledgements

This book has taken a long time to complete. Much longer than I, my wife, the Editor, or the publisher expected. The fact that I can write this acknowledgement means it's finally finished, and I'm heading for one of Munich's fine beer gardens.

Thanks are due to several people. Alan Mulquinn, sadly no longer with us, had the idea for the book. Indeed, it was he who convinced me to co-author it with him. Illness prevented Alan from completing it, but he is largely responsible for the layout, and for Chapters 3 and 9.

Lance Leventhal, the Editor, did a marvelous job of translating my pidgin English into barely intelligible American. His humorous approach to editing helped soften the blows!

Thanks to Janet Lunn at Data Based Solutions for facilitating the joint publication of the book through Slawson Communications and Data Based Advisor.

Thanks to Brian Russell for his encouragement and support in the early stages of the project when I worked at Nantucket.

Thanks to Joel Avni of Systems Ink., Tom Leylan of the Leylan Factor, and David Lehrer of Fidelio Software for helping with various Chapters and reviewing parts of the manuscript.

Thanks to my wife Laurell for proofreading and negotiating the project with Data Based Solutions. A very special person indeed.

1

Overview

This chapter provides an overview of Clipper. It discusses the differences between interpreters and compilers, and their effects on program construction. The Chapter also describes Clipper extensions to the original dBASE III language.

Interpreters and Compilers

As most of you probably know, dBASE III Plus is an interpreter, whereas Clipper is a compiler. Both follow directions written in a shared language and stored in program (PRG) files. Each time an application executes, dBASE translates instructions into a form the computer can understand. It does this one line at a time. This provides flexibility when you are developing a program and it is changing frequently. Once the program is working and no longer being modified, however, speed of execution becomes an issue. An interpreter is slow because of the continuing need to translate instructions each time.

Clipper, on the other hand, examines the instructions only once. It translates the original dBASE instructions from the source PRG file into a machine-readable object (OBJ) file. The intermediate format is then linked, either alone or with other object files derived from code written in Clipper, C, or assembly language, into an executable (EXE) file. The EXE file should run on any DOS machine, without either dBASE or Clipper being present.

The program that does the linking is called (cleverly!) a linker. Clipper includes a modified version of Phoenix Technologies' Plink86 (pronounced "pee link") linker. Plink86 is relatively slow, but quite versatile. Unlike many linkers, it can divide large applications into smaller modules, called *overlays*. The division lets you execute programs considerably larger than the available memory in your computer by swapping code during execution.

If you do not need overlays, you may want to use DOS' Link. It is faster than Plink86. Tlink, which is packaged with Borland compilers, is even faster. Either works with Clipper object modules, but remember that each uses its own syntax to actually link files.

One thing you will notice about an executable file is that it is big, often very big. Another thing is that it runs fast. The executable program consists of low-level machine instructions. Stripped of the overhead imposed by translation and fine tuned by Clipper and the linker, compiled programs run much faster than their interpreted counterparts. Furthermore, executable files encrypt the source code into a binary form almost impossible for a human to decipher. Your program is thus safe from prying eyes.

Programs have a way of growing, so no matter how you manage memory, a time will surely come when you do not have enough. As mentioned, Plink86 provides overlays that allow programs to be larger than the available memory. The Summer '87 manual provides adequate documentation for you to undertake overlays with confidence.

You may store overlays in OVL files for distribution as separate modules, or you may append them to the executable file. Either method works, although it can be puzzling to see an EXE file expand beyond 640K. The computer determines which part is loaded as the main program. It will only load the overlays when needed.

Let us now consider the two new steps in producing a compiled program: compilation and linking.

Compilation

You can easily compile simple applications from Clipper's command line. Just give the compiler the program's name, and it automatically includes all PRG files the program calls with the DO command.

For example, suppose a program ACCOUNTS calls subprograms SCREEN and REPORT with DO commands. Then

```
Clipper ACCOUNTS
```

will compile SCREEN and REPORT as well as ACCOUNTS itself. The compiler produces the file ACCOUNTS.OBJ in the current directory. If it cannot find a subprogram there, it reports the error "cannot open, assumed external" and continues processing.

When a program calls procedures or user-defined functions from another file, you tell the compiler where to find them with the SET PROCEDURE TO command. The compiler reads the file and compiles it as if it were included. Unlike the dBASE interpreter, Clipper need not be explicitly directed to procedures within a file. The SET PROCEDURE TO command has no effect at run time.

You can use command line switches to control the compiler, such as:

- The -m switch tells Clipper to compile only the named file. Thus invoking the compiler with:

  ```
  clipper ACCOUNTS -m
  ```

  will produce an OBJ file of ACCOUNTS, ignoring SCREEN and REPORT. You can compile them separately, then pass all OBJ files to the linker which then creates the executable file.

- If you compile programs in different subdirectories, invoke Clipper with the -o switch to create object files in a specified subdirectory. The command

```
clipper ACCOUNTS -m -o d:\objdir
```

adds ACCOUNTS.OBJ to a directory you use for linking, here D:\objdir.

- The -s switch checks syntax without producing an object file.
- The -l switch omits line numbers from the compiled code. This saves three bytes for each line containing a command, but should only be used after debugging. The compiler reports errors by line number, and the debugger needs the numbers to track and report its place in a procedure.
- The -t option puts the temporary file Clipper creates on a RAM disk, which can reduce compile time considerably. The instruction

  ```
  clipper ACCOUNTS -t d:
  ```

  uses drive D for the housekeeping file.

Clipper also lets you compile a group of programs together by explicitly naming each in a batch-type CLP file. Tell Clipper you are calling a CLP file by preceding its name with an @ (at symbol). For example, create the ASCII file COMP.CLP consisting of the two lines:

```
ACCOUNTS
REPORT
```

and compile it with the command

```
clipper @COMP
```

This will produce the file COMP.OBJ.

The compiler acts as though you were compiling each file with the -m option. The resulting object file does not include the instructions in the third program, SCREEN.PRG. This technique is useful when building a program from separate modules, such as with overlays, or when condensing a large program that uses more variables or constants than the compiler can handle in a single session. The linker can combine modules later.

Linking

The linker, or linkage editor, combines object files into an executable program in an EXE file.

The Plink86 supplied with Clipper is a modified version. It is tailored to Nantucket's use in that it automatically links CLIPPER.LIB.

Tlink and Link use the same command line format. The OBJ files come first, the EXE file next, then the MAP file, and finally the library files. Defaults are assumed for the EXE file and MAP file, but the Clipper library must be specified. Assuming that the files accounts.obj, report.obj, and screen.obj are already created, the following link line creates acct.exe, using the Microsoft linker:

```
link accounts report screen,acct,,\clipper\clipper
```

Tlink's syntax is the same.

If you use functions from the extend library, you must specify it, as in:

```
link accounts report screen,acct,,\clipper\clipper \clipper\extend
```

Plink86 requires a different format. Three commands provide most of the information it needs: files, which informs it which object files to process; library, which directs it to libraries the application may call; and output, the name of the executable file if it differs from the first object file. You may abbreviate these commands as fi, lib, and out. They also provide exactly the information the other two linkers require.

You can use Plink86 by typing its name at the DOS prompt. This brings up the = prompt, from which you can enter files, libraries, and output. Usually it is easier to call the linker by explicitly listing the required object files and libraries on the command line. To link the one object module accounts, assuming that it contains report and screen, issue the following command:

```
Plink86 file ACCOUNTS library EXTEND
```

This links the file ACCOUNTS.OBJ with the default CLIPPER.LIB, as well as EXTEND.LIB, into the file ACCOUNTS.EXE.

The command

```
Plink86 out ACCT fi ACCOUNTS lib EXTEND
```

would produce the file ACCT.EXE.

Most programmers keep all object files for an application in a single subdirectory. As with the compiler, this is usually the most convenient place to work if you include Plink's directory in the DOS path.

Plink86 recognizes paths in filenames. It looks for object and library files in paths identified by the DOS environment variable OBJ. For example, the DOS command

```
SET OBJ=\OBJS;\CLIPPER
```

tells Plink86 to search the directories \OBJS and \CLIPPER if it cannot find an OBJ file in the current directory. This makes it much easier to store object code and libraries in appropriate subdirectories.

As the list of instructions grows longer and more complex, and you repeat it during development and debugging, you will surely want to combine the linker directives in a LNK file, Plink's equivalent of the compiler's CLP file. This is the preferred way to link overlays.

For example, create the file ACCOUNTS.LNK:

```
fi ACCOUNTS
out ACCT
lib EXTEND
```

You can then call it with the command

```
Plink86 @ACCOUNTS
```

The Nantucket documentation describes the use of PLINK86 to create overlays.

Libraries

A library file is a convenient place to store commonly used routines. It basically consists of OBJ files and an index. The index specifies which routines each OBJ file defines. Storing OBJ files in a LIB file has the major advantage that, unless one of the OBJ file's routines is accessed, it is not included in the EXE. When it is, however, the linker includes the OBJ file, and any routines that it references. This is why commercial libraries, such as Tom Rettig's, consist of many small OBJ files. Accessing a function from the library causes only its OBJ (and any it may call) to be linked, saving space.

The LIB utility provided with Microsoft products allows programmers to build their own libraries. You can put many Clipper produced OBJs in a single, convenient LIB file. This is recommended programming practice.

As you know, CLIPPER.LIB is a library file. It contains several OBJ files, each of which does a group of related functions. There is one for indexing, one for networking, one for sorting, etc. Now you may ask, given this division, why does a one line statement such as:

```
x=1
```

generate a 160K file? Why doesn't Clipper produce an EXE file with just the required modules? This is a difficult question to answer. First, our example is contrived. Clipper is a serious database programming language, and even the simplest program will at least use a database. That means it needs the database processing and probably the indexing code. These routines need access to Clipper's internal stack handling and memory management code. That's four major pieces of code right there. Furthermore, assume an expression uses a macro. The compiler has no way of knowing which functions the program might access when it executes, so it must link all of them. A real program then includes most of the code, unlike trivial programs that count to 10. To write trivia, use BASIC instead.

However, Clipper undoubtedly could do better in limiting the size of its EXE files. A flag indicating that macro expansions did not call functions, or requiring you to define with EXTERNAL all built in functions not explicitly referenced would help. In the real world, when used with real applications, the program size is not bad. After the initial 160K or so overhead, additions cause relatively small increases in program size. Besides, what's a little memory in today's multimegabyte world?

The Clipper library ensures that most of its modules are linked, even though the OBJ may not explicitly reference any code or data in it. It does this by including a reference in every OBJ to a data area inside CLIPPER.LIB that references all required OBJ files in the library file. A little known fact about Clipper is that it excludes some OBJ files from the EXE file if they are not required. For example, it does not include the code for SORT (contained in one OBJ), if that verb is not used. Similarly, it does not include the code for REPORT and LABEL FORM (combined as one OBJ) if the program does not use them.

EXTERNAL

Clipper stores in each OBJ file the names of all procedures and functions that the PRG calls, but which it does not define. These are known as 'external references'. The linker ensures that all such references exist in the files it is processing. They may be in libraries or other OBJ files. If any external reference is not resolved, the linker reports an error.

Sometimes a procedure or function may be invoked without the compiler's knowledge. This can be the result of a macro expansion, or its naming in either a REPORT or a LABEL FORM. Since the compiler does not know the function is being called, it cannot produce an external reference for it. Thus, the linker does not guarantee its existence in the resulting EXE file. A subsequent call of a routine not present in the EXE file will produce a particularly unpleasant run time error. If the routines are in an OBJ file, the programmer can explicitly provide it to the linker. If it is a separate OBJ in a LIB file, however, there must be an explicit method of generating an external definition symbol. The EXTERNAL statement does just that.

Use EXTERNAL to define routines invoked through a macro expansion or from a REPORT or LABEL FORM, that would not otherwise be linked. The most common examples are the functions in extend.lib, such as HARDCR. FRM files often use HARDCR. You must declare it EXTERNAL if you do not use it explicitly elsewhere in the program.

Using Make

Summer '87 compiles much faster than previous versions of Clipper, but recompiling and relinking an entire application repeatedly can take a lot of time. Most strategies to solve this problem rely on the fact that typically one changes only a few modules at a time. Only these must be recompiled.

The Make utility included in the Summer '87 package allows the developer to devise a routine that traces the dates and times of all files involved in an application. Only ones that have been changed will be recompiled or linked. Tracing updated modules can be tedious without a Make utility.

Clipper's sophisticated version resembles the Make that

accompanies Microsoft languages. However, anyone familiar with the like named Borland or Unix utilities will have little difficulty learning the program.

The utility works by using a concept of dependencies; an object file depends on particular source files, and an executable file depends on certain object and library files. These dependencies are stored in a response file, which also lists rules to follow if the targets are dated earlier than their dependents.

If any dependent source files are dated later then their target object files, they must be recompiled according to the defined rules; similarly, dependent object or library files stored later than their target executable files must be relinked following their rules. We could write a make file for the sample system used in this chapter as:

```
accounts.obj: accounts.prg
    clipper accounts -m

screen.obj: screen.prg
    clipper screen -m

report.obj: report.prg
    clipper report -m

accts.exe: accounts.obj screen.obj report.obj
    link accounts screen report,accts,,\clipper\clipper \clipper\extend
```

The first rule states that accounts.obj depends on accounts.prg. The command to be executed if the PRG file is newer than the OBJ is:

```
clipper accounts -m
```

The next two rules give the same information for screen.prg and report.prg.

The fourth and final rule states that accts.exe depends on accounts.obj, screen.obj, and report.obj. If any of these OBJ files is more recent than accts.exe, the command:

```
link accounts screen report,accts,,\clipper\clipper \clipper\extend
```

is invoked.

Refer to the well written Nantucket documentation on Make. We strongly suggest that you invest the time required to master its use. You will find it to be highly worthwhile.

The Clipper Package

The Clipper package now has a rich set of tools to solve almost any database problem, as well as an elaborate set of hooks for modules written in other languages. If you need a command, write it. That's what Clipper is for and what this book will help you do.

Here are the tools you receive from Nantucket in the Summer '87 version, released early in 1988.

Disk One, the heart of the package, contains Clipper.exe, the compiler, and Plink86.exe, the standard linker. Then come the tools: debug.obj, the debugger; extend.lib, the compendium that holds most of Clipper's new features; and overlay.lib, which lets you divide enormous programs into merely huge sections. Clipper has a long history of burying some of its best tools in obscure disk files. Pore through the imploring READ_ME.1ST; it is the map to the entire trove of new features.

Clipper.lib, the library of standard features, is the only file every Clipper-compiled application must see at link time. It occupies most of Disk Two. Two important tools on the disk are me.prg, the source code for the Wordstar-like editor, and ndx.obj, for those who choose to work with the slower, dBASE-compatible indexes.

Disk Three contains three powerful new Clipper utilities: DBU, the all-purpose database manipulator; RL, a report form and label editor; and SWITCH, a program that chains executable modules together.

Disk Four is not the general wasteland you expect when you first see the directory of PRGs scroll on and on. Addendum.doc lists most new or improved functions that, as usual, did not quite make it into the current documentation. Please read this file.

The rest of the disk is rich with useful programs, procedures, and functions that demonstrate advanced programming techniques in Clipper.

Case Histories

Now that we have covered the basics, but before we delve into the details, here are some brief case studies of applications.

Case Study 1

Among the many systems developed by The Leylan Factor (Hollywood, CA) is one called the Submission Reporting System. Written for a large firm in the entertainment industry, the program keeps track of and reports on the hundreds of scripts and books received for review each month.

Particularly interesting are the 'locate' and 'range' modules which provide a menu-driven method for searching by, and reporting on, any field or group of fields for any condition.

Case Study 2

SourceMate Information Systems (Mill Valley, CA) produces a multi-user accounting system called AccountMate. It is written in dBASE III Plus, but can be compiled with Clipper. SourceMate provide the source code for the system, so the user can tailor it to his or her own needs.

The software is available in modules, including General Ledger, Accounts Receivable, Accounts Payable, and Payroll.

Case Study 3

Fidelio Software (Munich, West Germany) has a hotel package written in Clipper. It is installed in over 50 hotels in Europe. Fidelio's approach is to make everything user definable - even the language! This is done by an installation program that sets up a data dictionary and a configuration file. The application does not even know what fields are in the databases - the data dictionary defines them.

The package has an interface to a PBX for call accounting, and to cash registers located in the hotel's restaurants and bars. A dedicated communications server, running under the Novell network, handles the interfaces. The communications code is a combination of C, Clipper, and assembly language, interfacing to a database on the Novell server.

Fidelio offers a graphics package that runs on CGA, EGA, and VGA systems, using one of the popular Clipper add-on products.

Case Study 4

Redken Laboratories (Canoga Park, CA) uses a Clipper program on portable computers for their salespeople in the field. Every night, the portables download sales and customer information from MCI Mail, and update their local databases. Another Clipper program, running at the company's headquarters, sends the information, downloaded from a mainframe, into MCI Mail. The software splits the information as required, sending to each salesperson only the information concerning his or her customers.

Case Study 5

Techsoft (Bermuda Dunes, CA) uses a sophisticated Clipper program to maintain an electronic storage system. The system combines a high resolution screen with an optical disk drive, laser printer, and scanner, to allow documents to be scanned, saved on the optical disk drive, and retrieved at will.

Techsoft has rewritten the Clipper drivers so they can be used in a window on the high resolution screen, with the rest of the screen being used to display the document.

The device drivers, written in C and assembly language, interface with the controlling Clipper program through the extend system. The Clipper databases are used to index the images on the optical disk drive.

Summary

This Chapter has provided an overview of Clipper. It discussed compilation and linking, the Clipper package, and some case histories. Now, if you're ready for some advanced Clipper, turn the page!

2

The Clipper Language and Environment

This chapter covers the basic features of the Clipper language. It is background material for the rest of the book. An understanding of the subjects covered here is necessary to appreciate the other chapters.

Clipper novices should read the entire chapter in detail. More experienced users may want to skim sections to find areas of interest, or ones where they need a review.

Basics

! symbol

In Clipper, you can use the ! symbol instead of the .NOT. operator. For example, you can write

```
DO WHILE !eof( )
```

instead of

```
DO WHILE .NOT. eof( )
```

You can also use ! in the "not equal" operator !=. For example, you can use

```
DO WHILE x != 10
```

instead of

```
DO WHILE x <> 10
```

== symbol

Clipper uses the == (equality) operator to force an EXACT comparison. The result is the same as having SET EXACT ON. For example,

```
name = "Hetherington"
? name = "Hether"

? name == "Hether"

SET EXACT ON

? name = "Hether"
```

produces:

```
.T.
.F.
.F.
```

Because EXACT is OFF, the first expression is .T.. The second one does an EXACT comparison (forced by ==), so it returns .F.. The third one also does an EXACT comparison, as EXACT is now ON.

FOR NEXT

Clipper has a FOR NEXT loop, much like the ones in C, BASIC, and Pascal. It repeats a set of statements a fixed number of times, automatically initializing and incrementing the loop variable. For example,

```
FOR i = 1 TO 10
      •
      •
      •
NEXT
```

is the same as

```
i = 1
DO WHILE i <= 10
      •
      •
      •
      i = i + 1
ENDDO
```

The FOR loop is the best way to repeat a code section a fixed number of times. It uses less code, is easier to read, and runs faster.

The FOR command has a STEP option. It specifies the step in the loop control variable for each iteration.

An EXIT command inside the loop forces an immediate exit.

Looping

Clipper always re-evaluates the loop condition. You should therefore avoid using a complex expression or function call whose result does not change as the loop's limit. A common mistake, for example, is to write:

```
FOR i = 1 TO fcount( )

NEXT
```

If FCOUNT returns the same value on every iteration, the re-evaluations waste a lot of time. It is better to write:

```
num_fields = fcount( )

FOR i = 1 TO num_fields

NEXT
```

The same applies to WHILE loops, of course.

RULE

Clipper re-evaluates the loop condition on every iteration.

dBASE programmers often take the following approach to constructing loops:

```
DO WHILE .T.

     •
     •

     IF some_condition
          EXIT
     ENDIF
     •
     •

ENDDO
```

This is probably the fastest way to write the code. You don't have to determine the extent of the loop in advance. It is also the hardest to read and the least maintainable. To analyze the loop, you must read the entire block and figure out what causes it to exit. It is MUCH better to write:

```
some_condition = .F.
DO WHILE !some_condition


     some_condition = ...
ENDDO
```

WARNING

DO WHILE .T. loops are difficult to understand and maintain.

Now you can clearly see what the loop does at its head.

ELSEIF

The Summer '87 release introduced an ELSEIF option to the IF statement. By combining IF and ELSE statements, it saves the programmer from having to include a full IF ENDIF block inside an ELSE clause. For example, you can write:

```
IF x = 1
     •
     •
ELSEIF x = 2
     •
     •
ENDIF
```

instead of:

```
IF x = 1

     •
     •

ELSE
     IF x = 2

     •
     •

     ENDIF
ENDIF
```

This makes the code easier to read, as there is less nesting. However, you should only use it to two or three levels. Beyond that depth, a DO CASE is preferable.

( ) for File Names

Clipper lets you put a file name expression in parentheses, instead of using a macro. You can write:

```
USE (test)
```

instead of:

```
USE &test
```

The code will run faster. You can use ( ) anywhere a file name is required.

Macros

Clipper puts many restrictions on the macro operator. It only allows an expression in the macro string, not a command. For example, the following is correct:

```
mac = "a + b * c"
? &mac
```

but this is not:

```
mac = "LIST x"
&mac
```

The macro string may not contain a comma. The following, for example, generates an error:

```
fields = "name1, name2"
LIST &fields
```

Another limitation is that you may not apply the macro operator directly to a function result. For example:

```
f = &fieldname(1)
```

will fail. Instead, first save the result in a memory variable, as in:

```
fname = fieldname(1)
f = &fname
```

See Chapter 3 for a discussion of arrays and macros.

Variable number of parameters

Clipper lets you pass a variable number of parameters to procedures and user defined functions. The PCOUNT( ) function returns the number passed. You can check whether a particular one was passed by comparing its type to "U".

To make a routine accept a variable number of parameters, define the formal list with the maximum number. For example:

```
* test accepts up to 7 parameters.

PROCEDURE test

PARAM p1, p2, p3, p4, p5, p6, p7
PRIVATE num_params
```

```
num_params = pcount( )

DO CASE
      CASE num_params = 1
            * process one parameter

      CASE num_params = 2
            * process two parameters

      CASE num_params = 3
            * process three parameters

            •
            •
            •

ENDCASE

RETURN
```

Sandwell
Michael Li
Senior Programmer Analyst
Sandwell Inc.
Sandwell Swan Wooster Division
1190 Hornby Street
Vancouver, B.C., Canada
V6Z 2H6
Telephone: (604) 684-9311
Telex: 04-51275
Telefax: (604) 688-5913

A good way to write a function or procedure that accepts a variable number of parameters is to assign them all default values initially. You can do this with an immediate IF statement and the TYPE function. For example:

```
FUNCTION do_get

PARAM say_str, get_str

      say_str = IIF(type("say_str") = 'U', "SAY", say_str)
      get_str = IIF(type("get_str") = 'U', "", get_str)

      •
      •
```

assigns "SAY" as a default value to say_str, and a null string to get_str if they are not defined.

You can assign a default value to a parameter while still passing ones further down the list. Just pass an invalid type for the default parameter. The routine then compares the expected type of the parameter against the type actually passed. If they differ, it assigns it the default, as in the following example.

```
FUNCTION do_get

PARAM say_str, get_str

      say_str = IIF(type("say_str") != 'C', "SAY", say_str)
      get_str = IIF(type("get_str") != 'C', "", get_str)
```

Now, you can use the default value for say_str while passing a value for get_str. DBEDIT does this.

END

Clipper lets you use the keyword END instead of ENDIF, ENDDO, or NEXT. It ends the most recent block. Nantucket uses END in the errorsys.prg file (described later in this chapter). We prefer not to use it. Explicit termination of a block with its own end clause (ENDIF, ENDDO, or NEXT) makes its extent more evident.

User Defined Functions

Clipper lets you write your own functions. Once you define them, you can call them as if they were built in (such as CTOD). The FUNCTION statement defines a user function. The RETURN statement returns a value. You can call a function and use its result anywhere you can use a memory variable.

For example, Program 2 - 1 is a simple user defined function that returns .T. if the Escape key is pressed, and .F. otherwise.

Program 2-1. Simple User Defined Function† (See Note 1)

```
FUNCTION escape_hit
RETURN inkey( ) = 27
```

Program 2 - 1 returns a logical. You can use it anywhere a logical value could go. You can simply assign its value to a memory variable, as in:

```
carry_on = escape_hit( )
```

You can also use it as a while scope, as in:

```
REPORT FORM test WHILE !escape_hit( )
```

The user can then terminate the report by pressing the Escape key.

Since functions can appear in any expression, they provide great flexibility. In an expression, you can execute an arbitrary sequence of instructions. You can use them for index expressions, as a scope for batch commands (WHILE ufunc( )), in VALIDs, etc.

† (Note 1) — All program listings are available on disk. Please see page 649 for details.

You define parameters with a formal parameter list, the same as with procedures. A later section discusses the parameter passing method. As an example, Program 2-2 accepts a key as a parameter. You can then use it for any key value.

Program 2-2. Simple User-Defined Function with a Parameter

```
FUNCTION key_hit

PARAM key

RETURN inkey( ) = key
```

You do not need to use a function's return value. You can simply invoke it as:

```
test_func(p1, p2)
```

using it like a procedure, just to perform a sequence of steps.

Even if a function has no parameters, you must still put parentheses after its name, as in:

```
test_func( )
```

A function must return a value, even if it is meaningless. In cases where no value is necessary, return a logical constant such as .F. as a dummy. Or define a variable DUMMY or VOID, with a value of .F., and return it. It is then clear that the result is meaningless.

We employ user defined functions in every chapter of this book. They are preferable to PROCEDUREs when you need a value returned.

Logical Expressions

Clipper always evaluates a logical expression in full. For example, a WHILE loop such as

```
DO WHILE i < 10 .AND. ar[i] != "Brown"
```

always evaluates both sides of the expression, even if the first condition determines the outcome. This is annoying at times. For example, consider the following code:

```
PRIVATE ar[10]
•
•
•
i = 1
DO WHILE i <= 10 .AND. ar[i] != name
    •
    •
    •
    IF ar[i] != name
        i = i + 1
    ENDIF
ENDDO
```

If name is not in the array, the code will fail with a runtime array subscript error. i is 10 the last time through the loop. Since name is not found, it is incremented, and the loop returns to its head. Now, i is 11, and the first condition fails. Since Clipper reevaluates ar[i] != name, an error is generated.

C takes a different approach. It evaluates expressions from left to right, terminating as soon as the result is known. Clipper follows Pascal, where the evaluation is undefined.

The Clipper approach is also annoying when the second term does some processing. For example,

```
LIST s_no FOR p_no = "P1" .AND. qty > avg(j_no)
```

Clipper invokes the avg function regardless of p_no's value. We would rather have Clipper call the function only if p_no is "P1". With Clipper's approach, we must make avg return immediately if p_no is not "P1".

> **RULE**
>
> Clipper always evaluates logical expressions in full, even when early parts of the evaluation determine the result.

WHILE and FOR Conditions

The WHILE and FOR conditions on batch commands behave differently. FOR starts the operation at the beginning of file, whereas WHILE starts it from the current record. The FOR condition processes the entire file, whereas the WHILE condition terminates the command as soon as the condition is not met. For example:

```
USE test

LIST fname, lname FOR lname = "BROWN"
```

examines every record in the database, whereas:

```
USE test

LIST fname, lname WHILE lname = "BROWN"
```

terminates as soon as lname is not BROWN. When using a WHILE clause, you must be sure that the starting record matches the condition; otherwise, no records will be processed. In the example, if the first record in the database did not have lname = "BROWN", no records would be printed. A statement with a WHILE clause therefore is usually preceded by a LOCATE or a SEEK to initially position the record pointer, as in:

```
USE test

SEEK "BROWN"

LIST fname, lname WHILE lname = "BROWN"
```

If you must use a LOCATE (the database is not indexed on the required field), the WHILE condition loses some of its advantage. The records must be scanned sequentially to find the first one, a process similar to the FOR condition. WHILE conditions thus are better suited to processing indexed databases.

Scope of Variables

The scope of a variable or procedure name is the part of the program in which it is defined. In most compiled languages, the scope depends on where the name is declared. Since Clipper has no formal declaration statement, a name is declared when first used. This section discusses how declarations occur and what their scopes are.

Due to dBASE's origin as an interpreter, its features often differ from those of a compiled language. We doubt that the language designers thought much about scoping rules. They apparently evolved as a result of a line by line, interpretive language being forced into a program mode.

In C, a variable name is either global to a module or local to a routine contained within it. Furthermore, a global name may either be visible to other modules or local to one module. The only way to override these strict scoping rules is to pass a name as a parameter. All function names are declared at the same level, and are thus globally available within a module. Again, you can define functions as either local to a module (static), or global (available to other modules).

In Pascal, which supports nested procedures and functions, a name declared in one procedure is visible in all other procedures and functions lexically declared within it. Procedure and function names follow a similar scoping rule.

The strict rules in C and Pascal allow the compiler to enforce scoping. Unfortunately, even though Clipper is a compiler, it must adopt the dBASE scoping rules. This prohibits compile time enforcement.

The first use of a memory variable must assign it a value. PROCEDURE and FUNCTION statements declare procedures and user defined functions, respectively. A field name is declared when you first use its database. Field names have global scope. Once you open the database, you can reference its fields anywhere in the program. Similarly, procedure and function names have global scope. There is no restriction on where you may access them.

Clipper has no concept of modules. Once separate modules are linked, the Clipper run time system, which is responsible for enforcing the scoping rules, does not know the sources of the names. Furthermore, it does not care. The scoping rules in dBASE do not distinguish modules. So, when we define the scope of a name, we do not distinguish modules.

Once you declare a name in Clipper, where can you use it? We already know that procedures, user defined functions, and field names have global scope; our only concern therefore is memory variables. We will first define the scope of an ordinary memory variable, and then discuss the effects of the PUBLIC and PRIVATE commands.

Once declared, a memory variable is visible in the routine in which you declared it, and in all routines called from that routine, during THAT INVOCATION ONLY. A routine in Clipper is either a procedure or a user defined function. As far as a variable's scope goes, there is no difference.

For example, consider the sequence of commands in Program 2-3.

Program 2-3. Procedure Sequence Illustrating Scoping Rules

```
* outer level
glob = "def"

DO proc_a

* a is not visible here

DO proc_b

* b is not visible here

PROCEDURE proc_a

    * glob is visible here

    a = "abc"

    DO proc_b

    * b is not visible here

RETURN

PROCEDURE proc_b

    * glob is visible here

    * a is visible when this routine is called from proc_a,
    * but not when it is called from the outer level

    b = "ghi"

RETURN
```

The main routine first calls procedure proc_a, then proc_b. proc_a defines memory variable a, then calls proc_b. In this invocation of proc_b, a is visible. Proc_b's caller defines it. glob is visible in all routines, since it is declared in the outer level. All routines are called from there.

When the program returns to the main routine, a is not visible, nor is it visible in the subsequent call to proc_b. a's scope ends when proc_a exits. Since the subsequent call to proc_b is in the main routine, a is not redeclared. Clipper scope thus has the strange property that a name may be visible in a routine at some times, but not at others. It depends on where the routine was called. Clipper scope thus follows the calling sequence of the program.

If the call to proc_a preceded the declaration of "glob", "glob" would not be visible in the called routine.

A memory variable defined in the outermost level of the program has global scope. Since all calls emanate from there, it is available in every routine.

Effects of PRIVATE and PUBLIC

The PUBLIC statement changes the scope of the named memory variable to global. At the outermost level, of course, this has no effect. In procedures and functions, it does. For example, consider the sequence in Program 2-4.

Program 2-4. Procedure Sequence Illustrating the PUBLIC Statement

```
* outer level
glob = "def"

* a is not visible here

DO proc_a

* a is visible here

DO proc_b

* b is not visible here

PROCEDURE proc_a
        * glob is visible here

PUBLIC a

        a = "abc"

        DO proc_b

        * b is not visible here

RETURN

PROCEDURE proc_b

        * glob is visible here
```

```
        * a is visible here, regardless of whether this routine is
        * called from proc_a or the outer level.

        b = "ghi"

RETURN
```

The PUBLIC statement in proc_a makes a globally available. It is thus visible in the outer level after proc_a is executed. It is also available in proc_b now, regardless of the origin of the call.

Assignments made to a memory variable within its scope affect its value everywhere. This creates a problem if two routines use the same name. Imagine the difficulty if we had to examine each library routine and determine if it duplicated names in our programs or other routines. We obviously need a way to make variables local, i.e. to limit their scope to a single routine. PRIVATE is the statement that does this. It defines a memory variable distinct from any variable of the same name, declared at a higher level. It does not declare the variable, so it is undefined until the program assigns it a value.

Once we declare a variable as PRIVATE, its scope is limited to the current routine. On return to the calling routine, its value is lost. A variable of the same name in the calling routine would be unaffected.

Strictly speaking, you only need to define a variable as PRIVATE if a name conflict exists. However, you should declare all variables that are not to be seen outside a routine as PRIVATE. This simplifies the task of writing generic routines, and protects against inadvertent use of the name at a higher level. We follow this practice throughout the book.

> **TIP**
>
> Declare all local variables as PRIVATE

Program 2-5. Procedure Sequence Illustrating the PRIVATE Statement

```
a = "abc"

DO proc_a
```

```
* a still has the value "abc"

DO proc_b
DO proc_c

* a still has the value "abc"

PROCEDURE proc_a

PRIVATE a

        * a is undefined here

        a = "cde"
        DO proc_b

RETURN

PROCEDURE proc_b

* a has the value "cde" when called from proc_a, but the value
* "abc" when called from the outer level.

RETURN

PROCEDURE proc_c

* a has the value "abc" here

PRIVATE a
* a is undefined here

        a = "ghi"

RETURN
```

The assignments made to variable a in proc_a and proc_c do not affect its value in the calling routine. However, when proc_b is called from proc_a, a has its updated value since it is still in scope. Note that in proc_c, before the PRIVATE statement, a is defined. Immediately following this statement, however, a is undefined, and remains so until you assign it a value.

The PRIVATE statement thus does not define a new scope. It simply hides higher level declarations of a variable with the same name.

Once you have defined a memory variable in a routine, you cannot make it PUBLIC, for example:

```
DO proc_a

* x is undefined here.

PROCEDURE proc_a

    x = "abc"

    PUBLIC x

    * Clipper ignores the PUBLIC statement.
    * dBASE flags it as a syntax error.

RETURN
```

In the previous example, to make x visible in the outer level, the PUBLIC statement would have to precede its assignment.

Procedures and PRG Files

Like dBASE, Clipper lets you DO both a PROCEDURE and a PRG file. Unlike dBASE, Clipper does not have to be directed to the PROCEDURE file at run time. The compiler only uses SET PROCEDURE TO to open the file and compile it.

Since you can DO a PRG file, Clipper saves its name as a valid PROCEDURE in its run time symbol table. Thus you cannot define a PROCEDURE with the same name as a PRG file. A common error is to DO a PRG file when you meant to DO one of its PROCEDUREs. If there is no code at the head of the PRG file, it simply returns.

Don't forget to define a PRG file's local variables as PRIVATE, just as you would a PROCEDURE's.

Call by Value and Call by Reference

When you write a procedure or function, you define it to operate on formal parameters. When you call it, Clipper substitutes the actual parameters and the routine executes.

The terms "call by reference" and "call by value" describe the relationship between the actual and formal parameters. If you pass a parameter by reference, its address is passed (its reference). The routine then operates on the actual variable. Its value thus changes with any changes the routine makes to the formal parameter. If you pass a parameter by value, a new variable is created. The actual parameter's value is copied into the new variable when the routine is called. Any changes made to the formal parameter affect only the local copy. They do not affect the actual parameter.

RULES

- Parameters passed by reference can be changed.
- Parameters passed by value cannot be changed.

By default, Clipper passes parameters to procedures by reference, and to user defined functions by value.

DEFAULT RULES

- Parameters are passed to procedures by reference.
- Parameters are passed to functions by value.

You can override the default rules. To pass a procedure parameter by value, enclose it in parentheses. To pass a function parameter by reference, precede it with the @ symbol.

RULES

- Use the () operator to force call by value to a procedure.
- Use the @ operator to force call by reference to a user defined function.

Clipper passes arrays differently from ordinary memory variables. Refer to Chapter 3 for a discussion.

Fields must always be passed by value. If you try to pass them by reference, you will get a run time error.

Error Handling

The Summer '87 release introduced new error handling capabilities. The aim was to give the programmer more control over handling run time errors. However, this powerful feature is a double edged sword. Most program errors are mistakes in the code. The error handling routines in the Summer '87 release let the programmer fix problems at run time. If you do not use this powerful feature carefully, you can end up with a catastrophic mess. You should fix most problems in the original code, not at run time.

Some problems, however, are beyond the programmer's control. A printer going offline during the printing of a report is a common example. Perhaps it ran out of paper, the paper got jammed or misaligned, or someone cleverly tripped over the cable or power cord. Another annoying problem is a divide by zero interrupt. Although you can usually guard against it, you cannot in an AVERAGE command. If the number of records in the scope is 0, an error is generated. The new error handler lets you manage these problems.

When a program error occurs, the code should quit gracefully rather than trying to fix it. We show how to make the error handler save messages in a file for later review. The biggest advantage of the error handler is that you can control the program's exit.

Clipper classifies errors into the following categories:

- Database error
- Expression error
- Miscellaneous error
- Print error
- Open error
- Undefined error

These errors cause a Clipper routine to be called, as listed in Table 2-1.

Table 2-1. Clipper Error Handling Routines

ERROR	ROUTINE
Database	db_error( )
Expression	expr_error( )
Miscellaneous	misc_error( )
Open	open_error( )
Print	print_error( )
Undefined	undef_error( )

The error handlers are in the Clipper library. Nantucket provides their source in the file "errorsys.prg". They generally display the error and quit. We will examine their source in more detail later. By changing them and linking the revisions with your program, you can control error handling. Your routines have precedence over the Nantucket ones. Another file, "alterror.prg", includes the source to an alternative set of functions that call the debugger. We will concentrate on the errorsys file here.

Each routine receives the following parameters. Some get more - we will describe them in the routine-specific documentation.

- **name** — the name of the procedure or function that was executing when the error occurred. If the program was not inside a routine, the name of the PRG file is given.
- **line** — the number of the source line that caused the error.
- **info** — a character string describing the error.

These names are the ones Nantucket uses in its source code. Of course, you can use any names you want.

Clipper also has a new control structure, BEGIN SEQUENCE/END, to provide complete flexibility in error handling. We will first describe the functions. We will show the Nantucket source, and suggest modifications. We will then describe the control structure and show how to use it.

Database Error

db_error is called when a database error occurs. The info parameter describes the cause. It has one of the following values:

- **Database required** — an operation that requires a database, such as an APPEND BLANK, found none open.
- **Lock required** — an operation that requires either a file or record lock did not have one.
- **Exclusive required** — the operation requires the database to be open in EXCLUSIVE mode.
- **Field numeric overflow** — a REPLACE into a numeric field has a value that is too large.
- **Index file corrupted** — Clipper detected a corrupt index file.

db_error's parameters are name, line, and info. The returned value determines Clipper's response. .T. causes the operation to be retried, whereas .F. CLOSEs all files and the program terminates.

Program 2-6 contains the Nantucket supplied source code for db_error.

Program 2-6. Database Error Handler

```
***
* db_error(name, line, info)
*

FUNCTION db_error
PARAM name, line, info

     SET DEVICE TO SCREEN
     @ 0, 0
     @ 0, 0 SAY "Proc " + M->name + " line " + LTRIM(STR(M->line)) + ;
                                   ", " + M->info

     NOTE BREAK

     QUIT

RETURN .F.
```

The program first ensures that device is set to screen, displays its parameters on line zero, and then QUITs. It never executes the RETURN statement. For example, a database required error would be displayed as:

```
Proc TEST line 1, database required
```

There is no way to recover from a database error. With the exception of the corrupt index file, the errors are all the result of programmer mistakes. The best approach is to terminate gracefully, perhaps saving the error message. Program 2-7 shows this, displaying a polite (!) message, and then writing the error to a file. The programmer can then review it without relying on the user's description.

Program 2-7. Modified Database Error Handler

```
***
* db_error(name, line, info)
*
*     Modified version of Nantucket's routine. Saves error message in
* file "errs.txt", then quits.
*
FUNCTION db_error
```

```
PARAM name, line, info
PRIVATE err_handle

        SET DEVICE TO SCREEN

        CLEAR
        @ 0, 10 SAY "Internal error xx has occurred. Please call ..."

        * close all files to guarantee a handle.
        CLOSE ALL
        err_handle = fcreate("errs.err")
        x = "Proc " + M->name + " line " + LTRIM(STR(M->line)) +;
                                ", " + M->info

        fwrite(err_handle, x, len(x))
        fclose(err_handle)

        QUIT

RETURN .F.
```

Program 2-7 clears the screen and displays the message. It then creates an error file errs.txt, and writes the message to it. It writes what the Nantucket routine would print on the screen. Note that before creating the error file, it closes all files. This guarantees that a file handle is available for the FCREATE. Chapter 9 describes the file handling routines we use.

Expression Error

When expr_error is called, info contains one of the following messages:

- **Type mismatch** — operation on mismatched types, such as "abc" + 2. Here we are adding a numeric to a character string.
- **Subscript range** — attempt to access an array element with a subscript greater than the declared maximum.
- **Zero divide** — attempt to divide by zero. An AVERAGE command produce this error if no records match its scope.
- **Expression error** — a macro expansion contains an invalid expression.

In addition to name, line, and info, expr_error has four other parameters. Again we will use the Nantucket formal parameter names.

- **model** — model of the expression that failed. It shows a parameterized version of the expression that was being executed. The parameters are given the names _1, _2, _3 (these are valid variable names in Clipper). The names refer to the formal parameters of the routine. It is important that they have those names.
- **_1** — first term of the expression.
- **_2** — Second term of the expression.
- **_3** — Third term of the expression.

For example, assume the following expression was being evaluated:

```
x = "ABC" + 123
```

This will produce an error as it adds a character string to a numeric. expr_error will be called with info set to "type mismatch". The model parameter will contain the string:

```
"_1 + _2"
```

Parameter _1 will contain:

```
"ABC"
```

Parameter _2 will contain:

```
123
```

Using the model and the _1, _2, and _3 parameters, you can reconstruct the expression that caused the error. By applying a macro to the model parameter, you can also re-evaluate it (&model). If you intend to process the model parameter in any way, you must give the last three parameters the Nantucket names. The model parameter refers to them as variables.

The value returned by expr_error is used as the expression's value. If the previous example returned 0, x would be 0.

Program 2-8 contains the Nantucket supplied source code for expr_error.

Program 2-8. Expression Error Handler

```
***
* expr_error(name, line, info, model, _1, _2, _3)
*
FUNCTION expr_error
```

```
PARAM name, line, info, model, _1, _2, _3

        SET DEVICE TO SCREEN
        @ 0, 0
        @ 0, 0 SAY "Proc " + M->name + " line " + LTRIM(STR(M->line)) +;
                                        ", " + M->info

        QUIT

RETURN .F.
```

Just like db_error, expr_error displays the message and QUITs. It never executes RETURN.

All the errors except divide by zero are the result of programmer mistakes. Again, the program should do nothing except terminate gracefully. For the divide by zero error, however, it should return a predefined value, probably zero. Program 2-9 is a version of the function that returns zero. It writes the message to a file if the error is not divide by zero. This is the same action taken by Program 2-7, the modified db_error routine.

Program 2-9. Zero Divide Error Handler

```
***
* expr_error(name, line, info, model, _1, _2, _3)
*
*       Modified version of expr_error. It returns zero for a divide by
* zero error. Otherwise, it creates file "errs.err" and writes info
* to it.
*

FUNCTION expr_error
PARAM name, line, info, model, _1, _2, _3
PRIVATE err_handle

        IF info != "zero divide"

                SET DEVICE TO SCREEN
                CLEAR
                @ 0, 10 SAY "Internal error xx has occurred. Please call ..."

                CLOSE ALL
                err_handle = fcreate("errs.err")

                x = "Proc " + M->name + " line " + LTRIM(STR(M->line)) +;
                                        ", " + M->info
                fwrite(err_handle, x, len(x))
```

```
        fclose(err_handle)

        QUIT
    ENDIF

RETURN 0
```

A divide by zero error causes expr_error to be called with the info parameter set to "zero divide". In this case, expr_error exits, returning 0.

Miscellaneous Error

misc_error is called with info set to one of:

- **Type mismatch** — attempt to REPLACE a field with the wrong type.
- **RUN error** — a program cannot be run, either due to lack of memory or the fact that COMMAND.COM cannot be found.

In addition to the name, line, and info parameters, it receives:

- **model** — this contains the piece of Clipper code that caused the error. It cannot be evaluated with a macro like expr_error.

misc_error's return value tells Clipper what to do next. If the value is .T., Clipper retries the operation. If it is .F., Clipper quits.

Program 2-10 contains the Nantucket source code for misc_error.

Program 2-10. Miscellaneous Error Handler

```
***
* misc_error(name, line, info, model)
*

FUNCTION misc_error
PARAM name, line, info, model

    SET DEVICE TO SCREEN
    @ 0, 0
    @ 0, 0 SAY "Proc " + M->name + " line " + LTRIM(STR(M->line)) +;
                                ", " + M->info
```

```
        NOTE BREAK

        QUIT

    RETURN .F.
```

Again, the routine simply displays the error and QUITs. You may want to change it to write the error to a file as shown previously.

Open Error

The open_error routine is called when a file open fails. It could occur during USE, SET INDEX, REPORT FORM, or any other command that opens a file.

The info parameter always has the value "Open error". Two extra parameters are:

- **model** — piece of code executing when the error occurred. It contains something like "USE" or "SET INDEX".
- **_1** — Name of the file that could not be opened.

The routine can return .T. to cause the open to be retried, or .F. to continue without opening the file.

Program 2-11 shows the source for the Nantucket supplied function for open_error.

Program 2-11. Open Error Handler

```
***
* open_error(name, line, info, model, _1)
*

FUNCTION open_error
PARAM name, line, info, model, _1

    IF NETERR( ) .AND. model == "USE"
        RETURN .F.
    END

    SET DEVICE TO SCREEN
    @ 0, 0
    @ 0, 0 SAY "Proc " + M->name + " line " + LTRIM(STR(M->line)) +;
        ", " + M->info + " " + M->_1 + " (" + LTRIM(STR(DOSERROR( ))) + ")"
    @ 0, 65 SAY "Retry? (Y/N)"
```

```
        INKEY(0)

        DO WHILE .NOT. CHR(LASTKEY( )) $ "YyNn"
              INKEY(0)
        END

        IF .NOT. CHR(LASTKEY( )) $ "Yy"
              QUIT
        END

        @ 0,0

RETURN .T.
```

Program 2-11 first checks whether the error is the result of a network USE (NETERR( ) = .T.). If it is, the routine terminates with .F., instructing Clipper to continue without opening the file. Your network handling code then continues as usual. It should check NETERR( ) and act accordingly (see Chapter 10). Otherwise, the routine gives the user the option of retrying.

Print Error

Probably the most useful error handling function is print_error. It is called when a printing error, such as off-line or out of paper, occurs. This gives the programmer complete control over the printer. Previously, you could only ensure that the printer was ready before the operation started.

The info parameter contains the string "Printer error". No additional parameters are passed.

If print_error returns .T., Clipper retries the operation. If it returns .F., Clipper skips the printer access, and the program continues.

Program 2-12 contains the Nantucket source for the print error handler.

Program 2-12. Print Error Handler

```
***
*       print_error(name, line)
*

FUNCTION print_error
PARAM name, line
```

```
        SET DEVICE TO SCREEN
        @ 0, 0
        @ 0, 0 SAY "Proc " + M->name + " line " + LTRIM(STR(M->line)) +;
                                ", printer not ready"

        @ 0, 65 SAY "Retry? (Y/N)"

        INKEY(0)

        DO WHILE .NOT. CHR(LASTKEY( )) $ "YyNn"
              INKEY(0)
        END

        IF .NOT. CHR(LASTKEY( )) $ "Yy"
              QUIT
        END

        @ 0,0

    RETURN .T.
```

Program 2-12 displays a message and gives the user the option of retrying. If he or she agrees, the routine returns .T.. Otherwise, it QUITs. We extend this function in the next section.

Undefined Error

undef_error is the result of an invalid reference to a variable. There are three possible causes. info contains the message describing which one applies; it could be:

- **Undefined identifier** — referencing a variable before defining it.
- **Not an array** — referencing a memory variable as an array when it is not defined as such.
- **Missing EXTERNAL** — calling a nonexistent procedure or user defined function. This can be the result of a macro expansion, or a function being referenced in a report or label file (see Chapter 1).

If undef_error returns .T., Clipper retries the operation. If it returns .F., Clipper quits.

Program 2-13 shows the Nantucket supplied source code for the undefined error handler.

Program 2-13. Undefined Error Handler

```
***
* undef_error(name, line, info, model, _1)
*

FUNCTION undef_error
PARAM name, line, info, model, _1

    SET DEVICE TO SCREEN
    @ 0, 0
    @ 0, 0 SAY "Proc " + M->name + " line " + LTRIM(STR(M->line)) +;
                       ", " + M->info + " " + M->_1

    QUIT

RETURN .T.
```

The routine simply displays a message and QUITs. Table 2-2 summarizes the error handling routines.

Table 2-2. Formats and Return Values for Error Handling Routines

ERROR	ROUTINE	MODEL	RETURN
Database	db_error	db_error(name, line, info)	.T. - Retry .F. - Quit
Expression	expr_error	expr_error(name, line, info, model, _1, _2, _3)	Numeric for expression value
Miscellaneous	misc_error	misc_error(name, line, info_model)	.T. - Retry .F. - Quit
Open	open_error	open_error(name, line, info, mode, _1).	.T. - Retry .F. - Skip open
Print	print_error	print_error(name, line, info)	.T. - Retry .F. - Skip printer access
Undefined	undef_error	undef_error(name, line, info, model, _1).	.T. - Retry .F. - Quit

Before executing the first program statement, Clipper does a

```
DO errorsys
```

In errorsys.prg, you will see simply a return at the outermost level. In alterror.prg, you will see a PROCEDURE called errorsys. Since it overrides the errorsys procedure in the library, it gets called first. It contains a call to the debugger. You can place any startup code you want here.

BEGIN SEQUENCE

The Summer '87 release introduced a new control structure for use with error handling functions. You can delimit a block of code with the BEGIN SEQUENCE, END pair, as in:

```
BEGIN SEQUENCE
        •
        •
        •
END
```

A BREAK command, issued anywhere within the block or within a routine called from it, causes control to pass to the statement immediately following END.

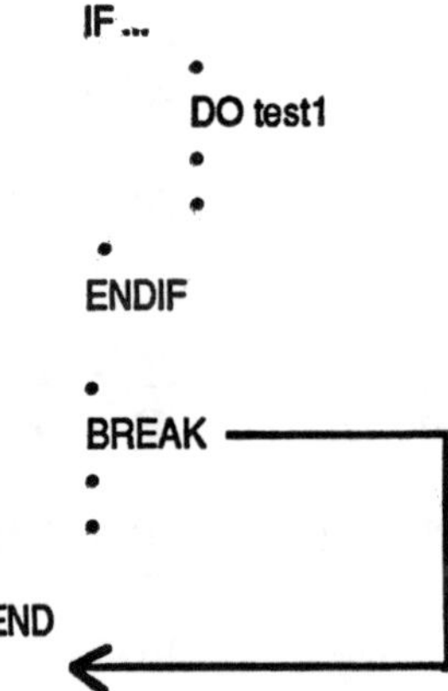

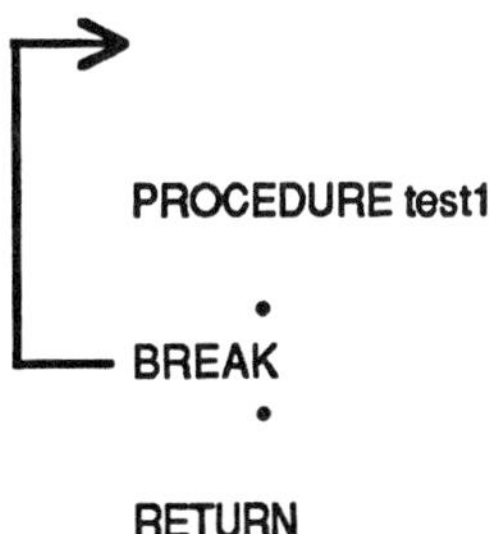

As you can see, the BREAK can jump out of procedures and functions. Furthermore, you can nest the blocks. The BREAK goes to the statement following the most recent END.

```
BEGIN SEQUENCE
     IF ...
          •
          DO test1
          •
          •
          •
     ENDIF
     BEGIN SEQUENCE
          •
          BREAK
          •
          •
     END
     •
     •
END

PROCEDURE test1
     •
     BREAK
     •
RETURN
```

If the BREAK command is issued from outside a BEGIN/END sequence, the program terminates.

This control structure will be new to most programmers. It is like the general purpose exception handling in the Ada language.

The structure has uses besides error handling. For example, you can use it to simulate a RETURN TO MASTER command (not supported by Clipper). This command transfers program control to the outermost procedure. Program 2-14 shows an outline of the idea.

Program 2-14. Simulated Return to Master Command

```
* Example of using BEGIN SEQUENCE/BREAK to simulate
* RETURN TO MASTER

* main program
escape = .F.

DO WHILE !escape

        BEGIN SEQUENCE
                CLEAR

                DO show_menu

                DO sel_menu

                DO proc_menu
        END

ENDDO

PROCEDURE proc_menu

        DO show_menu1

        DO sel_menu1

        DO proc_menu1

RETURN

PROCEDURE proc_menu1

        IF ...

                * now to return to master,
                BREAK
        ENDIF

RETURN
```

The BREAK command passes control to the closest BEGIN/END sequence. In Program 2-14, this is in the main routine. By setting the escape global variable, you can cause either the menu to be reissued, or the program to exit.

Since any routine called from within a BEGIN/END sequence can issue a BREAK, any error handling function may. Using the nesting capability of the BEGIN/END sequence then lets you write local error handlers. Different handlers can be invoked for the same error from different program levels.

For example, Program 2-15 handles a printer error using the BEGIN/END sequence and the print_error routine. When a print error occurs, we let the user retry up to 3 times. Afterward, we break to the END of the sequence.

Program 2-15. Printer Error Handler with a Maximum Number of Retries

```
* 1 - Set maximum and current number of retries
*

* 2 - BEGIN SEQUENCE
*
*       2.1 - print report
*
* 3 - END
*
* 4 - At this level can determine whether error occurred by checking
*       global p_err
*
*
* ON PRINT ERROR -
*
*       IF done maximum retries
*               SET global p_err
*               BREAK TO end
*       ELSE
*               Give option to retry
*
*

MAX_RETRIES = 3
num_retries = 0
p_err = .F.

BEGIN SEQUENCE

        DO print_report WITH ...
```

```
    •
    •
    •

END

IF p_err

        * ended with printer error.

ENDIF

***
* print_error(name, line)
*
* Modified version of Nantucket routine. Only allows 3 retries.
* Sets global flag p_err if exit with error
*

FUNCTION print_error
PARAM name, line

        IF num_retries < MAX_RETRIES
                SET DEVICE TO SCREEN
                @ 0, 0
                @ 0, 0 SAY "Proc " + M->name + " line " + LTRIM(STR(M->line)) +;

                                        ", printer not ready"

                @ 0, 65 SAY "Retry? (Y/N)"

                INKEY(0)

                DO WHILE .NOT. CHR(LASTKEY( )) $ "YyNn"
                        INKEY(0)
                END

                IF .NOT. CHR(LASTKEY( )) $ "Yy"
                        QUIT
                END

                @ 0,0
                num_retries = num_retries + 1
        ELSE
                p_err = .T.
                BREAK
        ENDIF

RETURN .T.
```

After retrying the specified number of times (MAX_RETRIES), Program 2-15 sets the global p_err and BREAKs. Control returns to the main routine following END where we check p_err. Setting a global from the error handling routines is the usual way to inform the main program how it arrived at the END.

The BREAK command is basically an uncontrolled GO TO statement. It allows jumps out of functions and procedures. As with all GO TO statements, use it with care. Abuse can lead to unreadable programs.

> **TIP**
>
> Use the error handling functions to exit gracefully from a program with errors. Change them to put the message in a file so you can see what caused the problem. Do not do elaborate error handling to get around your program's bugs. Use the BEGIN SEQUENCE structure to clearly define the scope of your error handling.

Environment

When loaded, Clipper produced EXE files look for an environment variable 'CLIPPER'. It specifies, among other things, how to configure the available memory. If it is not found, Clipper reverts to defaults. The CLIPPER variable can contain the following flags:

- **Vnnn** - The amount of memory, in K, to allocate for the memory variable table. In most applications, you can use V to reduce memory requirements. Each memory variable takes 22 bytes. By default, Clipper allocates 20% of available memory for the table, up to a maximum of 44K. This is enough room for 2048 memory variables (2048 * 22 = 44K, approximately), Clipper's maximum. If your application uses fewer, and even the largest usually do, reducing this value will save memory.

  The presence of expanded memory does not affect V as Clipper does not put memory variables in expanded memory.

- **Rnnn** - The amount of memory, in K, to allocate to index buffers and the RUN command. They share memory. When a program is run, the index buffers are discarded and the run command uses the memory to load the program. By default, Clipper allocates 33% of available memory for this parameter. A minimum of 16K is required.

Expanded memory affects R. If it is present, Clipper puts index buffers there (unless you set E000, see its description), and uses regular memory only for the RUN command. In this case, you may want to reduce R substantially.

- **Ennn** - The maximum amount of expanded memory, in K, to use. If you do not specify E, and expanded memory is present and available, Clipper will use up to 1 MB of it for buffer space. If E is 0, Clipper will not use expanded memory.
- **Xnnn** - The amount of memory to exclude from use. You may want to specify X to test a program in a smaller amount of memory. The memory is excluded before any percentage calculations are done. However, programs RUN will still use this memory to execute.
- **Fnnn** - The maximum number of files that can be opened at one time. F, and the DOS FILES variable, specify the maximum number of files that may be open at one time. The MINIMUM of the two values applies. This is only relevant for DOS versions 3.3 and above. DOS 3.3 supports a maximum of 255 open files.
- **Sn** - A value of 1 turns snow off on color monitors. Screen output will be slightly slower.

If you pass more than one flag, use semicolons to separate them. Do not put a space between CLIPPER and =.

Hints and Warnings

- Use PRIVATE for all local variables. Make sure you understand the scoping rules.
- Employ a user defined function rather than a procedure when you need to return a value.
- Use the CLIPPER environment variable to reduce the amount of memory your program needs.

- Variables are passed by reference to procedures, but by value to user defined functions. You can override the defaults with ( ) and @, respectively. Arrays are different (see Chapter 3). Fields must be passed by value.
- Clipper evaluates all elements of an expression, even if it can determine the value before reaching some of them.
- When using a filename, use ( ) to evaluate the expression rather than a macro.
- Use the FOR NEXT statement for loops that repeat a fixed number of times.

3

Arrays

This chapter covers the background material you need to use arrays. It discusses their declaration and scope, and describes how they are passed as parameters. It also explains the extend library's (extend.lib) array processing functions. They are written in C, so they are faster than comparable Clipper code. A separate section covers the powerful ACHOICE function. We show how to use it to browse a database, locking fields. We present a binary search algorithm and give practical tips concerning arrays and macros. The final section shows how to save arrays in MEM files and restore them, a feature missing from Clipper.

Arrays — Background

Clipper arrays are simply sets of memory variables with a common name, much like arrays in BASIC, C, Pascal, and other languages. Each individual variable has an index or subscript. It is a number that appears in square brackets after the name. You must state the number of elements explicitly when you declare an array. You do this either with a DECLARE statement, or with a PRIVATE or PUBLIC statement. The array's elements may be of different types, and can vary just like ordinary memory variables.

We use arrays in almost every chapter of this book. The user interface chapters use them to store prompts for pulldown menus, variables and coordinates for two dimensional GET processing, database records and totals for the spreadsheet interface, and buttons for dialog boxes. The text editing chapter uses arrays to save record numbers of memo fields that contain a certain key string. The efficient query methods chapter uses arrays to save field properties for database creation and empty fields for appending, and to speed up query routines. The direct file access chapter uses arrays to save file names in the text search program, and to save buffering information in the read buffering code. In general, arrays are useful because they store related data in a way that is easy to process with a loop. The same code can then handle data of widely varying sizes.

Declaring and Using Arrays

The following statement declares an array names of size 10:

```
DECLARE names[10]
```

We refer to element 3 of names as:

```
names[3]
```

As with memory variables, you must assign values to array elements before using them. The following statement assigns the value "Rick" to element 4 of names:

```
names[4] = "Rick"
```

The array subscript may be any numeric expression. For example, the following code initializes the ten elements of names to 0.

```
FOR i = 1 TO 10

    names[i] = 0

NEXT
```

FOR loops are an excellent way to process arrays. They repeat a fixed number of times, and the array is a fixed size. For example, Program 3-1 sorts an array "nums" into ascending order.

Program 3-1. Simple Sort Routine

```
* Sort routine to demonstrate array handling
* Algorithm works by continually scanning the array for adjacent
* elements out of order. Any found are swapped. If a scan
* does not swap any elements, the array is ordered
* and the routine terminates.

DECLARE nums[5]

* assign arbitrary test values
nums[1] = 3
nums[2] = -2
nums[3] = 1243
nums[4] = 32
nums[5] = 1

* force first iteration as if a previous one had swapped elements
swapped = .T.

* repeatedly scan array until no values are swapped.
DO WHILE swapped

    * haven't swapped any yet this scan
    swapped = .F.

    * scan entire array, swapping adjacent elements out of
    * order (continue only through next to last element)

    FOR i = 1 TO 4

        IF nums[i] > nums[i + 1]
            * swap elements

            temp = nums[i]
            nums[i] = nums[i + 1]
            nums[i + 1] = temp
            * indicate swap occurred so process will be
            * repeated
            swapped = .T.
        ENDIF

    NEXT

ENDDO
```

The number of elements in an array can be a variable, although it cannot change once the array is declared. The following lines, for example, are equivalent to the previous declaration.

```
MAX_NUMS = 5
DECLARE nums[MAX_NUMS]
```

This method is preferable. Subsequent code would use the "pseudo constant" max_nums to limit its operation. If later you need to change the array's size, all you must do is change the constant.

Once an array is declared, the "len" function determines its size. For example:

```
len(nums)
```

returns 5. You can pass array elements as parameters to len just like ordinary memory variables. The following code illustrates this:

```
ASIZE = 10
DECLARE names[ASIZE]

names[3] = "ABCDEF"

? len(nums[3])
```

The len function returns 6, the length of the string.

The type function returns "A" when its parameter is an array name. Thus

```
type("names")
```

returns "A", regardless of the type of the elements. The Summer '87 release lets you determine the type of an array element directly using the type function.

The memory occupied by an array returns to the free memory pool as soon as the array goes out of scope (its scope is discussed later). If the program must dispose of the array earlier, it can use the RELEASE statement just as with ordinary memory variables.

> **TIP**
>
> Use a FOR loop rather than a WHILE loop to process an array.

Arrays as Parameters

Chapter 2 defined call by reference and call by value. You may want to review the definitions briefly. Clipper allows two ways of passing arrays to procedures and user defined functions: as elements or as entire units. An example of the first approach is:

```
DO test1 WITH nums[3]
```

Here nums[3] is passed by value, so test1 cannot change it. An example of the second approach is:

```
DO test1 WITH nums
```

Here the array is passed by reference, so the function can change individual elements. These rules apply to both user defined functions and procedures. Contrast this with ordinary memory variables which are passed by reference to procedures, and by value to user defined functions.

You cannot change the rules by using either the @ operator to force a call by reference, or the () operator to force a call by value. The former causes a compiler error. The latter results in () being interpreted as a precedence operator and thus ignored.

> **RULE**
>
> Arrays are passed to procedures and functions by reference. Array elements are passed by value.

Program 3-2 is a procedural version of the exchange sort (Program 3-1).

Program 3-2. Array Sorting Procedure

```
* Sort routine to demonstrate array handling algorithm works by
* continually scanning the array for adjacent elements out of order and
* swapping them. If a scan does not swap any elements, the array is in
* order and the routine terminates.

PROCEDURE sort_arr

PARAMETERS aname
PRIVATE i, swapped, size

    * determine number of elements ...
    size = len(aname)

    * force first iteration as if a previous one had swapped elements
```

```
swapped = .T.

DO WHILE swapped

    * haven't swapped any yet this pass ...
    swapped = .F.

    * scan entire array, swapping adjacent elements out of
    * order (continue only through next to last element)

    FOR i = 1 TO size - 1

        IF aname[i] > aname[i + 1]
            * swap elements
            temp = aname[i]
            aname[i] = aname[i + 1]
            aname[i + 1] = temp

            * indicate swap occurred so process will be
            * repeated.
            swapped = .T.
        ENDIF

    NEXT

ENDDO
```

To emulate Program 3-1, call Program 3-2 with:

DO sort_arr WITH nums

The entire array is passed by reference. Otherwise, the procedure would only sort a local copy.

Scope of Arrays

The scope of arrays follows the same rules as the scope of ordinary memory variables. This is different from the Autumn '86 release in which arrays could not be made public. In the Summer '87 release, you can declare arrays using the PUBLIC and PRIVATE statements. For example,

```
PUBLIC ar[10]
```

declares a public array ar of size 10. Similarly,

```
PRIVATE ar[10]
```

declares a private array ar of size 10. Declaring an array with DECLARE gives it a private scope, and is thus equivalent to declaring it with PRIVATE.

You should use PRIVATE and PUBLIC for array declarations to be consistent with declarations of ordinary memory variables.

Array Handling Functions

The extend library provides functions for handling arrays. They are written in C, and therefore execute much faster than ones written in Clipper. To use them, you must include EXTEND.LIB when linking. We will now examine the functions one at a time.

ACHOICE

ACHOICE is a powerful function introduced in the Summer '87 release. It provides a pop - up menu for use in selecting an element from an array of character strings. The function allows the array to be larger than the window, scrolling vertically as necessary. It also allows for easy customization through an optional user defined function called after each keystroke. Still another feature is the limiting of selection (while still displaying unselectable items) by means of a user supplied array of logicals, corresponding to the elements in the selection array. If an element in the logical array is .T., the corresponding string in the selection array is selectable, and the highlight bar can be placed on it. If a logical element is .F., the corresponding string is unselectable, and the highlight bar cannot be placed on it.

ACHOICE terminates when the user presses either Escape or Enter, or when directed to do so by the user defined function. When Escape causes the exit, ACHOICE returns 0. When Enter is the cause, it returns the selected element number. When the function forces the exit, the return value depends on the circumstance. This is described in a moment.

ACHOICE takes the following nine parameters:

1 - The top left row of the window.

2 - The top left column of the window.

3 - The bottom right row of the window.

4 - The bottom right column of the window.

Parameters 1 through 4 specify two coordinates just as in the BOX command. They must all be numerics.

5- An array with elements of type character, containing the values to be displayed and selected.

6- An array of logicals, one corresponding to each selection element and indicating whether it can be selected. A single value of .T. or .F. for this parameter propagates through the entire array. The parameter is optional. If it is not specified, the default is all elements selectable.

7- The name of a user defined function that is called after each keystroke. The function receives three parameters:

a) Mode - ACHOICE's state when the function was called, defined as follows:

0 - Idle mode, caused by a cursor movement key not specified below.

1 - The user tried to move beyond the top of the list.

2 - The user tried to move beyond the end of the list.

3 - A keystroke not handled by ACHOICE, such as a function key, control key, or character key.

4 - No items are selectable.

b) Current element - the item selected when the function was called.

c) Relative position within the window. Its value is between 0 and the number of elements that fit in the window minus 1.

The function must return one of the following values:

0 - Causes ACHOICE to abort, as if the user had pressed Escape. ACHOICE returns zero.

1 - Causes ACHOICE to terminate, as if the user had pressed Enter. ACHOICE returns the selected element number.

2 - Causes ACHOICE to continue the selection process, in effect ignoring the key just pressed.

3 - Causes ACHOICE to go to the next element whose

initial character matches the last key pressed. This value would usually be returned when a character key has been pressed.

8 - The initially selectable array element. If specified, the default is the first available element (depending on the boolean array).

9 - The initial relative window row. This is the row offset from the start of the window. It is where the element defined in 8 should be displayed. The offsets are zero-based, that is, a zero value displays the element on the first row, a one value on the second row, etc. If not specified, the parameter defaults to zero. We discuss ACHOICE in detail in the next section. Use it when you need more control over the menu than MENU/PROMPT allows, or when you need to allow the menu to scroll vertically.

ACOPY

ACOPY is the fastest way to duplicate an array. It takes the following five parameters:

1 - Source array (the array to copy)

2 - The target array (the array to copy). It must be declared and be of the appropriate size.

3 - Starting position in the source array.

4 - Number of elements to copy, starting with 3 above.

5 - Starting element in the target array.

Parameters 3 through 5 are optional. If they are not specified, the entire array is copied starting with element 1 in both source and destination. Again, the programmer should resist the temptation to write custom code such as:

```
MAX_SIZE = 100

PRIVATE source[MAX_SIZE]
PRIVATE target[MAX_SIZE]

FOR i = 1 TO MAX_SIZE

      target[i] = source[i]

NEXT
```

Instead, use the ACOPY function, that is:

```
acopy(source, target)
```

Use ACOPY when you need to change elements in an array without destroying the original version.

ADEL

ADEL deletes an element. It takes 2 parameters: the array's name and an expression giving the element to delete. Array elements beyond the one being deleted are shifted down one, and the highest numbered element becomes undefined.

Example

```
ASIZE = 5

PRIVATE names[ASIZE]

* load 5 records from database ...

USE test

FOR i = 1 TO ASIZE

        names[i] = name             && field
        SKIP

NEXT

adel(names, 4)

* a[1] is record 1
* a[2] is record 2
* a[3] is record 3
* a[4] is record 5
* a[5] is undefined.
```

ADIR

ADIR fills arrays with the directory information for a sequence of file names matching a specification (possibly including wildcard characters). It returns the number of matching files. You could use ADIR to fill an array with the names of database files (*.DBF), then pass it to ACHOICE to let the user select a database. The RL utility does this with FRM and LBL files.

ADIR takes the following six parameters (contrast this with the Autumn '86 version's two parameters):

1 - The file specification - "*.dbf", "*.db?", etc.

2 - The array to receive the file names matching the specification. Each element is of type character.

3 - The array to receive the sizes of the files. Each element is of type numeric.

4 - The array to receive the date stamp of the files. Each element is of type date.

5 - The array to receive the time stamp of the files. Each element is of type character.

6 - The array to receive the attributes of the files. Possible attributes are the following characters:

   R - Read only

   H - Hidden

   S - System

   D - Directory

   A - Archive (i.e., ordinary)

All arrays must be declared previously. All parameters are optional except the first. If parameter 6 is included, ADIR returns all system, hidden, and directory files as well as ordinary files. Otherwise, ADIR returns only ordinary files.

If an array is too small, only as many elements as fit are returned; no error occurs. To declare arrays of the correct size, call ADIR twice. The first time, determine how many matching files exist. The second time, fill the arrays. In between the calls, declare the arrays. For example, the sequence

```
num_files = adir("*.dbf")

PRIVATE file_names[num_files]

adir("*.dbf", file_names)
```

declares an array with an element for each matching file. It then fills the array with the file names.

To omit a parameter, pass an empty string in its place. For example, to return the names, dates, and times of all DBF files in the current directory, but not their sizes, use the following code:

```
num_files = adir("*.dbf")

PRIVATE file_names[num_files]
PRIVATE file_dates[num_files]
PRIVATE file_times[num_files]

dummy = ""

adir("*.dbf", file_names, dummy, file_dates, file_times)
```

You can use ADIR to determine whether an index file is out of date with respect to its database. Do this by comparing the dates and times of the two files. The following code shows an example:

```
FUNCTION need_index

PARAM dbf_name, ntx_name

PRIVATE dbf_date[1], dbf_time[1], ntx_date[1], ntx_time[1]
PRIVATE dummy, ret_val

    dummy = ""

    * if index file does not exist, must index
    IF adir(ntx_name, dummy, dummy, ntx_date, ntx_time) = 0
        ret_val = .T.
    ELSE
        adir(dbf_name, dummy, dummy, dbf_date, dbf_time)
        IF dbf_date[1] > ntx_date[1]
            ret_val = .T.
        ELSEIF dbf_date[1] = ntx_date[1] .AND. ;
                    dbf_time[1] > ntx_time[1]
            ret_val = .T.
        ELSE
            ret_val = .F.
        ENDIF
    ENDIF

RETURN ret_val
```

Call need_index as follows:

```
IF need_index("test.dbf", "test.ntx")
    INDEX ON id TO id
ENDIF
```

need_index is useful when you are developing an application. For test purposes, you may want to modify the databases directly in dBASE. This does not update the Clipper indexes, as need_index will show. However, the function is inaccurate when used 'live' in a program. For example, editing a non-key field will cause the date and time of the database to be updated, but not the index. need_index would then return .T., although the index is up to date.

Use the need_index function during development, but remove it from the final version to avoid unnecessarily recreating index files.

You should use the ADIR function whenever you need file or directory information.

AFIELDS

AFIELDS fills arrays with the four values that define the fields of a database - name, type, size, and decimal places. It returns the number of fields in the database, and fills each element of the arrays with information about the corresponding field. The function thus takes four array parameters. The first receives the field names, the second the field types, the third the field widths, and the fourth the field decimal places. To omit a parameter, pass an empty string in its place. For example, to get the names and lengths, but not the types of the fields in the currently active database, issue the following sequence of commands:

```
num_fields = fcount()
PRIVATE fnames[num_fields], flens[num_fields]

dummy = ""

afields(fnames, dummy, flens)
```

You can produce the equivalent of a DISP STRU command by displaying the values returned by AFIELDS.

AFIELDs is useful in writing generic routines that must work with any database structure. By calling it, you can quickly obtain the current structure.

AFILL

AFILL is the fastest way to initialize all or part of an array with a specified value. It takes four parameters: the array's name, the value (which can be of any type), and two indexes bounding the part of the array to be filled. If the latter two parameters are omitted, AFILL fills the entire array. The programmer should resist the temptation to write custom code such as:

```
size_test = 50
PRIVATE test[size_test]

FOR i = 1 TO size_test

     test[i] = 0

NEXT
```

Instead, use the AFILL function, that is,

```
afill(test, 0)
```

AINS

AINS is basically the inverse of ADEL - it makes room for a new element at a specified position by shifting the current element and all higher ones up one position. The new element is undefined until assigned, and the previous last element is lost.

AINS takes two parameters: the array's name and an expression defining the position of the insert. Program 3-3 uses AINS to perform an insertion sort on array nums. The result is placed in the array new_nums.

Program 3-3. Insertion Sort Using AINS

```
NUM_ELEMS = 5

* array to sort
PRIVATE nums[NUM_ELEMS]

* array to sort into
PRIVATE new_nums[NUM_ELEMS]

* assign arbitrary test values
nums[1] = 3
nums[2] = 2
nums[3] = 1243
nums[4] = 32
nums[5] = 1

* initialize destination array to 0
afill(new_nums, 0)

* place every item from the nums array in the new_nums array
```

```
* at the appropriate place ...

FOR source = 1 TO NUM_ELEMS

    * find where nums[source] belongs ...
    dest = 1

    DO WHILE nums[source] < new_nums[dest] .AND. dest < source

        dest = dest + 1

    ENDDO

    * dest now has correct position, insert source element here
    ains(new_nums, dest)
    new_nums[dest] = nums[source]
NEXT
```

ASCAN

ASCAN is a high speed searching function. Since it works sequentially, a binary search written in Clipper is faster if the array is large and ordered. We show such a routine later in this chapter. In all other cases, ASCAN is preferable to custom routines.

ASCAN takes four parameters: the array's name, the value to search for, and two indexes that bound the search. If the last two parameters are omitted, the search covers the entire array. The array to be searched may contain elements of different types. If the search succeeds, ASCAN returns the value's element number. Otherwise, it returns zero.

The programmer should use

```
x = ascan(ar, "string", 1, ASIZE)
```

rather than custom code such as:

```
ASIZE = 20
x = 1
DO WHILE x <= ASIZE .AND. ar[x] != "string"
    x = x + 1
ENDDO

IF x > ASIZE
    x = 0
ENDIF
```

ASORT

ASORT is a high speed sorting function, much faster than anything that could be custom written in Clipper. It sorts an array into ascending order. The elements must all be of the same type. ASORT takes three parameters: the array's name, the starting element, and the number of elements to sort. The defaults for the last two arguments are 1, and the size of the array, respectively, providing a sort of the entire array.

Table 3 - 1 summarizes Clipper's array handling functions.

Table 3 - 1. Clipper Array Handling Functions

NAME	PARAMETERS	RESULT	FUNCTION
ACHOICE	Top left row, top left column, bottom right row, bottom right column, character array, logical array, user defined function, initial element, initial relative row.	Selected element.	Light bar menu with vertical scrolling.
ACOPY	Source array, target array, starting element, number of elements, starting element in destination.	None.	Copies an array.
ADEL	Array, element number.	None.	Deletes an element.
AFIELDS	Names array, types array, widths array, decimals array	None.	Fills arrays with current database structure.
AINS	Array, element number.	None.	Inserts empty element.
ASCAN	Array, search value, start element, last element.	Element number where found or 0 if not found.	Sequentially searches for element.
ASORT	Array, start element, number of elements.	None.	Sorts an array into ascending order

Using ACHOICE

ACHOICE is so powerful and important that it merits separate discussion. First we show a few simple calls. The following code allows the selection of any element from array "choice". The array is filled with the f_name field from the first 40 records of database test.

```
CLEAR
AR_MAX = 40

PRIVATE choice[AR_MAX]

USE test

FOR i = 1 TO AR_MAX

        choice[i] = f_name    && character field in database
        SKIP

NEXT

? achoice(10, 10, 20, 20, choice)
```

Now assume another field in the database, status, classified according to the f_name field. To allow only fields with a status greater than 10 to be selected, use the following code:

```
AR_MAX = 40

PRIVATE choice[AR_MAX]
PRIVATE on_off[AR_MAX]

USE test

FOR i = 1 TO AR_MAX

        choice[i] = f_name    && character field in database

        IF status > 10
                on_off[i] = .T.
        ELSE
                on_off[i] = .F.
        ENDIF

        SKIP

NEXT

? achoice(10, 10, 20, 20, choice, on_off)
```

To illustrate the user defined function, let's start with the one in Program 3-4. It displays its parameters, and then returns the continue code.

Program 3-4. Trial ACHOICE Function that Displays Its Parameters

```
AR_MAX = 40

PRIVATE choice[AR_MAX]
PRIVATE on_off[AR_MAX]

USE test

FOR i = 1 TO AR_MAX

    choice[i] = f_name    && character field in database

    IF status > 10
        on_off[i] = .T.
    ELSE
        on_off[i] = .F.
    ENDIF

    SKIP

NEXT

? achoice(10, 10, 20, 20, choice, on_off, "acfunc")

FUNCTION acfunc

PARAMETER mode, cur_elem, rel_pos

    @ 24, 20 SAY mode
    @ 24, 30 SAY cur_elem
    @ 24, 40 SAY rel_pos

RETURN 2
```

If you run the code, you will find that it provides no exit (except via Alt-C). This is because it instructs ACHOICE to continue the selection process, regardless of the input. To allow the Escape and Enter keys to perform their default actions, you must change the function and its calling environment as shown in Program 3-5.

Program 3-5. Trial ACHOICE Function Allowing Select and Abort

```
AR_MAX = 40

PRIVATE choice[AR_MAX]
PRIVATE on_off[AR_MAX]
```

```
USE test

FOR i = 1 TO AR_MAX

        choice[i] = f_name    && character field in database

        IF status > 10
                on_off[i] = .T.
        ELSE
                on_off[i] = .F.
        ENDIF

        SKIP

NEXT
DO init_consts

? achoice(10, 10, 20, 20, choice, on_off, "acfunc")


FUNCTION acfunc

PARAMETER mode, cur_elem, rel_pos
PRIVATE ret_val, key

        DO CASE

                CASE mode = AC_EXCEP
                        key = lastkey()

                        DO CASE

                                CASE key = ESC
                                        ret_val = AC_ABORT

                                CASE key = ENTER
                                        ret_val = AC_SELECT

                                OTHERWISE
                                        ret_val = AC_CONTINUE
                        ENDCASE

                OTHERWISE
                        ret_val = AC_CONTINUE

        ENDCASE

RETURN ret_val

PROCEDURE init_consts

PUBLIC AC_IDLE, AC_TOP, AC_BOT, AC_EXCEP, AC_NOITEM, AC_ABORT,;
```

```
AC_SELECT
PUBLIC AC_CONTINUE, AC_GO_MATCH, ESC, ENTER

    AC_IDLE  = 0
    AC_TOP = 1
    AC_BOT = 2
    AC_EXCEP = 3
    AC_NOITEM  = 4

    AC_ABORT  = 0
    AC_SELECT  = 1
    AC_CONTINUE = 2

    AC_GO_MATCH = 3

    ESC = 27
    ENTER = 13

RETURN
```

Pressing the Enter and Escape keys causes the ACHOICE user defined function to be called with an "exception" mode. The function detects this, and returns the abort code for Escape or the select code for Enter. These codes both cause the function to exit; abort causes it to return 0, select to return the selected element.

We define constants such as keystroke values, ACHOICE modes, and return values as memory variables. The code thus becomes far more readable at the (small) expense of using a few extra memory variables. We will expand this 'init_consts' function in later chapters where more 'constants' are defined.

Parameters 8 and 9 allow an arbitrary initial state. This is most useful when we need to suspend ACHOICE temporarily to do something. It allows the function to be reinvoked in exactly the state in which it was suspended. This gives a windowing effect. For example, Program 3-6 shows an entry to ACHOICE, a choice being made, a menu being placed on top of the ACHOICE window, and then ACHOICE being reentered with the display in the same state.

Program 3-6. Using ACHOICE's Initial State Parameters

```
* 1 - Declare arrays
*
* 2 - Load records into array, setting parallel boolean array
*
* 3 - Initialize constants
*
* 4 - Invoke ACHOICE
```

```
*
* 5 - DO UNTIL ACHOICE left with Escape
*
*       5.1 - Save screen
*
*       5.2 - Issue prompts
*
*       5.3 - Perform selected action
*
*       5.4 - Restore screen
*
*       5.5 - Reinvoke ACHOICE in same state
*
ASIZE = 40
PRIVATE choice[ASIZE], on_off[ASIZE]
USE test

* build arrays as before
FOR i = 1 TO ASIZE

    choice[i] = f_name    && character field in database

    IF status > 10
        on_off[i] = .T.
    ELSE
        on_off[i] = .F.
    ENDIF

    SKIP

NEXT

CLEAR
DO init_consts

* initial state variables ...
chosen = 1
init_row = 0

* frame the achoice window ...
@ 9, 9 TO 21, 21

* initial invocation ...
chosen = achoice(10, 10, 20, 20, choice, on_off, "acfunc", ;
                         chosen, init_row)

* loop until Escape ...
DO WHILE chosen != 0

    SAVE SCREEN TO x          && should be partial save

    * initial prompt
```

```
        i = 1

        * frame the prompt area ...
        @ 7, 4 TO 11, 13

        @ 8, 5 PROMPT "Delete"
        @ 9, 5 PROMPT "Edit "
        @ 10, 5 PROMPT "Insert"
        MENU TO i

        * perform appropriate action ...
        DO CASE
            CASE i = 1
                do_delete()

            CASE i = 2
                do_edit()

            CASE i = 3
                do_insert()
        ENDCASE

        RESTORE SCREEN FROM x  && also should be partial

        * reinvoke achoice in state it was in when last left ...
        chosen = achoice(10, 10, 20, 20, choice, on_off, "acfunc", ;
                                chosen, init_row)

    ENDDO

    * function now saves the relative position in global init_row
    * when Enter pressed. This is used to re-invoke achoice in same state
    * next time.

    FUNCTION acfunc

    PARAMETER mode, cur_elem, rel_pos
    PRIVATE ret_val, key

        DO CASE

            CASE mode = AC_EXCEP
                key = lastkey()

                DO CASE

                    CASE key = ESC
                        ret_val = AC_ABORT

                    CASE key = ENTER
                        ret_val = AC_SELECT
                            && set global
```

```
                    init_row = rel_pos

                OTHERWISE
                    ret_val = AC_CONTINUE
            ENDCASE

        OTHERWISE
            ret_val = AC_CONTINUE

    ENDCASE

RETURN ret_val
```

When the user selects an element with the Enter key, the rel_pos parameter is saved in the global init_row. When ACHOICE is subsequently re-invoked, the element selected (as returned by the previous ACHOICE) is again selected. It is displayed in the window at offset init_row, the same as before. Note that if we could not specify a relative row position, the selected item would have to be positioned at offset 0 inside the window. The DBEDIT function described in Chapter 8 suffers from this problem.

Program 3-6 lets the user choose a record to work with from those matching the selection criteria (status > 10, recno() <= 40). After selecting the record, he or she is prompted for an action to perform: delete, edit, or insert. When that action is finished, the program returns to the record list.

We can use this method of exiting and re-entering to implement a horizontal pan feature. When the function detects that the user wants to pan left or right, it returns a value that directs ACHOICE to exit. ACHOICE's caller then re-invokes it with a new array, containing values arranged just as if the old array had been horizontally scrolled within the window. Program 3-7 shows this, using the left and right arrow keystrokes to indicate a horizontal pan request.

Program 3-7. Horizontal Scrolling With ACHOICE

```
* 1 - Declare and build arrays
*
* 2 - Initialize constants
*
* 3 - Set current view to initial
*
```

```
* 3 - DO UNTIL Escape or Enter pressed
*
*       3.1 - Invoke ACHOICE with current view
*
*       3.2 - If ACHOICE was terminated by left or right arrow,
*             change current view
*

ASIZE = 50

* declare 6 arrays for viewing
PRIVATE test1[ASIZE], test2[ASIZE], test3[ASIZE], test4[ASIZE]
PRIVATE test5[ASIZE], test6[ASIZE]

* arrays that are combinations of previous ones
PRIVATE pan1[ASIZE], pan2[ASIZE], pan3[ASIZE]

* build the arrays
FOR i = 1 TO ASIZE

        * fill arrays with arbitrary values
        test1[i] = str(100 + i, 5)
        test2[i] = str(200 + i, 5)

        test3[i] = str(300 + i, 5)
        test4[i] = str(400 + i, 5)
        test5[i] = str(500 + i, 5)
        test6[i] = str(600 + i, 5)

        * set up 3 views

        * view 1 is test1 and test2
        pan1[i] = test1[i] + " " + test2[i]

        * view 2 is test3 and test4
        pan2[i] = test3[i] + " " + test4[i]

        * view 3 is test5 and test6
        pan3[i] = test5[i] + " " + test6[i]
NEXT

CLEAR
DO init_consts

* initial view
pan = 1

* initial achoice state
init_row = 0
choice = 1

* frame achoice area
```

```
@ 9, 9 TO 21, 21

* until Escape or Enter is pressed ...
* note lastkey() initially returns zero if no keys have been
* pressed. If this code followed user input, a global would
* have to be used which was initially set to 0 to allow initial
* entry to loop

DO WHILE lastkey() != ESC .AND. lastkey() != ENTER

    * get view number as character for use in macro expansion
    cpan = ltrim(str(pan))

    * show current view
    choice = achoice(10, 10, 20, 20, pan&cpan, .T., "acfunc", ;
                choice, init_row)

    * if achoice exit was due to right arrow, and not on rightmost
    * view, go to next view
    IF lastkey() = RT_ARROW .AND. pan != 3
        pan = pan + 1
    ELSEIF lastkey() = LT_ARROW .AND. pan != 1
        * exit was due to left arrow and not on first view
        pan = pan - 1
    ENDIF

ENDDO

* now, in addition to Escape and Enter forcing exit, allow left and
* right arrow to cause exit. Main code will determine which caused
* exit with a call to lastkey()

FUNCTION acfunc

PARAMETER mode, cur_elem, rel_pos
PRIVATE ret_val, key

    DO CASE

        CASE mode = AC_EXCEP
            key = lastkey()

            DO CASE
                CASE key = ENTER
                    ret_val = AC_SELECT

                CASE key = ESC
                    ret_val = AC_ABORT

                CASE key = LT_ARROW
                    ret_val = AC_SELECT
                    init_row = rel_pos
```

```
                    CASE key = RT_ARROW
                         ret_val = AC_SELECT
                         init_row = rel_pos

                    OTHERWISE
                         ret_val = AC_CONTINUE
               ENDCASE

          OTHERWISE
               ret_val = AC_CONTINUE

     ENDCASE

RETURN ret_val
```

You must add the following two assignments to the init_consts routine:

```
LT_ARROW = 19
RT_ARROW = 4
```

You must also make LT_ARROW and RT_ARROW PUBLIC.

The routine pans among three different views. The function exits when the user presses either the Escape or the Enter key. In the latter case, choice contains the element selected. In the former, it contains 0. In either case, pan contains the number of the pan array (1, 2, or 3) which was in view when the function terminated.

If we filled the arrays with fields from a database, the interface is similar to DBEDIT. As an example, consider the following database structure:

```
*** structure of database merch_dis.dbf ***

Last update 88 1 7

Data offset 641
Record size 100
Number of records 4

NAME          TYPE  LEN  DEC

DIST_ID        N     3    0
MERCH1_ID      N     2    0
MERCH1_86      N     7    2
MERCH1_87      N     7    2
MERCH2_ID      N     2    0
MERCH2_86      N     7    2
```

```
MERCH2_87      N   7   2
MERCH3_ID      N   2   0
MERCH3_86      N   7   2
MERCH3_87      N   7   2
MERCH4_ID      N   2   0
MERCH4_86      N   7   2
MERCH4_87      N   7   2
MERCH5_ID      N   2   0
MERCH5_86      N   7   2
MERCH5_87      N   7   2
MERCH6_ID      N   2   0
MERCH6_86      N   7   2
MERCH6_87      N   7   2
```

merch_dis.dbf contains a distributor identification code and identification codes and 1986 and 1987 sales figures for six merchants. For each distributor, there is one record in the database. The database tracks the distributor's yearly sales history for the top 6 merchants. Program 3-8 builds the arrays for each view.

Program 3-8. Horizontal Scrolling of Database Fields Using ACHOICE

```
USE merch_dis

num_recs = reccount()

PRIVATE pan1[num_recs]

PRIVATE pan2[num_recs]
PRIVATE pan3[num_recs]

* first view is distributor id, merchant1, and merchant 2
FOR i = 1 TO num_recs
        pan1[i] = str(dist_id) + " ";
                        + str(merch1_id) + " " + str(merch1_86) + " ";
                        + str(merch1_87) + " " + str(merch2_id) + " ";
                        + str(merch2_86) + " " + str(merch2_87)
        SKIP
NEXT

GOTO TOP

* second view is merchant 3 and merchant 4
FOR i = 1 TO num_recs
        pan2[i] = str(merch3_id) + " " + str(merch3_86) + " " + ;
                        str(merch3_87) + " " + str(merch4_id) + " " + ;
                        str(merch4_86) + " " + str(merch4_87)
        SKIP
```

```
NEXT

GOTO TOP

* third view is merchant 5 and merchant 6
FOR i = 1 TO num_recs
      pan3[i] = str(merch5_id) + " " + str(merch5_86) + " " + ;
                  str(merch5_87) + " " + str(merch6_id) + " " + ;
                  str(merch6_86) + " " + str(merch6_87)
      SKIP
NEXT
```

If we change the size of the window with:

```
@ 9, 9 TO 21, 52
```

and

```
choice = achoice(10, 10, 20, 51, pan&cpan, .T., "acfunc", ;
            choice, init_row)
```

the code from the previous example will work the same with these arrays in place of the ones defined there.

The first view has the distributor id, plus the id, 86, and 87 fields for merchants 1 and 2. The second view has the id, 86, and 87 fields for merchants 3 and 4; the third view has the id, 86, and 87 fields for merchants 5 and 6. Note that for views 2 and 3, the code adds four spaces to keep a constant width.

We can now easily modify the code to lock some fields while panning others, a feature missing from DBEDIT. This is useful when some fields provide key information. In this case, the distributor identification uniquely identifies the record. It is important that it be visible at all times so the user can determine the distributor to whom the current view refers. We do this by including the locked fields in all views. Program 3-9 shows the array building part, keeping the dist_id field locked.

Program 3-9. Horizontal Scrolling of Database Fields with Locked Field

```
USE merch_dis
num_recs = reccount()

PRIVATE pan1[num_recs]
PRIVATE pan2[num_recs]
PRIVATE pan3[num_recs]

* first view is distributor id, merchant 1, and merchant 2
```

```
FOR i = 1 TO num_recs
      pan1[i] = str(dist_id) + " " ;
                    + str(merch1_id) + " " + str(merch1_86) + " " ;
                    + str(merch1_87) + " " + str(merch2_id) + " " ;
                    + str(merch2_86) + " " + str(merch2_87)
      SKIP
NEXT

* second view is distributor id, merchant 3, and merchant 4
GOTO TOP
FOR i = 1 TO num_recs
      pan2[i] = str(dist_id) + " " ;
                    + str(merch3_id) + " " + str(merch3_86) + " " ;
                    + str(merch3_87) + " " + str(merch4_id) + " " ;
                    + str(merch4_86) + " " + str(merch4_87)
      SKIP
NEXT

* third view is distributor id, merchant 5, and merchant 6
GOTO TOP
FOR i = 1 TO num_recs
      pan3[i] = str(dist_id) + " " ;
                    + str(merch5_id) + " " + str(merch5_86) + " " ;
                    + str(merch5_87) + " " + str(merch6_id) + " " ;
                    + str(merch6_86) + " " + str(merch6_87)
      SKIP
NEXT
```

Unlike many array handling functions, ACHOICE does not allow parameters that define a starting point or the extent of the array. They would allow the function to work on an array subset. Although ACHOICE has a parameter indicating the initial element to be selected, there is nothing to stop the user from scrolling backward. Even if elements are unselectable (their boolean counterparts are .F.), they can still be seen. These two omissions are unfortunate, particularly the first. The problem is that programmers often do not know how many elements are needed in advance. They therefore define arrays to be much larger than is actually required, and use the calculated maximum element to restrict array operations.

Since ACHOICE will not operate on an array subset, some manipulation is necessary. One approach is to use ACOPY to copy to another array of the correct size. Another is to rely on the fact that ACHOICE will not process "undefined" array elements; it limits its scope to the last defined element. This latter approach does not work if the array has already been used, and an element higher than the new maximum was assigned previously.

Although ACHOICE may seem to be complex, it is very powerful.

You should spend the time required to master its use. In Chapter 7 we use ACHOICE to process memo fields, and in Chapter 6 we use it to develop a "spreadsheet-like" user interface.

Binary Search

The ASCAN function scans the array sequentially. While this is more efficient than an equivalent programmed directly in Clipper, it is still slow for large arrays. If the array is ordered, a Clipper routine that does a binary search may be faster.

The binary search algorithm takes advantage of the array's ordering. It first compares the search value with the middle element. If the value is less and it is present, it can only be in the left half of the array. If it is greater, it can only be in the right half. We then apply the process repetitively, continually halving the array until we either find the element or run out of items to search. Program 3-10 shows a binary search of array a.

Program 3-10. Binary Search of an Array

```
ASIZE = 200
PRIVATE a[ASIZE]

* fill the array with test values
FOR i = 1 TO ASIZE

      a[i] = i * i

NEXT

* ask user what to search for
srch_for = 0
INPUT "search for " TO srch_for

* initial search area is entire array
low = 1
high = ASIZE
mid = int((low + high) / 2)

* while not found and more to search, search between low and high ...
DO WHILE a[mid] != srch_for .AND. low <= high

      IF srch_for > a[mid]
            * Must be in right side - next search is between mid + 1
            * and high
```

```
            low = mid + 1
      ELSE
            * must be in left side - next search is between low and
            * mid - 1
            high = mid - 1
      ENDIF

      * new middle between new extremes
      mid = int((low + high) / 2)
ENDDO

* did we find what we were looking for ?
IF a[mid] = srch_for
      * yes
      ? "Found at ", mid
ELSE
      * no
      ? "not found"
ENDIF
```

Program 3-10 first fills the array with numeric values. It then reads a numeric using the INPUT command, and searches the array for it. If it finds the value, the program displays the array element that contained it. Otherwise, it reports "not found".

We can modify this special purpose code to produce a general purpose function that accepts an array and a value as parameters. The function (Program 3-11) returns the element number if the value is found, or a zero if not.

Program 3-11. Binary Search Function

```
FUNCTION binsrch

PARAM a, srch_for
PRIVATE i, low, high, mid

      * bounds for search, initially entire array
      low = 1
      high = len(a)
      mid = int((low + high) / 2)
      * while not found and more to search for, search between low
      * and high
      DO WHILE a[mid] != srch_for .AND. low <= high

            IF srch_for > a[mid]
                  * must be in rhs - next search is between mid + 1 and
                  * high
                  low = mid + 1
```

```
        ELSE
            * must be in lhs - next search is between low and
            * mid - 1
            high = mid - 1
        ENDIF

        * new middle between new extremes
        mid = int((low + high) / 2)
    ENDDO

    * if didn't find it, return 0
    IF a[mid] != srch_for
        mid = 0
    ENDIF

RETURN (mid)
```

We can invoke Program 3-11 as follows:

```
ASIZE = 200
PRIVATE a[ASIZE]

FOR i = 1 TO ASIZE

    a[i] = i * i

NEXT

srch_for = 0
INPUT "search for " TO srch_for

where = binsrch(a, srch_for)

IF where != 0
    ? "Found at ", mid
ELSE
    ? "not found"
ENDIF
```

The number of comparisons required to determine whether a value is in an array of size N is at most $\log_2 N$. This is a maximum value. A sequential search, on the other hand, requires N/2 comparisons on the average. When N is about 20 or more, the binary search is preferable.

Multidimensional Arrays

Clipper arrays are one-dimensional, that is, they have only one index. However, we can write an "indexer" function to simulate multidimensional arrays. Assume, for example, that we want a 10 by 10 array for a multiplication lookup table. Program 3-12 declares the array, fills it with the products, and prints them in tabular form.

Program 3-12. Simulation of a Two Dimensional Array

```
num_rows = 10
num_cols = 10
PRIVATE table[num_rows * num_cols]

FOR i = 1 TO num_rows

    FOR j = 1 TO num_cols

        x = aindex(i, j)
        table[aindex(i, j)] = i * j

    NEXT

NEXT

CLEAR

* print column headings
FOR j = 1 TO num_cols
    @ 1, j * 5 SAY ltrim(str(j))
NEXT

* print table
FOR i = 1 TO num_rows

    @ i + 2, 0 SAY ltrim(str(i))

    FOR j = 1 TO num_cols
        @ i + 2, j * 5 say ltrim(str(table[aindex(i, j)]))
    NEXT

NEXT

FUNCTION aindex
PARAMETERS row, col

RETURN ((row - 1) * num_cols + col)
```

The AINDEX function converts the two-dimensional index to a one-dimensional index. This function is used every time the array is accessed. Figure 3-1 shows the relationship between the function and the array index.

Figure 3-1. Two Dimensional Array

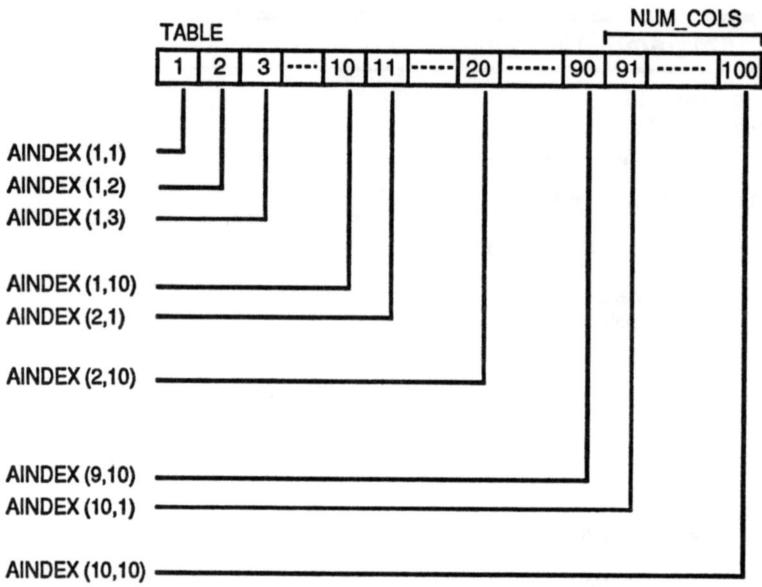

As Figure 3-1 shows, the AINDEX function maps row 1 column 1 to index 1, row 1 column 2 to index 2, row 10 column 10 to index 100, etc. This is just how compilers map multidimensional arrays into a computer's one-dimensional memory.

Arrays and Macros

We can use a macro to create an array name. This is useful in generic coding that must maintain a variable number of arrays. Since the code may not know in advance how many are required, they can be created on the fly with a name generated from a macro expansion. Assume, for example, that for a given database, we want to declare name, type, and length arrays identified by the prefixes "nm", "ty", and "le", respectively, followed by the database's name. If the name of the database is in the memory variable fname, the following code does this:

```
USE (fname)

num_fields = FCOUNT()
```

```
PRIVATE nm&fname[num_fields]
PRIVATE ty&fname[num_fields]
PRIVATE le&fname[num_fields]
```

The following code initializes the arrays. In practice we would use AFIELDS.

```
FOR i = 1 TO num_fields

    name = fieldname(i)
    nm&fname[i] = name
    ty&fname[i] = type(name)
    DO CASE

        CASE ty&fname[i] = "M"
            le&fname[i] = 10

        CASE ty&fname[i] = "L"
            le&fname[i] = 1

        CASE ty&fname[i] = "D"
            le&fname[i] = 8

        CASE ty&fname[i] = "N"
            le&fname[i] = len(str(&name))

        OTHERWISE
            le&fname[i] = len(&name)

    ENDCASE

NEXT
```

Having the macro expansion code within the loop is time-consuming. In fact, the expansion has the same effect on every iteration - it gets the name of the array. It would be better if we could do the expansion once for each array, and then use the result with a subscript. Unfortunately, there is no syntax for this - it would require something like Pascal's WITH statement. However, there is a way around the limitation - expand the macro to give the array's name, and then pass the name to a procedure or function. For example, we could rewrite the above code as:

```
DO ainit WITH nm&fname, ty&fname, le&fname

PROCEDURE ainit

PARAMETERS names, types, lengths
PRIVATE i, name
```

```
        FOR i = 1 TO num_fields

            name = fieldname[i]
            names[i] = name
            types[i] = type(name)

            DO CASE

                CASE types[i] = "M"
                    lengths[i] = 10

                CASE types[i] = "L"
                    lengths[i] = 1

                CASE ty&fname[i] = "D"
                    lengths[i] = 8

                CASE ty&fname[i] = "N"
                    lengths[i] = len(str(&name))

                OTHERWISE
                    lengths[i] = len(&name)

            ENDCASE

            le&fname[i] = len(dummy)

        NEXT

    RETURN
```

Since entire arrays are passed by reference, this code is correct. The solution is cumbersome, but the time savings are tremendous.

The previous example used a macro to generate the array's name. However, we cannot define the size in a macro expansion. The following code, for example,

```
mac = "ar[10]"
PRIVATE &mac
```

would give a "Not an array" run time error. We would have to recode it as:

```
mac = "ar"
PRIVATE &mac[10]
```

We could then access it with:

```
FOR i = 1 TO 10
    &mac[i] = i
```

```
NEXT

? &mac[1]

* this generates a 1
```

We cannot use the value of an array element in a macro expansion. For example:

```
PRIVATE test[2]

num = 123
test[2] = "num"
? &test[2]
```

produces the run time error message:

```
Type mismatch error
```

We must recode it as:

```
PRIVATE test[2]

num = 123
test[2] = "num"

temp = test[2]
? &temp
```

Saving Arrays on Disk

The SAVE TO and RESTORE FROM commands, used to save and restore memory variables to and from disk files, ignore arrays. Any in scope at the time of the SAVE command are not saved. This is unfortunate, but we can easily develop Clipper code for saving and restoring arrays.

The two functions we present combine all elements of an array into a large string, and save and restore it to or from a MEM file. Since array elements can have different types and sizes, we include this information in the string. It has the following structure:

```
<num_elems><type><len><string><type><len><string>...<type><len><string>
```

(the < and > characters delimit parts of the string definition, and are not actually present).

The sequence <type><len><string> repeats for each element. <num_elems> is the number of elements in the saved array. It occupies four bytes.

<type> is the type of an array element. It occupies one byte.
<len> is the length of the following string. It occupies four bytes.
<string> is the character representation of the array element. The preceding <len> field defines its size.

The total information cannot exceed 64K, the maximum size of a string.

Program 3-13. Saving Arrays in a MEM File

```
* 1 - Determine number of elements in array
*
* 2 - Store array size as first element in string
*
* 3 - For each element
*
*       3.1 - Get its type
*
*       3.2 - Store its type in string
*
*       3.3 - Depending on type, store length and data in string
*
* 4 - Save just this string in the MEM file
*

FUNCTION save_arr

PARAM ar, fname

PRIVATE num_elems, fstring, i, len_elem, etype

    num_elems = len(ar)

    * store num_elems field in destination string
    fstring = str(num_elems, 4)

    * for each array element
    FOR i = 1 TO num_elems
        etype = type("ar[i]")

        * add the type field to the string
        fstring = fstring + etype

        * store in string depending on type
        DO CASE
            CASE etype = "C"
                * character string just goes straight in
                len_elem = len(ar[i])

                fstring = fstring + str(len_elem, 4)
                fstring = fstring + ar[i]
```

```
                    CASE etype = "N"
                         * numeric gets converted to strings with str
                         * note default values here, programmer may want
                         * to change them

                         * store length (13)
                         fstring = fstring + str(13, 4)

                         * store numeric string
                         fstring = fstring + str(ar[i], 13, 2)

                    CASE etype = "D"
                         * dates get changed with dtoc

                         * store length (8)
                         fstring = fstring + str(8, 4)

                         * store actual date
                         fstring = fstring + dtoc(ar[i])

                    CASE etype = "L"
                         * logicals go in as T or F

                         * store length (1)
                         fstring = fstring + str(1, 4)

                         * char representation of logical
                         fstring = fstring + IF(ar[i], "T", "F")
               ENDCASE
          NEXT

          * save on disk
          SAVE TO (fname) ALL LIKE fstring

     RETURN (.T.)
```

We use dtoc to convert date types to strings, and str to convert numbers. Logicals appear as either "T" or "F". Although the sizes of all three types are known (8, 13, and 1, respectively), we include them for consistency (normal character strings must have a size).

The "save_arr" function takes two parameters, the array's name and the MEM file's name. You invoke it as follows:

```
ASIZE = 20
PRIVATE arr1[ASIZE]
arr1[1] = ...
•
•
•

save_arr(arr1, "arr1")
```

This creates a file "arr1.mem" with one memory variable "fstring".

To restore elements from the file, just do the inverse operation. Restore the "fstring" memory variable and extract the elements. The "rest_arr" function, defined later, takes two parameters: the array's name and the mem file's name. If the sizes of the array parameter and the array in the mem file do not match, the function returns .F. and no restoration occurs. If the sizes match, the individual elements are restored and the function returns .T..

Program 3-14. Restoring Arrays from a MEM File

```
* 1 - Restore string from MEM file
*
* 2 - Extract size from string
*
* 3 - Verify array to receive is same size as array saved
*
* 4 - Restore every element
*
*       4.1 - Extract type and length
*
*       4.2 - Extract data dependent on type and length
*
*       4.3 - Store in array


FUNCTION rest_arr

PARAM ar, fname
PRIVATE fstring, num_elems, arlen, i, fsindex, artype

        * retrieve fstring from disk, note use of ADDITIVE!!
        RESTORE FROM (fname) ADDITIVE

        * number of elements saved
        num_elems = val(substr(fstring, 1, 4))

        * if not same as array to receive, return
        IF num_elems != len(ar)
                RETURN (.F.)
        ENDIF

        * index into string
        fsindex = 5

        * restore every element
        FOR i = 1 TO num_elems

                * type
                artype = substr(fstring, fsindex, 1)
```

```
            fsindex = fsindex + 1

            * length
            arlen = val(substr(fstring, fsindex, 4))
            fsindex = fsindex + 4

            * retrieve particular type
            DO CASE
                CASE artype = "C"
                    * character string comes straight out
                    ar[i] = substr(fstring, fsindex, arlen)

                CASE artype = "N"   && len 13
                    * numeric gets converted with val
                    ar[i] = val(substr(fstring, fsindex, arlen))

                CASE artype = "L"   && len 1
                    * logical was either "T" or "F"
                    ar[i] = ;
                        IF(substr(fstring, fsindex, arlen) = "T", .T., .F.)

                CASE artype = "D"   && len 8
                    * date gets converted with ctod
                    ar[i] = ctod(substr(fstring, fsindex, arlen))
            ENDCASE

            fsindex = fsindex + arlen
        NEXT

RETURN (.T.)
```

To restore the example array, invoke rest_arr with:

```
PRIVATE arr2[20]

rest_arr(arr2, "arr1")
```

You should use Programs 3-13 and 3-14 to save and restore arrays.

Hints and Warnings

- Define the limits of an array with a "pseudo constant" and use it in all array processing code.
- Use the built in array processing functions whenever possible.

- Declare arrays with the PUBLIC and PRIVATE statements rather than with the DECLARE statement.

- Remember that array elements are passed to user defined functions and procedures by value. Entire arrays are passed by reference.

- When using ADIR, call it twice—first to determine the number of matching files, and again to obtain the directory information.

- When using a macro to generate an array name, process the array in a procedure or function whenever possible. This avoids repetitive macro expansion.

- When searching large ordered arrays, use the binary search routine developed in this Chapter rather than the ASCAN function.

4

SET KEY TO: The Key to Help and More

Clipper lets you access help files by pressing the F1 function key. Programmers can also assign keys to other purposes. The SET KEY function lets the programmer define a procedure to be executed from any wait state, in response to a designated key. This chapter shows how to use SET KEY effectively.

Operation of SET KEY

The syntax for SET KEY is:

```
SET KEY <expN> TO [<procedure>]
```

<expN> is the INKEY value of the designated key, and <procedure> is the name of the program or procedure to be executed when the key is pressed during a wait state. SET KEY <expN> TO without a procedure name cancels the assignment.

The following commands produce a wait state:

```
WAIT
READ
ACCEPT
INPUT
MENU TO
```

When the program is executing one of these, pressing a key defined with a SET KEY causes the designated procedure to be executed. Note that INKEY, discussed in Chapter 5, does not produce a wait state. We discuss the use of SET KEY from INKEY later in this chapter.

Although we could designate any key, in practical situations the ones not otherwise in use are the function keys (all 40), <Alt> and <Ctrl> combinations (e.g., Alt-H or Ctrl-C), and the directional keys. SET KEY's ability to transfer control on the press of a key opens up a whole new world in dBASE programming.

Help Key (F1)

By default, Clipper assigns the F1 key on startup to look for a program or procedure called HELP. The effect is the same as if the program had issued the command:

```
SET KEY 28 TO help
```

No error occurs if there is no help procedure.

If the default is satisfactory, no SET KEY command is necessary. If, however, you want to assign a different key to invoke help, you can use SET KEY. For example, the following lines assign help to Alt-h.

```
SET KEY 28 TO           && Turn off F1 default
SET KEY 291 TO help     && Turn on Alt-h
```

Not issuing the SET KEY 28 TO command makes both F1 and Alt-h access help. Of course, you can change the name of the help procedure or, more important, jump to a procedure that performs some other function. SET KEY is thus more than a way of implementing help. It is a general purpose tool for building applications.

Context Sensitive Help

The Clipper manual distinguishes between generalized and context sensitive help. Essentially, they are the same. Writing a help program basically consists of querying variables, either the ones that SET KEY passes automatically, or ones you have set up yourself. The SET KEY command passes three parameters to the procedure it calls. They are (in order):

1. A character variable containing the name of the calling program or procedure
2. A numeric variable containing the source code line number of the pending wait state (READ, ACCEPT, etc.)
3. A character variable containing the name of the variable or field that is awaiting user input.

The Clipper functions PROCNAME, PROCLINE, and READVAR are the sources of this information.

One exception is WAIT TO <mvar>. It sends a null as the variable name. The procedure and variable names are especially useful in constructing context sensitive help. Using a DO CASE to interrogate the input variable (parameter 3) lets the program respond appropriately. Program 4-1 illustrates this.

Program 4-1. Querying the Input Variable for Context Sensitive Help

```
* querying input variable for context sensitive help

PROCEDURE help

PARAMETERS prog_name,line_num,input_var

    DO CASE
        CASE input_var = "LASTNAME"   &&character parameters
                                      && are passed in uppercase
            ? "Enter last name"

        CASE input_var = "FIRSTNAME"
            ? "Enter first name"

        OTHERWISE
            ? "No help available."
    ENDCASE
RETURN
```

Often, context sensitive help is unnecessary, and generalized help is sufficient. Depending on your programming style, you can provide it in either of two ways:

- by querying the procedure name sent by SET KEY
- by setting a general help variable

If you write well-defined procedures or subprograms, you can easily determine which one is calling help and provide direction. Remember that Clipper passes the name of the procedure being processed. Program 4-2 shows an example in which the help routine recognizes two names in a DO CASE statement.

Program 4-2. Querying Procedure Name for Context Sensitive Help

```
* querying program / procedure name for context sensitive help

PROCEDURE help

PARAMETERS prog_name,line_num,input_var

    DO CASE
        CASE prog_name = "GEN_LEDG"
```

```
            ? "This is the general ledger portion of the "
            ? "program. Here's what you're supposed to do..."

        CASE prog_name = "PAYROLL"
            ? "This is the payroll portion of the program. "
            ? "Here's what you're supposed to do..."
    ENDCASE

RETURN
```

If you put everything in a MAIN.PRG, you can define a (public) variable that changes value depending on position in the program. You may then provide help according to the variable's value. The former method is preferable, as it promotes modularity.

In a typical help facility, the program displays information and waits for the user to respond, perhaps by pressing a key to indicate that he or she has read the instructions. Another possibility, however, is that the user might press the help key again. This, of course, would start the procedure over; it has called itself, a process known as recursion. Unfortunately, it can be fatal to your program. To assure that the user will never be more than one level deep in the help procedure, you should include the following code at the beginning.

```
IF prog_name = "HELP"
    RETURN
ENDIF
```

Another approach is to deactivate the help key (SET KEY <number> TO) upon entering the help procedure, and turn it back on just before exiting (SET KEY <number> TO help.)

> **TIP**
>
> If you plan to have context sensitive help, divide your program into well defined procedures and functions.

Recursion and Multi-Level Help

You can use Clipper's ability to handle recursion to provide multi-level help. The first invocation of the help procedure would display very specific help. Another invocation from inside the existing help would display a more general help. This is the "help on help" facility many programs offer. You can extend it to as many levels as required.

The help procedure obviously must be able to determine the level of invocation. The best way to do this is with a global variable. The main part of the program initializes it to 0, and the procedure increments it upon entry, and decrements it just before exiting. The variable thus holds the nesting depth. The procedure would then switch on its value and call the appropriate help routine. Program 4-3 shows how to call different procedures through a DO CASE statement.

Program 4-3. Using Recursion for Multi-Level Help

```
* using recursion for multi-level help

help_level = 0            && in main routine ...
•
•
•
PROCEDURE help

PARAMETERS prog_name,line_num,input_var

     help_level = help_level + 1

     DO CASE

          CASE help_level = 1
               DO detail_1

          CASE help_level = 2
               DO detail_2

          CASE help_level = 3
               DO detail_3

          •
          •
          •
          OTHERWISE
               * no more help available ...
     ENDCASE

     help_level = help_level - 1

RETURN
```

```
* the most detailed help

PROCEDURE detail_1

        •
        •
        •

RETURN

* a less detailed help

PROCEDURE detail_2

        •
        •
        •

RETURN

* the most general help

PROCEDURE detail_3

        •
        •
        •

RETURN
```

TIP

Use recursive help for a multi-level help system.

Saving the Program State

Interrupting the normal flow of a program at the press of a key leads to a new set of programming problems. The procedure executed as a result of the hot key must not disturb the context of the calling program. Assume, for example, that the program is executing a READ when a hot key is pressed. If the routine uses another database, it must restore the main program's database before returning to it. This is one element of the calling program's context. Other elements include:

- All the SETs, that is, CURSOR, EXACT, COLOR, etc.
- The current database state. This includes the selection number, the current record number, open indexes, etc.
- Other SET KEYs. It may be necessary to turn off other SET KEYs when the procedure activated by one is being executed.
- The current GET list
- The current screen

This state, or the program's view of the current system, must be maintained. Clipper helps in some areas. It provides functions that return and save some elements. For example, the SETCOLOR function returns the current color setting. SAVESCREEN and RESTSCREEN can be used for the screen. In most areas, however, Clipper leaves programmers to their own devices. This is unfortunate. Functions that save and restore the system state would greatly enhance the language.

A common way to save elements is to use a function call. The function executes the required command and sets a global variable that tracks the state. To record the state of the cursor, for example, you would invoke the following routine:

```
FUNCTION cursor

PARAMETER new_state

    st_cursor = new_state      && set the global

    IF st_cursor = 0           && turn it off

        SET CURSOR OFF
    ELSE
        SET CURSOR ON
    ENDIF

RETURN .T.
```

The global 'st_cursor' (standing for 'state cursor') must initially be set to Clipper's default for the variable (ON in this case). To check the cursor's state, you would simply examine the global. To save, change, and then restore it, as is necessary during the activation of a SET KEY, you would execute the following code:

```
OFF=0
•
•

* save current setting
old_cursor = st_cursor

* turn it off
cursor(OFF)
* now perform the required processing with cursor off
•
•

* now restore original state

cursor(old_cursor)
```

A problem with this solution is that it requires a separate function and global variable for each state element. Upon entry, the 'hot key' routine would then either save the states of the variables it changes, or execute a general function that saves everything. Before exiting, it would perform the inverse function.

Neither solution is elegant, however, and this is surely one of Clipper's weak points. Chapter 11 offers elegant, fast solutions to the problem. By processing some of Clipper's internal, but public, variables, we can manage important state elements.

However, you cannot maintain the GET list without support from Clipper. Although it is technically possible to do this by processing Clipper internal variables, it requires detailed knowledge of Clipper internals. The inability to maintain this list makes nested READs impossible. A function or procedure executed as the result of a hot key from a READ, or a VALID function (see Chapter 5), cannot do another READ. This is another shortcoming of Clipper. Appendix C shows code that simulates the GET and READ commands, allowing them to be nested.

Another problem with executing a hot key procedure from a READ is that, upon return, the cursor is placed on the first character of the GET, regardless of where it was when the hot key was called. This happens regardless of whether the procedure does any screen output. The best way to solve the problem is to use the KEYBOARD command (discussed in Chapter 5) to stuff right arrows into the keyboard buffer before the procedure returns. These characters return the cursor to the position where it was when the routine was called. The trick lies in knowing how many to stuff. For a simple character field with no picture clause formatting, you can compute the number by recording the current column position on entry (using the COL function), and determining how far it is from the start of the current GET. For dates, numerics, and any type formatted with a picture clause, the problem is more complex. It is difficult to write a general purpose routine to solve it - the picture clause is not passed as a parameter to the hot key procedure. It is necessary to hard code the picture strings in the routine and treat each one as a special case. You may want to simply accept this as another Clipper shortcoming.

If your hot key procedure needs to clear the screen, use the CLEAR SCREEN command. Issuing a CLEAR causes pending GETs to be cancelled.

> **TIP**
> On entry to a SET KEY procedure, save the state of anything the procedure changes. Restore it before exiting.

SET KEY and INKEY

Although a key defined by SET KEY interrupts normal program execution from any wait state, it has no effect on INKEY. INKEY simply returns the key code value and continues. This is particularly unfortunate for help, as many programmers use INKEY to determine a user's desires (such as menu choice). It is convenient to allow the user access to help during the input process. Fortunately, the problem has an easy solution. Suppose the program is looping, waiting for the user to choose among three options - 1, 2, or 3. Program 4-4 lets the user pick any valid option or press F1 for help.

Program 4-4. Using SET KEY from INKEY

```
* Allow 1, 2, 3, or F1 to be pressed. 1, 2, or 3 exits, F1 calls help

DO WHILE .T.
```

```
        pressed = 0
        DO WHILE pressed <> 49 .AND. pressed <> 50 ;
         .AND. pressed <> 51 .and. pressed <> 28  &&pass 1,2,3, & F1

                pressed = inkey()

        ENDDO

        IF pressed = 49 .OR. pressed = 50 .OR. pressed = 51
                EXIT
        ELSE
                DO help WITH procname(), procline(), readvar()
        ENDIF
ENDDO
```

Program 4-4 determines why the loop terminated. If the reason was that the F1 key was pressed, it calls the HELP procedure. Otherwise, it exits.

A general solution is to follow INKEY with a DO CASE that checks all the keys that are set. Program 4-5 shows the procedure for three hot keys.

Program 4-5. Generalized Use of SET KEY with INKEY

```
* Alt_F1 calls help1
* Alt_F2 calls help2
* Alt_F3 calls help3

SET KEY ALT_F1 TO help_1
SET KEY ALT_F2 TO help_2
SET KEY ALT_F3 TO help_3

•
•
•
•

hot_key = .T.
DO WHILE hot_key
        key = inkey(0)
        DO CASE
                CASE key = ALT_F1
                        DO help_1

                CASE key = ALT_F2
                        DO help_2

                CASE key = ALT_F3
                        DO help_3

                OTHERWISE
```

```
                * hot key was not pressed, exit loop
                hot_key = .F.
        ENDCASE
    ENDDO
```

Although the function is called correctly, the parameters are not passed. We could use the PROCNAME function to pass the name of the current procedure, but we cannot pass the line number without hard coding it. Hardly a technique to be recommended. Similarly, there is no READ variable.

If this code must repeat several times in the program, you should write it as a general function, called instead of INKEY when the SET KEYs are allowed. For the keys set in Program 4-5, the routine would look like Program 4-6.

Program 4-6. Procedure to Handle SET KEY from INKEY

```
* General function to allow hot keys from INKEY

FUNCTION pressed

PRIVATE hot_key, key

    hot_key = .T.

    DO WHILE hot_key
        key = inkey(0)

        DO CASE
            CASE key = ALT_F1
                DO help_1

            CASE key = ALT_F2
                DO help_2

            CASE key = ALT_F3
                DO help_3

            OTHERWISE
                * hot key was not pressed, so exit routine
                hot_key = .F.
        ENDCASE
    ENDDO

RETURN key
```

The routine returns the value of the key pressed. You call it as follows:

```
key = pressed()
```

The routine only returns when the user presses a key that is not hot. All hot keys have been processed.

> **TIP**
> If you need to allow hot keys from an INKEY, write a general function to do the job.

User Defined Help

In many applications, users want to write their own context sensitive help. You can allow this by using the memo editor (discussed in Chapter 7) together with a SET KEY and a database. The database stores the help text in a memo field. The help is made specific by including the name of the READ variable in the database. If different GETs use the same variable and each requires distinct help, then the database must include a means of distinguishing them. The current row and column position as returned by the ROW and COL functions is a good choice. The programmer must decide exactly what uniquely identifies the help text for the application, and include it in the database. As an example, consider the following database structure:

```
    Field Field Name    Type          Width   Dec
        1 VAR           Character        10
        2 ROW           Numeric           2
        3 HELPTEXT      Memo             10
** Total **                              23
```

This database would be indexed on var + str(row, 2). Now, when the user presses the help key, the hot key procedure (Program 4-7) seeks the indexed database for the var/row key. If it does not find the key, it appends a record to the database and replaces the var field with the current READ variable. It replaces the row field with the value returned by the ROW function. MEMOEDIT is then invoked, and the user creates his or her own help text. Finally, the procedure replaces the result of the edit into the database.

If the procedure finds the key, it invokes MEMOEDIT with the memo field (which must have been created previously). Program 4-7 lets the user edit the text both when it is created initially, and when it is recalled later. You may prefer to allow recall only to view the text (this is easy with the Summer '87 version of MEMOEDIT. Again, see Chapter 7), and invoke edit with a separate hot key.

Program 4-7. User Defined Help Code.

```
* helpcode.prg
*
* This is sample driver code for user defined help
*
*       1 - Open database, build index if necessary
*
*       2 - Point key to user defined help procedure
*
*       3 - Set up GETs and do READ
*


CLEAR

USE help

* build index if necessary
IF !file("help.ntx")
        INDEX ON var + str(row, 2) TO help
        GOTO TOP
ELSE
        SET INDEX TO help
ENDIF


* point key to routine
F1 = 28

SET KEY F1 TO do_help

* now display sample gets on screen
room_num = 0
res_date = CTOD("")
num_days = 0

@ 10, 10 SAY "room    " GET room_num
```

```
@ 11, 10 SAY "date   " GET res_date
@ 12, 10 SAY "# days " GET num_days

READ


* do_help
*
*  The routine to implement user defined help
*
*  1 - Turn key off
*
*  2 - Seek for this variable and row
*
*  3 - If not found, add record to database
*
*  4 - Save screen where text will be shown / edited
*
*  5 - Call MEMOEDIT, replacing into database
*
*  6 - Restore screen
*
*  7 - Turn key back on

PROCEDURE do_help

PARAMETERS prog_name, line_num, input_var

PRIVATE r, win_save, help_x, help_y, help_u, help_v

      * avoid recursion
      SET KEY F1 TO

      r = row()

      * check to see if this help already exists
      SEEK pad(input_var, 10) + str(r, 2)

      IF !found()

            * doesn't exist, so add to database

            APPEND BLANK

            REPLACE var WITH input_var
            REPLACE row WITH r
            REPLACE helptext WITH ""

      ENDIF

      * define location of help box
      help_x = 10                  && top row
```

```
        help_y = 40                     && top col
        help_u = 20                     && bottom row
        help_v = 70                     && bottom col

        * now save this area in case anything is overwritten
        win_save = savescreen(help_x, help_y, help_u, help_v)

        * save state of cursor here, see Chapter 11

        * force cursor ON for MEMOEDIT.
        SET CURSOR ON

        * frame the edit window
        @ help_x, help_y TO help_u, help_v

        * now allow help text to be edited, or created if was not found.
        REPLACE helptext WITH memoedit(helptext, help_x + 1, help_y + 1, ;
                                       help_u - 1, help_v - 1)

        * restore cursor here. Again, see Chapter 11

        * now restore screen
        restscreen(help_x, help_y, help_u, help_v, win_save)

        * turn help key back on
        SET KEY F1 TO do_help
RETURN

* pad string on right hand side with spaces to specified length

FUNCTION pad

PARAMETERS string, size

RETURN (string + space(size - len(string)))
```

Note that Program 4-7 pads the 'input_var' parameter, the name of the memory variable read, with spaces to a length of 10 for the SEEK. As received, this parameter only occupies as many bytes as required. However, the SEEK cannot find the correct record unless the variable has a length of 10.

The program uses the SAVESCREEN and RESTSCREEN functions to save and restore only the part of the screen that was changed. This creates a windowing effect.

When using this help with a MENU TO command, you must use the row and column to uniquely identify the wait state. Every prompt causes the same READ variable to be passed to the procedure. Using the row and column then allows the context sensitive help to distinguish different prompts.

This function can serve as the basis for your own user defined help system. This chapter's summary describes extensions that are easy to make.

> **TIP**
>
> When using the variable name parameter of a SET KEY procedure as an index, pad it with spaces to a width of 10.

SET KEY and Macros

Chapter 1 explained why a procedure or function accessed through a macro should be declared as EXTERNAL. This is so the linker can guarantee it will be placed in the EXE file. The same applies to SET KEY procedures. If they are accessed by a macro, declare them as external. For example, the following code accesses hotkey1 through a macro:

```
* access hot key routine with a macro
x = "hotkey1"

SET KEY -1 TO &x

•
•

PROCEDURE hotkey1

    •
    •

RETURN
```

In this case, there is no problem, but if hotkey1 had been defined in a separate LIB file, it would need to be declared as EXTERNAL. It is good practice to do this for any procedure or function accessed with a SET KEY.

Other Uses for SET KEY

As we said earlier, you can use the SET KEY command to do other tasks besides providing help. Program 4-8 is part of an application that simplifies data entry from a reverse telephone directory. Since the listings are by street address, the only information that constantly changes is the street number. From time to time, of course, the street name changes as do less frequently, the Zip Code, city, and state. The user wants the street, city, state, and Zip Code information to stay the same until he or she acts to change it. The cursor returns to the street number field after the user enters a new record.

Program 4-8. Using SET KEY for GET Handling

```
* Program.: REV_GETS.PRG
* Author..: Alan Mulquinn
* Date....: 03/04/87
* Notice..: Copyright 1987, Alan Mulquinn, All Rights Reserved
* Version.: Clipper, Summer 1987
* Notes...: GET <fields/memvars> for DIRECTRY.DBF
*
* SAY state, city, street and Zip Code information in reverse
* video so it will appear the same as GETs.

SET COLOR TO N/W
@ 7,29 SAY mState PICTURE "!!"
@ 8,29 SAY mcity
@ 9,29 SAY mstreet
@ 10,29 SAY mzip     PICTURE "99999-9999"
SET COLOR TO W/N
SET COLOR TO ,N/W

*SET F10 key to call the procedure moregets when pressed
SET KEY -9 TO moregets

* GET street number, name, and telephone.
@ 11,29 GET mnumber
@ 12,29 GET mname
@ 13,29 GET mphone       PICTURE "(999)-999-9999"
READ
* Turn off F10
SET KEY -9 TO
SET COLOR TO

RETURN
* EOF: REV_GETS.PRG
```

```
PROCEDURE moregets

PARAMETERS a,b,c

    * SET KEY does not allow another READ so first we
    * clear the pending GETs and start over.
    DO CASE

        * CASE we were GETting street number when called, move back
        * to Zip Code.
        CASE trim(c) = "MNUMBER"
            @ 10,29 GET mzip    PICTURE "99999-9999"
            @ 11,29 GET mnumber
            @ 12,29 GET mname
            @ 13,29 GET mphone
                PICTURE "(999)-999-9999"

            READ

        * CASE we were GETting Zip Code when called, move back
        * to street name.
        CASE trim(c) = "MZIP"
            @  9,29 GET mstreet
            @ 10,29 GET mzip    PICTURE "99999-9999"
            @ 11,29 GET mnumber
            @ 12,29 GET mname
            @ 13,29 GET mphone
                PICTURE "(999)-999-9999"
            READ

        * CASE we were GETting street name when called, move back
        * to city.
        CASE trim(c) = "MSTREET"
            @  8,29 GET mcity
            @  9,29 GET mstreet
            @ 10,29 GET mzip    PICTURE "99999-9999"
            @ 11,29 GET mnumber
            @ 12,29 GET mname
            @ 13,29 GET mphone
                PICTURE "(999)-999-9999"
            READ

        * CASE we were GETting city when called, move back
        * to state.
        CASE trim(c)="MCITY"
            @  7,29 GET mState PICTURE "!!"
            @  8,29 GET mcity
            @  9,29 GET mstreet
            @ 10,29 GET mzip    PICTURE "99999-9999"
            @ 11,29 GET mnumber
            @ 12,29 GET mname
            @ 13,29 GET mphone
```

```
                    PICTURE "(999)-999-9999"
                READ

        ENDCASE
    RETURN
```

Program 4-8 lets the user press F10 to change information that normally stays the same. Pressing F10 causes the program to move back one field.

Three functions in the Summer '87 release let the programmer redefine keys. They are ACHOICE, DBEDIT, and MEMOEDIT. The programmer supplies a user defined function as a parameter to the routine. It is called after every keystroke. However, functions can only redefine certain keys. For example, none lets you redefine the up or down arrow keys. This is unfortunate, but you can overcome it by using SET KEY; it has precedence over the function's key requirement. This means that if you have the down arrow key set to a procedure and ACHOICE is invoked, the hot key procedure is called, and ACHOICE never sees the key. You can thus use SET KEY to gain complete control of keystrokes in the three functions.

SET KEY is frequently used to provide utility 'pop-ups'. When a key is pressed, a utility 'pops' onto the screen, and the user can perform some function. This is allowed anywhere within the program, so pop-ups can be overlaid. Typical uses are a calculator, a calendar, and an appointment book.

In Chapter 5 (see Program 5-10), we use SET KEY in a pull-down menu system to allow horizontal movement. Another use is to tie a function key to a procedure that displays the amount of free RAM using the memory 0 function. At any time during program execution, the programmer can see just how little RAM is still available. You can also use SET KEY during a READ to display a list of choices. For example, the user may press F2 to get a pop-up window with a list of valid choices.

Hints and Warnings

- Save state upon entry to a hot key procedure and restore it upon exit. Refer to Chapter 11 for helpful routines. For the screen, only save the area that is modified. This is faster, uses less memory, and produces a windowing effect. Use the partial screen save and restore functions described in Chapter 5.

- Since you may not reference SET KEY procedures directly in your code, declare them as EXTERNAL to ensure that the linker requests them.
- The variable name received as a parameter to a SET KEY routine is not necessarily of length 10. Pad it with spaces to give it this length if you intend to use it as an index key. Remember that the name is passed in uppercase.
- Remember that INKEY does not produce a wait state. Use the techniques discussed in this Chapter to handle hot keys from INKEY.
- When using overlays and SET KEY, remember that a routine in one overlay cannot call one that is part of a different module in the same overlay area. This applies to routines called through a SET KEY as well.
- When writing help code, consider allowing the help text to be moved to a different area of the screen. The user can then decide where to have the help text appear and, therefore, what information it overwrites.
- When using MEMOEDIT with help text, consider an option that lets the user vary the text size. This is easy to implement with MEMOEDIT (see Chapter 7).
- Consider letting the user write his or her own help. You can easily modify the basic code in this chapter to allow him or her to define the color and position of the MEMOEDIT text, and the keys used to access it. You can also use this approach to pass bug reports, comments, and suggestions from user to programmer.
- Use SET KEY to redefine keys that ACHOICE, MEMOEDIT, and DBEDIT would otherwise handle.
- Don't issue a CLEAR command from inside a procedure invoked via SET KEY. This will cancel all pending GETs. Use the CLEAR SCREEN command instead.

5

User Interface: Basics

This Chapter describes Clipper extensions to the dBASE III language for screen and keyboard handling. In my opinion, they are among Clipper's most important features - indeed, they are most often the reason why programmers are willing to sacrifice dBASE compatibility.

Simple Menus

The MENU and PROMPT commands work together much as GET and READ do. First, PROMPT places PROMPTs on the screen. Then, MENU lets the user navigate through the PROMPTs with the cursor keys, and select one with its first character or the Enter key. If the first characters are not unique, MENU selects the first PROMPT that starts with the character.

PROMPTs are simply text strings placed where the programmer indicates, in the same way as GETs are. The MENU TO memvar command then saves the selected PROMPT number in memvar. The value is zero if an Escape is used to terminate.

The following code fragment shows a simple menu with three choices:

```
CLEAR

@ 10, 10  PROMPT "Sales history"
@ 11, 10  PROMPT "Appointments"
@ 12, 10  PROMPT "Calculator"

i=1
MENU TO i
```

If the user selects "Sales history", i is 1. If he or she selects "Appointments", i is 2. If he or she selects "Calculator", i is 3. Terminating the menu with an Escape makes i zero. If you are not familiar with the MENU and PROMPT commands, you should compile, link, and run the sample program, printing the value of i after MENU TO.

The PROMPTs are traversed in the order of execution, regardless of where they appear on the screen. The MENU command starts the highlight bar on the PROMPT corresponding to memvar's initial value. The example sets i to 1, so the bar starts on the first PROMPT. The bar moves according to the order of execution of the PROMPTs. So, if you have them out of sequence, the behavior will be peculiar. For example, say you add an extra PROMPT on line 9, but place it at the end as in

```
CLEAR

@ 10, 10 PROMPT "Sales history"
```

```
@ 11, 10 PROMPT "Appointments"
@ 12, 10 PROMPT "Calculator"
@ 9,  10 PROMPT "Calendar"

i=1
MENU TO i
```

The highlight bar would start on line 10 (the first PROMPT). Pressing the down arrow key repeatedly would move it to line 11, then to line 12, and finally to line 9. This is the order in which the PROMPTs were issued. The down arrow key thus means "move to the next prompt." Similarly, the up arrow key means "move to the previous prompt."

> **RULE**
>
> PROMPTs are traversed in the order in which they are issued, not according to their screen position.

The left and right arrow keys have the same effect as the up and down arrow keys, respectively. The PgUp and PgDn keys terminate the MENU command just as the Enter key does. The Home and End keys move the highlight bar to the first and last PROMPTs, respectively. Table 5-1 summarizes the keys' actions.

Table 5-1. Key Actions for MENU/PROMPT

KEY	ACTION
Up Arrow	Move to previous PROMPT.
Left Arrow	Move to previous PROMPT.
Down Arrow	Move to next PROMPT.
Right Arrow	Move to next PROMPT.
PgUp	Select current PROMPT and exit from MENU.
PgDn	Select current PROMPT and exit from MENU.
Enter	Select current PROMPT and exit from MENU.
Escape	Exit from MENU, returning zero.
Home	Move to first PROMPT.
End	Move to last PROMPT.

If the PROMPTs vary in length, you may want to pad them with spaces for appearance. This keeps the highlight bar's length constant. For example, we could recode

```
CLEAR

@ 10, 10 PROMPT "Payables"
@ 11, 10 PROMPT "Taxes"
@ 12, 10 PROMPT "Receivables"

i=1
MENU TO i
```

as

```
CLEAR

prompt_size = 12

@ 10, 10 PROMPT menu_pad("Payables", prompt_size)
@ 11, 10 PROMPT menu_pad("Taxes", prompt_size)
@ 12, 10 PROMPT menu_pad("Receivables", prompt_size)

i=1
MENU TO i

FUNCTION menu_pad

PARAMETERS string, size

RETURN (string + space(size - len(string)))
```

The menu_pad function adds spaces to the string to give it the specified width.

You can, of course, create horizontal menus, just by placing the PROMPTs on the same line. For example:

```
CLEAR

@ 0, 01 PROMPT "DBFS"
@ 0, 11 PROMPT "NTXS"
@ 0, 21 PROMPT "NDXS"
@ 0, 31 PROMPT "DBTS"
@ 0, 41 PROMPT "FRMS"
@ 0, 51 PROMPT "LBLS"
i=1
MENU TO i
```

puts a horizontal menu bar across the top of the screen.

The MESSAGE option makes Clipper display a message whenever the PROMPT is selected. The message appears on the line specified by a preceding SET MESSAGE TO memvar command. The following code fragment shows this:

```
CLEAR
SET MESSAGE TO 24

@ 0, 01 PROMPT "DBFS" MESSAGE "SELECT THIS OPTION TO DISPLAY DBF FILES"
@ 0, 11 PROMPT "NTXS" MESSAGE "SELECT THIS OPTION TO DISPLAY NTX FILES"
@ 0, 21 PROMPT "NDXS" MESSAGE "SELECT THIS OPTION TO DISPLAY NDX FILES"
@ 0, 31 PROMPT "DBTS" MESSAGE "SELECT THIS OPTION TO DISPLAY DBT FILES"
@ 0, 41 PROMPT "FRMS" MESSAGE "SELECT THIS OPTION TO DISPLAY FRM FILES"
@ 0, 51 PROMPT "LBLS" MESSAGE "SELECT THIS OPTION TO DISPLAY LBL FILES"

i=1
MENU TO i
```

Once again, if you do not understand how this code operates, run it and see.

Appending the keyword CENTER to the SET MESSAGE command centers the message, as in:

```
SET MESSAGE TO 24 CENTER
```

The MENU code centers messages of different lengths by adding spaces to make everything the length of the longest message. This eliminates residues from previous messages. However, the extra spaces are not always desirable. If the line contains other characters (such as underscores used for framing), the spaces will destroy them. The next section describes how to overcome this.

> You can display messages when PROMPTs are selected by using the MESSAGE option and the SET MESSAGE TO command.

Pulldown menus combine a horizontal menu and a vertical menu. Program 5-1 illustrates this.

Program 5-1. Simple Pulldown Menu

```
* simple pulldown menu code

CLEAR

* horizontal MENU
```

```
@ 0, 01 PROMPT "DBFS"
@ 0, 11 PROMPT "NTXS"
@ 0, 21 PROMPT "NDXS"

i = 1
MENU TO i

DO CASE

     * Now, depending on horizontal menu selected, issue vertical menu

     CASE i = 1

          @ 02, 01 PROMPT "test1.dbf"
          @ 03, 01 PROMPT "test2.dbf"
          @ 04, 01 PROMPT "test3.dbf"

          i = 1          && actually redundant, but clearer this way
          MENU TO i

     CASE i = 2

          @ 02, 11 PROMPT "test1.ntx"
          @ 03, 11 PROMPT "test2.ntx"
          @ 04, 11 PROMPT "test3.ntx"
          @ 05, 11 PROMPT "test4.ntx"
          @ 06, 11 PROMPT "test5.ntx"

          i = 1
          MENU TO i

     CASE i = 3

          @ 02, 21 PROMPT "test1.ndx"
          @ 03, 21 PROMPT "test2.ndx"

          i = 1
          MENU TO i

ENDCASE
```

Depending on the choice from the initial horizontal menu, the corresponding vertical menu appears below (it is "pulled down"). The program then lets the user select from the vertical menu.

Programmers often use the ADIR function (described in Chapter 3) with a MENU/PROMPT sequence to select a file. The following code is an example:

```
CLEAR

num_files = adir("*.dbf")
```

```
PRIVATE file_names[num_files]

adir("*.dbf", file_names)

FOR i = 1 TO num_files

    @ i + 1, 10 PROMPT file_names[i]

NEXT

i = 1
MENU TO i
```

Using this technique, we can rewrite the pulldown menu code of Program 5-1 to determine which files are available rather than hard coding them. Program 5-2 shows a typical implementation.

Program 5-2. Pulldown Menu with ADIR

```
* Pulldown menu code to allow selection of DBF, NTX, and NDX
* files present in current directory.
*
* 1 - Declare and fill arrays for dbf, ntx, and ndx files.
*       Use adir function.
*
* 2 - Issue PROMPTS, get selection.
*
* 3 - Issue appropriate pulldown
*

CLEAR

prompt_size = 12                && make all PROMPTs this width

* Get DBF file names
num_dbfs = adir("*.dbf")
PRIVATE dbfs[num_dbfs]
adir("*.dbf", dbfs)

* Get NTX file names
num_ntxs = adir("*.ntx")
PRIVATE ntxs[num_ntxs]
adir("*.ntx", ntxs)

* Get NDX file names
num_ndxs = adir("*.ndx")
PRIVATE ndxs[num_ndxs]
adir("*.ndx", ndxs)

* Place initial horizontal MENU
```

```
@ 0, 01 PROMPT "DBFS"
@ 0, 11 PROMPT "NTXS"
@ 0, 21 PROMPT "NDXS"
i = 1
MENU TO i

* Now switch to appropriate pulldown.
DO CASE

    CASE i = 1

        * issue pulldown for DBFs

        FOR i = 1 TO num_dbfs
            @ i + 1, 01 PROMPT menu_pad(dbfs[i], prompt_size)
        NEXT

        i = 1
        MENU TO i

    CASE i = 2

        * issue pulldown for NTXs

        FOR i = 1 TO num_ntxs
            @ i + 1, 11 PROMPT menu_pad(ntxs[i], prompt_size)
        NEXT

        i = 1
        MENU TO i

    CASE i = 3

        * Issue pulldown for NDXs

        FOR i = 1 TO num_ndxs
            @ i + 1, 21 PROMPT menu_pad(ndxs[i], prompt_size)
        NEXT

        i = 1
        MENU TO i

ENDCASE

FUNCTION menu_pad

PARAMETERS string, size

RETURN (string + space(size - len(string)))
```

The SET WRAP ON/OFF command controls how the highlight bar operates at the boundary PROMPTs. If SET WRAP is ON, the bar wraps from one side to the other. If it is OFF (the default), no wraparound occurs and attempts to move the bar beyond its limits have no effect.

TIPS

- Pad PROMPTs to the same width for appearance.
- You can create pulldown menus by combining horizontal and vertical MENUs.

BOX

The BOX command draws a box around a rectangle. The programmer specifies two positions, the top left corner and the bottom right corner. The box will be drawn from the first position to the second. A string of 9 characters tells Clipper which characters to use to draw the box. The first eight specify the four sides and the four corners, as in:

```
122223
8    4
8    4
8    4
766665
```

The numbers are the character's position in the string. The optional ninth character is a fill character. If it is not present, the inside of the box is left as it was. For example, the command:

```
@ 10, 10, 15, 18 BOX "ABCDEFGHZ"
```

produces a box like:

```
ABBBBBBBC
HZZZZZZZD
HZZZZZZZD
HZZZZZZZD
HZZZZZZZD
GFFFFFFFE
```

with the A positioned at 10, 10, and the E at 15, 18.

Passing a null string to a BOX command clears the area. For example, we could clear the box we just drew with:

```
@ 10, 10, 15, 18 BOX ""
```

Programmers often use the BOX command with the IBM PC's graphics characters to produce single line or double line boxes. A good program editor will let you insert the characters directly. (Brief, published by Underware, lets you enter them by pressing the Alt key along with the ASCII values.) Lacking this facility, you can use the CHR function to create the string. For example,

```
SL_BOX = chr(218) + chr(196) + chr(191) + chr(179) + chr(217) + ;
         chr(196) + chr(192) + chr(179)
```

and

```
SL_BOX = "┌─┐│┘─└│"
```

have the same effect, and produce a box with the following format:

For simple single or double line boxes, you may also use the

```
@ x, y TO x1, y1
```

and

```
@ x, y TO x1, y1 DOUBLE
```

commands. You need not specify the box characters. To create more exotic boxes or join boxes, you must use the BOX command. For consistency, we use BOX even for simple boxes.

The following diagrams show common boxes and their ASCII characters:

chr(201) + chr(205) + chr(187) + chr(186) +
chr(188) + chr(205) + chr(200) + chr(186)

chr(213) + chr(205) + chr(184) + chr(179) +
chr(217) + chr(196) + chr(192) + chr(179)

chr(213) + chr(205) + chr(184) + chr(179) +
chr(190) + chr(205) + chr(212) + chr(179)

chr(218) + chr(196) + chr(191) + chr(179) +
chr(190) + chr(205) + chr(212) + chr(179)

Take special care when joining boxes - use the "overlapping" or "tailed" graphic characters at the junctions. The following boxes show this:

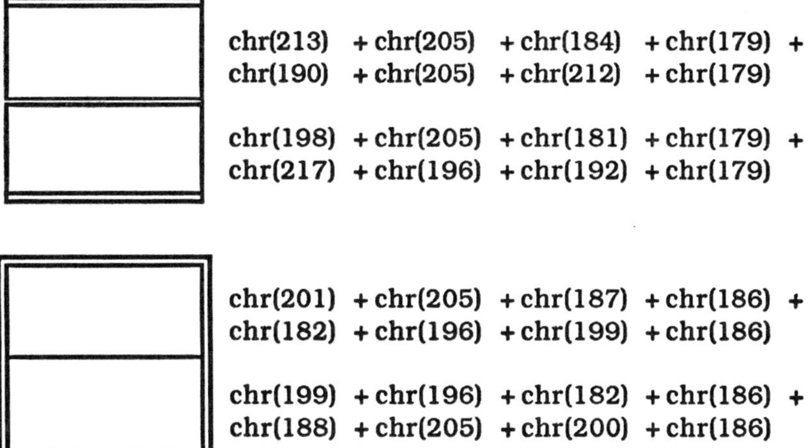
chr(213) + chr(205) + chr(184) + chr(179) +
chr(190) + chr(205) + chr(212) + chr(179)
chr(198) + chr(205) + chr(181) + chr(179) +
chr(217) + chr(196) + chr(192) + chr(179)
chr(201) + chr(205) + chr(187) + chr(186) +
chr(182) + chr(196) + chr(199) + chr(186)
chr(199) + chr(196) + chr(182) + chr(186) +
chr(188) + chr(205) + chr(200) + chr(186)

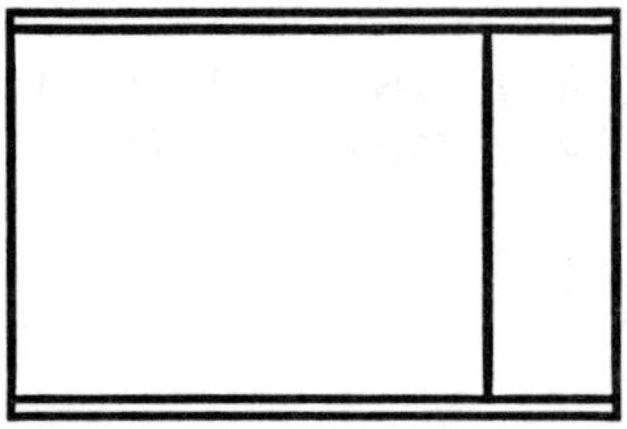

chr(213) +chr(205) +chr(209) +
chr(179) +chr(207) +chr(205) +
chr(212) +chr(179)

chr(209) +chr(215) +chr(184) +
chr(179) +chr(190) +chr(205) +
chr(207) +chr(179)

The ninth character in the box string is usually a "background" character, such as ASCII 177 or 178. Program 5-3 is a version of Program 5-2 with a single line box drawn around the pulldown menus, and around the entire screen. The background is filled with ASCII 177.

Program 5-3. Pulldown Menus with Boxes Drawn around Them

```
* Pulldown menu code to allow selection of DBF, NTX, and NDX
* files from the current directory. Screen filled with ASCII 177,
* single line boxes drawn around pulldowns and entire screen.
*
* 1 - Declare and fill arrays for dbf, ntx, and ndx files.
*       Use adir function.
*
* 2 - Frame screen and fill with background character

*
* 3 - Issue PROMPTS, get selection.
*
* 4 - Issue appropriate pulldown
*

CLEAR

* Get DBF file names
num_dbfs = adir("*.dbf")
PRIVATE dbfs[num_dbfs]
adir("*.dbf", dbfs)

* Get NTX file names
num_ntxs = adir("*.ntx")
PRIVATE ntxs[num_ntxs]
adir("*.ntx", ntxs)

* Get NDX file names
```

```
num_ndxs = adir("*.ndx")
PRIVATE ndxs[num_ndxs]
adir("*.ndx", ndxs)

prompt_size = 12                        && make all prompts this width

* Frame screen and fill with background character
sl_box = chr(218) + chr(196) + chr(191) + chr(179) + chr(217) + ;
               chr(196) + chr(192) + chr(179)

@ 0, 0, 24, 79 BOX sl_box + chr(177)

* Place initial horizontal MENU

@ 0, 02 PROMPT "DBFS"
@ 0, 12 PROMPT "NTXS"
@ 0, 22 PROMPT "NDXS"

i = 1
MENU TO i

* Now switch to appropriate pulldown
DO CASE

     CASE i = 1

          * issue pulldown for DBFs and frame it

          @ 01, 01, num_dbfs + 2, 14 BOX sl_box

          FOR i = 1 TO num_dbfs
               @ i + 1, 02 PROMPT menu_pad(dbfs[i], prompt_size)
          NEXT

          i = 1
          MENU TO i

     CASE i = 2

          * issue pulldown for NTXs and frame it

          @ 01, 11, num_ntxs + 2, 24 BOX sl_box

          FOR i = 1 TO num_ntxs
               @ i + 1, 12 PROMPT menu_pad(ntxs[i], prompt_size)
          NEXT

          i = 1
          MENU TO i

     CASE i = 3
```

```
        * Issue pulldown for NDXs and frame it

        @ 01, 21, num_ndxs + 2, 34 BOX sl_box

        FOR i = 1 TO num_ndxs
              @ i + 1, 22 PROMPT menu_pad(ndxs[i], prompt_size)
        NEXT

        i = 1
        MENU TO i

ENDCASE

FUNCTION menu_pad

PARAMETERS string, size

RETURN (string + space(size - len(string)))
```

Carefully note the coordinates in the BOX commands. In this example, we shifted the PROMPTs one character right to account for the box around the screen.

SET MESSAGE's CENTER option conflicts with the box around the screen, and with the background character. As discussed previously, the CENTER option pads the message with spaces to make it the length of the longest message. If all messages are the same length, there is no problem. If not, however, we want to pad them with the overwritten characters rather than with spaces. To do this, we must write a function that pads the message string to a length of 80 with the appropriate characters.

In Program 5-3, the actual characters to be padded are line-dependent. On line 23, for example, we would pad the string with the background character and a corner character at each end. Program 5-4 shows this.

Program 5-4. Padding a MESSAGE with Backgound Characters

```
FUNCTION center_msg

PARAMETER mess

PRIVATE l_spaces, r_spaces, msg_len

      msg_len = len(mess)
```

```
        l_spaces = int((78 - msg_len) / 2)
        r_spaces = l_spaces

        IF r_spaces + l_spaces + msg_len != 78
                l_spaces = l_spaces + 1
        ENDIF

RETURN (chr(192) + replicate(chr(177), l_spaces) + mess + ;
                replicate(chr(177), r_spaces) + chr(217))
```

On line 24, we must pad the string with the box character used on the bottom line, and add a corner character at each end. Program 5-5 shows this.

Program 5-5. Padding a MESSAGE with Frame Characters

```
FUNCTION center_msg

PARAMETER mess

PRIVATE l_spaces, r_spaces, msg_len

        msg_len = len(mess)
        l_spaces = int((78 - msg_len) / 2)
        r_spaces = l_spaces

        IF r_spaces + l_spaces + msg_len != 78
                l_spaces = l_spaces + 1
        ENDIF

RETURN (chr(192) + replicate(chr(196), l_spaces) + mess + ;
                replicate(chr(196), r_spaces) + chr(217))
```

We would call the functions as follows:

```
@ 10, 10 PROMPT "Select a file" MESSAGE center_msg("Choose a file")
```

> **TIP**
>
> The CENTER option of the SET MESSAGE TO command conflicts with framing characters. Use a function to return the string instead.

To cover the entire screen with a background character, we use it as the edges as well, for example:

```
@ 0, 0, 24, 79 BOX replicate(chr(177), 9)
```

We often want to center a message on either the top or the bottom line of a box. Program 5-6 draws a box and centers the message on the top line. Its parameters are the box's string, the coordinates, the message, a logical specifying whether to display the message in high intensity mode, and two color strings, one for high intensity and one for normal.

Program 5-6. Centering a Message on the Top Line of a BOX

```
* box_top.prg
*
* Draw box with message centered on top line. If intense flag .T.,
* display message in 'bright'.
*
* 1 - Draw box
*
* 2 - Calculate gap on left and right side
*
* 3 - Draw characters in left side
*
* 4 - Draw message (in intense color if specified) on top line of box
*
* 5 - Draw characters in right side

PROCEDURE box_top_msg

PARAM t, l, b, r, box_str, str, intense, norm, bright
PRIVATE l_spaces, r_spaces, msg_len

        @ t, l, b, r BOX box_str

        msg_len = len(str)
        l_spaces = int(((r - l - 1) - msg_len) / 2)
        r_spaces = l_spaces
        * adjust left side if not equal
        IF r_spaces + l_spaces + msg_len != (r - l - 1)
                l_spaces = l_spaces + 1
        ENDIF

        @ t, l SAY substr(box_str, 1, 1)
        @ t, l + 1 SAY replicate(substr(box_str, 2, 1), l_spaces)

        IF intense
                SET COLOR TO &bright
                @ t, l + l_spaces + 1 SAY str
```

```
        SET COLOR TO &norm
    ELSE
        @ t, l + l_spaces + 1 SAY str
    ENDIF

    @ t, l + l_spaces + 1 + len(str) SAY ;
            replicate(substr(box_str, 2, 1), r_spaces)

    @ t, r SAY substr(box_str, 3, 1)

RETURN
```

In Program 5-6, note that we must retrieve the characters to pad the sides from the box string - we cannot hard code values.

To produce the following box with "TAXES" displayed in normal mode:

call Program 5-6 with

```
bright = "W+/ "
norm = "W/ "

box1 = chr(213) + chr(205) + chr(184) + chr(179) + ;
        chr(217) + chr(196) + chr(192) + chr(179)

DO box_top_msg WITH 10, 10, 15, 20, box1, "TAXES", .F., ;
  norm, bright
```

Program 5-7 is similar, except that it displays the string on the bottom line.

Program 5-7. Centering a Message on the Bottom Line of a BOX

```
* box_bot.prg
*
* Draw box with message centered on bottom line. If intense flag .T.,
* display message in 'bright'.
*
* 1 - Draw box
*
```

```
* 2 - Calculate gap on left and right side
*
* 3 - Draw characters in left side
*
* 4 - Draw message (in intense color if specified) on top line of box
*
* 5 - Draw characters in right side

PROCEDURE box_bot_msg

PARAM t, l, b, r, box_str, str, intense, norm, bright
PRIVATE l_spaces, r_spaces, msg_len

    @ t, l, b, r BOX box_str

    msg_len = len(str)
    l_spaces = int(((r - l - 1) - msg_len) / 2)
    r_spaces = l_spaces

    * adjust left side if not equal
    IF r_spaces + l_spaces + msg_len != (r - l - 1)
        l_spaces = l_spaces + 1
    ENDIF

    @ b, l SAY substr(box_str, 7, 1)
    @ b, l + 1 SAY replicate(substr(box_str, 6, 1), l_spaces)

    IF intense
        SET COLOR TO &bright
        @ b, l + l_spaces + 1 SAY str
        SET COLOR TO &norm
    ELSE
        @ b, l + l_spaces + 1 SAY str
    ENDIF

    @ b, l + l_spaces + 1 + len(str) SAY ;
        replicate(substr(box_str, 6, 1), r_spaces)
    @ b, r SAY substr(box_str, 5, 1)

RETURN
```

To produce the following box with "TAXES" displayed in high intensity:

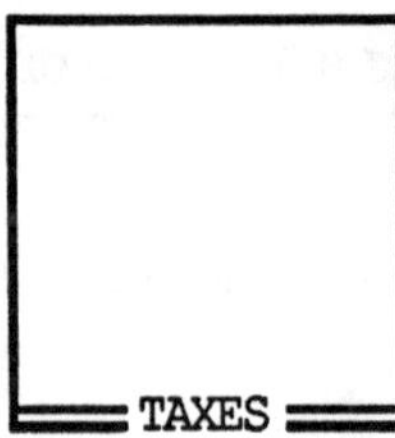

call Program 5-7 with

```
bright = "W+/ "
norm = "W/ "

box2 = chr(218) + chr(196) + chr(191) + chr(179) + ;
            chr(190) + chr(205) + chr(212) + chr(179)

DO box_bot_msg WITH 10, 10, 15, 20, box2, "TAXES", .T., ;
  norm, bright
```

TIPS

- Use BOX to frame distinct screen areas such as MENUs and messages.
- The background characters such as ASCII 177 and 178 produce an attractive background for BOXes.
- Use the 'box_top_msg' and 'box_bot_msg' routines to display centered messages in BOXes.

Key Handling

Any code you write that processes keys directly needs to know the value of the key just pressed. The INKEY and LASTKEY functions can determine it. INKEY can operate in several modes. When called with no parameter, it returns immediately with the value of the key if one was waiting, or 0 if not. When called with a zero parameter, it waits for a key if none is available. It treats any other parameter as the length of time it should wait (to the nearest tenth of a second) before returning if no key is available. If it times out without finding a key, it returns zero. LASTKEY simply returns the value of the last key pressed. A common use is to determine what key was pressed to exit from a READ or MENU command. If LASTKEY is called before any key has been pressed, it returns zero. This is convenient, as it lets you write code such as:

```
DO WHILE lastkey() != 27

    ....

ENDDO
```

We know that the loop will be entered initially because LASTKEY will return zero the first time through.

These functions are like the dBASE READKEY function, but return different values. Most often, the programmer is concerned with the function keys, and special keys such as arrows, Page Up, etc. Table 5-2 lists commonly tested key values.

Table 5-2. LASTKEY Values

Key	LASTKEY Value	Key	LASTKEY Value
F1	28	Shift F1	-10
F2	-1	Shift F2	-11
F3	-2	Shift F3	-12
F4	-3	Shift F4	-13
F5	-4	Shift F5	-14
F6	-5	Shift F6	-15
F7	-6	Shift F7	-16
F8	-7	Shift F8	-17
F9	-8	Shift F9	-18
F10	-9	Shift F10	-19
Ctrl F1	-20	Alt F1	-30
Ctrl F2	-21	Alt F2	-31
Ctrl F3	-22	Alt F3	-32
Ctrl F4	-23	Alt F4	-33
Ctrl F5	-24	Alt F5	-34
Ctrl F6	-25	Alt F6	-35
Ctrl F7	-26	Alt F7	-36
Ctrl F8	-27	Alt F8	-37
Ctrl F9	-28	Alt F9	-38
Ctrl F10	-29	Alt F10	-39
End	6	Home	1
Ctrl End	23	Up Arrow	5
Enter	13	Down Arrow	24
Right Arrow	4	Left Arrow	19
PgDn	3	Ctrl Home	29
PgUp	18	Ctrl Left Arrow	26
Ctrl PgDn	3	Ctrl Right Arrow	2
Ctrl PgUp	31	Esc	27

You should define key values as memory variables. For example, it is much clearer to write

```
UP_ARROW = 5

IF key = UP_ARROW
      •
      •
```

rather than:

```
IF key = 5
```

To do this, we must write a function to assign the values to PUBLIC memory variables. We also include here other frequently used 'constants' such as box and color strings. We first did this in Chapter 3 with the constants used for ACHOICE. We will expand the function here. (Appendix A describes a Clipper preprocessor that allows REAL constants to be defined).

Program 5-8. Expanded Constant Initialization

```
* Routine to initialize memory variable 'pseudo constants'
* Call it before any of them are accessed

FUNCTION init_consts

PUBLIC SL_BOX, ESC, UP_ARROW, PG_UP, DOWN_ARROW, PG_DOWN, CTRL_END
PUBLIC END_KEY, HOME, CTRL_HOME, ENTER, F1, F2, F3, F4, F5, F6, F7
PUBLIC F8, F9, F10, LT_ARROW, RT_ARROW, CTRL_W, CTRL_Y, CTRL_T
PUBLIC AC_IDLE, AC_TOP, AC_BOT, AC_EXCEP, AC_NOITEM, AC_ABORT
PUBLIC AC_CONTINUE, BRIGHT, NORM, ENH, AC_GO_MATCH, AC_SELECT

    * achoice modes - See Chapter 3
    AC_IDLE  = 0
    AC_TOP   = 1
    AC_BOT   = 2
    AC_EXCEP = 3
    AC_NOITEM = 4

    * achoice return values - See Chapter 3
    AC_ABORT  = 0
    AC_SELECT  = 1
    AC_CONTINUE = 2
    AC_GO_MATCH = 3


    * color values for BW screen
    BRIGHT = "W+/ "
```

```
    NORM = "W/ "
    ENH = " /W"

    * single line box
    SL_BOX = chr(218) + chr(196) + chr(191) + chr(179) + chr(217) + ;
                chr(196) + chr(192) + chr(179)

    * some key values from INKEY, see Table 5 - 2
    ESC = 27
    UP_ARROW = 5
    PG_UP = 18
    DOWN_ARROW = 24
    PG_DOWN = 3
    CTRL_END = 23
    END_KEY = 6
    HOME = 1
    CTRL_HOME = 29
    ENTER = 13
    LT_ARROW = 19
    RT_ARROW = 4
    F1 = 28
    F2 = -1
    F3 = -2
    F4 = -3
    F5 = -4
    F6 = -5
    F7 = -6
    F8 = -7
    F9 = -8
    F10 = -9
    CTRL_W = 23
    CTRL_Y = 25
    CTRL_T = 20

RETURN (.T.)
```

We will refer to Program 5-8 and these values throughout the book. Note that we use capital letters for the memory variable 'constants' . This distinguishes them from ordinary variables.

We can use the following routine to test a key returned from INKEY or LASTKEY:

```
CLEAR

key = 0
ALT_F1 = -30

* loop until Alt F1 hit

DO WHILE key != ALT_F1
```

```
        key = inkey(0)
        ? key

    ENDDO
```

The routine displays the INKEY value of the key pressed; it terminates when you press Alt-F1.

The following routine does the same thing, but only waits for five seconds, displaying the "No key" message if no key was pressed.

```
    CLEAR

    key = 0
    ALT_F1 = -30

    * loop until Alt F1 pressed

    DO WHILE key != ALT_F1

        key = inkey(5)
        IF key = 0
            ? "No key"
        ELSE
            ? key
        ENDIF

    ENDDO
```

The following code prints the value of the key used to exit from a READ:

```
    x = 12
    @ 10, 10 SAY "x ? " GET x

    y = 7
    @ 11, 10 SAY "y ? " GET y

    z = 5
    @ 12, 10 SAY "z ? " GET z

    READ

    ? lastkey()
```

TIP

Define frequently used INKEY return values as pseudo constants. Capitalize their names to distinguish them from ordinary memory variables.

Cursor Management

Interfaces that do not require text input should turn the cursor off to avoid distraction. The MENU command does this automatically. If you write your own menu code that uses the cursor keys to 'point', or an interface that only uses function keys, you should turn the cursor off. Program 5-9, for example, waits for a key to be pressed, then invokes the appropriate routine. If the key is invalid, no action occurs. This interface is like the Autumn '86 version of the DBU utility.

Program 5-9. Menuless User Interface

```
* Function key driven user interface
*
* 1 - Initialize constants
*
* 2 - DO UNTIL ESC pressed
*
*       2.1 - Show options
*
*       2.2 - Wait for key
*
*       2.3 - If key valid, call appropriate routine   (F1 .. F4)
init_consts()

key = 0

DO WHILE key != ESC

      CLEAR
      @ 0, 20 SAY "F1"
      @ 1, 20 SAY "OPEN"

      @ 0, 30 SAY "F2"
      @ 1, 30 SAY "CLOSE"

      @ 0, 40 SAY "F3"
      @ 1, 40 SAY "INDEX"

      @ 0, 50 SAY "F4"
      @ 1, 50 SAY "SET"

      key = inkey(0)

      DO CASE
            CASE key = F1
                  f_open()
```

```
        CASE key = F2
            f_close()

        CASE key = F3
            f_index()

        CASE key = F4
            f_set()

    ENDCASE
ENDDO
```

The cursor (sitting after SET on line 1) is annoying. In this menuless user interface, where one selects options with a hotkey (one linked to a processing operation), the cursor should not be visible. The SET CURSOR ON/OFF command does the job.

Chapter 11 presents a routine that lets the programmer set the cursor to an arbitrary size, by specifying its start and end line. Chapter 7 also discusses this.

> **TIP**
>
> Turn the cursor off when it is not required.

Stuffing the Keyboard Buffer

The KEYBOARD command stuffs the keyboard buffer with a sequence of keystrokes. As far as the program is concerned, the result is just as if someone had pressed the keys. Although overuse of this command can lead to unstructured, unreadable programs, there are cases where it makes programs shorter. There are also cases where KEYBOARD is absolutely essential, usually due to some inadequacy in Clipper.

One example involves stuffing the keyboard buffer with a value just before an ACCEPT. This makes the ACCEPT act like GET. The previous value appears initially. The following code shows this:

```
x = "initial value"

KEYBOARD x

ACCEPT TO x
```

Another use is with the pulldown menu code in Programs 5-1 through 5-3. In a MENU command, the left and right arrows have the same effects as up and down arrows, respectively. In a pulldown menu interface, we want the left and right arrows to cause horizontal movement. We can do this by making the left and right arrow keys call a function when pressed (with the SET KEY command, see Chapter 4). The function must stuff the keyboard buffer with the key values necessary to produce horizontal movement. Program 5-10, based on Program 5-3, shows this.

Program 5-10. Using SET KEY for Horizontal Scrolling in a Pulldown Menu

```
* Pulldown menu code to allow selection of DBF, NTX, and NDX
* files present in current directory. Screen filled with ASCII 177,
* single line boxes drawn around pulldowns and entire screen.
* Left and right arrow keys perform horizontal movement.
*
*
* 1 - Declare and fill arrays for dbf, ntx, and ndx files.
*       Use adir function.
*
* 2 - Frame screen and fill with background character
*
* 3 - Issue PROMPTS, get selection.
*

* 4 - Issue appropriate pulldown
*


* Get DBFs
num_dbfs = adir("*.dbf")
PRIVATE dbfs[num_dbfs]
adir("*.dbf", dbfs)

* Get NTXs
num_ntxs = adir("*.ntx")
PRIVATE ntxs[num_ntxs]
adir("*.ntx", ntxs)

* Get NDXs
num_ndxs = adir("*.ndx")
PRIVATE ndxs[num_ndxs]
adir("*.ndx", ndxs)

init_consts()

* Make all PROMPTs this width
prompt_size = 12
```

```
* Initial prompt for horizontal MENU
horiz = 1

* Do until escape from horizontal menu

DO WHILE horiz != 0

        CLEAR

        * Frame and fill screen
        @ 0, 0, 24, 79 BOX SL_BOX + chr(177)

        @ 0, 02 PROMPT "DBFS"
        @ 0, 12 PROMPT "NTXS"
        @ 0, 22 PROMPT "NDXS"

        * 'hot' keys are OFF here
        MENU TO horiz

        * Set 'hot' keys, left and right arrow
        SET KEY LT_ARROW TO left_arrow
        SET KEY RT_ARROW TO right_arrow

        DO CASE

          CASE horiz = 1
                * Issue pulldown for DBFs and frame it

                @ 01, 01, num_dbfs + 2, 14 BOX SL_BOX

                FOR i = 1 TO num_dbfs
                        @ i + 1, 02 PROMPT menu_pad(dbfs[i], prompt_size)
                NEXT

                i = 1
                MENU TO i

          CASE horiz = 2
                * Issue pulldown for NTXs and frame it

                @ 01, 11, num_ntxs + 2, 24 BOX SL_BOX

                FOR i = 1 TO num_ntxs
                        @ i + 1, 12 PROMPT menu_pad(ntxs[i], prompt_size)
                NEXT

                i = 1
                MENU TO i

          CASE horiz = 3
                * Issue pulldown for NDXs and frame it
                @ 01, 21, num_ndxs + 2, 34 BOX SL_BOX
```

```
                    FOR i = 1 TO num_ndxs
                        @ i + 1, 22 PROMPT menu_pad(ndxs[i], prompt_size)
                    NEXT

                    i = 1
                    MENU TO i

          ENDCASE

          * Turn keys off to avoid recursion
          SET KEY RT_ARROW TO
          SET KEY LT_ARROW TO

     ENDDO

* Hot key routine for left arrow

PROCEDURE left_arrow

PARAMETERS a, b, c

PRIVATE move_left

     * stuff esc, up arrow, enter
     move_left = chr(ESC) + chr(UP_ARROW) + chr(ENTER)
     KEYBOARD move_left

RETURN


* Hot key routine for right arrow

PROCEDURE right_arrow

PARAMETERS a, b, c

PRIVATE move_right

     * stuff esc, down arrow, enter
     move_right = chr(ESC) + chr(DOWN_ARROW) + chr(ENTER)

     KEYBOARD move_right

RETURN


FUNCTION menu_pad

PARAMETERS string, size

RETURN (string + space(size - len(string)))
```

To move the bar right, we stuff the buffer with an Escape character to exit from the pulldown menu, a down arrow to move right, and then an Enter to select the new pulldown menu. We could also use the right arrow key.

To move the bar left, we stuff the buffer with an Escape character to exit from the pulldown menu, an up arrow to move left, and then an Enter to select the new pulldown.

Note that the routine turns off the hot keys after it invokes the pulldown. Although this is not strictly necessary, it would avoid an endless loop if we were stuffing the left and right arrow keys. The SET KEY would be executed which would stuff the keyboard with the same hot key. Once this key was processed, the SET KEY key would again be executed. It would stuff the buffer with the same key, etc., ad infinitum.

Turning off the SET KEY avoids this problem because a SET KEY is only invoked from a wait state, NOT when the key enters the buffer (as when stuffed). Even though we would stuff the key from its own routine, there would be no recursion because the key would not be processed until the next MENU TO, when the SET KEY is OFF. See Chapter 4 for more information on SET KEY.

After the horizontal move occurs, the routine executes the new pulldown menu code, positioning the highlight bar on the first menu. We may prefer to start the new pulldown menu at the current level on the adjacent menu. For example, if the highlight bar were at the third PROMPT in the second pulldown menu, and a move was made to the right, we would then start the third pulldown menu at level 3. Program 5-11 shows this.

Program 5-11. Pulldown Menu with Horizontal Scrolling to Same Position

```
* Pulldown menu code to allow selection of DBF, NTX, and NDX
* files present in current directory. Screen filled with ASCII 177,
* single line boxes drawn around pulldowns and entire screen.
* Left and right arrow keys perform horizontal movement, moving to
* same level in adjacent menus.
*
*
* 1 - Declare and fill arrays for dbf, ntx, and ndx files.
*       Use adir function.
*
* 2 - Frame screen and fill with background character
*
* 3 - Issue PROMPTS starting at 'vertical', get selection.
*
```

```
* 4 - Issue appropriate pulldown
*

* Get DBFs
num_dbfs = adir("*.dbf")
PRIVATE dbfs[num_dbfs]
adir("*.dbf", dbfs)

* Get NTXs
num_ntxs = adir("*.ntx")
PRIVATE ntxs[num_ntxs]
adir("*.ntx", ntxs)

* Get NDXs
num_ndxs = adir("*.ndx")
PRIVATE ndxs[num_ndxs]
adir("*.ndx", ndxs)

init_consts()

prompt_size = 12            && make all prompts this width

* Maintains currently selected horizontal
horiz = 1

* Maintains currently selected vertical
vertical = 1

* Do until escape from horizontal menu

DO WHILE horiz != 0

    CLEAR

    * frame and fill screen
    @ 0, 0, 24, 79 BOX SL_BOX + chr(177)

    @ 0, 02 PROMPT "DBFS"
    @ 0, 12 PROMPT "NTXS"
    @ 0, 22 PROMPT "NDXS"

    * hot keys are OFF here
    MENU TO horiz

    * set left and right arrow hot keys
    SET KEY LT_ARROW TO left_arrow
    SET KEY RT_ARROW TO right_arrow

    DO CASE

        CASE horiz = 1
            * Issue pulldown for DBFs and frame it
```

```
                @ 01, 01, num_dbfs + 2, 14 BOX SL_BOX

                FOR i = 1 TO num_dbfs
                        @ i + 1, 02 PROMPT menu_pad(dbfs[i], prompt_size)
                NEXT

                MENU TO vertical

        CASE horiz = 2
                * Issue pulldown for NTXs and frame it

                @ 01, 11, num_ntxs + 2, 24 BOX SL_BOX

                FOR i = 1 TO num_ntxs
                        @ i + 1, 12 PROMPT menu_pad(ntxs[i], prompt_size)
                NEXT

                MENU TO vertical

        CASE horiz = 3
                * Issue pulldown for NDXs and frame it

                @ 01, 21, num_ndxs + 2, 34 BOX SL_BOX

                FOR i = 1 TO num_ndxs
                        @ i + 1, 22 PROMPT menu_pad(ndxs[i], prompt_size)
                NEXT

                MENU TO vertical

      ENDCASE
      * Turn keys off to avoid recursion
      SET KEY RT_ARROW TO
      SET KEY LT_ARROW TO

  ENDDO


PROCEDURE left_arrow

PARAMETERS a, b, c

PRIVATE move_left

      * stuff Enter, up arrow, Enter

      move_left = chr(ENTER) + chr(UP_ARROW) + chr(ENTER)
      KEYBOARD move_left

RETURN
```

```
PROCEDURE right_arrow

PARAMETERS a, b, c

PRIVATE move_right

        * stuff Enter, down arrow, Enter

        move_right = chr(ENTER) + chr(DOWN_ARROW) + chr(ENTER)
        KEYBOARD move_right

RETURN

FUNCTION menu_pad

PARAMETERS string, size

RETURN (string + space(size - len(string)))
```

Program 5-11 differs in two ways from Program 5-10. First, it uses a common variable, "vertical", to keep track of the last position on the pulldown menu. Second, by stuffing the keyboard with an Enter as the first character, rather than an Escape, the pulldown menu terminates and fills "vertical" with the PROMPT number that was active when the hot key was pressed. In the previous version, "i" was zero since we terminated the menu with an Escape.

Note that Clipper lets you start a MENU command with an initial PROMPT value greater than the number of PROMPTs issued. It simply starts on the last one. Program 5-11 relies on this when moving horizontally - it does not validate the new initial PROMPT (in "vertical").

If you wanted the horizontal move to go to the previously selected PROMPT it was on, rather than to the same level, each prompt would need a separate variable.

Program 5-11 only demonstrates vertical and horizontal movement in pulldown menus. It does not DO anything. Typically, after a pulldown menu is executed, the code would use the selected value to DO a PROCEDURE, as in:

```
CASE horiz = 3

        @ 01, 21, num_ndxs + 2, 34 BOX SL_BOX

        FOR i = 1 TO num_ndxs
                @ i + 1, 22 PROMPT menu_pad(ndxs[i], prompt_size)
        NEXT
```

```
MENU TO vertical

DO CASE

     CASE vertical = 1
          DO ndx_menu1

     CASE vertical = 2
          DO ndx_menu2

ENDCASE
```

This conflicts with the new method of horizontally traversing the menus. Stuffing the buffer with Enter instead of Escape causes one case to be executed. An alternative method is necessary. The solution lies in using the procedure to set a global logical memory variable that indicates a horizontal move is required. The routine tests the variable before entering the CASE structure. Program 5-12 shows this.

Program 5-12. Pulldown Menu with Processing

```
* Pulldown menu code to allow selection of DBF, NTX, and NDX
* files present in current directory. Screen filled with ASCII 177,
* single line boxes drawn around pulldowns and entire screen.
* Left and right arrow keys perform horizontal movement, moving to
* same level in adjacent menus.
*
* Allow processing to take place using global horiz_move to indicate
* move required
*


* 1 - Declare and fill arrays for dbf, ntx, and ndx files
*       Use adir function
*
* 2 - Frame screen and fill with background character
*
* 3 - Issue PROMPTS starting at 'vertical', get selection
*
* 4 - Perform action
*
* 5 - Issue appropriate pulldown
*


* Get DBFs
num_dbfs = adir("*.dbf")
PRIVATE dbfs[num_dbfs]
adir("*.dbf", dbfs)
```

```
* Get NTXs
num_ntxs = adir("*.ntx")
PRIVATE ntxs[num_ntxs]
adir("*.ntx", ntxs)

* Get NDXs
num_ndxs = adir("*.ndx")
PRIVATE ndxs[num_ndxs]
adir("*.ndx", ndxs)

init_consts()

* Make all prompts this width
prompt_size = 12

* maintains currently selected horizontal
horiz = 1

* maintains currently selected vertical
vertical = 1

* Do until escape from horizontal menu

DO WHILE horiz != 0

    CLEAR

    * Frame and fill screen
    @ 0, 0, 24, 79 BOX SL_BOX + chr(177)

    @ 0, 02 PROMPT "DBFS"
    @ 0, 12 PROMPT "NTXS"
    @ 0, 22 PROMPT "NDXS"

    MENU TO horiz

    * activate hot keys
    SET KEY LT_ARROW TO left_arrow

    SET KEY RT_ARROW TO right_arrow
    horiz_move = .F.

    DO CASE

      CASE horiz = 1
            * Issue pulldown for DBFs and frame it

            @ 01, 01, num_dbfs + 2, 14 BOX SL_BOX

            FOR i = 1 TO num_dbfs
                @ i + 1, 02 PROMPT menu_pad(dbfs[i], prompt_size)
            NEXT
```

```
            MENU TO vertical

            * If we didn't leave pulldown with left or right arrow,
            * process selection
            IF !horiz_move
                  DO CASE
                        CASE vertical = 1
                              •
                              •

                        CASE vertical = 2
                              •
                              •

                        OTHERWISE
                              •
                              •

                  ENDCASE
            ENDIF

      CASE horiz = 2
            * Issue pulldown for NTXs and frame it

            @ 01, 11, num_ntxs + 2, 24 BOX SL_BOX

            FOR i = 1 TO num_ntxs
                  @ i + 1, 12 PROMPT menu_pad(ntxs[i], prompt_size)
            NEXT

            MENU TO vertical

            * If we didn't leave pulldown with left or right arrow,
            * process selection
            IF !horiz_move
                  DO CASE
                        CASE vertical = 1
                              •
                              •

                        CASE vertical = 2

                              •
                              •

                        OTHERWISE
                              •
                              •
                  ENDCASE
            ENDIF

      CASE horiz = 3
```

```
                    * Issue pulldown for NDXs and frame it

                    @ 01, 21, num_ndxs + 2, 34 BOX SL_BOX

                    FOR i = 1 TO num_ndxs
                        @ i + 1, 22 PROMPT menu_pad(ndxs[i], prompt_size)
                    NEXT

                    MENU TO vertical

                    * If we didn't leave pulldown with left or right arrow,
                    * process selection
                    IF !horiz_move
                        DO CASE
                            CASE vertical = 1
                                @ 20, 20 SAY "one"

                            CASE vertical = 2
                                @ 20, 20 SAY "two"

                            OTHERWISE
                                @ 20, 20 SAY "more"
                        ENDCASE
                    ENDIF
        ENDCASE

        SET KEY LT_ARROW TO
        SET KEY RT_ARROW TO

    ENDDO


    PROCEDURE left_arrow

    PARAMETERS a, b, c

    PRIVATE move_left

        horiz_move = .T.
        move_left = chr(ENTER) + chr(UP_ARROW) + chr(ENTER)
        KEYBOARD move_left

    RETURN


    PROCEDURE right_arrow

    PARAMETERS a, b, c

    PRIVATE move_right

        horiz_move = .T.
```

```
        move_right = chr(ENTER) + chr(DOWN_ARROW) + chr(ENTER)

        KEYBOARD move_right

RETURN

FUNCTION menu_pad

PARAMETERS string, size

RETURN (string + space(size - len(string)))
```

The pulldown menu code in Program 5-1 has grown much larger. However, it is still a simple program. Table 5-3 summarizes the different versions.

Table 5-3. Pulldown Menu Programs

PROGRAM	FUNCTION
5-1	Basic pulldown menu code with hard coded file names
5-2	Pulldown menu code using ADIR to get file names
5-3	Pulldown menu code with framing. Screen is filled with background character
5-10	Pulldown menu code as 5-3, using KEYBOARD and SET KEY to allow horizontal movement
5-11	As 5-10, except horizontal movement stays at same level in adjacent pulldowns
5-12	As 5-11, but allows processing of selected pulldown
5-13	As 5-12, but uses partial screen saves for speed

The KEYBOARD command is not additive. For example, the sequence:

```
KEYBOARD chr(ENTER)

KEYBOARD chr(ENTER)
```

puts just one ENTER key in the keyboard buffer. The second KEYBOARD statement overwrites the first one. To put two ENTERs in the buffer, you must write:

```
KEYBOARD chr(ENTER) + chr(ENTER)
```

KEYBOARD has many other uses. For example, we can simulate the RETURN TO MASTER command, not supported by Clipper. The dBASE RETURN TO MASTER command causes control to return to the main program. This is allowed from any nesting depth. We can do this in Clipper by stuffing the keyboard buffer with the characters necessary to return to the main level. If "backtracking" involves repainting the screen, as with nested menus, then the user will see the screen redrawing. You can usually program around this with a "backtrack" flag and the necessary IF statements. Still another use is in creating self-running demonstration versions of applications. Rather than developing a separate program, we can change the original application to stuff the keyboard buffer with the keys required to run it. You can intersperse the KEYBOARD commands with calls to the INKEY(x) function to slow things down.

TIPS

- Take care to avoid endless recursion when stuffing a 'hot key' from its own procedure.
- Hot keys stuffed with the KEYBOARD command do not cause the routine to be executed until a WAIT state is reached (for example, the result of a subsequent READ or MENU TO).
- Combine keys to be stuffed into one string. The KEYBOARD command is not additive.

SAVE SCREEN/RESTORE SCREEN

Clipper lets you save screens in memory variables and restore them. The SAVE SCREEN TO <memvar> and RESTORE SCREEN FROM <memvar> commands do this. On an IBM PC or compatible system, a screen contains 80 * 25 = 2000 characters. Since each character has an associated attribute byte, it takes 4000 characters to save a screen. The memvar created by a SAVE SCREEN will thus be 4000 bytes long. A common use of SAVE SCREEN is to temporarily display a message box over the top of the screen, giving a windowing effect. To do this, the programmer draws the screen, saves a copy of it, displays the message box on top of it, and restores the screen when the user finishes with the message. This is exactly what we must do to allow context specific help as described in Chapter 7.

SAVE SCREEN and RESTORE SCREEN are particularly useful in generic routines. They allow routines to be written without concern for the current screen content. The screen is saved initially and restored afterwards. For example, the following code checks whether the printer is ready. If not, it saves the screen, and then displays a message box. It waits for the user to press a key indicating that the printer is ready, or an Escape to abort the process. It restores the screen, and if the Escape key was not pressed, invokes the procedure "report".

```
IF !isprintr()
        SAVE SCREEN TO screen1

        message = "Printer not ready, press any key when ready or ESC to
                        abort"

        @ 10, 30, 12, len(message + 4) BOX sing_box
        @ 11, 32 SAY message
        key = 0

        * wait for a key or printer ready
        WHILE !isprinter .OR. key = ESC
                key = inkey(0)
        ENDDO

        RESTORE SCREEN FROM screen1

        IF key != ESC
                DO report
        ENDIF
ENDIF
```

If we wrote this as a routine, it could be called from anywhere in the program. The screen would not be disturbed.

The SAVE SCREEN and RESTORE SCREEN commands can produce the same effect as true overlapping windows. For example, the following code draws four overlapping windows, and then restores the underlying windows one at a time:

```
SAVE SCREEN TO dos_screen

col = col()
```

```
row = row()

CLEAR

init_consts()

@ 0, 0, 8, 8 BOX SL_BOX + "*"

SAVE SCREEN TO screen1

@ 4, 4, 12, 12 BOX SL_BOX + chr(1)

SAVE SCREEN TO screen2

@ 8, 8, 16, 16 BOX SL_BOX + chr(2)

SAVE SCREEN TO screen3

@ 12, 12, 20, 20 BOX SL_BOX + chr(14)

inkey(2)
RESTORE SCREEN FROM screen3

inkey(2)
RESTORE SCREEN FROM screen2

inkey(2)
RESTORE SCREEN FROM screen1

inkey(2)
RESTORE SCREEN FROM dos_screen

@ row, col SAY ""
```

If you do not understand this code, run it and see how it works.

Some programmers like to save the screen immediately upon entry to a program and restore it upon exit. This leave the "DOS" screen intact. Note that you must also save and restore the cursor position.

It is wasteful and time-consuming to save the entire screen when all you need is a small rectangle. The Summer '87 release has partial screen saves and restores. They involve two new functions, "SAVESCREEN" and "RESTSCREEN". SAVESCREEN takes four parameters, specifying the coordinates of the rectangle to be saved, and returns the screen area as its result. RESTSCREEN takes five parameters, four defining the coordinates of the rectangle to be restored, and a fifth the memory variable containing the window to be restored.

RESTSCREEN requires a memory variable returned from a

SAVESCREEN, since it contains the bytes used to define the attributes of the characters. The RESTSCREEN routine can, however, restore the window in a different area. For example, the following code draws a box, and then lets the arrow keys move it:

```
CLEAR

init_consts()

SET CURSOR OFF

x = 10
y = 10

key = 0

* save an empty window ...
empty_win = savescreen(x, y, x + 4, y + 4)

@ x, y, x + 4, y + 4 BOX SL_BOX

box_win  = savescreen(x, y, x + 4, y + 4)

DO WHILE key != ESC

    key = inkey(0)

    * clear old window
    restscreen(x, y, x + 4, y + 4, empty_win)

    DO CASE

        CASE key = UP_ARROW
            x = x - 1

        CASE key = DOWN_ARROW
            x = x + 1

        CASE key = LT_ARROW
            y = y - 1

        CASE key = RT_ARROW
            y = y + 1

    ENDCASE

    restscreen(x, y, x + 4, y + 4, box_win)

ENDDO

SET CURSOR ON

CLEAR
```

Note the technique of saving an empty window, and then using it to delete a window of the same size.

Program 5-12 cleared the screen and redrew the horizontal prompts after executing the MENU TO command on the pulldown menu. On an IBM PC-XT, this causes a noticeable delay. Once again, there is no need to clear the entire screen. All that is necessary is to save the area overwritten by the pulldown menu, and then restore it afterwards. Program 5-13 actually saves only a copy of the empty background; all three windows contain the same values. We programmed the code in a general manner deliberately.

Program 5-13. Pulldown Menu Code with Partial Screen Save and Restore

```
* Pulldown menu code to allow selection of DBF, NTX, and NDX
* files present in current directory. Screen filled with ASCII 177,
* single line boxes drawn around pulldowns and entire screen.
* Partial screen save and restore used to save underlying areas.
* Left and right arrow keys perform horizontal movement to adjacent
* pulldown at same depth
*
* 1 - Declare and fill arrays for dbf, ntx, and ndx files
*        Use adir function
*
* 2 - Frame screen and fill with background char
*
* 3 - Issue PROMPTS starting at 'vertical', get selection
*
* 4 - Issue appropriate pulldown
*

CLEAR

* Get DBFs
num_dbfs = adir("*.dbf")
DECLARE dbfs[num_dbfs]
adir("*.dbf", dbfs)

* Save its window
dbfs_win = savescreen(1, 0, num_dbfs + 3, 13)

num_ntxs = adir("*.ntx")
DECLARE ntxs[num_ntxs]
adir("*.ntx", ntxs)

ntxs_win = savescreen(1, 10, num_ntxs + 3, 23)

num_ndxs = adir("*.ndx")
DECLARE ndxs[num_ndxs]
```

```
adir("*.ndx", ndxs)

ndxs_win = savescreen(1, 20, num_ndxs + 3, 33)
init_consts()

* Maintains currently selected horizontal
horiz = 1

* Maintains currently selected vertical
vertical = 1

* Do until escape from horizontal menu

DO WHILE horiz != 0

    @ 0, 01 PROMPT "DBFS"
    @ 0, 11 PROMPT "NTXS"
    @ 0, 21 PROMPT "NDXS"

    MENU TO horiz

    SET KEY LT_ARROW TO left_arrow
    SET KEY RT_ARROW TO right_arrow

    DO CASE

      CASE horiz = 1

            @ 01, 00, num_dbfs + 2, 13 BOX SL_BOX

            FOR i = 1 TO num_dbfs
                @ i + 1, 01 PROMPT menu_pad(dbfs[i], 12)
            NEXT

            MENU TO vertical

            restscreen(1, 0, num_dbfs + 3, 13, dbfs_win)

      CASE horiz = 2

            @ 01, 10, num_ntxs + 2, 23 BOX SL_BOX

            FOR i = 1 TO num_ntxs
                @ i + 1, 11 PROMPT menu_pad(ntxs[i], 12)
            NEXT

            MENU TO vertical

            restscreen(1, 10, num_ntxs + 3, 23, ntxs_win)

      CASE horiz = 3
```

```
                @ 01, 20, num_ndxs + 2, 33 BOX SL_BOX

                FOR i = 1 TO num_ndxs
                        @ i + 1, 21 PROMPT menu_pad(ndxs[i], 12)
                NEXT

                MENU TO vertical

                restscreen(1, 20, num_ndxs + 3, 33, ndxs_win)

        ENDCASE

        SET KEY RT_ARROW TO
        SET KEY LT_ARROW TO

ENDDO

PROCEDURE left_arrow

        * stuff Enter, left, Enter
        KEYBOARD chr(ENTER) + chr(UP_ARROW) + chr(ENTER)

RETURN

PROCEDURE right_arrow

        * stuff Enter, right arrow, Enter
        KEYBOARD chr(ENTER) + chr(DOWN_ARROW) + chr(ENTER)

RETURN

FUNCTION menu_pad

PARAMETERS string, size

RETURN (string + space(size - len(string)))
```

You can use Program 5-13 as a basis for a customized, efficient pulldown menu system. To allow it to process the selected menu item, add the CASE and the 'horiz_move' variable as in Program 5-12.

TIPS

- Use 'SAVESCREEN' and 'RESTSCREEN' to save just the changed part of the screen.
- Use these functions in generic routines to avoid disturbing the current screen.

Screen and MEM Files

Since full and partial screens can be saved in memory variables, they can also be saved in and restored from MEM files. This is very useful, as drawing a complex screen can be time consuming. Changing colors, drawing boxes, etc. are all very "user intensive" operations. The user is actually seeing something happen rather slowly. A program that has many complex screens can benefit greatly from storing them in MEM files. They can be restored, and thus the screen redrawn, in a fraction of the time it takes to draw the screen initially. The programmer can either ship applications with the MEM files already built, containing the screens, or can draw the screens and construct the MEM files the first time the application is run. Program 5-14 shows an example.

Program 5-14. Transferring a Screen to and from a MEM File.

```
CLEAR

SET COLOR TO G+/R
@ 0, 10 SAY "C"

SET COLOR TO G/R
@ 0, 11 SAY "HOICE 1"

SET COLOR TO G+/GR
@ 0, 20 SAY "C"

SET COLOR TO G/GR
@ 0, 21 SAY "HOICE 2"

SET COLOR TO GR+/BG
@ 0, 30 SAY "C"

SET COLOR TO GR/BG
@ 0, 31 SAY "HOICE 3"

SET COLOR TO R+/B
@ 0, 40 SAY "C"

SET COLOR TO R/B
@ 0, 41 SAY "HOICE 4"

SET COLOR TO B+/GR
@ 0, 50 SAY "C"

SET COLOR TO B/GR
```

```
@ 0, 51 SAY "HOICE 5"

SET COLOR TO GR+/W
@ 0, 60 SAY "C"
SET COLOR TO GR/W
@ 0, 61 SAY "HOICE 6"

line1 = savescreen(0, 1, 0, 79)

CLEAR

SAVE TO testm ALL LIKE line1
RESTORE FROM testm

restscreen(0, 1, 0, 79, line1)
```

Program 5-14 draws the first line of the screen in various colors, saves it in a memory variable, and then in a MEM file. It then saves the screen and later restores the variable from the MEM file to the screen.

Summary

This chapter shows the basics of using Clipper to write efficient, elegant user interfaces. The next chapter continues this theme, showing Clipper's more advanced features. Some points you should note from this chapter are:

- Save and restore partial screens rather than full screens whenever possible.
- Use the BOX command to clearly define the borders of menus, messages, text, etc.
- Consider saving screens in MEM files and restoring them, rather than building them from scratch.
- Use the KEYBOARD command with care. It can lead to incomprehensible code. Most of its use in this book is to overcome inadequacies in Clipper.
- When using the MESSAGE option of the PROMPT command, use a function to create the entire line.
- Define all key values symbolically as PUBLICs. This saves you from having to continually refer to an INKEY chart,

and makes the code more readable. Appendix A discusses using a preprocessor with Clipper.

- Modify the pulldown menu code developed here for your own use. Consider making a database-driven version of this code.

6

User Interface: Advanced Features

This chapter covers advanced aspects of user interfaces and illustrates Clipper extensions. Become familiar with the commands used here and in Chapter 5. The user interface is often a critical part of a successful application.

Much of this chapter deals with GET, probably the most important command in the dBASE language. Later parts develop scrolling routines that let you browse through arrays and databases. We discuss the RL program and show how to use its source code to create dialog boxes. We also present a spreadsheet interface that is well structured and easy to tailor to your own needs.

GET Processing

Clipper has made many extensions to the dBASE language for processing GETs. It allows GETs on fields from an unselected database. It also allows horizontal scrolling of the GET variable with the S picture clause option, and European number formatting with the E option. The Clipper documentation describes these extensions adequately. This section focuses on the VALID option, the UPDATED function, and on a system we call "two dimensional GET processing."

UPDATED

When returning from a GET/READ sequence, the program often must determine whether the user changed any fields. This could indicate the end of an editing process, or prevent the redundant updating of a database. The usual approach is to compare a saved copy of the original data with the new values. Program 6-1 shows the source of an "append" routine. The database records have the following structure:

```
NAME    TYPE    LEN   DEC

S_NO     C       4
P_NO     C       4
J_NO     C       4
QTY      N       5     0
```

The name of the database is SPJ.

Program 6-1. Sample Append

```
* APPEND routine
*

* 1 - LOOP WHILE changed
*
*       1.1 - Append blank record
*
*       1.2 - Copy blank fields to memory variables
*
```

```
*       1.3 - Place GETs and do READ
*
*       1.4 - If changed
*
*               1.4.1 - Update record

USE spj

changed = .T.

CLEAR
DO WHILE changed

        APPEND BLANK

        m_s_no = s_no
        m_p_no = p_no
        m_j_no = j_no
        m_qty = qty

        changed = .F.

        @ 10, 10 SAY "S_NO " GET m_s_no
        @ 11, 10 SAY "P_NO " GET m_p_no
        @ 12, 10 SAY "J_NO " GET m_j_no
        @ 13, 10 SAY "QTY  " GET m_qty

        READ

        IF s_no != m_s_no .OR. p_no != m_p_no .OR. j_no != m_j_no ;
          .OR. qty != m_qty

                REPLACE s_no WITH m_s_no
                REPLACE p_no WITH m_p_no
                REPLACE j_no WITH m_j_no
                REPLACE qty  WITH m_qty

                changed = .T.
        ENDIF
ENDDO
```

Before replacing the record, the code verifies that a change occurred. If not, the loop simply terminates. This prevents unnecessary updates.

We can use the UPDATED function to simplify the code as shown in Program 6-2. UPDATED returns a .T. value if any data was changed, and .F. otherwise.

Program 6-2. Sample Append Using UPDATED

```
* APPEND routine using UPDATED
*
* 1 - LOOP WHILE changed
*
*       1.1 - Append blank record
*
*       1.2 - Copy blank fields to memory variables
*
*       1.3 - Place GETs and do READ
*
*       1.4 - If changed
*
*             1.4.1 - Update record

USE spj

changed = .T.

CLEAR

DO WHILE changed

      APPEND BLANK

      m_s_no = s_no
      m_p_no = p_no
      m_j_no = j_no
      m_qty = qty

      changed = .F.

      @ 10, 10 SAY "S_NO " GET m_s_no
      @ 11, 10 SAY "P_NO " GET m_p_no
      @ 12, 10 SAY "J_NO " GET m_j_no
      @ 13, 10 SAY "QTY  " GET m_qty

      READ

      IF updated()

            changed = .T.
            REPLACE s_no WITH m_s_no
            REPLACE p_no WITH m_p_no
            REPLACE j_no WITH m_j_no
            REPLACE qty  WITH m_qty

      ENDIF
ENDDO
```

We replaced the IF statement with code that uses UPDATED to check for differences. Since UPDATED initially returns a .F. value, we cannot use it as the loop control variable.

The append code has a side effect that experienced Clipper programmers should recognize — it always adds an extra blank record at the end of the database. We append the record to get blank memory variables of the correct size and type. Chapter 8 suggests ways to eliminate the extra record and develops a general purpose append routine.

VALID

GET's VALID option uses the keyword "VALID" followed by a logical expression (which may be a user defined function returning a logical). The expression is used to validate the GET. The user can exit only when the expression returns a .T., or by pressing Esc with SET ESCAPE ON.

This feature makes GET far more user friendly, as it allows for immediate correction of entry errors. Previously, a typical sequence of program steps to validate GETs would be:

```
... get mem1
... get mem2
... get mem3

READ

validate mem1
validate mem2
validate mem3

IF .NOT. all_validated
```

An overall WHILE loop is necessary. If a field is invalid, the program reissues the GETs. This involves re-painting the screen, which although not time consuming, is highly visible to the user. Furthermore, the user does not learn about the error until after he or she has entered all the data. Imagine validating a screen of 20 or 30 GETs this way! It could take virtually forever.

The following example shows a simple use of the VALID option. It requires the input from a single character GET to be either M or F. Those belonging to other sexes beware!

```
sex = "M"

@ 10, 10 GET sex PICTURE "@!" VALID sex $ "MF"
READ
```

The alternative without VALID is:

```
sex = "M"
@ 10, 10 GET sex PICTURE "@!"
READ

DO WHILE .NOT. sex $ "MF"
     @ 10, 10 GET sex PICTURE "@!"
     READ
ENDDO
```

Besides allowing line by line validation of GETs, the VALID option also allows a user defined function to be called at each GET line, thereby giving the programmer control over processing. You can display error messages, issue prompts, count or "stuff" keys, or do other operations from within the GET/VALID cycle.

Program 6-3 verifies that the state abbreviation is CA, WA, or NY. If not, the routine displays a message and gives the user the option of quitting or retrying. To quit, the routine uses the KEYBOARD command to stuff the keyboard buffer with an Escape. Note that this only works with SET ESCAPE ON. Upon return from the READ, the main program uses the LASTKEY function to check how the GET terminated.

Program 6-3. Using a User Defined Function with VALID

```
* Example of a VALID user defined function
*

CLEAR

ESC = 27
state = "CA"

@ 10, 10 GET state PICTURE "@!" VALID good_state(state)
READ

IF lastkey() = ESC
     ? "Get terminated with Escape"
ELSE
     ? "Get terminated normally"
ENDIF

FUNCTION good_state

PARAMETER state

PRIVATE ret_val, save_win, key
```

```
        ret_val = (state = "CA" .OR. state = "WA" .OR. state = "NY")
        IF !ret_val

                save_win = savescreen(23, 0, 24, 79)

                @ 24, 10 SAY "Invalid state, retry? "
                key = inkey(0)

                IF key = asc("N") .OR. KEY = asc("n")
                        KEYBOARD chr(ESC)
                ENDIF

                restscreen(23, 0, 24, 79, save_win)

        ENDIF

RETURN (ret_val)
```

Note that we must read the key with INKEY, not GET. Clipper does not allow nested GETs. Appendix C shows GET code to overcome this limitation.

As another example, assume we want to validate the state abbreviation from a database, "state_ab", indexed on the two character field "state". The following user defined function does the job.

```
FUNCTION good_ab

PARAMETER state_ab
PRIVATE ret_val, save_sel

        save_sel = select()
        SELECT 0
        USE state_ab INDEX state

        SEEK &state_ab

        ret_val = found()

        * This close is important, as it avoids opening a new copy of the
        * file with every call
        USE

        SELECT (save_sel)

RETURN (ret_val)
```

As yet another example, let us rewrite append code for the SPJ database to validate each field. We assume that:

- Information about part numbers is in the "parts" database, indexed on the "p_no" field.

- Information about suppliers is in the "supplier" database, indexed on the "s_no" field.
- Information about projects is in the "project" database, indexed on the "j_no" field.

Program 6-4 shows the code.

Program 6-4. Validation of Fields from a Database

```
* APPEND routine using UPDATED and VALIDation from a database
*
* 1 - Open databases with indexes
*
* 2 - LOOP WHILE changed
*
*       2.1 - Append blank record
*
*       2.2 - Copy blank fields to memory variables
*
*       2.3 - Place GETs with VALIDs and do READ
*
*       2.4 - If changed
*
*             2.4.1 - Update record


CLEAR

SELECT 0
USE parts INDEX p_no

SELECT 0
USE supplier INDEX s_no

SELECT 0
USE project INDEX j_no

SELECT 0
USE spj

ESC = 27
key = 0
changed = .T.

DO WHILE changed

       APPEND BLANK
       m_s_no = s_no
       m_p_no = p_no
```

```
        m_j_no = j_no
        m_qty = qty

        changed = .F.

        @ 10, 10 SAY "S_NO " GET m_s_no VALID good_s_no(m_s_no)
        @ 11, 10 SAY "P_NO " GET m_p_no VALID good_p_no(m_p_no)
        @ 12, 10 SAY "J_NO " GET m_j_no VALID good_j_no(m_j_no)
        @ 13, 10 SAY "QTY  " GET m_qty  VALID m_qty > 0

        READ

        IF updated()

                changed = .T.
                REPLACE s_no WITH m_s_no
                REPLACE p_no WITH m_p_no
                REPLACE  j_no WITH m_j_no
                REPLACE qty  WITH m_qty

        ENDIF
ENDDO

FUNCTION good_s_no

PARAMETER s_num
PRIVATE save_sel, ret_val

        save_sel = select()
        SELECT supplier

        seek s_num
        ret_val = found()

        SELECT (save_sel)

RETURN (ret_val)


FUNCTION good_p_no

PARAMETER p_num
PRIVATE save_sel, ret_val

        save_sel = select()
        SELECT parts

        seek p_num
        ret_val = found()

        SELECT (save_sel)
```

```
RETURN (ret_val)

FUNCTION good_j_no

PARAMETER j_num
PRIVATE save_sel, ret_val

        save_sel = select()
        SELECT project

        seek j_num
        ret_val = found()

        SELECT (save_sel)

RETURN (ret_val)
```

Note that for speed, Program 6-4 opens the required databases and then reselects them, rather than reusing them in every invocation of the functions. Also note that upon return from a function, the same selection is active as when the function was called. This is important as the calling routine relies on spj being the active database.

Using VALID for Processing

Sometimes we use the VALID option with a function that simply returns a .T. value. The function does something after every GET. Program 6-5 has a function that keeps a running total of computer expenses.

Program 6-5. Using the VALID Function to Maintain a Running Total

```
* 1 - Initialize items and totals
*
* 2 - Issue GETs with "do_tot" as the VALID
*
* 3 - do_tot UDF
*
*       3.1 - Add items and calculate totals
*
*       3.2 - Display totals

hardware = 000.00
software = 000.00
books = 000.00

sub_total = 000.00
```

```
total = 000.00
tax = 00.00

CLEAR

* Don't allow other gets to be seen until selected
SET COLOR TO W/N, N/W,,,W/N

@ 4, 10 SAY "hardware"
@ 4, 20 GET hardware VALID do_tot()

@ 5, 10 SAY "software"
@ 5, 20 GET software VALID do_tot()

@ 6, 10 SAY "books"
@ 6, 20 GET books VALID do_tot()

@ 8, 10 SAY "sub total"
@ 8, 20 SAY sub_total

@ 10, 10 SAY "tax"
@ 10, 20 SAY tax

@ 12, 10 SAY "total"
@ 12, 20 SAY total

READ

FUNCTION do_tot

PARAM value
PRIVATE i

      sub_total = hardware + software + books
      @ 8, 20 SAY sub_total

      tax = sub_total * 6.5 / 100
      @ 10, 20 SAY tax

      total = sub_total + tax
      @ 12, 20 SAY total

RETURN (.T.)
```

Every GET calls the function "do_tot" which calculates the subtotal, tax, and total, and displays them. The routine initially sets the "unselected" color, another Clipper extension, so only the currently selected GET appears in reverse video.

> **TIP**
>
> You can use a VALID function to do other tasks besides validation.

Disallowing Exit with Unsatisfied VALIDs

VALID prevents a single GET from terminating unless it returns .T.. However, there is a way to exit a sequence of GETs without all the VALID conditions being met. Study the following example:

```
CLEAR

hardware = 0.00
@ 10, 10 SAY "Hardware   " GET hardware VALID hardware > 0

software = 0.00
@ 12, 10 SAY "Software   " GET software

books = 0.00
@ 14, 10 SAY "Books      " GET books VALID books > 0 .AND. books < 500

disks = 0.00
@ 16, 10 SAY "Disks      " GET disks VALID disks < 20
READ
```

The GET for software has no VALID clause. Pressing a key that exits a READ on this particular GET will leave books and disks with invalid data. To only allow exits when all VALIDs are satisfied, each GET without a VALID must have a VALID clause that calls a function. The function disallows the exit by returning a .F. when one of those keys was pressed. It then stuffs the keyboard with an Enter key to terminate the current GET and go to the next one.

The following keys cause a READ command to exit:

PageUp	(18)	(same value as Ctrl-R)
PageDn	(3)	(same value as Ctrl-C)
Ctrl-W	(23)	(same value as Ctrl-End)
Esc	(27)	(only when SET ESCAPE IS ON)
Enter	(13)	(only when on last GET)
Ctrl-Y	(24)	(only from last GET when READEXIT is .T.)
Ctrl-X	(25)	(only from last GET when READEXIT is .T.)

Although Ctrl-End and Ctrl-W have the same INKEY value, they behave differently in a READ. Ctrl-W exits, whereas Ctrl-End moves to the last GET. Checking for a key value of 23 will trap both combinations. Program 6-6 does this.

Program 6-6. Using VALID to Disallow Exit

```
CLEAR

init_consts()
```

```
hardware = 0.00
@ 10, 10 SAY "hardware   " GET hardware VALID hardware > 0

software = 0.00
@ 12, 10 SAY "software   " GET software VALID no_exit()

books = 0.00
@ 14, 10 SAY "books      " GET books VALID books > 0 .AND. books < 500

disks = 0.00
@ 16, 10 SAY "disks      " GET disks VALID disks < 20
READ

FUNCTION no_exit

PRIVATE key, ret_val

     key = lastkey()
     IF key = PG_UP .OR. key = PG_DOWN .OR. key = CTRL_W ;
       .OR. (readexit() .AND. (key = UP_ARROW .OR. key = DOWN_ARROW))
          KEYBOARD chr(ENTER)
          ret_val = .F.
     ELSE
          ret_val = .T.
     ENDIF

RETURN (ret_val)
```

The function is invoked twice when the user presses one of the above keys. The first call causes it to return .F.. However, the call also stuffs the keyboard with an Enter key, so the function is immediately re-invoked, and returns a .T. value. If you want the function to stay on the same GET, remove the KEYBOARD command.

Program 6-6 prevents exits through GETs without VALIDs. However, you can still exit the READ by filling a GET that does not contain a call to no_exit with a valid value, and then pressing a terminating key combination. To overcome this, we must put the no_exit function call on every VALID, as shown in Program 6-7.

Program 6-7. Using VALID to Disallow Exit from Any GET

```
CLEAR

init_consts()

hardware = 0.00
@ 10, 10 SAY "hardware " GET hardware VALID hardware > 0 .AND. no_exit()
```

```
software = 0.00
@ 12, 10 SAY "software    " GET software VALID no_exit()

books = 0.00
@ 14, 10 SAY "books       " GET books VALID books > 0 .AND. books < 500 ;
                                  .AND. no_exit()
disks = 0.00
@ 16, 10 SAY "disks       " GET disks VALID disks < 20 .AND. no_exit()
READ

FUNCTION no_exit

PRIVATE key, ret_val

     key = lastkey()
     IF key = PG_UP .OR. key = PG_DOWN .OR. key = CTRL_W,
       .OR. (readexit() .AND. (key = UP_ARROW .OR. key = DOWN_ARROW))

          KEYBOARD chr(ENTER)
          ret_val = .F.
     ELSE
          ret_val = .T.
     ENDIF

RETURN (ret_val)
```

Restrictions on VALID

There are restrictions on expressions with VALID, and on what you can pass to a VALID function. Since the parameter is evaluated when the READ occurs, not when the GET is processed, the parameter cannot depend on the values of any variables at the time of the GET. The most common example is the use of an index variable for an array subscript as in:

```
PRIVATE gets[5]

afill(gets, 1)

CLEAR

FOR i = 1 TO 5

     @ 10 + i, 10 GET gets[i] VALID gets[i] > 2

NEXT

READ
```

As soon as the first VALID is invoked, a run time "array subscript error" occurs since i is 6 after the FOR loop terminates. However, because of the new way the Summer '87 release handles macros, their use in VALIDs does not cause a problem. The following code, for example, works correctly:

```
gets1 = 1
gets2 = 1
gets3 = 1
gets4 = 1
gets5 = 1

CLEAR

FOR i = 1 TO 5
        stri = ltrim(str(i))

        @ 10 + i, 10 GET gets&stri VALID gets&stri > 2

NEXT

READ
```

You can, of course, use array elements with GETs, as long as the index expression at the time of the GET is the same as at the time of the READ. We could rewrite the above code, for example, as:

```
PRIVATE gets[5]

@ 11, 10 GET gets[1] VALID gets[1] > 2
@ 12, 10 GET gets[2] VALID gets[2] > 2
@ 13, 10 GET gets[3] VALID gets[3] > 2
@ 14, 10 GET gets[4] VALID gets[4] > 2
@ 15, 10 GET gets[5] VALID gets[5] > 2

READ
```

The VALID clause is a powerful extension to the dBASE language. Besides allowing data validation before the READ exits, it gives the programmer control over the GET processing.

Two Dimensional GETs

Clipper processes GETs in the order they are issued, regardless of their screen positions. Pressing the down arrow key makes the READ proceed to the next GET. Similarly, the up arrow makes it proceed to the previous GET. You can allow these keys to cause the

READ to terminate by using the READEXIT function. The left and right arrow keys move the cursor within the current GET - they do not move it from one GET to another.

This one dimensional operation is often restrictive. The up and down arrow keys do not behave as one would intuitively expect when GETs are positioned horizontally. We often want to let the user navigate with the cursor keys and select with the Enter key. In this system, the cursor keys operate as one would expect - in a two-dimensional way. The left and right arrow keys cause horizontal movement, and the up and down arrow keys cause vertical movement.

The first stage in developing this system is to write a navigation routine. It moves a selection bar according to the cursor keys. We will make the routine navigate through fields from a database with the following structure:

```
*** structure of database cust.dbf ***

Last update 87 11 29

Data offset 865
Record size 515
Number of records 2

NAME          TYPE   LEN   DEC

CUST_ID        C      10
CUST_NAME      C      23
ADD1           C      30
ADD2           C      30
ADD3           C      30
ADD4           C       3
PHONE          C      14
CREDIT_LIM     N      12     2
OPEN_AR        N      12     2
LAST_ODATE     D       8
YTD_SALES      N      12     2
LAST_YSALE     N      12     2
MTD_SALES      N      12     2
C1_NAME        C      20
C1_PHONE       C      14
C1_COMMENT     C      40
C2_NAME        C      20
C2_PHONE       C      14
C2_COMMENT     C      40
C3_NAME        C      20
C3_PHONE       C      14
C3_COMMENT     C      40
C4_NAME        C      20
```

```
C4_PHONE      C    14
C4_COMMENT    C    40
COMMENTS      M    10
```

The fields C1_NAME .. C4_COMMENT contain the name, telephone number, and comments for four contacts. Assume we want to display them on the screen as follows:

```
C1_NAME      C1_PHONE      C1_COMMENT
C2_NAME      C2_PHONE      C2_COMMENT
C3_NAME      C3_PHONE      C3_COMMENT
C4_NAME      C4_PHONE      C4_COMMENT
```

The navigation routine must know the field name and screen location of each item, the number of fields to display per line, the total number of fields, and the enhanced and normal color strings (so it can highlight fields and remove the highlight as necessary). For the example shown above, the parameters would be set up as Program 6-8a shows.

Program 6-8a. Setting up Variables for Navigate Routine

```
****
* NAV1.PRG
*
*  Set up field names, coordinates, and colors for NAVIGATE routine
*

USE cust

CLEAR

init_consts()

num_fields = 12
first_field = 14
fields_line = 3

PRIVATE fnames[num_fields], rows[num_fields], cols[num_fields]

FOR i = first_field TO first_field + num_fields - 1
      fnames[i - first_field + 1] = fieldname(i)
NEXT

* set up get coordinates
FOR i = 1 TO num_fields / fields_line
```

```
        rows[fields_line * (i - 1) + 1] = 9 + i
        cols[fields_line * (i - 1) + 1] = 2
        rows[fields_line * (i - 1) + 2] = 9 + i
        cols[fields_line * (i - 1) + 2] = 23
        rows[fields_line * (i - 1) + 3] = 9 + i
        cols[fields_line * (i - 1) + 3] = 38

NEXT

norm = "W/ "
enh  = " /W"
```

We would call the routine with:

```
DO navigate WITH fnames, rows, cols, enh, norm, fields_line, num_fields
```

Program 6-8b shows the navigate routine.

Program 6-8b. Two-Dimensional Navigate

```
* The navigate function
*
* 1 - Draw box and SAY fields inside it
*
* 2 - DO UNTIL user presses Enter
*
*       2.1 - Highlight current field
*
*       2.2 - Wait for a key
*
*       2.3 - Remove highlight from current field
*
*       2.4 - Switch on key to call cursor movement routine

PROCEDURE navigate

PARAM fnames, rows, cols, enh, norm, fields_line, num_fields

PRIVATE key, current_get, fname, last_rec, first_rec

        DO draw_screen

        key = 0

        current_get = 1

        SET CURSOR OFF
```

```
        DO WHILE (key != ENTER)
                fname = fnames[current_get]
                * highlight current selection
                SET COLOR TO &enh
                @ rows[current_get], cols[current_get] SAY &fname
                SET COLOR TO &norm

                key = inkey(0)

                * remove the highlight
                @ rows[current_get], cols[current_get] SAY &fname

                DO CASE
                        CASE key = DOWN_ARROW
                                DO dn_arrow_proc

                        CASE key = UP_ARROW
                                DO up_arrow_proc

                        CASE key = LT_ARROW
                                DO lt_arrow_proc

                        CASE key = RT_ARROW
                                DO rt_arrow_proc
                ENDCASE

        ENDDO

        SET CURSOR ON

RETURN

PROCEDURE dn_arrow_proc

        * If not on last line, go down by number of lines specified
        * by fields_line : 3 in this case
        IF current_get <= num_fields - fields_line

                current_get = current_get + fields_line

        ENDIF

RETURN

PROCEDURE up_arrow_proc

        * If not on top line, go up by number of lines specified
        * by fields_line : 3 in this case

        IF current_get > fields_line
```

```
            current_get = current_get - fields_line

        ENDIF

    RETURN

    PROCEDURE lt_arrow_proc

        * If not at first get, go back one
        IF current_get > 1

            current_get = current_get - 1

        ENDIF

    RETURN

    PROCEDURE rt_arrow_proc

        * If not at last get, go forward one
        IF current_get < num_fields

            current_get = current_get + 1

        ENDIF

    RETURN

    PROCEDURE draw_screen

    PRIVATE fname

        FOR i = 1 TO num_fields

            fname = fnames[i]
            @ rows[i], cols[i] SAY &fname

        NEXT

    RETURN
```

Using Program 6-8b as a base, we can allow the editing of a field selected with the Enter key as shown in Program 6-9.

Program 6-9. Navigate Allowing Editing

```
    * The navigate function
    *
    * 1 - Draw box and SAY fields inside it
    *
```

```
* 2 - DO UNTIL user presses Escape
*
*       2.1 - DO UNTIL user presses Escape or Enter
*
*               2.1.1 - Highlight current field
*
*               2.1.2 - Wait for a key
*
*               2.1.3 - Remove highlight from current field
*
*               2.1.3 - Switch on key to call cursor movement routine
*
*       2.2 - IF key was Enter
*
*               2.2.1 - Issue GET on current field and READ

PROCEDURE nav_edit

PARAM fnames, rows, cols, enh, norm, fields_line, num_fields

PRIVATE key, current_get, fname

        DO draw_screen

        key = 0
        current_get = 1

        * starting navigate mode ...

        DO WHILE key != ESC

                * for inner loop ...
                key = 0

                SET CURSOR OFF

                * select get to edit or escape
                DO WHILE (key != ENTER .AND. key != ESC)

                        fname = fnames[current_get]

                        SET COLOR TO &enh
                        @ rows[current_get], cols[current_get] SAY &fname
                        SET COLOR TO &norm

                        key = inkey(0)

                        * remove the highlight
                        @ rows[current_get], cols[current_get] SAY &fname
                        DO CASE
                                CASE key = DOWN_ARROW
                                        DO dn_arrow_proc
```

```
                    CASE key = UP_ARROW
                          DO up_arrow_proc

                    CASE key = LT_ARROW
                          DO lt_arrow_proc

                    CASE key = RT_ARROW
                          DO rt_arrow_proc
               ENDCASE

          ENDDO

          SET CURSOR ON

          IF key <> ESC
               * starting edit mode ...

               fname = fnames[current_get]

               @ rows[current_get], cols[current_get] GET &fname
               READ

               * note, since we don't assign to "key" here, an ESC
               * will not exit DO WHILE ! escape loop
          ENDIF

     ENDDO

RETURN
```

If the user presses Enter, a single GET is issued, followed by a READ. As soon as the READ is terminated, the routine resumes its navigate mode. The user terminates the mode by pressing the Escape key.

We can modify these routines in many ways. We can easily allow the user to skip records with the PgUp and PgDn keys. The CASE statement must change to recognize the two keys and call a function.

```
DO CASE
     CASE key = DOWN_ARROW
          DO dn_arrow_proc
     CASE key = UP_ARROW
          DO up_arrow_proc
     CASE key = LT_ARROW
          DO lt_arrow_proc
     CASE key = RT_ARROW
          DO rt_arrow_proc
```

```
        CASE key = PG_DOWN
              DO pg_down_proc
        CASE key = PG_UP
              DO pg_up_proc

    ENDCASE
```

The page up and down routines do a SKIP and redraw the screen.

```
    PROCEDURE pg_down_proc

          IF recno() != last_rec

                SKIP
                DO draw_screen

          ENDIF

    RETURN

    PROCEDURE pg_up_proc

          IF recno() != first_rec

                SKIP -1
                DO draw_screen

          ENDIF

    RETURN
```

The initialization must first set up first_rec and last_rec.

```
    PROCEDURE nav_edit

    PARAM fnames, rows, cols, enh, norm

    PRIVATE key, current_get, fname, last_rec, first_rec

          DO draw_screen

          key = 0
          current_get = 1

          GOTO BOTT
          last_rec = recno()

          GOTO TOP
          first_rec = recno()

          •
          •
          •
```

The initial navigate code, NAV1, lets the left arrow key wrap to the preceding line, and the right arrow key to the following line. To prohibit this, recode the routines using the modulus operator % as:

```
PROCEDURE lt_arrow_proc

    * If not at first get on line ...
    IF (current_get % fields_line) != 1

        current_get = current_get - 1

    ENDIF

RETURN

PROCEDURE rt_arrow_proc

    * If not at last get on line ...
    IF (current_get % fields_line) != 0

        current_get = current_get + 1

    ENDIF

RETURN
```

The new left arrow routine prohibits movement when the current GET is the first on a line. Similarly, the right arrow routine prohibits movement when the current GET is the last on a line. To allow the up and down arrow keys to skip records when pressed on the first and last line, respectively, rewrite the routines as:

```
PROCEDURE dn_arrow_proc

    * If not on last line, go down number of lines given by
    * fields_line
    IF current_get <= num_fields - fields_line

        current_get = current_get + fields_line

    ELSE
        IF recno() != last_rec
            DO pg_down_proc
            current_get = (current_get - 1) % fields_line + 1
        ENDIF
    ENDIF

RETURN

PROCEDURE up_arrow_proc

    * If not on top line
    IF current_get > fields_line

        current_get = current_get - fields_line
```

```
    ELSE

        IF recno() != first_rec
            DO pg_up_proc
            current_get = current_get + num_fields - fields_line
        ENDIF
    ENDIF

RETURN
```

The routine for the down arrow key first determines whether there is room to skip, and then does the page down processing. The one for the up arrow key first determines whether the highlight bar is currently at the beginning of the file, and then does the page up processing.

As a final modification, we remove the requirement of selecting a field before editing is allowed. The routine allows editing to occur whenever a "non-movement" key, such as a letter or digit, is pressed. The press is detected by including an OTHERWISE clause in the CASE statement, and forcing the DO WHILE loop to terminate with an EXIT statement.

```
DO CASE
    CASE key = DOWN_ARROW
        DO dn_arrow_proc

    CASE key = UP_ARROW
        DO up_arrow_proc

    CASE key = LEFT_ARROW
        DO lt_arrow_proc

    CASE key = RIGHT_ARROW
        DO rt_arrow_proc

    CASE key = PG_DOWN
        DO pg_down_proc

    CASE key = PG_UP
        DO pg_up_proc

    OTHERWISE
        EXIT

ENDCASE
```

The code now falls through to the edit mode where the key just pressed is stuffed.

```
IF key <> ESC

    IF key != ENTER
        KEYBOARD chr(key)
    ENDIF
```

```
        fname = fnames[current_get]

        @ rows[current_get], cols[current_get] GET &fname
        READ

        * note, since we don't assign to "key" here, an ESC will
        * not exit DO WHILE ! escape loop
ENDIF
```

Use this technique to design screens without the limitations of Clipper's one dimensional GET processing.

Spreadsheet Interface

A spreadsheet is basically a matrix of numbers with separate totals for columns and rows. The user can navigate it, entering numbers at will with the totals being updated immediately. Changing the value in one cell affects two totals, the row and the column. Program 6-10 presents a spreadsheet with the structure defined by Figure 6-1.

Figure 6-1. Simple Spreadsheet Screen

```
              Jan  Feb  Mar  Apr  May  Jun  Jul  Aug  Sep  Oct  Nov  Dec
Supplier 1
Supplier 2
Supplier 3
Supplier 4
Supplier 5
Supplier 6
Supplier 7
Supplier 8
Supplier 9
Supplier 10
Supplier 11
Supplier 12
Supplier 13
Supplier 14
Supplier 15
Supplier 16
Supplier 17
Supplier 18
Supplier 19
Supplier 20
Supplier 21
```

We store the cells in a simulated two dimensional array "spreadsheet" (see Chapter 3 for details). The totals for each row are in the array "row_totals", and the totals for each column are in "col_totals". The screen is navigated just as in the preceding section.

Program 6-10. Simple Spreadsheet Using Arrays

```
* Spreadsheet routine
*
* 1 - Declare arrays and initialize totals to 0
*
* 2 - Draw screen
*
* 3 - Navigate as before
*
* 4 - On EDIT:
*

*       4.1 - Get cell from spreadsheet
*
*       4.2 - Issue GET and READ
*
*       4.3 - Update row and column totals, display them

PRIVATE months[12]

months[1] = "Jan"
months[2] = "Feb"
months[3] = "Mar"
months[4] = "Apr"
months[5] = "May"
months[6] = "Jun"
months[7] = "Jul"
months[8] = "Aug"
months[9] = "Sep"
months[10] = "Oct"
months[11] = "Nov"
months[12] = "Dec"

SET SCOREBOARD OFF
CLEAR

init_consts()

num_cols = 12
num_rows = 21

PRIVATE spreadsheet[num_cols * num_rows]
PRIVATE row_totals[num_rows]
```

```
PRIVATE col_totals[num_cols]

afill(spreadsheet, 0)
afill(row_totals, 0)
afill(col_totals, 0)

key = 0
current_row = 1
current_col = 1

@ 1, 10 TO 23, 70

FOR  i = 1 TO num_rows

        @ i + 1, 1 SAY "Supp. " + str(i, 2)

NEXT

FOR i = 1 TO num_cols

        @ 0, 12 + (i - 1) * 5 SAY months[i]

NEXT
* starting navigate mode ...
DO WHILE key != ESC

        * for inner loop ...
        key = 0

        SET CURSOR OFF

        * select cell to edit or escape
        DO WHILE (key != ENTER .AND. key != ESC)

                cell = spreadsheet[aindex(current_row, current_col)]

                SET COLOR TO &enh
                @ current_row + 1, 11 + (current_col - 1) * 5 SAY cell ;
                        PICT "@z 9999"
                SET COLOR TO &norm

                key = inkey(0)

                * remove highlight ...
                @ current_row + 1, 11 + (current_col - 1) * 5 SAY cell ;
                        PICT "@z 9999"

                DO CASE
                        CASE key = DOWN_ARROW
                                DO dn_arrow_proc

                        CASE key = UP_ARROW
```

```
                DO up_arrow_proc

            CASE key = LT_ARROW
                DO lt_arrow_proc

            CASE key = RT_ARROW
                DO rt_arrow_proc

            CASE key >= asc('0') .AND. key <= asc('9')
                EXIT
        ENDCASE

ENDDO

SET CURSOR ON

IF key <> ESC
        * starting edit mode ...

        IF key != ENTER
                KEYBOARD chr(key)
        ENDIF

        cell = spreadsheet[aindex(current_row, current_col)]

        save_cell = cell
        @ current_row + 1, 11 + (current_col - 1) * 5 GET cell PICT;
                "@z 9999"
        READ

        IF updated()

                row_totals[current_row] = row_totals[current_row] + cell ;
                        - save_cell

                col_totals[current_col] = col_totals[current_col] + cell ;
                        - save_cell

                SET COLOR TO &bright

                @ current_row + 1, 71 SAY row_totals[current_row] ;
                        PICT "99999"

                @ 24, 10 + (current_col - 1) * 5 SAY ;
                                col_totals[current_col] PICT "99999"

                SET COLOR TO &norm

        ENDIF

        spreadsheet[aindex(current_row, current_col)] = cell
        * note, since we don't assign to "key" here, an ESC will
```

```
            * not exit DO WHILE !escape loop
        ENDIF

ENDDO

PROCEDURE dn_arrow_proc

        * If not on last line, go down by fields_line
        IF current_row < num_rows

            current_row = current_row + 1

        ENDIF

RETURN

PROCEDURE up_arrow_proc

        * If not on top line
        IF current_row > 1

            current_row = current_row - 1

        ENDIF

RETURN

PROCEDURE lt_arrow_proc

        * If not at first get ...
        IF current_col > 1

            current_col = current_col - 1

        ELSEIF current_row > 1      && current_col = 1

            * Go to last column on previous row
            current_col = num_cols
            current_row = current_row - 1

        ENDIF
RETURN

PROCEDURE rt_arrow_proc

        * If not at last get ...
        IF current_col < num_cols

            current_col = current_col + 1

        ELSEIF current_row < num_rows

            * Go to first column on next row
            current_row = current_row + 1
```

```
          current_col = 1

     ENDIF

RETURN

FUNCTION aindex
PARAMETERS row, col

RETURN ((row - 1) * num_cols + col)
```

A more useful interface keeps the values in a database with the following structure:

```
*** structure of database spr.dbf ***
Last update 88 1 21

Data offset 417
Record size 49
Number of records 12

NAME      TYPE LEN  DEC

JAN        N    4    0
FEB        N    4    0
MAR        N    4    0
APR        N    4    0
MAY        N    4    0
JUN        N    4    0
JUL        N    4    0
AUG        N    4    0
SEP        N    4    0
OCT        N    4    0
NOV        N    4    0
DEC        N    4    0
```

21 blank records (the number of visible rows) are initially appended to the database. We then update the records at will. For speed, Program 6-11 uses arrays to save the totals.

Program 6-11. Spreadsheet Routine Using a Database

```
* Spreadsheet routine with database
*
* 1 - Get cells from database, displaying and building totals
*
* 2 - Display totals
*
* 3 - Navigate as before
```

```
*
* 4 - On EDIT:
*
*       4.1 - Get cell from database
*
*       4.2 - Issue GET and READ
*
*       4.3 - Update row and column totals, display them
*
*       4.4 - Update database

SET SCOREBOARD OFF
CLEAR

USE spr

init_consts()

num_cols = fcount()

num_rows = 21

PRIVATE row_totals[num_rows]
PRIVATE col_totals[num_cols]

afill(row_totals, 0)
afill(col_totals, 0)

key = 0
current_row = 1
current_col = 1

@ 1, 10 TO 23, 70

* Calculate totals and draw screen
* for each row
FOR  current_row = 1 TO num_rows

     * this row's title
     @ current_row + 1, 1 SAY "rec # " + str(current_row, 2)

     * For each column
     FOR current_col = 1 TO num_cols

          fname = fieldname(current_col)
          row_totals[current_row] = row_totals[current_row] + &fname
          col_totals[current_col] = col_totals[current_col] + &fname

          * display this cell
          @ current_row + 1, 11 + (current_col - 1) * 5 SAY &fname ;
                    PICT "@z 9999"
     NEXT
```

```
        * this row's total
        SET COLOR TO &bright

        @ current_row + 1, 71 SAY row_totals[current_row] PICT "99999"

        SET COLOR TO &norm

        SKIP
NEXT

* Now display column totals

FOR current_col = 1 TO num_cols

        fname = fieldname(current_col)

        * this column's title
        @ 0, 12 + (current_col - 1) * 5 SAY substr(fname, 1, 4)

        SET COLOR TO &bright

        @ 24, 10 + (current_col - 1) * 5 SAY col_totals[current_col] ;
                    PICT "99999"

        SET COLOR TO &norm

NEXT

current_col = 1
current_row = 1

GOTO TOP

* starting navigate mode ...
DO WHILE key != ESC

        * for inner loop ...
        key = 0

        SET CURSOR OFF

        * select cell to edit or escape
        DO WHILE (key != ENTER .AND. key != ESC)

                fname = fieldname(current_col)
                cell = &fname

                SET COLOR TO &enh
                @ current_row + 1, 11 + (current_col - 1) * 5 SAY cell ;
                        PICT "@z 9999"
                SET COLOR TO &norm
```

```
		key = inkey(0)

		* Remove highlight ...
		@ current_row + 1, 11 + (current_col - 1) * 5 SAY cell ;
			PICT "@z 9999"

		DO CASE
			CASE key = DOWN_ARROW
				DO dn_arrow_proc

			CASE key = UP_ARROW
				DO up_arrow_proc

			CASE key = LT_ARROW
				DO lt_arrow_proc

			CASE key = RT_ARROW
				DO rt_arrow_proc

			CASE key >= asc('0') .AND. key <= asc('9')
				EXIT
		ENDCASE

	ENDDO

	SET CURSOR ON

	IF key <> ESC
		* starting edit mode ...

		IF key != ENTER
			KEYBOARD chr(key)
		ENDIF
		fname = fieldname(current_col)
		cell = &fname

		save_cell = cell
		@ current_row + 1, 11 + (current_col - 1) * 5 GET cell PICT "@z 99 99"
		READ

		IF updated()

			row_totals[current_row] = row_totals[current_row] + cell ;
				- save_cell

			col_totals[current_col] = col_totals[current_col] + cell ;
				- save_cell

			SET COLOR TO &bright

			@ current_row + 1, 71 SAY row_totals[current_row] ;
										PICT "99999"
```

```
                @ 24, 10 + (current_col - 1) * 5 SAY ;
                            col_totals[current_col] PICT "99999"

                SET COLOR TO &norm

                REPLACE &fname WITH cell

            ENDIF

            * note, since we don't assign to "key" here, an ESC will
            * not exit DO WHILE !escape loop
        ENDIF

    ENDDO

    PROCEDURE dn_arrow_proc

        * If not on last line, go down by fields_line
        IF current_row < num_rows

            current_row = current_row + 1

            SKIP

        ENDIF

    RETURN

    PROCEDURE up_arrow_proc

        * If not on top line
        IF current_row > 1

            current_row = current_row - 1

            SKIP -1

        ENDIF

    RETURN

    PROCEDURE lt_arrow_proc

        * If not at first get ...
        IF current_col > 1

            current_col = current_col - 1

        ELSEIF current_row > 1     && current_col = 1

            * Go to last column on previous row
```

```
            current_col = num_cols
            current_row = current_row - 1

            SKIP -1

        ENDIF
RETURN

PROCEDURE rt_arrow_proc

        * If not at last get ...
        IF current_col < num_cols

            current_col = current_col + 1

        ELSEIF current_row < num_rows

            * Go to first column on next row
            current_row = current_row + 1
            current_col = 1
            SKIP

        ENDIF

RETURN
```

The database record pointer is at the record representing the row where the highlight bar is.

Dialog Boxes

The Summer '87 release combines the report and label utilities as RL. The release disk contains the source code for the functions that form the utility. As they are written entirely in Clipper, you can include them in an application and let the user modify report and label formats under program control.

RL's user interface relies heavily on "dialog boxes", used extensively on the Apple Macintosh computer. RL dialog boxes have the following screen layout:

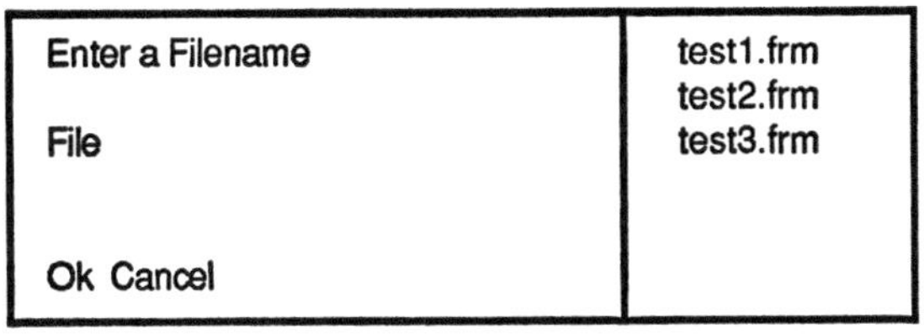

Enter a Filename File Ok Cancel	test1.frm test2.frm test3.frm

The highlight bar starts on the first field in the field list. The code basically does an ACHOICE. The user selects a file from the list (it scrolls when necessary) with the Enter key. On selection, the program puts the name after "file" in the left window, and places the highlight bar on "Ok". Now the user can either confirm the choice by selecting "Ok", or cancel it. If he or she confirms the selection, the utility then allows the editing of either the report or label file. If the user cancels the selection, or presses Escape during either selection or confirmation, the utility returns to its main menu. Pressing the left arrow key from the file selection mode lets the user enter the file name manually.

This is an attractive, easy to use interface. Since the source code is included, you can use dialog boxes directly in an application. The code for the function and its subroutines is in the file "RLDIALOG.PRG", and the code that uses it (RL's front end) is in the file "RLFRONT.PRG". By studying these two files, you can learn about the calling conventions and environment.

The main function of the dialog box routine is "multi_box". It takes three parameters that define the dialog box (top row, top column, and height). Remember that the width is predefined (45). multi_box also requires the following parameters:

- An array of functions that implement states of the dialog box ("buttons"). You usually can use the functions already defined in the rldialog.prg file to give the default operation.

- Element in array "buttons" where the highlight bar appears initially.

Studying the rlfront code shows that rl_main calls "multi_box" with the following parameters:

1) Top row = 7.

2) Top column = 17.

3) Box height = 7.

4) Initial button = 5 (described subsequently).

5) A five element function array with the following values:

   [1] "enter_title(sysparam)"

   [2] "rl_getfil(sysparam)"

   [3] "ok_button(sysparam)"

   [4] "cancel_button(sysparam)"

   [5] "filelist(sysparam)"

Each array element is a function that implements a state of the dialog box. The programmer can also use his or her own routines. The main function "multi_box" just acts as a "controller", the ultimate in flexibility. The default functions in the rldialog file are:

"enter_title" displays the text "Enter a filename".

"rl_getfil" reads a field name, if not selected from the file list.

"ok_button" handles the "Ok" button.

"cancel_button" handles the "Cancel" button.

"filelist" handles the list of file names with an ACHOICE.

sysparam is a memory variable private to multi_box. It maintains the internal state.

Setting the initial button to 5 causes the highlight bar to appear initially at the right hand side of the dialog box (the "filelist" routine). multi_box also depends on three global variables:

1) "files" - an array of file names, used in the file list.

2) "filename" - the name of the selected file.

3) "okee_dokee" - a routine that multi_box invokes once a file has been selected. The rlfront code sets it to "do_it()", another routine in the dialog box code. It completes the selection process.

Program 6-12 invokes multi_box in the same way as the report front end code:

Program 6-12. Using RL's Dialog Box Routines

```
PRIVATE file_box[5]

file_box[1] = "enter_title(sysparam)"
```

```
file_box[2] = "rl_getfil(sysparam)"
file_box[3] = "ok_button(sysparam)"
file_box[4] = "cancel_button(sysparam)"
file_box[5] = "filelist(sysparam)"

num_files = adir("*.*")
PRIVATE files[num_files]
adir("* *", files)

filename = SPACE(64)
okee_dokee = "do_it()"

CLEAR

multibox(7, 17, 7, 5, file_box)
```

If no file is selected, multi_box returns 0. Otherwise, it returns 4 (an internal state), and sets filename to the name of the selected file.

To specify a default selection for the file name, simply set filename to it, as in:

```
filename = "test.frm"
```

Now, to start the highlight bar on the "ok" button with the default file name specified, pass a 3 (ok_button) for the fourth parameter (initial button).

Vertical Scrolling

SCROLL, a procedure in the EXTEND library, implements high speed scrolling of a rectangle on the screen. This is helpful when the user must select from an unspecified number of items (such as database files on a disk). We can allocate a fixed sized area on the screen and scroll within it.

The scroll procedure takes the following parameters: starting row, starting column, ending row, ending column, and number of lines. A positive value for number of lines indicates a downward scroll, a negative value indicates an upward scroll, and zero clears the area.

The following call scrolls the rectangle from 10, 10 to 20, 20 up one line:

```
scroll(10, 10, 20, 20, -1)
```

The programmer usually frames the area to be scrolled with a BOX command, as in:

```
@ 9, 9, 21, 21 BOX singbox

scroll(10, 10, 20, 20, -1)
```

A SCROLL function with zero lines clears the area. This is the fastest clearing method, as it uses a direct call to the ROM-BIOS.

> **TIP**
>
> Use the SCROLL function with zero lines to clear part of the screen.

Browsing Arrays

The SCROLL function can be the basis for a high speed "browse" routine. It creates a window filled with data from an array. If the user presses the up arrow key when the highlight bar is on the top line, the window scrolls. This is much faster than redrawing it. It also scrolls if the user presses the down arrow key when the highlight bar is on the bottom row. The function terminates if the user presses either the Escape or the Enter key. The Escape key makes the function return 0. The Enter key makes it return the selected element number. Program 6-13 shows this general "array browse" function.

Program 6-13. Browsing an Array

```
****
* BRA.PRG
*
* Browse of an array
*
* 1 - Draw box, fill array, display first window full of array, highlight
*        initial element
*
* 2 - DO UNTIL user presses Escape or Enter
*
*        2.1 - Remove highlight from current element
*
*        2.2 - Move according to key pressed, scrolling as necessary
*
*        2.3 - Highlight new active element, displaying ^X and ^Y
```

```
*                  if the items can now be scrolled

FUNCTION abrowse

PARAMETERS ar, num_elems, start_row, start_col, end_row, end_col

PRIVATE num_disp_rows, floor, ceiling, key, highlight, width, cur_disp_rows

        IF num_elems = 0
                RETURN (0)
        ENDIF

        SET CURSOR OFF

        @ start_row, start_col, end_row, end_col BOX SL_BOX
        num_disp_rows = end_row - start_row - 1

        width = end_col - start_col - 1

        floor = 1
        highlight = 1

        cur_disp_rows = afill_box(ar, start_row, start_col, end_row, ;
                                                    end_col, floor)

        ceiling = cur_disp_rows + floor - 1

        IF ceiling < num_elems
                SET COLOR TO /W

                @ end_row, start_col SAY chr(25)
                SET COLOR TO W/
        ENDIF

        SET COLOR TO  /W

        * Highlight active element
        @ start_row + highlight, start_col + 1 SAY ;
                                pad(ar[floor + highlight - 1], width)
        SET COLOR TO W/

        key = inkey(0)
        DO WHILE (key != ESC) .AND. (key != ENTER)

                * remove highlight from active element
                @ start_row + highlight, start_col + 1 SAY ;
                                pad(ar[floor + highlight - 1], width)

                DO CASE
                        CASE key = UP_ARROW
                                IF highlight > 1
                                        highlight = highlight - 1
```

```
            ELSE
                  IF floor > 1
                        floor = floor - 1

                        scroll(start_row + 1, start_col + 1, ;
                                end_row - 1, end_col - 1, -1)
                        * this leaves highlight row empty

                        cur_disp_rows = min(num_disp_rows, ;
                                     num_elems - floor + 1)

                        ceiling = floor + cur_disp_rows - 1

                  ENDIF
            ENDIF

      CASE key = DOWN_ARROW
            IF highlight < cur_disp_rows
                  highlight = highlight + 1
            ELSE
                  IF ceiling < num_elems
                        floor = floor + 1

                        scroll(start_row + 1, start_col + 1, ;
                                     end_row - 1, end_col - 1, 1)

                        * This leaves highlight row empty

                        cur_disp_rows = min(num_disp_rows, ;
                                     num_elems - floor + 1)
                        ceiling = floor + cur_disp_rows - 1

                  ENDIF
            ENDIF

      CASE key = PG_UP
            IF floor > 1
                  floor = max(floor - num_disp_rows, 1)
                  ceiling = afill_box(ar, start_row, start_col, end_row,   ;
                              end_col, floor)
                  cur_disp_rows = ceiling - floor + 1
            ENDIF

      CASE key = PG_DOWN
            IF ceiling < num_elems
                  floor = min(floor + num_disp_rows, num_elems)
                  cur_disp_rows = afill_box(ar, start_row, start_col, ;
                              end_row, end_col, floor)
                  ceiling = cur_disp_rows + floor - 1
                  highlight = min(highlight, cur_disp_rows)
            ENDIF
```

```
        CASE key = HOME
            highlight = 1

        CASE key = END_KEY
            highlight = cur_disp_rows

        CASE key = CTRL_HOME
            highlight = 1
            floor = 1
            cur_disp_rows = afill_box(ar, start_row, start_col, ;
                        end_row, end_col, floor)
            ceiling = cur_disp_rows + floor - 1

        CASE key = CTRL_END
            IF ceiling = num_elems
                highlight = cur_disp_rows
            ELSE
                floor = num_elems - num_disp_rows + 1
                cur_disp_rows = afill_box(ar, start_row, start_col, ;
                            end_row, end_col, floor)
                ceiling = cur_disp_rows + floor - 1
                highlight = cur_disp_rows
            ENDIF
    ENDCASE

    * highlight active element
    SET COLOR TO /W
    @ start_row + highlight, start_col + 1 SAY ;
                    pad(ar[floor + highlight - 1], width)
    SET COLOR TO W/

    IF floor > 1
        SET COLOR TO /W
        @ start_row, start_col SAY chr(24)
        SET COLOR TO W/
    ELSE
        @ start_row, start_col SAY chr(218)
    ENDIF

    IF ceiling < num_elems
        SET COLOR TO /W
        @ end_row, start_col SAY chr(25)
        SET COLOR TO W/
    ELSE
        @ end_row, start_col SAY chr(192)
    ENDIF

    key = inkey(0)
ENDDO
```

```
        SET CURSOR OFF
RETURN (IF (lastkey() = ESC, 0, floor + highlight - 1))

FUNCTION afill_box

PARAMETERS ar, start_row, start_col, end_row, end_col, floor

PRIVATE num_disp, num_rows, i, width

        num_rows = end_row - start_row - 1
        width = end_col - start_col - 1
        num_disp = min(num_rows, num_elems - floor + 1)

        FOR i = 1 TO num_disp
                @ start_row + i, start_col + 1 SAY pad(ar[floor + i - 1], width)
        NEXT

        FOR i = num_disp + 1 TO num_rows
                @ start_row + i, start_col + 1 SAY space(width)
        NEXT

RETURN (num_disp)

FUNCTION pad

PARAMETERS str, width

        IF len(str) > width
                str = substr(str, 1, width)
        ELSE
                str = str + space(width - len(str))
        ENDIF

RETURN (str + space(width - len(str)))
```

Program 6-13's parameters are the array name, the number of elements to "browse" (may be less than the total number), and the coordinates of the browse box. The following code invokes the routine:

```
size = 20

PRIVATE ar[size]

FOR i = 1 TO size

        ar[i] = str(i)

NEXT
init_consts()
CLEAR

sel = abrowse(ar, size, 10, 10, 20, 42)
```

Figure 6-2 shows the states of the variables at various points during the activation of the routine. Note that the expression

ELEMENT SELECTED = FLOOR + HIGHLIGHT - 1

is maintained throughout.

Figure 6-2. Array Browse Diagrams

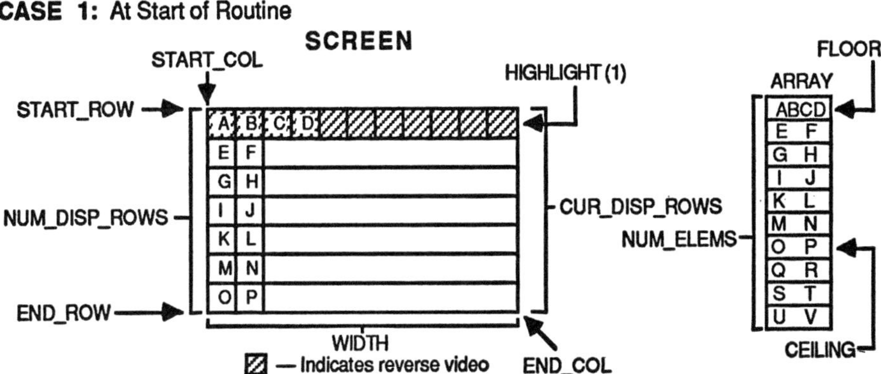

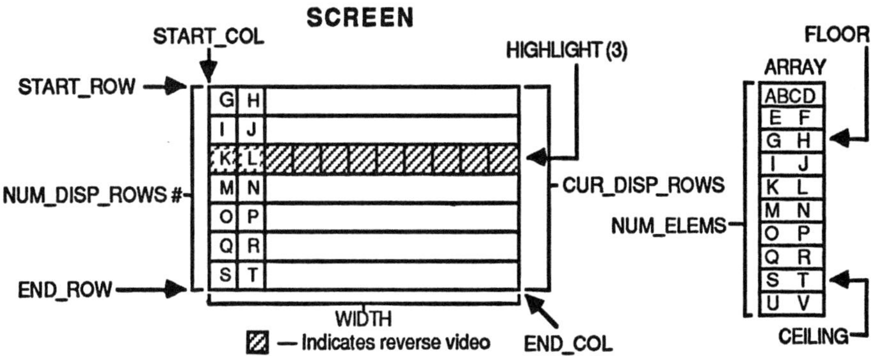

CASE 3: Only Part of Box Displayed After a Page Down

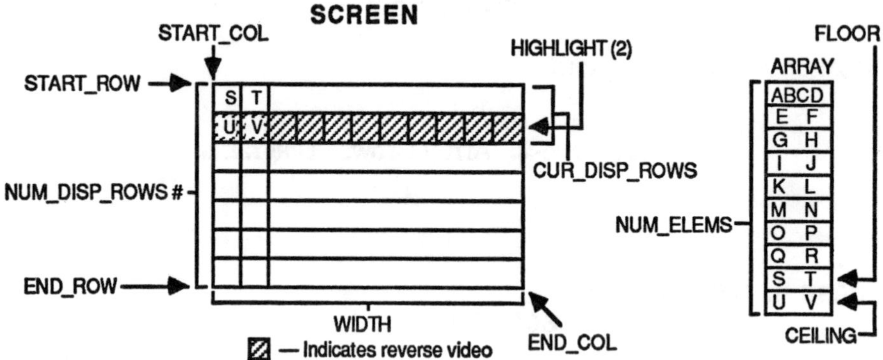

Browsing Simple Databases

A simple modification to Program 6-13 allows it to be used on a database file. An expression is passed which evaluates to the fields of a database. The routine uses it with the SKIP command to display the database's records. Whenever the "floor" variable is repositioned, the record pointer is set with the GOTO command. The maximum element to be displayed, "len(ar)" in the array version, is now "reccount", the number of records. To highlight the active element, the code skips to this record so that "&expr" returns the correct value.

Program 6-14. Browsing a Simple Database

```
****
* DBR.PRG
*
* Browse of a database with no index or set filter
*
* 1 - Draw box, display first window full from database, highlight
*        initial element
*
* 2 - DO UNTIL user presses Escape or Enter
*
*        2.1 - Remove highlight from current element
*
*        2.2 - Move according to key pressed, scrolling as necessary
*
*        2.3 - Highlight new active element, displaying ^X and ^Y
*                if the items can now be scrolled
```

```
FUNCTION browse

PARAMETERS expr, start_row, start_col, end_row, end_col

PRIVATE num_disp_rows, floor, ceiling, key, highlight, width, cur_disp_rows

     SET CURSOR OFF

     IF (reccount() = 0)
          RETURN (0)
     ENDIF

     @ start_row, start_col, end_row, end_col BOX SL_BOX
     num_disp_rows = end_row - start_row - 1

     width = end_col - start_col - 1

     floor = 1

     highlight = 1

     cur_disp_rows = dfill_box(expr, start_row, start_col, end_row, end_col , ;
                                        floor)

     ceiling = cur_disp_rows + floor - 1

     IF ceiling != reccount()
          SET COLOR TO /W
          @ end_row, start_col SAY chr(25)
          SET COLOR TO W/
     ENDIF

     * Highlight active element
     SET COLOR TO  /W
     SKIP highlight - 1
     @ start_row + highlight, start_col + 1 SAY ;
                                        pad(&expr, width)
     SKIP -(highlight - 1)
     SET COLOR TO W/

     key = inkey(0)
     DO WHILE (key != ESC) .AND. (key != ENTER)

          * Remove highlight from active element
          SKIP highlight - 1
          @ start_row + highlight, start_col + 1 SAY pad (&expr, width)
          SKIP -(highlight - 1)

          DO CASE
               CASE key = UP_ARROW
                    IF highlight > 1
                         highlight = highlight - 1
```

```
            ELSE
                IF floor > 1
                    SKIP -1
                    floor = floor - 1

                    scroll(start_row + 1, start_col + 1, ;
                            end_row - 1, end_col - 1, -1)
                    * this leaves highlight row empty

                    cur_disp_rows = min(num_disp_rows, ;
                                reccount() - floor + 1)

                    ceiling = floor + cur_disp_rows - 1

                ENDIF
            ENDIF

        CASE key = DOWN_ARROW
            IF highlight < cur_disp_rows
                highlight = highlight + 1
            ELSE
                IF ceiling < reccount()
                    SKIP

                    floor = floor + 1

                    scroll(start_row + 1, start_col + 1, ;
                            end_row - 1, end_col - 1, 1)
                    * This leaves highlight row empty

                    cur_disp_rows = min(num_disp_rows, ;
                                reccount() - floor + 1)
                    ceiling = floor + cur_disp_rows - 1

                ENDIF
            ENDIF

        CASE key = PG_UP
            IF floor > 1
                floor = max(floor - num_disp_rows, 1)
                GOTO floor
                cur_disp_rows = dfill_box(expr, start_row, start_col,;
                        end_row, end_col, floor)
                ceiling = cur_disp_rows + floor - 1
            ENDIF

        CASE key = PG_DOWN
            IF ceiling < reccount()
                floor = min(floor + num_disp_rows, reccount())
                GOTO floor

                cur_disp_rows = dfill_box(expr, start_row, start_col,;
```

```
                    end_row, end_col, floor)

                ceiling = cur_disp_rows + floor - 1

                highlight = min(highlight, cur_disp_rows)
            ENDIF

        CASE key = HOME
            highlight = 1

        CASE key = END_KEY
            highlight = cur_disp_rows

        CASE key = CTRL_HOME
            highlight = 1
            floor = 1
            GOTO floor
            cur_disp_rows = dfill_box(expr, start_row, start_col, ;
                        end_row, end_col, floor)
            ceiling = cur_disp_rows + floor - 1

        CASE key = CTRL_END
            IF ceiling = reccount()
                highlight = cur_disp_rows
            ELSE
                floor = reccount() - num_disp_rows + 1
                GOTO floor
                cur_disp_rows = dfill_box(expr, start_row, start_col,;
                        end_row, end_col, floor)
                ceiling = cur_disp_rows + floor - 1
                highlight = cur_disp_rows
            ENDIF
    ENDCASE

    * Highlight active element
    SET COLOR TO  /W
    SKIP highlight - 1
    @ start_row + highlight, start_col + 1 SAY pad(&expr, width)
    SKIP -(highlight - 1)
    SET COLOR TO W/

    IF floor != 1
        SET COLOR TO /W
        @ start_row, start_col SAY chr(24)
        SET COLOR TO W/
    ELSE
        @ start_row, start_col SAY chr(218)
    ENDIF

    IF ceiling != reccount()
        SET COLOR TO /W
        @ end_row, start_col SAY chr(25)
```

```
                SET COLOR TO W/
            ELSE
                @ end_row, start_col SAY chr(192)
            ENDIF

            key = inkey(0)

        ENDDO

        SET CURSOR ON

    RETURN (IF (lastkey() = ESC, 0, floor + highlight - 1))

    FUNCTION dfill_box

    PARAMETERS expr, start_row, start_col, end_row, end_col, floor

    PRIVATE num_disp, num_rows, i, width, ret_val

        num_rows = end_row - start_row - 1
        width = end_col - start_col - 1
        num_disp = min(num_rows, reccount() - floor + 1)

        FOR i = 1 TO num_disp
            @ start_row + i, start_col + 1 SAY pad(&expr, width)
            SKIP
        NEXT

        ret_val = recno()
        FOR i = num_disp + 1 TO num_rows
            @ start_row + i, start_col + 1 SAY space(width)
        NEXT

        GOTO floor

    RETURN (num_disp)
```

The routine's parameters are an expression and the window's coordinates. The expression must contain the fields to browse, combined in a character string. The following call simply uses the field "names":

```
USE test

expr = "names"

CLEAR
init_consts()

? browse(expr, 10, 10, 20, 22)
```

This call browses through three fields: a character (names), a numeric (nums), and a date (dates).

```
USE test

expr = "names + str(nums) + dtoc(dates)"

CLEAR
init_consts()

? browse(expr, 10, 10, 20, 50)
```

The "expr" string may include string constants. For example,

```
USE test

expr = "'RECORD ' + str(recno(), 3) + names + str(nums) + dtoc(dates)"

CLEAR
init_consts( )

? browse(expr, 10, 10, 20, 60)
```

is acceptable.

Browsing Complex Databases

The preceding browse code does not work correctly when the database is indexed, when a set filter is active, or when DELETED is on. The problems are:

1) The first record may not be record 1. The way to get the first record number is to do a GOTO TOP followed by a RECNO().

2) The last record may not be "lastrec()". The way to get the last record number is to do a GOTO BOTTOM followed by a RECNO().

3) You cannot do arithmetic on record numbers. Instead, SKIP the database the correct number of times and get the new record number with the "RECNO()" function. This is the way to set "floor" and "ceiling".

4) The UP_ARROW code sets "cur_disp_rows" to the minimum of the maximum number of rows that can be displayed, and the number that can be displayed from the current "floor" record. This latter value is calculated using

record number arithmetic which is impossible with an active index or set filter. Instead, we use the fact that "cur_disp_rows" can only change by growing when the previous value was less than the maximum. Similarly, in the PG_DOWN code we realize that "cur_disp_rows" cannot change. The code was actually redundant.

Program 6-15 is a general purpose "browse" routine that handles the above problems.

Program 6-15. Browsing Complex Databases

```
****
* DBRI.PRG
*
* Browse of a database which may be indexed, have a filter set, or
* have deleted on
*
* 1 - Draw box, display first window full from database, highlight
*       initial element
*
* 2 - DO UNTIL user presses Escape or Enter
*
*       2.1 - Remove highlight from current element
*
*       2.2 - Move according to key pressed, scrolling as necessary
*
*       2.3 - Highlight new active element, displaying ^X and ^Y
*               if the items can now be scrolled


FUNCTION dbibrows

PARAMETERS expr, start_row, start_col, end_row, end_col

PRIVATE num_disp_rows, floor, ceiling, key, highlight, width, cur_disp_rows
PRIVATE ret_val

        GOTO BOTTOM
        last = recno()

        GOTO TOP
        first = recno()
        floor = first

        IF eof()
                RETURN (0)
        ENDIF

        SET CURSOR OFF
```

```
@ start_row, start_col, end_row, end_col BOX SINGBOX
num_disp_rows = end_row - start_row - 1

width = end_col - start_col - 1

highlight = 1

cur_disp_rows = fill_box(expr, start_row, start_col, end_row, end_col,  ;
                                  floor)

SKIP cur_disp_rows - 1
ceiling = recno()
SKIP - (cur_disp_rows - 1)

IF ceiling != last
        SET COLOR TO /W
        @ end_row, start_col SAY chr(25)
        SET COLOR TO W/
ENDIF

* Highlight active element
SET COLOR TO  /W
SKIP highlight - 1
@ start_row + highlight, start_col + 1 SAY ;
                                pad(&expr, width)
SKIP -(highlight - 1)
SET COLOR TO W/

key = inkey(0)
DO WHILE (key != ESC) .AND. (key != ENTER)

        * Remove highlight from active element
        SKIP highlight - 1

        @ start_row + highlight, start_col + 1 SAY pad (&expr, width)
        SKIP -(highlight - 1)

        DO CASE
                CASE key = UP_ARROW
                        IF highlight > 1
                                highlight = highlight - 1
                        ELSE
                                IF floor != first
                                        SKIP -1
                                        floor = recno()

                                        scroll(start_row + 1, start_col + 1, ;
                                                end_row - 1, end_col - 1, -1)
                                        * this leaves highlight row empty

                                        * grow ??
                                        IF cur_disp_rows < num_disp_rows
```

```
                        cur_disp_rows = cur_disp_rows + 1
                    ENDIF

                    SKIP cur_disp_rows - 1
                    ceiling = recno()
                    SKIP -(cur_disp_rows - 1)
                ENDIF
            ENDIF

        CASE key = DOWN_ARROW
            IF highlight < cur_disp_rows
                highlight = highlight + 1
            ELSE
                IF ceiling != last
                    SKIP
                    floor = recno()

                    scroll(start_row + 1, start_col + 1, ;
                            end_row - 1, end_col - 1, 1)
                    * This leaves highlight row empty

                    * cur_disp_rows cannot have changed here

                    SKIP cur_disp_rows - 1
                    ceiling = recno()
                    SKIP -(cur_disp_rows - 1)
                ENDIF
            ENDIF

        CASE key = PG_UP
            IF floor > first
                SKIP -num_disp_rows
                floor = recno()

                cur_disp_rows = fill_box(expr, start_row, start_col, ;
                                         end_row, end_col, floor)
                SKIP cur_disp_rows - 1

                ceiling = recno()
                SKIP -(cur_disp_rows - 1)
            ENDIF

        CASE key = PG_DOWN
            IF ceiling != last
                SKIP num_disp_rows
                floor = recno()

                cur_disp_rows = fill_box(expr, start_row, start_col, ;
                                         end_row, end_col, floor)

                SKIP cur_disp_rows - 1
                ceiling = recno()
```

```
                SKIP -(cur_disp_rows - 1)
                highlight = min(highlight, cur_disp_rows)
            ENDIF

        CASE key = HOME
            highlight = 1

        CASE key = END_KEY
            highlight = cur_disp_rows

        CASE key = CTRL_HOME
            highlight = 1
            GOTO TOP
            floor = recno()

            cur_disp_rows = fill_box(expr, start_row, start_col, ;
                        end_row, end_col, floor)

            SKIP cur_disp_rows - 1
            ceiling = recno()
            SKIP -(cur_disp_rows - 1)

        CASE key = CTRL_END
            IF ceiling = last
                highlight = cur_disp_rows
            ELSE
                GOTO BOTTOM
                SKIP -(num_disp_rows - 1)
                floor = recno()

                cur_disp_rows = fill_box(expr, start_row, start_col, ;
                        end_row, end_col, floor)

                ceiling = last
                highlight = cur_disp_rows
            ENDIF
ENDCASE

* Highlight active element
SET COLOR TO /W
SKIP highlight - 1

@ start_row + highlight, start_col + 1 SAY pad(&expr, width)
SKIP -(highlight - 1)
SET COLOR TO W/

IF floor != first
    SET COLOR TO /W
    @ start_row, start_col SAY chr(24)
    SET COLOR TO W/
ELSE
    @ start_row, start_col SAY chr(218)
```

```
            ENDIF
            IF ceiling != last
                  SET COLOR TO /W
                  @ end_row, start_col SAY chr(25)
                  SET COLOR TO W/
            ELSE
                  @ end_row, start_col SAY chr(192)
            ENDIF

            key = inkey(0)

      ENDDO

      IF lastkey() = ESC
            ret_val = 0
      ELSE
            SKIP highlight - 1
            ret_val = recno()
      ENDIF

      SET CURSOR ON
RETURN (ret_val)

FUNCTION fill_box

PARAMETERS expr, start_row, start_col, end_row, end_col, floor

PRIVATE num_disp, num_rows, i, width, ret_val

      num_rows = end_row - start_row - 1
      width = end_col - start_col - 1

      num_disp = 0
      DO WHILE !eof() .AND. num_disp < num_rows
            @ start_row + num_disp + 1, start_col + 1 SAY pad(&expr, width)
            SKIP
            num_disp = num_disp + 1
      ENDDO

      ret_val = recno()

      FOR i = num_disp + 1 TO num_rows
            @ start_row + i, start_col + 1 SAY space(width)
      NEXT

      GOTO floor

RETURN (num_disp)
```

We call Program 6-15 (DBRI) just like the simpler version. Figure 6-3 explains the relationship between the variables.

Figure 6-3. Browse of a Complex Database

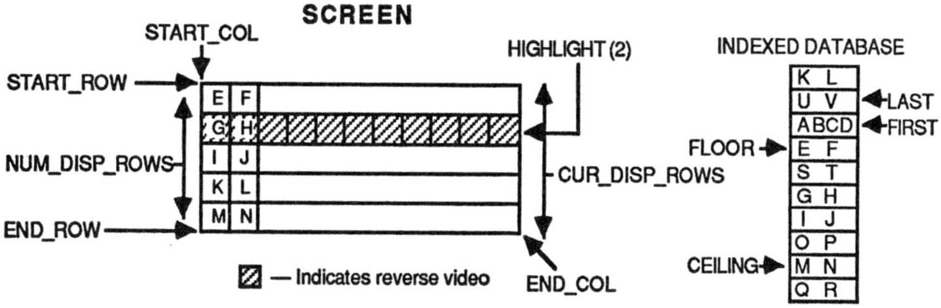

Complex Database Browse Diagram

The above code is rather complex, but then so is the problem. This version is the easiest to understand that we have seen, although it is not necessarily the most efficient.

Hints and Warnings

- Use the routines defined in this chapter as building blocks for your applications.
- Tailor the spreadsheet interface to your own use or extend it into a general purpose spreadsheet.
- Use dialog boxes to display error messages, unusual circumstances, etc. You may also want to use them for file selection rather than a pulldown menu.
- Use GET's VALID clause to provide of control. Use the "no_exit" function to disable an exit from a GET list with unsatisfied VALIDs.
- Use the two dimensional GET routines to overcome the one-dimensional limitation imposed by Clipper.
- Use the scroll routines rather than ACHOICE and DBEDIT when you need more control over handling the keys. A

useful extension to the database browse routine would be to pass a scope as a parameter. While records can be filtered out by setting a filter before the routine is called, this does not restrict the scope. A SKIP in a 50,000 record database can be slow. Using a scope with the SKIP speeds operations considerably.

- Study the screen saving and loading to and from disk files shown in Chapter 9. This can reduce your application's memory requirements at the cost of a slight reduction in performance.

7

Memo Fields: Care and Feeding

This chapter deals with memo fields. They let users save notes, comments, and other free-form text in a database. Clipper has many new features for managing and processing memo fields. They are no longer a loosely connected appendage as they are in dBASE III. Instead, Clipper makes them into an integral part of the database and lets you apply almost all commands to them, either directly or through conversion to a character field. Clipper adds special functions besides, including a full-featured text editor that can be customized with a user function.

The chapter also delves into the mechanics of memo fields. It compares their storage needs with those of text files. It also shows how Clipper implements them and how the implementation differs from that of dBASE III.

Introduction

Memo fields hold text of variable length, such as notes, comments, remarks, and special instructions. Clipper lets them be up to 64K in size. A nice feature is that you need not define the size in advance. The fields grow as needed when you edit them with the memo editor, or process them with code.

Clipper stores memo fields in a separate disk file with the same name as the database file, but with a DBT extension. If a memo field is empty, Clipper does not allocate space in the DBT file. Nonempty fields occupy as much space as they need, in units of 512 bytes. A memo field uses 10 bytes in every record in the database file, regardless of whether it contains data. This points to the start of the field in the DBT file.

Many applications have avoided dBASE's poor implementation of memo fields. However, Clipper has solved the following problems:

- In dBASE, you must dedicate the entire screen to edit a memo. In Clipper, you can use a window of any size at any location.
- In dBASE, you cannot assign the memo field to a memory variable. Thus, you cannot search through it, extract data from it, or process it arbitrarily. Clipper does not impose this restriction - it treats memo fields just like other fields.
- In dBASE, the DBT file grows every time you edit a record. In Clipper, it grows only when the field reaches a 512 byte boundary. Neither dBASE nor Clipper automatically reclaims pages no longer in use.

In the Summer '87 release, the Clipper functions for processing memo fields are in the EXTEND.LIB library file. You must include it when linking to use them.

Memo fields are dynamic; they grow as required. Since Clipper allocates no space for them if they contain no data, the DBT file does not grow when you append to a database containing a memo field. It only grows when you update a memo field with the REPLACE command.

One result of the 512 byte units is wasted space for short memo fields. Thus, you should use memo fields only after studying the data carefully.

This Chapter first discusses when to use memo fields. It then shows how to edit, process, view, and display them. It also shows how to customize the memo editor with its user defined function.

When to Use Memo Fields

If your application must store free-form text, you must decide whether to use a large character string or a memo field. This section discusses which to choose.

What are the differences? A large character field occupies a defined amount of space in a database file, regardless of whether it is used. A memo field only takes space when used, but requires a minimum of 512 bytes. A character field has a fixed size; you cannot change it without rebuilding the entire database. Traditionally then, designers make the field large enough for the longest foreseeable data plus some margin for error. On the average, space is wasted. A memo field may also waste space because of the 512 byte units.

Thus do not think of a memo field as a large character field with the added flexibility of unrestrained growth. The best use of memo fields is in situations where they seldom contain anything, but may be quite long when they are used.

To decide whether to use a memo field, we must consider the following four variables:

- The typical number of records in the database ("num_recs").
- The average size of the memo field's data ("avg_size").
- The maximum size of the data ("max_size").
- The percentage of records that use the memo field ("usage").

A fixed size character field would require:

```
num_recs * max_size
```

bytes to hold the data. A memo field would require

```
num_recs * 10 + (INT((avg_size + 511) / 512) * 512)  * num_recs * usage / 100
```

bytes. This approximation is based on the average size of the data. The first term, "num_recs * 10", accounts for the 10 bytes used in each record in the database file. The second term is the size of the DBT file, the typical size of each memo field (rounded up to the nearest 512 bytes), multiplied by the expected number of records containing data. The formula does not consider fragmentation in the DBT file (discussed later).

Here are typical cases:

CASE 1) Database of 100 records, average record size of 75 bytes, maximum size 100, percentage use 100:

Using character field: 10,000 bytes

Using memo field: 52,200

Since this file uses every record, and both the maximum and the average size of the field are less than 512 bytes, memo fields offer no advantage.

CASE 2) Database of 1000 records, average record size of 75 bytes, maximum size 100, percentage usage 25:

Using character field: 100,000 bytes

Using memo field: 138,000 bytes

Here, even though only 25% of the records actually use the memo field, the wastage makes the memo field solution less space efficient than a character field.

CASE 3) Database of 1,000 records, average record size of 75 bytes, maximum size 200, percentage usage 10:

Using character field: 200,000 bytes

Using memo field: 61,200 bytes

Here, the small usage factor (10%) makes the memo field attractive. The character field method is wasteful since it allocates 200 bytes for each record, even though only 75 are used on the average.

CASE 4) Database of 100 records, average record size of 500 bytes, maximum size 750, percentage usage 90:

Using character field: 75,000 bytes

Using memo field: 47,080 bytes

In this case, even with a high usage factor (90%), the memo field is still attractive because of the difference between the maximum size and the average size of the record. The average size allows the data to be stored in one memo file record. Note that if this were not true, the balance would shift toward the character field. For example:

Database of 100 records, average record size of 513 bytes, maximum size 750, percentage usage 90:

Using character field: 75,000 bytes

Using memo field: 93,160 bytes

You can use Program 7-1 to test different combinations.

Program 7-1. Compare Sizes of Memo Fields and Character Fields

```
* Program to estimate file sizes with and without memo fields

CLEAR
more = .T.

DO WHILE more

     more = .F.
     num_recs = 0
     max_size = 0
     usage = 0
     avg_size = 0

     @ 10, 10 SAY "num_recs " GET num_recs
     @ 11, 10 SAY "max_size " GET max_size
     @ 12, 10 SAY "usage % " GET usage
     @ 13, 10 SAY "avg size " GET avg_size

     READ

     IF updated()
          @ 15, 10 SAY "As a character field " + str(num_recs * max_size)

          @ 16, 10 SAY "As a memo field     "

          s = num_recs * 10 + (INT((avg_size + 511) / 512) * 512) * ;
               num_recs * usage / 100

          @ row(), col() SAY s
```

```
            more = .T.

            WAIT
        ENDIF

    ENDDO
```

Editing Memo Fields

The MEMOEDIT function provides interactive editing of memo fields. It is a "full screen", "WordStar/dBASE" like editor. Editing occurs in a user defined window that you can put anywhere on the screen, and make any size. MEMOEDIT scrolls the text as required, both vertically and horizontally, to handle large fields. The function now takes up to 13 parameters. The first six are the same as in the Autumn '86 release. The remaining seven were introduced in the Summer '87 release. The parameters are:

1) Memo field
2) Top left row
3) Top left column
4) Bottom right row
5) Bottom right column

   If you do not specify parameters 2 through 5, MEMOEDIT uses the entire screen.

6) Update flag of type logical, which specifies whether you can update the memo field, or just view it. A .T. value allows updating, and places the MEMOEDITor in an edit mode. A .F. indicates viewing only, and places the editor in a browse mode where you can use the cursor keys to scroll. Contrast this with the Autumn '86 release where a false update flag made the computer simply display the first window full of text and then exit. The default value of this parameter is .T., allowing editing.
7) User defined function that handles keystrokes. It is invoked just like the function in DBEDIT. This chapter contains several examples of its use.

8) Virtual width of the window. By default, it is the size of the line defined by the window, but you can change it to allow editing or browsing of longer lines. In this mode, MEMOEDIT performs horizontal scrolling as required.

9) Tab size (also enables real tabs).

10) Cursor's initial line number in the memo field. Initial values are useful when the user function causes MEMOEDIT to exit, and be re-entered later. Examples will illustrate this. The parameter is ONE BASED, i.e., a value of 1 puts the cursor on the first line of the memo.

11) Cursor's initial column in the memo field. It is ZERO BASED, i.e., a value of 0 puts the cursor in the first column of the memo.

12) Cursor's initial row relative to the start of the window. It allows the line specified in 10 to be located arbitrarily within the window. The default is 0, indicating the first row.

13) Cursor's initial column, relative to the start of the window. It allows the column specified in 11 to be located arbitrarily within the window. The rows can then be initially scrolled right. The default is 0, indicating the first column.

All parameters are optional.

Parameters 10 and 11 specify the row and column that appears in the top left corner of the MEMOEDIT window. You can think of parameters 12 and 13 as offsetting this point from the top left corner.

The following code edits a memo field, "comments", in record 2, in a window extending from coordinates 10, 10 to 20, 20. It allows the field to be updated.

```
USE cust
GOTO 2

REPLACE comments WITH memoedit(comments, 10, 10, 20, 20, .T.)
```

The Nantucket documentation describes the keys that you can use to edit the memo field.

Running the code shows that the memo editor does not frame its window. So, the programmer usually issues a BOX command before MEMOEDIT to define the window clearly. The following code shows this:

```
USE cust
GOTO 2

SL_BOX = chr(218) + chr(196) + chr(191) + chr(179) + chr(217) + ;
            chr(196) + chr(192) + chr(179)

CLEAR

@ 9, 9, 21, 21 BOX SL_BOX
REPLACE comments WITH memoedit(comments, 10, 10, 20, 20, .T.)
```

You can use the box_top_msg procedure from Chapter 5 to center a header within the memo field frame. The following code shows this, with the header "COMMENTS" displayed in high intensity on the top line:

```
USE cust
GOTO 2

bright = "W+/ "
norm = "W/ "
SL_BOX = chr(218) + chr(196) + chr(191) + chr(179) + chr(217) + ;
            chr(196) + chr(192) + chr(179)

CLEAR

DO box_top_msg WITH 9, 9, 21, 21, SL_BOX, "COMMENTS", .T., norm, bright

* memo field is called comments
REPLACE comments WITH memoedit(comments, 10, 10, 20, 20, .T.)
```

The Summer '87 release introduced the READINSERT function which you can use to check for, and toggle, the insert mode. Invoking the function without a parameter returns the current mode setting, whereas invoking it with a logical parameter makes it set the mode. By default, the insert mode is off. When you invoke MEMOEDIT, it is thus in overstrike mode. Before READINSERT was available, you had to press the insert key to switch modes. Calling the function with a .T. parameter before calling MEMOEDIT starts it in insert mode.

MEMOEDIT is simply a function that returns a value - that of the updated string or memo field passed as a parameter. In the last example, the value returned is REPLACEd into the memo field "comments". This is how the updating occurs. As with any other function, you need not use the return value. The following code, for example, lets the user edit a blank string. It does not use the return value, so the second call also invokes it with an empty string.

```
SL_BOX = chr(218) + chr(196) + chr(191) + chr(179) + chr(217) + ;

         chr(196) + chr(192) + chr(179)

CLEAR

@ 9, 9, 21, 21 BOX SL_BOX
s = ""
memoedit(s, 10, 10, 20, 20, .T.)

memoedit(s, 10, 10, 20, 20, .T.)
```

Since the memo field editor lets the programmer define the window's dimensions, it automatically formats the lines as required. For example, if you create the memo field in a window with a width of 20, and then edit it in a window of width 30, the editor will reformat the lines as necessary. Run the following code to demonstrate this:

```
SL_BOX = chr(218) + chr(196) + chr(191) + chr(179) + chr(217) + ;
         chr(196) + chr(192) + chr(179)

CLEAR

@ 9, 9, 21, 21 BOX SL_BOX
s = ""
s = memoedit(s, 10, 10, 20, 20, .T.)

CLEAR
@ 4, 4, 23, 23 BOX SL_BOX
memoedit(s, 5, 5, 22, 22, .T.)
```

Note that the editor keeps carriage returns typed by the user, but not ones inserted for formatting purposes. Be careful, however, as this does not occur if word wrap is off.

> **RULE**
>
> MEMOEDIT reformats lines as necessary.

Parameter 8 is the virtual width for the editing. It lets you edit the memo field in an area larger than the defined window. The lines scroll horizontally. To specify a value for this parameter without specifying a user function (parameter 7), pass an empty string for the function name.

GETting a Memo Field

In Clipper, performing a GET on a memo field causes it to be skipped. dBASE displays only the word 'memo'. To access the memo editor, you must press Ctrl-PgDn. This is only allowed when the memo GET is the currently selected one. To emulate this behavior in Clipper, you must program it manually. There is no GET function that disallows editing, allowing only set keys to be executed.

To GET a memo field, you must create a variable with the string 'memo' as its contents. You need a separate variable for each memo field. You must then issue GETs on the variables and set the Ctrl-PgDn key to a procedure that calls the memo editor. It should check that the active GET variable is one of those created with the 'memo' string. If so, it should execute MEMOEDIT on the appropriate field. If not, it ignores the key. Program 7-2 shows this.

Program 7-2. Simulating dBASE's GET on a Memo Field

```
* Sample code to allow GETs on database with two memo fields,
* 'comments1' and 'comments2'
*
*       1 - Open database
*
*       2 - Set Ctrl-PgDn hot key
*
*       3 - Set up two memory variables with the string 'memo'.
*
*       4 - Issue GETs and READ.

USE \mci\cust
CLEAR

CTRL_PG_DOWN = 30
SET KEY CTRL_PG_DOWN TO do_memo_edit

* Note, these are not the contents of the memo fields. We just
* use them as memory variables to emulate dBASE.

memo1 = "memo"
memo2 = "memo"

@ 10, 10 GET c1_name
@ 11, 10 GET memo1
@ 12, 10 GET memo2
@ 13, 10 GET c2_name
```

```
      READ
      SET KEY CTRL_PG_DOWN TO

      PROCEDURE do_memo_edit

      PARAMETERS prog, line, var
      PRIVATE save_lines

            IF var = "MEMO1"
                  save_lines = savescreen(14, 10, 22, 70)
                  REPLACE comments1 WITH memoedit(comments1, 14, 10, 22, 70)
                  restscreen(14, 10, 22, 70, save_lines)
            ELSEIF var = "MEMO2"
                  save_lines = savescreen(14, 10, 22, 70)
                  REPLACE comments2 WITH memoedit(comments2, 14, 10, 22, 70)
                  restscreen(14, 10, 22, 70, save_lines)
            ENDIF

RETURN
```

The 'cust' database contains the memo fields comments1 and comments2. It is taken from an application that maintains back orders for several customers. The memo field comments1 is used by the salesman to keep general comments about the client (for example, "Laurell is the boss. She is tough to pin down. Her secretary, Joe, handles the details."). The field comments2 holds comments about specific back orders (for example, "Order 12-123 was late because we were out of widgets again.") In Program 7-2, they are related to the variables 'memo1' and 'memo2', which are checked when the function is executed.

Use this method when editing or appending records that contain memo fields.

Memo Handling with the User Function

In the Autumn '86 version of the memo editor, pressing Esc during edit caused the "Abort edit (y/n)" message to appear, regardless of whether you had changed the memo. The Summer '87 release simply exits if you press the Esc key and the memo has not changed. Unfortunately, this is not always what you want. You may want to display the message in a different location, or with control over re-painting all or part of the screen.

MEMOEDIT's seventh parameter, its user defined function, gives you this control. It is called just like DBEDIT's function after every keystroke. You can use it to detect that the Esc key has been pressed and perform the appropriate action. First, let us examine how to invoke it.

The parameter is the name of a function. It must be a character string. The routine receives three parameters:

1) mode - the state from which it was called:

   - mode = 0, idle, a keystroke that cannot be reconfigured.
   - mode = 1, a reconfigurable keystroke, the memo field has not yet been changed since the routine was invoked.
   - mode = 2, a reconfigurable keystroke, the memo field has been altered, but not necessarily by this keystroke.
   - mode = 3, a startup mode, called on startup until it returns zero. It allows the function to return multiple initial values to the memo editor.

2) line - the current line number, starting from 1.

3) col - the current column number, starting from 0.

The function must return one of the following values to MEMOEDIT:

0 - perform default action for this key.

1 - 31 perform the action corresponding to the returned value. For example, 22 = Ins, toggle insert mode.

32 - Ignore current key.

33 - Process the current key as data. This allows control characters to be embedded in the memo field.

34 - Toggle word wrap mode.

35 - Toggle scrolling.

The return values are significant only when the function is called with a nonzero mode. A key that causes the function to be called with a zero mode cannot be reconfigured. For example, you cannot disable or reconfigure cursor keys, Enter, Backspace, Tab, Del, or any character key.

Before implementing an actual user defined function, first

develop a trial function like Program 7-3. It simply displays its parameters and returns a "default action" value of 0.

Program 7-3. Simple User Defined Function for MEMOEDIT

```
* Program to call MEMOEDIT with a user defined function
* The function displays its parameters and returns

USE cust

CLEAR
i=0
DEFAULT_ACTION = 0

memoedit(comments, 10, 10, 20, 20, .T., "ufunc")

FUNCTION ufunc

PARAM mode, line, col

    i=i+1

    @ 22, 10 SAY mode
    @ 22, 25 SAY line
    @ 22, 40 SAY col
    @ 22, 65 SAY i

RETURN DEFAULT_ACTION
```

Note that all keys that cannot be reconfigured generate a call with a mode value of 0. They are the arrow keys, page keys, etc. Also note that column numbers start at 0, whereas row numbers start at 1. The character in the top left corner of the box is therefore at 1, 0, relative to the start of the editing box.

As ufunc returns a value directing MEMOEDIT to perform the default action for all keys, its operation is unaltered with a minor exception. Without the user function, pressing the Esc key causes the "Abort edit (y/n)" prompt to appear if the memo has been modified. With the user function, however, the function aborts without issuing the prompt. Of course, the function can detect the Escape key and issue the prompt itself. A later example shows how.

An improved user defined function (Program 7-4) disables the Escape key. It returns the value 32 to tell MEMOEDIT to ignore the key.

Program 7-4. MEMOEDIT Function to Disable Escape Key

```
* Program to call MEMOEDIT with user function to disable the
* Escape key. It does this by returning the "ignore key" value,
* 32, when the key is pressed.

USE cust

CLEAR

ESC = 27
IGNORE_KEY = 32
DEFAULT_ACTION = 0

MODE_NOT_CHANGED = 1
MODE_CHANGED = 2

MODE_STARTUP = 3

MEMOEDIT(comments, 10, 10, 20, 20, .T., "ufunc")

FUNCTION ufunc

PARAM mode, line, col
PRIVATE ret_val

    IF mode = MODE_STARTUP
        ret_val = DEFAULT_ACTION
    ELSEIF lastkey() = ESC
        ret_val = IGNORE_KEY
    ELSE
        ret_val = DEFAULT_ACTION
    ENDIF

RETURN ret_val
```

Program 7-4 defines the "constants" as memory variables. In practice, you would define them in the "init_consts" routine, shown in Chapters 3 and 5.

The function first checks for a startup value. If it finds one, it returns the default action value (DEFAULT_ACTION = 0). The function must check for this mode before issuing a LASTKEY function call. If the mode is the startup value, LASTKEY returns the value of the key pressed before MEMOEDIT was entered.

To disable the Escape key, the function detects it and returns an IGNORE_KEY value. In all other cases, it returns a DEFAULT_ACTION value.

Program 7-5 issues the "Abort edit (y/n)" message on detecting the Escape key. According to the response, it either resumes or aborts editing.

Program 7-5. MEMOEDIT User Function with Query for Abort

```
* MEMOEDIT user function to prompt "Abort edit (y/n)" when Escape key is
* pressed. It saves the line before issuing the message and restores
* it when finished.

FUNCTION ufunc

PARAM mode, line, col
PRIVATE ret_val, msg, save_line

        IF mode = MODE_STARTUP
                ret_val = DEFAULT_ACTION
        ELSEIF lastkey() = ESC

                save_line = SPACE(160 * 2)

                save_line = savescreen(0, 0, 1, 79)

                msg = "Abort edit (y/n)?"
                @ 0, 60 SAY msg

                inkey(0)
                IF chr(lastkey()) $ "Yy"
                        ret_val = DEFAULT_ACTION
                ELSE
                        ret_val = IGNORE_KEY
                ENDIF

                restscreen(0, 0, 1, 79, save_line)
        ELSE
                ret_val = DEFAULT_ACTION
        ENDIF

RETURN ret_val
```

If the user responds with yes to the "Abort edit" question, the function returns a default action value to MEMOEDIT, causing it to abort.

To avoid disrupting the screen display, the code saves line 0 before displaying the message, and restores it upon exit.

Program 7-6 displays the message only if the memo field has actually changed; it allows the exit otherwise.

Program 7-6. MEMOEDIT Function with Query for Abort if Memo Has Changed

```
* MEMOEDIT user function to prompt "Abort edit (y/n)" when Escape key
* pressed if memofield has changed.
* It saves the line before issuing the message and restores
* it when finished.

FUNCTION ufunc

PARAM mode, line, col
PRIVATE ret_val, msg, save_line

        IF mode = MODE_STARTUP
                ret_val = DEFAULT_ACTION

        ELSEIF lastkey() = ESC .AND. mode = MODE_CHANGED

                * If memo was altered and abort was attempted ...

                save_line = SPACE(160 * 2)

                save_line = savescreen(0, 0, 1, 79)

                msg = "Abort edit (y/n)?"
                @ 0, 60 SAY msg

                inkey(0)
                IF chr(lastkey()) $ "Yy"
                        ret_val = DEFAULT_ACTION
                ELSE
                        ret_val = IGNORE_KEY
                ENDIF

                restscreen(0, 0, 1, 79, save_line)

        ELSE
                ret_val = DEFAULT_ACTION
        ENDIF

RETURN ret_val
```

The only change here verifies that the mode is "changed". We could extend this easily to provide the option to write the memo field and then exit. The sample program "ME.PRG" on the Clipper release disk does this.

The function can also recognize the Ins key and change the cursor to half height rather than displaying the <insert> message on line 0. This makes the mode more obvious and frees line 0 for other messages. Program 7-7 shows this, using the "setcurs" routine defined in Chapter 11 to change the cursor.

Program 7-7. Changing the Cursor Shape for Insert

```
* MEMOEDIT function to switch cursor shape between underscore and half
* height when Ins key is pressed. Use readinsert() function to switch
* editing modes and keep track of current state. Cursor shape matches
* this. Setcurs routine is defined in Chapter 11

ESC = 27
IGNORE_KEY = 32
DEFAULT_ACTION = 0

MODE_NOT_CHANGED = 1
MODE_CHANGED = 2
MODE_STARTUP = 3

INS = 22

@ 9, 9 TO 21, 21
MEMOEDIT("", 10, 10, 20, 20, .T., "ufunc")

setcurs(12, 13) && set underscore cursor back in case it was changed

FUNCTION ufunc

PARAM mode, line, col
PRIVATE ret_val

    IF mode = MODE_STARTUP
        ret_val = DEFAULT_ACTION
    ELSEIF lastkey() = INS
        ret_val = IGNORE_KEY

        * Toggle insert mode
        readinsert(!readinsert())

        IF readinsert()
            * change cursor to half height
            setcurs(7, 13)
        ELSE
            * change cursor to underscore
            setcurs(12, 13)
        ENDIF
    ELSE
        ret_val = DEFAULT_ACTION
    ENDIF

RETURN ret_val
```

Upon detecting the Ins key, Program 7-7 toggles the insert mode by issuing the function call:

```
readinsert(!readinsert())
```

This gets the mode's status, inverts it, and then resets it. An IGNORE_KEY value is returned to prevent the usual <insert> message from appearing on the scoreboard line. The setcurs function takes two parameters: the start and end lines for the cursor. The line numbers refer to the one character box in which the cursor is displayed, not the display line (0 through 24). On an IBM monochrome card, each character consists of 14 lines, numbered from 0 to 13, with 0 at the top. To get a half height cursor, you must set the start and end lines to 7 and 13, respectively. The standard underscore cursor is defined with a start line of 12 and an end line of 13.

With a color card, a character consists of only 8 lines. They are numbered from 0 to 7, starting with 0 at the top. An underscore cursor is formed by line 7 only. A half height cursor is formed by lines 4 through 7.

Reconfiguring the keys lets the programmer specify what actions they cause. To redefine a key, we must recognize that it has been pressed, and then return the translated value to the memo editor. For example, Program 7-8 invokes the memo editor with the following keys defined.

ACTIVE KEY	ACTION	TRANSLATED VALUE
F2	Save and exit	Ctrl-W
F3	Abort (exit with no save)	Esc
F4	Delete line	Ctrl-Y
F5	Delete word right	Ctrl-T

Program 7-8. Redefining Keys with MEMOEDIT's User Function

```
* MEMOEDIT function redefining Esc, Ctrl-W, Ctrl-Y, and Ctrl-T

USE cust
init_consts()
```

```
IGNORE_KEY = 32
DEFAULT_ACTION = 0

MODE_NOT_CHANGED = 1
MODE_CHANGED = 2
MODE_STARTUP = 3

REPLACE comments WITH MEMOEDIT(comments, 10, 10, 20, 20, .T., "memo_func")

FUNCTION memo_func

PARAM mode, line, col
PRIVATE ret_val, key

    IF mode = MODE_STARTUP
        ret_val = DEFAULT_ACTION
    ELSE
        ret_val = DEFAULT_ACTION
        key = lastkey()
        IF key = ESC .OR. key = CTRL_W .OR. key = CTRL_T ;
                    .OR. key = CTRL_Y
            ret_val = IGNORE_KEY
        ELSE
            DO CASE
                CASE key = F2
                    ret_val = CTRL_W

                CASE key = F3
                    ret_val = ESC

                CASE key = F4
                    ret_val = CTRL_Y

                CASE key = F5
                    ret_val = CTRL_T

            ENDCASE
        ENDIF
    ENDIF
RETURN (ret_val)
```

To disable the default actions of the specified control and Esc keys, the function returns a value instructing MEMOEDIT to ignore them. To enable the function keys, it returns the values required by MEMOEDIT to perform those operations. The "init_consts" routine, defined in Chapters 3 and 5, should be available to the linker when building this routine. It simply defines a public memory variable for key values, box strings, etc. It would be a good idea to include the values defined here for the actions and calling modes. We would add the following PUBLICs and assignment statements:

```
PUBLIC IGNORE_KEY, DEFAULT_ACTION, MODE_NOT_CHANGED
PUBLIC MODE_CHANGED, MODE_STARTUP

    IGNORE_KEY = 32
    DEFAULT_ACTION = 0

    MODE_NOT_CHANGED = 1
    MODE_CHANGED = 2
    MODE_STARTUP = 3
```

TIP

Define the MEMOEDIT function modes and return values as pseud-constants.

Clipper calls the user defined function repeatedly upon startup (before processing any keys) until it returns zero. In the previous examples, the function returned zero (the default action value) when called in this mode. However, if you must set states such as word wrap, Insert, or Scroll before editing starts, the function must return the values to MEMOEDIT before returning zero. Since a function can only return one value to its caller, a public variable must keep track of the "state" of the initialization process, and which variable should be returned next. Note that this is necessary even when the function only needs to set one state. You must first return a value to set the state, then 0 to terminate initialization. For example, Program 7-9 forces word wrap off (it is on by default).

Program 7-9. Using a State Variable for MEMOEDIT Initialization

```
* Allow editing as in Program 7-8 except initialization code forces
* word wrap OFF. It is on by default. Global init_state keeps
* track of initialization state - 0 makes routine return value to turn
* word wrap off, 1 makes it return DEFAULT ACTION to end initialization
USE cust
init_consts()

CLEAR

init_state = 0

REPLACE comments WITH MEMOEDIT(comments, 10, 10, 20, 20, .T., "memo_func")
```

```
FUNCTION memo_func

PARAM mode, line, col
PRIVATE ret_val, key

          * default return value ...
          ret_val = DEFAULT_ACTION
          IF mode = MODE_STARTUP
                    DO CASE

                              CASE init_state = 0  && turn word wrap off
                                        ret_val = 34
                                        init_state = init_state + 1

                              CASE init_state = 1
                                        ret_val = DEFAULT_ACTION

                    ENDCASE
          ELSE
                    * default return value ...
                    ret_val = DEFAULT_ACTION

                    key = lastkey()
                    IF key = ESC .OR. key = CTRL_W .OR. key = CTRL_T;
                                        .OR. key = CTRL_Y
                              ret_val = IGNORE_KEY
                    ELSE
                              DO CASE

                                        CASE key = F2
                                                  ret_val = CTRL_W
                                        CASE key = F3
                                                  ret_val = ESC
                                        CASE key = F4
                                                  ret_val = CTRL_Y
                                        CASE key = F5
                                                  ret_val = CTRL_T

                              ENDCASE
                    ENDIF
          ENDIF
RETURN (ret_val)
```

TIP

To set an initial state for MEMOEDIT, you must maintain a "state" variable.

Processing Memo Fields

Clipper lets you treat a memo field just like a character memory variable. You can then use string handling functions such as AT, SUBSTR, etc, directly on MEMO fields. You can search them, concatenate them, and do anything you can do to a character variable. For example, consider the following code:

```
USE memot

DO WHILE !eof()

    IF due > 30
        s = "This concerns account # 31. It is 30 days past due "

        REPLACE ac_status WITH s

    ENDIF

    SKIP

ENDDO
```

This updates the memofield 'ac_status' with the text when the due field is greater than 30. The memo field is replaced with a character variable in the same way you would update a character field.

When you pass a memo field to the type function, it returns "M" for memo. However, when you assign the field to a memory variable and then ask for its type, the function returns "C" for character. Internally, Clipper converts the field from a memo type to a character on assignment, and back to a memo on REPLACE. The character functions can be used with either characters or memos. This is because of the way Clipper encodes the type information (discussed in Chapter 11).

We can use the AT function to search every record in the database. Program 7-10 saves the numbers of records where the memo field contains a specified string, and then uses the numbers to restrict editing.

Program 7-10. Using the AT Function to Search All Memo Field Records

```
Program to search for records with memo fields containing a given
* string and allow them to be edited separately
*
```

```
*
*       1 - Read string to search for
*
*       2 - For each record:
*
*               2.1 - If memo record contains the string, add it to array
*
*       3 - For each record containing the string
*
*               3.1 - GOTO it
*
*               3.2 - Allow it to be edited

USE memot

PRIVATE rec_nums[reccount()]   && maximum size

search_for = space(10)

CLEAR

@ 10, 10 SAY "Enter string to search for " GET search_for
READ

search_for = rtrim(search_for)

num_found = 0

* search every record

DO WHILE !eof()
        IF in_memo(memo, search_for)
                num_found = num_found + 1
                rec_nums[num_found] = recno()
        ENDIF

        SKIP

ENDDO

IF num_found != 0
        * if found any, edit them

        SL_BOX = chr(218) + chr(196) + chr(191) + chr(179) + chr(217) + ;
                    chr(196) + chr(192) + chr(179)
        @ 9, 9, 21, 21 BOX SL_BOX

        this_rec = 1

        DO WHILE this_rec <= num_found

                GOTO rec_nums[this_rec]
```

```
            REPLACE memo WITH MEMOEDIT(memo, 10, 10, 20, 20, .T.)
            this_rec = this_rec + 1

        ENDDO
ELSE
        ? "Did not find any memos containing the search string"
ENDIF


FUNCTION in_memo

PARAMETERS memo, string

RETURN (IIF ((AT(string, memo) != 0), .T., .F.))
```

Rather than editing the memo fields separately, we could combine them into a large string, and then edit it. Program 7-11 shows this.

Program 7-11. Combining Memo Fields Containing a Specified String

```
* Program to search for records with memo fields containing a given string
* and allow them to be edited at the same time
*
*
*       1 - Read string to search for
*
*       2 - Initialize empty target string
*
*       3 - For each record:
*
*               3.1 - If memo record contains the string, concatenate it
*                     to the target string.
*
*       4 - Allow target string to be edited

USE memot

search_for = space(10)

CLEAR

@ 10, 10 SAY "Enter string to search for " GET search_for
READ

search_for = rtrim(search_for)

* target string
```

```
new_memo = ""
found_one = .F.

DO WHILE !eof()

        IF in_memo(memo, search_for)
                found_one = .T.
                this_memo = memo

                * concatenate this memo, separating with RECORD string
                new_memo = new_memo + chr(13) + CHR(10) + "RECORD " + ;
                                ltrim(str(recno())) + chr(13) + chr(10) + this_memo
        ENDIF

        SKIP

ENDDO

IF found_one

        CLEAR

        SL_BOX = chr(218) + chr(196) + chr(191) + chr(179) + chr(217) + ;
                        chr(196) + chr(192) + chr(179)

        @ 9, 9, 21, 21 BOX SL_BOX

        MEMOEDIT(new_memo, 10, 10, 20, 20, .T.)

ENDIF

FUNCTION in_memo
PARAMETERS memo, string

RETURN (IIF ((AT(string, memo) != 0), .T., .F.))
```

We separate the individual memo fields by inserting a line with the database record number. Note that we simply combine fields with the + operator.

We can use the LEN function to determine the length of the memo field. For example, the following sequence returns a value of 25:

```
USE memot

APPEND BLANK

REPLACE memo WITH "This concerns account #31"

? len(memo)
```

You can restrict the size of a memo field with the SUBSTR function. The following code allows the editing of a memo field. It restricts the size to 511 bytes, so the field fits in one record of the memo file (we use 511 rather than 512 because the memo editor adds the 1A marker to the end of the string).

```
USE memot

REPLACE memo WITH substr(MEMOEDIT(memo, 10, 10, 20, 20, .T.), 1, 511)
```

The MEMOEDIT function should have a parameter that specifies how much a memo field may grow. As it stands, there is nothing to stop the user from creating a memo field of any size up to 64K.

> **NOTE**
>
> You can use the character handling functions on memo fields.

MLCOUNT and MEMOLINE Functions

The MLCOUNT and MEMOLINE functions can operate either on memo fields or character strings, but were specifically designed for use with memos.

The MEMOLINE function returns a line from a memo field. You pass it the line's number and width as parameters. A call such as

```
mline = memoline(comments, LINE_WIDTH, line_num)
```

assigns to mline the line at line number line_num from the memo field comments. The memo is interpreted with a line width of LINE_WIDTH. Note that this value need not be the same as the width in which it was created (if it was created with the memo editor). This is important, as it allows you to print a memo in any width. For example, if you create a memo field in a window of width 30, you can display it with a width of 50 simply by using MEMOLINE with the larger width. It reformats the lines to the new width.

MLCOUNT returns the number of lines of a given width in the specified memo field or character variable. You typically use it as the limit of a loop calling MEMOLINE.

The following code uses these two functions to save every line of the memo comments in a separate element of the array lines. It then uses array to display the memo on the screen. This is the simplest way to display a memo field.

```
* Simple memo field display routine using an array and mlcount
* / memoline

USE memot
LINE_WIDTH = 10

num_memo_lines = mlcount(comments, LINE_WIDTH)

PRIVATE lines[num_memo_lines]

FOR i = 1 TO num_memo_lines

        lines[i] = memoline(comments, LINE_WIDTH, i)

NEXT

FOR i = 1 TO num_memo_lines

        ? lines[i]

NEXT
```

We can use the ACHOICE function, described in Chapter 3, with the MLCOUNT and MEMOLINE functions to implement a routine that lets the user find all lines in the memo field that contain a certain string. Program 7-12 shows this.

Program 7-12. Using ACHOICE to Show Selected Lines from a MEMO

```
* Program to demonstrate use of achoice with mlcount / memoline
* to allow browsing of memo field lines containing specified string

MAX_LINES = 1024
LINE_WIDTH = 60

CLEAR
ACCEPT "Enter string to search for : " TO search_for

USE memot

num_lines = MIN(mlcount(memo, LINE_WIDTH), MAX_LINES)
```

```
PRIVATE lines[num_lines]
PRIVATE in_line[num_lines]

* Build ACHOICE's Boolean array

FOR i = 1 TO num_lines

        lines[i] = memoline(memo, LINE_WIDTH, i)
        in_line[i] = AT(search_for, lines[i]) != 0

NEXT

SL_BOX = chr(218) + chr(196) + chr(191) + chr(179) + chr(217) + ;
                chr(196) + chr(192) + chr(179)

@ 3, 9, 21, 10 + LINE_WIDTH BOX SL_BOX

* Don't allow other "ON" elements to be seen until selected
SET COLOR TO W/N, N/W,,,W/N

ACHOICE(4, 10, 20, 10 + LINE_WIDTH - 1, lines, in_line)
```

The user enters a search string. The code fills each element with a line from the memo field using the MEMOLINE function, and searches the line for the string. If the search succeeds, the code sets the corresponding element in the logical array to .T.. ACHOICE will then allow it to be selected. Otherwise, the element is set to .F.. For more information on ACHOICE, see Chapter 3.

Searching from within MEMOEDIT

Program 7-12 showed a stand-alone method of searching a memo field. However, to search from within MEMOEDIT, we must employ the user function and MEMOLINE. Program 7-13 illustrates this. The database cust in the mci directory contains a memo field called comments. It contains general comments about a salesperson's customers. During MEMOEDIT, the user can activate a search by pressing the Alt and S keys. The user function detects this and asks for a search string. It then causes the function to terminate by returning the code for Ctrl-W. The memo field is then searched for the specified string. If the search succeeds, MEMOEDIT is reentered with the cursor at the string's location. Otherwise, MEMOEDIT is reentered with the cursor at its original position.

Program 7-13. Searching from within MEMOEDIT

```
* Memo field search function
*
*       1 - open database, do initializations
*
*       2 - DO WHILE search_active
*
*               2.1 - search_active = .F.
*
*               2.1 do memoedit with cursor starting on search string
*                       (start of memo if first time - no search)
*
*               2.2 memoedit function has set search_active, srch_str,
*                       init_row, init_col, init_rel_row, and init_rel_col
*                       if a search was issued (this caused memoedit to exit)
*
*               2.3 If we need to search:
*
*                       2.3.1 search every line from current position with AT
*                               until found or end of data
*
*                       2.3.2 if found, set new init_row, init_col, init_rel_row,
*                               and init_rel_col. memoedit will then be started
*                               at this place

USE \mci\cust

init_consts()

ALT_S = 287
srch_str = space(80)

CLEAR
search_active = .T.

* coordinates for edit window

x = 10
y = 10
u = 20
v = 20

* frame window
@ x - 1, y - 1 TO u + 1, v + 1

init_row = 1
init_col = 0

init_rel_row = 0
```

```
init_rel_col = 0

* while we are searching, or first time ....
DO WHILE search_active
	search_active = .F.

	REPLACE comments WITH memoedit(comments, x, y, u, v, .T., "ufunc", ;
				"", "", init_row, init_col, init_rel_row, init_rel_col)

	IF search_active
		* first check remainder of current line
		new_col = at(trim(srch_str), substr(memoline( ;
				comments, v - y + 1, init_row), init_col + 1))
		IF new_col != 0
			* found in same line
			init_col = new_col - 1 + init_col
			init_rel_col = init_col
			@ 24, 10 SAY "FOUND     "
		ELSE
			* Not found, so search rest of file
			num_lines = mlcount(comments, v - y + 1)
			new_col = 0

			* while not found and more lines, keep searching ...
			i = init_row + 1
			DO WHILE new_col = 0 .AND. i <= num_lines
				new_col = at(trim(srch_str), memoline( ;
							comments, v - y + 1, i))

				* didn't find it, go to next line
				IF new_col = 0
					i = i + 1
				ENDIF

			ENDDO

			IF new_col != 0
				init_col = new_col - 1
				init_rel_col = init_col
				init_row = i
				init_rel_row = (i - 1) % (u - x + 1)

				@ 24, 10 SAY "FOUND     "

			ELSE
				@ 24, 10 SAY "NOT FOUND"
			ENDIF
		ENDIF
	ENDIF
ENDDO
```

```
FUNCTION ufunc

PARAM mode, line, col
PRIVATE ret_val, save_line

    IF mode = MODE_STARTUP
        ret_val = DEFAULT_ACTION
    ELSEIF lastkey() = ALT_S
        init_row = line
        init_col = col
        init_rel_row = row() - x
        init_rel_col = col() - y

        save_line = savescreen(23, 0, 24, 79)
        @ 24, 10 SAY "Search for" GET srch_str PICT "@s40K"
        READ

        ret_val = CTRL_W
        search_active = .T.
        restscreen(23, 0, 24, 79, save_line)
    ELSE
        ret_val = DEFAULT_ACTION
    ENDIF

RETURN ret_val
```

The search has two parts. The first checks only from the current position to the end of the line. The second part checks the remainder of the line. Note the setting of the 'init_rel_row' variable when the string is found, and it is not on the first line. The modulus operator sets the relative row variable so that, when MEMOEDIT is reentered, the line containing the field is displayed at an offset from the start of the window. This works as if the user had pressed the page down key. If the line was already in the window, however, the screen is unchanged.

We can extend the basic search function in many ways. For example, we could implement a find next or translate function.

Browsing MEMO Fields

In the Autumn '86 version of the memo editor, a false update flag caused the first window of the memo field to be displayed, and the function terminated. To view more than one window without allowing editing, one needed a custom routine. In the Summer '87 release, a false update flag puts the memo editor in a "browse" mode in which only the cursor keys are active, allowing browsing but not editing.

Another technique for browsing memo fields uses the ACHOICE, MEMOLINE, and MLCOUNT functions. ACHOICE's highlight bar highlights the entire line. Program 7-14 shows this.

Program 7-14. Using ACHOICE to Browse a Memo Field

```
* Memo field view routine using ACHOICE
*
* 1 - Fill each element of array with a line from memo field
*
* 2 - Frame window
*
* 3 - Pass this to ACHOICE to allow viewing

MAX_LINES = 1024
LINE_WIDTH = 60

CLEAR

USE memot

num_lines = MIN(mlcount(memo, LINE_WIDTH), MAX_LINES)

PRIVATE lines[num_lines]

FOR i = 1 TO num_lines

        lines[i] = memoline(memo, LINE_WIDTH, i)

NEXT

SL_BOX = chr(218) + chr(196) + chr(191) + chr(179) + chr(217) + ;
                chr(196) + chr(192) + chr(179)

@ 3, 9, 10, 10 + LINE_WIDTH BOX SL_BOX

* Don't allow other "ON" elements to be seen until selected
SET COLOR TO W/N, N/W,,,W/N

ACHOICE(4, 10, 9, 10 + LINE_WIDTH - 1, lines)        && default to all seen
```

The code creates an array element for each line of the memo field. It then passes the elements to ACHOICE, allowing the memo to be viewed.

We can also modify the "browse" code developed in Chapter 6 for memo fields. Progam 7-15 is a modified version of Program 6-13 using MLCOUNT and MEMOLINE to implement the browse.

Program 7-15. Custom Code for Browsing a Written Memo Field

```
* Browse of a memo field. Modified version of 6-13 using memoline
* and mlcount. Init_consts must have been called.
*
*       1 - Determine number of lines in memo field
*
*       2 - Frame window
*
*       3 - Display first window full
*
*       4 - Highlight currently selected line
*
*       5 - Repeat until Esc or Enter key pressed
*
*               5.1 - Remove highlight from currently selected line
*
*               5.2 - Move according to key just pressed
*
*               5.3 - Highlight new line

FUNCTION mbrowse

PARAMETERS memo, start_row, start_col, end_row, end_col

PRIVATE num_disp_rows, floor, ceiling, key, highlight, width, cur_disp_row s
PRIVATE SL_BOX, num_lines

        width = end_col - start_col - 1

        num_lines = mlcount(memo, width)
        IF (num_lines = 0)
                RETURN (0)
        ENDIF

        @ start_row, start_col, end_row, end_col BOX SL_BOX
        num_disp_rows = end_row - start_row - 1

        floor = 1

        highlight = 1

        cur_disp_rows = mfill_box(memo, start_row, start_col, end_row, end_col , ;
                                        floor)

        ceiling = cur_disp_rows + floor - 1
```

```
IF ceiling != num_lines
        SET COLOR TO /W
        @ end_row, start_col SAY chr(25)
        SET COLOR TO W/
ENDIF

* Highlight active element
SET COLOR TO /W
@ start_row + highlight, start_col + 1 SAY ;
                        memoline(memo, width, floor + highlight - 1)
SET COLOR TO W/

key = inkey(0)
DO WHILE (key != ESC) .AND. (key != ENTER)

        * Remove highlight from active element
        @ start_row + highlight, start_col + 1 SAY ;
                        memoline(memo, width, floor + highlight - 1)

        DO CASE
                CASE key = UP_ARROW
                        IF highlight > 1
                                highlight = highlight - 1
                        ELSE
                                IF floor > 1
                                        floor = floor - 1

                                        scroll(start_row + 1, start_col + 1, ;
                                                end_row - 1, end_col - 1, - 1)

                                        * this leaves highlight row empty

                                        cur_disp_rows = min(num_disp_rows, ;
                                                        num_lines - floor + 1)

                                        ceiling = floor + cur_disp_rows - 1

                                ENDIF
                        ENDIF

                CASE key = DOWN_ARROW
                        IF highlight < cur_disp_rows
                                highlight = highlight + 1
                        ELSE
                                IF ceiling < num_lines
                                        floor = floor + 1

                                        scroll(start_row + 1, start_col + 1, ;
                                                end_row - 1, end_col - 1, 1)

                                        * This leaves highlight row empty
```

```
                    cur_disp_rows = min(num_disp_rows, ;
                          num_lines - floor + 1)

                    ceiling = floor + cur_disp_rows - 1

              ENDIF
        ENDIF

  CASE key = PG_UP
        IF floor > 1
              floor = max(floor - num_disp_rows, 1)
              cur_disp_rows = mfill_box(memo, start_row, start_col, ;
                                          end_row, end_col, floor)
              ceiling = cur_disp_rows + floor - 1
        ENDIF

  CASE key = PG_DOWN
        IF ceiling < num_lines
              floor = min(floor + num_disp_rows, num_lines)

              cur_disp_rows = mfill_box(memo, start_row, start_col, ;
                                          end_row, end_col, floor)

              ceiling = cur_disp_rows + floor - 1

              highlight = min(highlight, cur_disp_rows)
        ENDIF

  CASE key = HOME
        highlight = 1

  CASE key = END_KEY
        highlight = cur_disp_rows

  CASE key = CTRL_HOME
        highlight = 1
        floor = 1
        cur_disp_rows = mfill_box(memo, start_row, start_col, ;
                          end_row, end_col, floor)
        ceiling = cur_disp_rows + floor - 1

  CASE key = CTRL_END
        IF ceiling = num_lines
              highlight = cur_disp_rows
        ELSE
              floor = num_lines - num_disp_rows + 1

              cur_disp_rows = mfill_box(memo, start_row, start_col, ;
                    end_row, end_col, floor)
              ceiling = cur_disp_rows + floor - 1

              highlight = cur_disp_rows
```

```
                ENDIF
            ENDCASE

            * Highlight active element
            SET COLOR TO /W
            @ start_row + highlight, start_col + 1 SAY ;
                        memoline(memo, width, floor + highlight - 1)
            SET COLOR TO W/

            IF floor != 1
                SET COLOR TO /W
                @ start_row, start_col SAY chr(24)
                SET COLOR TO W/
            ELSE
                @ start_row, start_col SAY chr(218)
            ENDIF

            IF ceiling != num_lines
                SET COLOR TO /W
                @ end_row, start_col SAY chr(25)
                SET COLOR TO W/
            ELSE
                @ end_row, start_col SAY chr(192)
            ENDIF

            key = inkey(0)

        ENDDO
RETURN (IF (lastkey() = ESC, 0, floor + highlight - 1))


FUNCTION mfill_box

PARAMETERS memo, start_row, start_col, end_row, end_col, floor

PRIVATE num_disp, num_rows, i, width

        num_rows = end_row - start_row - 1
        width = end_col - start_col - 1
        num_disp = min(num_rows, num_lines - floor + 1)

        FOR i = 1 TO num_disp
            @ start_row + i, start_col + 1 SAY ;
                memoline(memo, width, floor + i - 1)
        NEXT

        FOR i = num_disp + 1 TO num_rows
            @ start_row + i, start_col + 1 SAY space(width)
        NEXT

RETURN (num_disp)
```

Program 7-15 determines the number of lines in the memo field and saves it in the memory variable "num_lines". The MEMOLINE function is used like an array index - we simply specify the line number we want from a memo field with a given width. The same variables are used as in Program 6-13 to save positions, so Figure 6-2 applies here. Note that the absolute line number is always given by the expression "floor + highlight - 1". Refer to Figure 6-2 to see the relationship between the variables.

We could call Program 7-15 as follows:

```
CLEAR
USE memot

init_consts()  && initialize box string, key values, etc.

size = 30

mbrowse(memo, 10, 10, 20, 10 + size + 1)
```

Although the memo editor now has a browse mode, this routine is useful when you need more control than MEMOEDIT provides.

Displaying MEMO Fields

We can emulate the behavior of the Autumn '86 'browse' mode with a user function as shown in Program 7-16.

Program 7-16. Emulating Autumn '86's Memo Display Mode

```
CLEAR

IGNORE_KEY = 32
DEFAULT_ACTION = 0

MODE_NOT_CHANGED = 1
MODE_CHANGED = 2
MODE_STARTUP = 3

ESC = 27

USE cust

memoedit(comments, 10, 10, 20, 20, .T., "no_browse")

? inkey(0)      && to pause display ...
```

```
FUNCTION no_browse

PRIVATE ret_val
PARAM mode, line, col

        ret_val = DEFAULT_ACTION

        IF mode = MODE_STARTUP
            KEYBOARD chr(ESC)
        ENDIF

RETURN ret_val
```

Remember that Clipper calls the user function repeatedly upon initialization with a STARTUP mode, until it returns a default action value. In this case, the function returns a default action value but also stuffs an Escape character into the keyboard buffer. The default action value causes the memo editor to terminate its initialization phase, and the stuffed Escape key causes the function to be immediately recalled with a mode of 1. The function then again returns the default action value, causing the MEMOEDIT function to exit (the default action for an Escape key). This mode lets you display the first window but not edit or browse it. You could then use a SET KEY to allow the edit or browse, while allowing other SET KEYs to perform other functions.

A previous section showed how MEMOEDIT automatically formats the memo field to the required width. To start a new line, it puts a "soft" carriage return (character 141) in the memo text. This is also stored in the DBT file when you REPLACE into the memo field. A hex dump of the file shows the value. For example, if we dump a memo field with the following screen format:

```
This is a
memo
field.
This is
record
number 1
of this
memo
field.
```

the following values appear:

```
400: 54 68 69 73 20 69 73 20 61 20 8D 0A 6D 65 6D 6F This is a ..memo
410: 20 8D 0A 66 69 65 6C 64 2E 20 8D 0A 54 68 69 73 ..field ...This
420: 20 69 73 20 8D 0A 72 65 63 6F 72 64 20 8D 0A 6E is ..record ..n
430: 75 6D 62 65 72 20 31 20 8D 0A 6F 66 20 74 68 69 umber 1 ..of thi
440: 73 20 8D 0A 6D 65 6D 6F 20 66 69 65 6C 64 2E 1A s..memo field..
```

Note the sequence 8D 0A (141 and 10 decimal), corresponding to each line break on the screen. The 8D is simply a 0D (carriage return) with the most significant bit set.

To display the field, we must use Program 7-17 to replace soft carriage returns with hard carriage returns.

Program 7-17. General-Purpose Character Conversion

```
* General purpose translation function - used to convert
* soft carriage returns to hard carriage returns

FUNCTION strtran

PARAMETER source, search_for, replace_with
PRIVATE len_source, index, destination, where

     len_source = len(source)

     index = 1
     destination = ""

     * while not at end of string...
     DO WHILE index <= len_source

          * look for next occurrence of source string
          where = AT(search_for, substr(source, index, ;
                         len_source - index + 1))

          IF where != 0
               * found one so replace it in output string

               destination = destination + ;
                              substr(source, index, where - 1)

               destination = destination + replace_with
               index = index + where

          ELSE
               * didn't find one so add to output string and terminate
               destination = destination + ;
                              substr(source, index, len_source - index + 1)
```

```
                * force termination
                index = len_source + 1
            ENDIF

        ENDDO

    RETURN (destination)
```

You would call Program 7-17 with:

```
USE memot

? strtran(this_memo, chr(141), chr(13))
```

strtran is a Clipper implementation of a faster C routine, hardcr, available in the extend library. Since hardcr's only job is to translate soft carriage returns into hard carriage returns, it takes only the text string as a parameter. You call it with:

```
USE memot

? hardcr(memo)
```

This method will only format the fields in the same width as they were created. To display them in an arbitrary width, you must use the MLCOUNT and MEMOLINE functions. Program 7-18 shows how to print a memo field in a given width.

Program 7-18. Printing a Memo Field in a Given Width

```
* Display memo field in given width using memoline

FUNCTION memo_print

PARAM memo, width

PRIVATE line_num, num_lines

    num_lines = mlcount(memo, width)

    FOR line_num = 1 TO num_lines

        ? memoline(memo, width, line_num)

    NEXT

RETURN .F.
```

To format the field "notes" for a width of 20, call the function with:

```
USE memot

memo_print(notes, 20)
```

Do not print the function's return value, i.e., do not call it with:

```
? memo_print(memo, 20)
```

The REPORT FORM code handles memo fields in a special way. Since it must display everything in a specified width, it must reformat the memo fields. First, it ignores soft carriage returns. It deletes occurrences of the sequence 8D 0A (hex) from the field entirely. Second, to format the field in the desired width, it breaks lines (just as the memo editor does) - at a space if possible, otherwise at the specified width. It maintains any hard carriage returns (those typed by the user).

To display the memo field in the format in which it was created, i.e., with the soft carriage returns in place, use the hardcr function in the report utility. You must declare hardcr as EXTERNAL in the main program, to ensure that the linker includes it in the EXE file.

Since the report generator removes soft carriage returns, it may combine lines without even a space between them. Sometimes this may not be what you want. Another C function, MEMOTRAN, in the extend library, is the C language equivalent of the strtran function (Program 7-17). In its default mode, MEMOTRAN translates hard carriage returns into semicolons (which cause the report generator to issue a new line), and soft carriage return/line feed pairs into spaces. You can change the default behavior by passing two arbitrary strings, the first the one to be replaced, the second the replacement. If you use MEMOTRAN in a report form, you must declare it as EXTERNAL in a PRG file so the linker will include it.

Implementation and Growth of MEMO Fields

This section gives an overview of the DBT file structure. It shows the relationship between the DBF file and the DBT file, and explains why the DBT file can grow so large. Further details are in Chapter 12.

As we have mentioned, Clipper reserves 10 bytes in every database record for each memo field. The bytes are an ASCII string that specifies the record in the DBT file where the memo field starts. A zero value indicates no memo for this record. The value does not appear when you LIST the database - Clipper simply displays "memo". Chapter 12 presents the source code for a C program, dbflist, that displays the record numbers. We will use it to explain the growth pattern. The EXE file is on the program disk for this book.

When a database is first created, Clipper creates a DBT file with the same name, consisting of a 512 byte header block, followed by an end of file marker (1A hex). The first four bytes of the header contain the number of 512 byte records in the file. This number is stored as a C long, with the least significant byte first. In the initial DBT file, the value is 1, as the file contains only one record. As records are added, the value is updated.

Now, assume we have a new database containing a memo field. The database file has no records, and the DBT file has only the 512 byte header. Now we do an APPEND BLANK command. The database now contains one blank record, but the DBT file remains the same size. Running the DBFLIST program would produce a value of 0 for the memo field entry. Now suppose that the user does a REPLACE memo WITH MEMOEDIT on this record, and then enters text of 200 bytes. The dbflist now shows a record number of 2, since the memo field record was placed at record number 2, the first free record. If we did a hex dump on the DBT file, we would see the memo field data just entered starting at offset 400 (hex), or 1024 decimal. This is what dbflist told us. It said that this memo field started at record number 2, or offset 2 * 512 = 1024 as each record is 512 bytes.

Every record in the DBT file ends with 1A (hex), the end of file marker. Since this is the last record, the file terminates here. The last record is not padded to a 512 byte boundary.

So, the DBT file now contains three records. Record 0 is the header and record 2 is the data just entered. But what is record 1? In fact, it is unused. Clipper reserved it for a future enhancement which has yet to occur! dBASE would allocate this record to the first memo field, and so in this case, its memo file would be 512 bytes smaller than Clipper's.

Now, assume we do another APPEND BLANK followed by a REPLACE memo WITH MEMOEDIT. The user again enters text of length less than 512 bytes. A dbflist would now show the memo field from database record 1 at memo file record 2 (the same as before), and the new memo field from database record 2 at memo file record 3. Clipper has simply appended to the end of the DBT file. A hex dump would show the new text at offset 600 (hex) (1536 decimal, 3 * 512). The previous record has been padded to reach a 512 byte boundary. This is why a memo field of 1 byte occupies 512 bytes in the DBT file. The 1A still remains at the end of the first record, so we can find the end of the valid data (Figure 7-1).

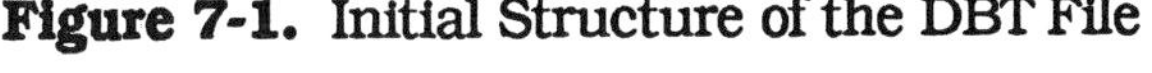

Figure 7-1. Initial Structure of the DBT File

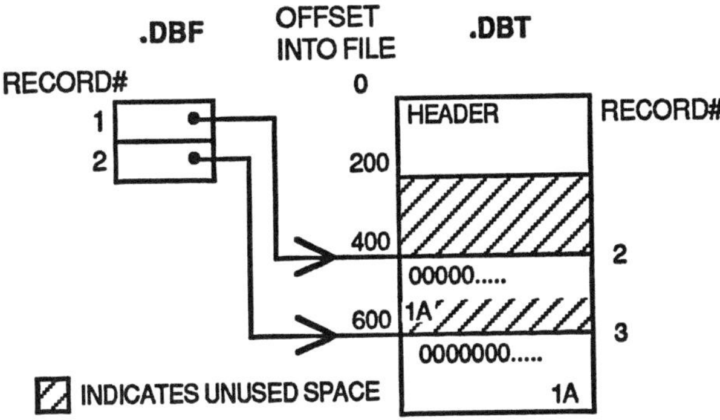

Now assume we do another APPEND BLANK, but this time we leave the memo field blank. Then, assume we do another APPEND BLANK and REPLACE memo WITH MEMOEDIT, but this time the user enters 1100 bytes of text. It occupies three memo file blocks. Figure 7-2 shows the new structure.

Figure 7-2. DBT File after a Large APPEND

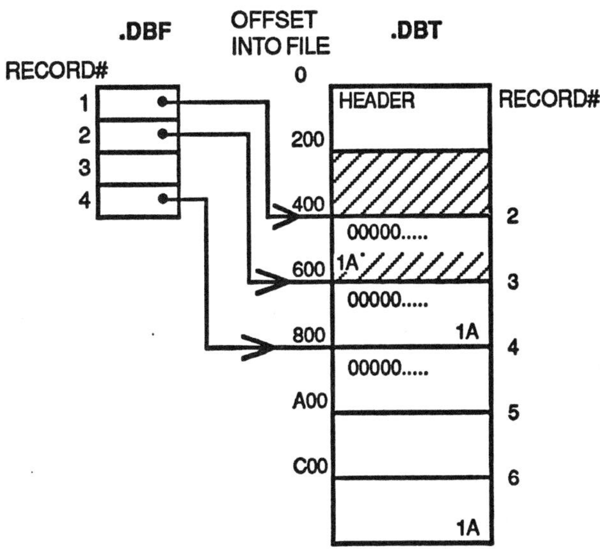

Since record 3 does not yet have an associated memo field, the dbflist shows a DBT record number of 0. No space has been reserved in the DBT file. The new memo field, from database record 4, starts at the next 512 byte boundary, with the preceding record again being padded.

Now, assume that we edit database record 3, and add a memo field of size 30 bytes. Figure 7-3 shows the new structure.

Figure 7-3. DBT File after a Small Insert

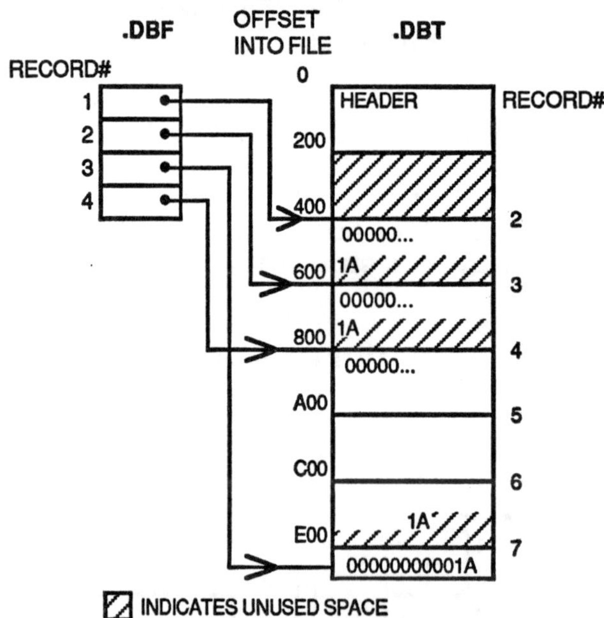

Figure 7-3 shows that Clipper does not necessarily order DBT records in the same sequence as the corresponding DBF records. In fact, it simply appends new DBT records to the end of the DBT file.

So far, dBASE and Clipper have worked similarly. The only difference is that Clipper does not allocate DBT record 1 to a memo field, whereas dBASE does. Now, a major difference appears. Let us assume that we access the memo field in record 1 and add 10 bytes. This does not cause it to overflow the 512 byte block, and so Clipper simply updates it in place — the DBT file does not grow. dBASE, however, appends the updated record to the end of the DBT file, and sets the DBF record pointer to this new location. The previous contents of the memo field from record 1 are still in the DBT file, but no database record points to it. It now appears as a "hole" in the DBT file, and is never reused. Figure 7-4 shows the results of this edit in Clipper and dBASE.

Figure 7-4. DBT File after an Edit

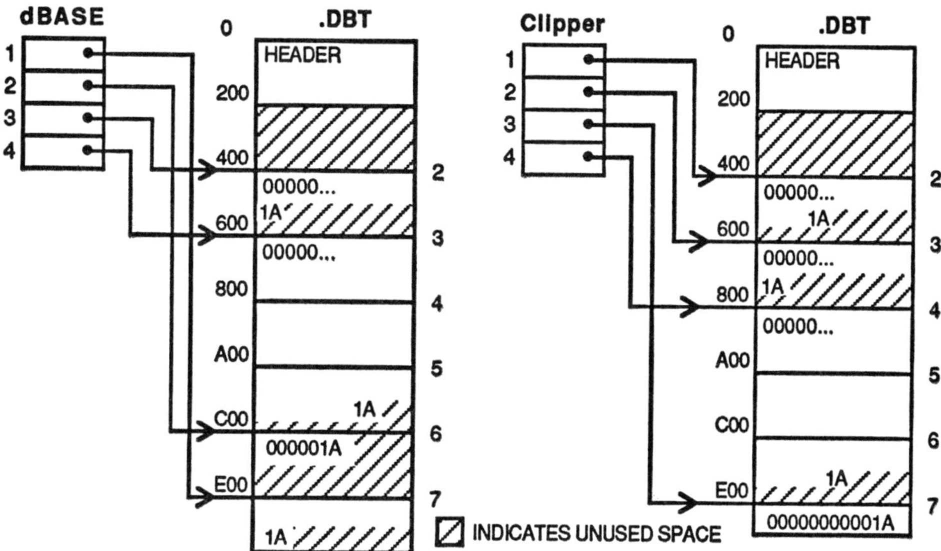

In Clipper, editing a memo field only causes the DBT file to grow when the memo field overflows a 512 byte boundary. In this case, the new memo field is appended to the end of the DBT file, and the previously occupied area also appears as a "hole", again never to be reused.

So, both dBASE and Clipper memo files will eventually end up with "holes". Clipper performs better than dBASE, but it still could do better. The "holes" could be linked into a free chain, and reallocated as necessary. Neither product performs this "garbage collection."

The traditional way to pack the DBT file is to copy the database. This creates a new DBT file with no holes - it is "packed" as tightly as possible. Chapter 12 contains the source for a C routine that packs a memo file without copying the database. It moves the memo fields, updating the database record pointers as necessary.

This section has described the implementation and growth of memo fields. Use the DBFLIST program in Chapter 12 to study your memo files. Pack them when necessary by either copying the database, or using the pack routine, also shown in Chapter 12.

> **TIP**
>
> Memo fields can grow rapidly. Don't forget to PACK them periodically.

Import/Export

MEMOREAD and MEMOWRIT simplify the import and export of character data. Like MEMOEDIT, they were designed for use with memo fields, but can be used with character strings.

As an example of importing data, assume there is a text file "notes.txt" in the current directory. We want to read it into a memory variable and then edit it with MEMOEDIT. The following code does the job:

```
CLEAR

SL_BOX = chr(218) + chr(196) + chr(191) + chr(179) + chr(217) + ;
             chr(196) + chr(192) + chr(179)
@ 9, 9, 21, 21 BOX SL_BOX

str = memoread("notes.txt")
str = memoedit(str, 10, 10, 20, 20, .T.)
```

Now assume that we want to return the edited text to the notes file. In this case, we use MEMOWRIT, as in:

```
CLEAR

SL_BOX = chr(218) + chr(196) + chr(191) + chr(179) + chr(217) + ;
             chr(196) + chr(192) + chr(179)

@ 9, 9, 21, 21 BOX SL_BOX

str = memoread("notes.txt")
```

```
str = memoedit(str, 10, 10, 20, 20, .T.)
memowrit("notes.txt", str)
```

We could code this more concisely as:

```
CLEAR

SL_BOX = chr(218) + chr(196) + chr(191) + chr(179) + chr(217) + ;
            chr(196) + chr(192) + chr(179)

@ 9, 9, 21, 21 BOX SL_BOX

memowrit("notes.txt", memoedit(memoread("notes.txt"), ;
            10, 10, 20, 20, .T.))
```

The Clipper programmer thus has access to a general purpose editor. You can make a function out of it, passing the name of the file and the coordinates of the editing window as parameters. Program 7-19 implements this.

Program 7-19. General Purpose Text Editor Using MEMOEDIT

```
FUNCTION text_editor

PARAMETER file, tl_row, tl_col, br_row, br_col
PRIVATE singbox

      singbox = chr(218) + chr(196) + chr(191) + chr(179) + chr(217) + ;
                  chr(196) + chr(192) + chr(179)

      @ tl_row - 1, tl_col - 1, br_row + 1, br_col + 1 BOX singbox

      memowrit(file, memoedit(memoread(file), ;
                  tl_row, tl_col, br_row, br_col, .T.))
RETURN (.T.)
```

A useful addition is to pass a browse flag that prevents editing, but allows browsing. Program 7-20 shows this.

Program 7-20. General Purpose Text Editor Allowing Browse Only

```
FUNCTION text_editor

PARAMETER file, tl_row, tl_col, br_row, br_col, browse_only
PRIVATE singbox, update

      singbox = chr(218) + chr(196) + chr(191) + chr(179) + chr(217) + ;
                  chr(196) + chr(192) + chr(179)
```

```
        @ tl_row - 1, tl_col - 1, br_row + 1, br_col + 1 BOX singbox

        IF browse_only
              update = .F.
        ELSE
              update = .T.
        ENDIF

        memowrit(file, memoedit(memoread(file), ;
                    tl_row, tl_col, br_row, br_col, update, .T.))

  RETURN (.T.)
```

An interesting use of the code is to view a report directed to a file with a SET ALTERNATE TO command, or as a result of a REPORT FORM TO command. For example:

```
USE test
REPORT FORM test TO test.txt

CLEAR

text_editor("test.txt", 10, 10, 20, 50, .T.)
```

You can then view a report without printing it. This is useful for proofreading and final checks. Note that the text_editor reformats the text to match the window size. It is important that the report is generated in a format consistent with this; otherwise, the lines will overflow.

Hints and Warnings

- Only use a memo field after careful consideration. Use Program 7-1 to evaluate the consequences.
- Do not forget that you can use MEMOEDIT on ordinary strings. This gives the Clipper programmer access to a general purpose text editor.
- Frame the MEMOEDIT window with a box before calling the editor. This clearly identifies the edit area.
- When writing general purpose editing or appending code, remember that memo fields require special handling in GETs. Use the VALID method described in this chapter to emulate the dBASE memo GET.

- Remember how memo fields grow. Use COPY or the memo pack routine to eliminate holes in the file.
- When using the memo function, define all return values and modes as pseudo constants for readability.
- When using the MEMOLINE function, use a pseudo constant to define the line size. This allows the routine to be modified easily.

8

Efficient Query Methods

This chapter describes Clipper features used in programming efficient database queries. The presentation involves a series of examples, increasing in complexity, that operate on a sample database. We will first describe the sample system, then the commands and functions used in the programs. Finally, we describe the examples themselves. This chapter is long, but you can study each example independently.

Sample Database System

Our sample database system contains information about parts and suppliers. It is based on the example used by C.J. Date in his books on relational databases (see references 1 and 2). It has four databases: PARTS, SUPPLIER, PROJECT, and a linking database called SPJ. Figures 8-1 through 8-4 show the structures of the databases, along with sample data.

Figure 8-1. Structure and Sample Values for PARTS Database

PARTS.DBF:

Field	Field Name	Type	Width	Dec
1	P_NO	Character	4	
2	PNAME	Character	15	
3	COLOR	Character	10	
4	WEIGHT	Numeric	5	1
5	PCITY	Character	15	
	**Total **		50	

RECORD#	P_NO	PNAME	COLOR	WEIGHT	PCITY
1	P1	NUT	RED	12.0	LONDON
2	P2	BOLT	GREEN	17.0	PARIS
3	P3	SCREW	BLUE	17.0	ROME
4	P4	SCREW	RED	14.0	LONDON
5	P5	CAM	BLUE	12.0	PARIS
6	P6	COG	RED	19.0	LONDON

Figure 8-2. Structure and Sample Values for SUPPLIER Database

SUPPLIER.DBF:

Field	Field Name	Type	Width	Dec
1	S_NO	Character	4	
2	SNAME	Character	10	
3	STATUS	Numeric	3	
4	SCITY	Character	15	
	** Total **		33	

Record#	S_NO	SNAME	STATUS	SCITY
1	S01	SMITH	20	LONDON
2	S02	JONES	10	PARIS

3	S03	BLAKE	30	PARIS
4	S04	CLARK	20	LONDON
5	S05	ADAMS	30	ATHENS
6	S06	PLATT	20	CHICAGO
7	S07	BAKER	40	LOS ANGELES
8	S08	THOMAS	20	LONDON
9	S09	BROWN	40	KANSAS CITY
10	S10	BRENNON	40	DUBLIN
11	S11	BROWN	30	MEMPHIS
12	S12	SPENCE	40	LONDON
13	S13	BRACK	20	CHICAGO
14	S14	RUTGER	50	BRISTOL
15	S15	CHILES	30	RENO
16	S16	SMYTH	40	WICHITA
17	S17	ABBOTT	30	NEW YORK

Figure 8-3. Structure and Sample Values for PROJECT Database.

PROJECT.DBF:

Field	Field Name	Type	Width	Dec
1	J_NO	Character	4	
2	JNAME	Character	15	
3	JCITY	Character	15	
	** Total **		35	

RECORD#	J_NO	JNAME	JCITY
1	J1	SORTER	PARIS
2	J2	PUNCH	ROME
3	J3	READER	ATHENS
4	J4	CONSOLE	ATHENS
5	J5	COLLATOR	LONDON
6	J6	TERMINAL	OSLO
7	J7	TAPE	LONDON
8	J8	REEL	ST.LOUIS
9	J9	CRT	DENVER

Figure 8-4. Structure and Sample Values for Linking (SPJ) Database

SPJ.DBF:

Field	Field Name	Type	Width	Dec
1	S_NO	Character	4	
2	P_NO	Character	4	
3	J_NO	Character	4	
4	QTY	Numeric	5	
	** Total **		18	

Record#	S_NO	P_NO	J_NO	QTY
1	S01	P1	J1	200
2	S01	P1	J4	700
3	S02	P3	J3	400
4	S02	P3	J2	200
5	S02	P3	J1	200
6	S02	P3	J4	600
7	S02	P3	J5	600
8	S02	P3	J6	400
9	S02	P3	J7	800
10	S02	P5	J2	100
11	S03	P3	J1	200
12	S03	P4	J2	500
13	S04	P6	J3	300
14	S04	P6	J7	300
15	S05	P2	J2	200
16	S05	P2	J4	100
17	S05	P5	J5	500
18	S05	P5	J7	100
19	S05	P6	J2	200
20	S05	P1	J4	1000
21	S05	P3	J4	1200
22	S05	P4	J4	800
23	S05	P5	J4	400
24	S05	P6	J4	500
25	S06	P4	J2	400
26	S02	P7	J7	100

Opening Databases

SELECT

When you USE a database, Clipper assigns it an area. Clipper allows up to 250 areas. However, before Version 3.3, DOS limited the number of open files to 20. Now Clipper can support 250 open files. The maximum number in practice is the minimum of the FILES environment variable, specified in CONFIG.SYS, and the F parameter set in the Clipper environment variable. Chapter 2 describes F.

Clipper assigns a newly USEd database to the area given by the current selection number. It is initially 1, and using the SELECT command changes it. For example, the following code opens databases in areas 3, 4, and 5.

```
SELECT 3
USE spj
```

```
SELECT 4
USE parts

SELECT 5
USE supplier
```

Executing a USE command in an area with an open database closes it, making it inaccessible. Using more than one database requires the SELECT command.

In a complex system, keeping track of which areas are in use can be a programming nightmare. This is particularly true when writing generic code that will work in many situations. Clipper provides an elegant solution with a little known (but documented) extension of the SELECT command. You can use area 0 to mean the lowest numbered, unused area. We could therefore write code such as:

```
SELECT 0
USE spj

SELECT 0
USE parts

SELECT 0
USE supplier
```

If no area was previously used, these statements would allocate area 1 to SPJ, area 2 to PARTS, and area 3 to SUPPLIER. Now, if you close the PARTS database by selecting area 2 and performing a USE, as in:

```
SELECT 2
USE
```

the next SELECT 0 command selects area 2 since it is the lowest numbered, unused area. The next SELECT 0 selects area 4 (remember, 3 is already in use). Executing a CLOSE DATABASES or CLOSE ALL command, of course, causes the next SELECT 0 command to select area 1.

When a database is USEd, its area gets a name, called an "alias". You can define it explicitly, as in:

```
SELECT 3
USE spj ALIAS sjoin
```

This assigns alias SJOIN to area 3. Clipper can also assign it, as in:

```
SELECT 3
USE sjoin
```

This assigns the default alias SPJ (the name of the database) to area 3. You can later use the alias to refer to the area with the SELECT command, as in:

```
SELECT sjoin
```

You can also use it to refer to a field in a database in an unselected area, as in:

```
? sjoin -> p_no
```

Using SELECT 0 and aliases totally removes the responsibility of keeping track of areas from the programmer, giving it to the system where it belongs.

The default alias identifies the database being used. A distinctive alias is unnecessary. Since the database name never appears except in the USE command, it cannot be confused with the alias. As far as we are concerned, they are identical.

TIP

Use SELECT 0 before opening databases, then always refer to them by their default aliases.

Another Clipper extension to SELECT is "indirect selection". Enclosing a numeric memory variable in parentheses causes the selection of an area by value, rather than by name. For example,

```
sel_area = 1

SELECT (sel_area)
```

selects area 1, rather than an area with the alias sel_area. It replaces the following cumbersome code:

```
sel_area = 1
str_sel_area = str(sel_area)

SELECT &str_sel_area
```

It also saves a macro expansion.

Clipper provides two functions for use with aliases and areas, ALIAS() and SELECT(). ALIAS(n), where n is a numeric expression, returns the alias of area n. SELECT(c), where c is a character expression, returns the selection number of the specified alias, or 0 if it is not currently in use. SELECT() with no parameters returns the alias of the currently selected area. Consider, for example, the following code:

```
SELECT 0
? "FIRST select "
?? select()
USE spj
? "FIRST alias "
?? alias()

SELECT 0
? "SECOND select "
?? select()
USE supplier
? "SECOND alias "
?? alias()

? "alias(1) "
?? alias(1)

SELECT spj                    && reuse this area

USE parts
? "THIRD select "
?? select()
? "THIRD alias "
?? alias()
```

It produces the following output:

```
FIRST select  1
FIRST alias SPJ
SECOND select  2
SECOND alias SUPPLIER
alias(1) SPJ
THIRD select  1
THIRD alias PARTS
```

You can use the SELECT function to determine whether a database is open. Program 8-1 opens the passed database only if it is not already open. If it is, the program selects it as the primary database. The return value is a logical, indicating whether SELECT had to open the database.

Program 8-1. Open a Database if It Is Not Already Open

```
FUNCTION dbf_open

PARAM alias_name
```

```
PRIVATE sel_num
        sel_num = select(alias_name)

        IF sel_num != 0
                SELECT (sel_num)
        ELSE
                SELECT 0
                USE (alias_name)
        ENDIF

RETURN (sel_num = 0)
```

You must call Program 8-1 with the database's name, as in:

```
dbf_open("test")
```

Note that dbf_open assumes that the database is opened with the default alias.

Suppose you have opened all databases in a program in areas determined by SELECT 0 statements. Further suppose that you have not selectively closed any with the USE statement. You can determine the number of open database files with:

```
FUNCTION open_dbfs

        SELECT 0

RETURN (select() - 1)
```

The following code produces a list of aliases and areas:

```
num_dbfs = open_dbfs()
FOR i = 1 TO num_dbfs

        ?i
        ?? alias(i)

NEXT
```

Note that issuing several SELECT 0 commands without any USE commands does not increment the current selection number. We could thus call the open_dbfs function many times without using up areas. The function does have a nasty side effect that many programmers overlook. It unselects the selected database. You should rewrite the code as shown in Program 8-2 to avoid this.

Program 8-2. Determine Number of Open Database Files

```
FUNCTION open_dbfs
PRIVATE save_sel, num_dbfs

    save_sel = select()

    SELECT 0
    num_dbfs = select() - 1

    SELECT (save_sel)

RETURN (num_dbfs)
```

Note the technique of saving the current selection, operating on a different one, and then restoring the original. It is a basic method used by authors of generic code. It lets a user defined function called from a processing command open and do searches on other databases. We use this capability later.

> **TIP**
>
> In generic database code, save the selection area on entry and restore it upon exit.

Alias Functions

In releases before Summer '87, to invoke a database function in another area, you had to first select the area, then apply the function. The Summer '87 release now lets functions operate on open databases in unselected areas. You simply use the alias to select the function, and enclose it in parentheses. For example, to display the end of file status of alias "test", we can write:

```
? test -> (eof())
```

You can display the file's record number with:

```
? test -> (recno())
```

As a practical example, consider updating the SPJ database from an update database SPJ_UPD. The update database has the same format as SPJ. The expression "s_no + p_no + j_no" identifies records uniquely. If the SPJ database contains a record with the same expression as a record in the update database, Program 8-3 updates the qty field. If not, it adds the update record to the database. This is the classical file update problem.

Program 8-3. Updating the SPJ Database from an Update Database

```
SELECT 0
USE spj_upd

SELECT 0
USE spj
INDEX ON s_no + p_no + j_no TO s_no

GOTO TOP

DO WHILE !spj_upd -> (eof())

        SEEK spj_upd -> s_no + spj_upd -> p_no + spj_upd -> j_no

        IF !found()
                APPEND BLANK

                REPLACE s_no WITH spj_upd -> s_no
                REPLACE p_no WITH spj_upd -> p_no
                REPLACE j_no WITH spj_upd -> j_no
                REPLACE qty  WITH spj_upd -> qty
        ELSE
                REPLACE qty  WITH spj_upd -> qty
        ENDIF

        SKIP ALIAS spj_upd

ENDDO
```

The SKIP ALIAS command moves the update database's record pointer to the next record.

You can use aliases with the following functions:

```
BOF()
DELETED()
EOF()
FCOUNT()
LASTREC()
RECCOUNT()
RECNO()
RECSIZE()
```

These "alias functions" eliminate the need to select a database. We use them in the examples at the end of the chapter.

Opening Files More than Once

In contrast to dBASE, Clipper allows a database file to be open in more than one area. To access the files symbolically, you must give each a unique alias. The following code opens the SPJ database in three areas:

```
SELECT 0
USE spj

SELECT 0
USE spj ALIAS spj1

SELECT 0
USE spj ALIAS spj2
```

In this situation, Clipper only guarantees read operations to work. Writes are a totally different matter. Again, examples appear at the end of the chapter.

Searching for Values

FOUND

After a SEEK, FIND, LOCATE, or CONTINUE command, the FOUND function tests whether the search succeeded. It returns a logical value. For example, we can code the query:

```
"List all suppliers located in LONDON"
```

as follows:

```
USE supplier
LOCATE FOR sname = "LONDON"

DO WHILE found()

    ? sname
    CONTINUE

ENDDO
```

FOUND's result is reset to .F. whenever the record pointer moves. For example:

```
use spj
LOCATE for s_no = "S1"

? found()
? found()

skip

? found()
? found()

LOCATE for s_no = "S!@#"

? found()
? found()
```

produces

```
.T.
.T.
.F.
.F.
.F.
.F.
```

The first LOCATE succeeds, so FOUND returns .T.. If you call FOUND again without moving the record pointer, it returns the same value. After the SKIP, FOUND returns .F. because the record pointer moved. The final LOCATE fails, so once again FOUND returns .F..

FOUND's result is specific to the current area. You can use it in one area without affecting its value in others. The following code shows this:

```
SELECT 0
USE supplier

SELECT 0
USE spj
INDEX ON s_no TO s_no

SEEK "S01"

? found()

SELECT supplier
? found()
```

```
SELECT spj
? found()
```

The results are:

```
.T.
.F.
.T.
```

The SEEK succeeds, so FOUND returns .T. We then select a new area and call FOUND again. This time it returns .F. When we later reselect the original area, FOUND returns .T., as the record pointer has not moved.

Continuing SEEK

Unfortunately, SEEK (unlike LOCATE) has no "CONTINUE" command. To process all records matching a condition in an indexed database, you must do the comparisons manually, using SKIP to advance the record pointer. The following code shows this, listing all SPJ records for supplier S02:

```
USE spj
INDEX ON s_no TO s_no

SEEK "S02"

DO WHILE s_no = "S02" .AND. !eof()

    ? s_no, p_no, j_no, qty
    SKIP

ENDDO
```

The WHILE loop guarantees that the SEEK condition is maintained.

SOFTSEEK

The SET SOFTSEEK command introduced in the Summer '87 release allows relative seeking of records. If SOFTSEEK is OFF, its default value, an unsuccessful SEEK leaves the pointer at EOF, as in previous releases. With SOFTSEEK ON, however, the pointer ends up at the record just beyond where it would have been if the SEEK had succeeded. This is the record with the next higher key.

SOFTSEEK is particularly useful when seeking dates. If a particular date is not found, the pointer ends up at the next later date. A SKIP -1 will then move it to the record with the latest date before the one being sought.

Another interesting use of SOFTSEEK is to extract records from an indexed database with values above a specified level, say "X". We set SOFTSEEK ON, and then SEEK a record with a key immediately following X. The database pointer then moves to the first required record. The actual value "immediately following" X depends on X's type. For a numeric, it is X plus the smallest possible increment. If X has no decimal places, the increment is 1; if X has 2 decimal places, it is .01. For a date, it is X + 1. For a character variable, we must add 1 to the last character in the string.

The following code moves the SPJ database pointer to the record with the next higher supplier code than "S01":

```
SELECT 0
USE spj

INDEX ON s_no TO s_no

seeker = "S01 "

* Add 1 to last character of string
seeker = substr(seeker, 1, 3) + chr(asc(substr(seeker, 4, 1)) + 1)

SET SOFTSEEK ON

SEEK seeker
```

In this case, SEEK sets the pointer to record 3 with supplier code "S02". Note that to add 1 to a character, you must first get its ASCII value with the ASC function.

> **TIP**
>
> To SOFTSEEK for a character key greater than X, use SOFTSEEK with:
>
> substr(x, 1, len(x) - 1) + chr(asc(substr(x, len(x), 1))+ 1)

The SOFTSEEK SET is system wide, so it applies to every open index file in every area.

Make sure you understand SOFTSEEK. The examples at the end of the chapter use it extensively.

Linking Databases through Relations

Clipper's relational features are among its least understood, but most powerful. It is definitely worth spending the time required to master them.

Single Relation

SET RELATION lets the programmer link databases based on a common field. dBASE allows only one such relation per database, whereas Clipper allows 8. Let us start with a simple, single relation example that would work in dBASE. Assume we want to LIST all SPJ records along with the supplier's name. The name is not in the SPJ database, but we can easily determine it by looking up the supplier code in the SUPPLIER database. Without SET RELATION, you could not use LIST. Instead, you would have to write a routine that printed every SPJ record, and then looked up the supplier name and printed it. The following code does the job using SET RELATION:

```
SELECT 0
USE supplier
INDEX ON s_no TO s_no

SELECT 0
USE spj
SET RELATION TO s_no INTO supplier

LIST s_no, supplier->sname, p_no, j_no, qty
```

SET RELATION defines a relationship between the currently selected database (SPJ) and the one specified by the INTO clause (SUPPLIER). We call the database from which the relation is set the parent, and the one into which it is set as the child. In this case, for example, SPJ is the parent, and SUPPLIER is the child. The relationship is based on a common field, called the key field, in this case S_NO. Note that S_NO appears in both databases and is the same size in each. The child database must be indexed on it. Here we create the index, but this is unnecessary if the database is indexed and the index is up to date. Figure 8-5 shows the relationship between the two databases.

Figure 8-5. Initial SET RELATION Diagram

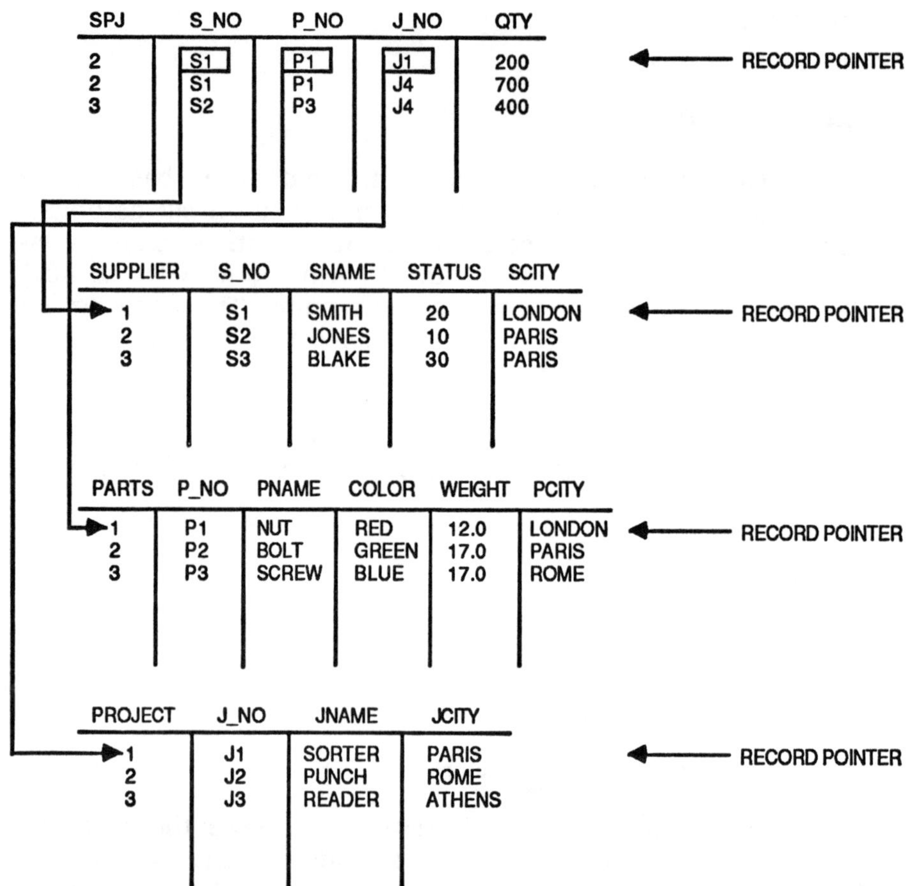

If we issue GOTO 10 on the parent database, the relationship looks like Figure 8-6.

Figure 8-6. SET RELATION Diagram after Parent Moves

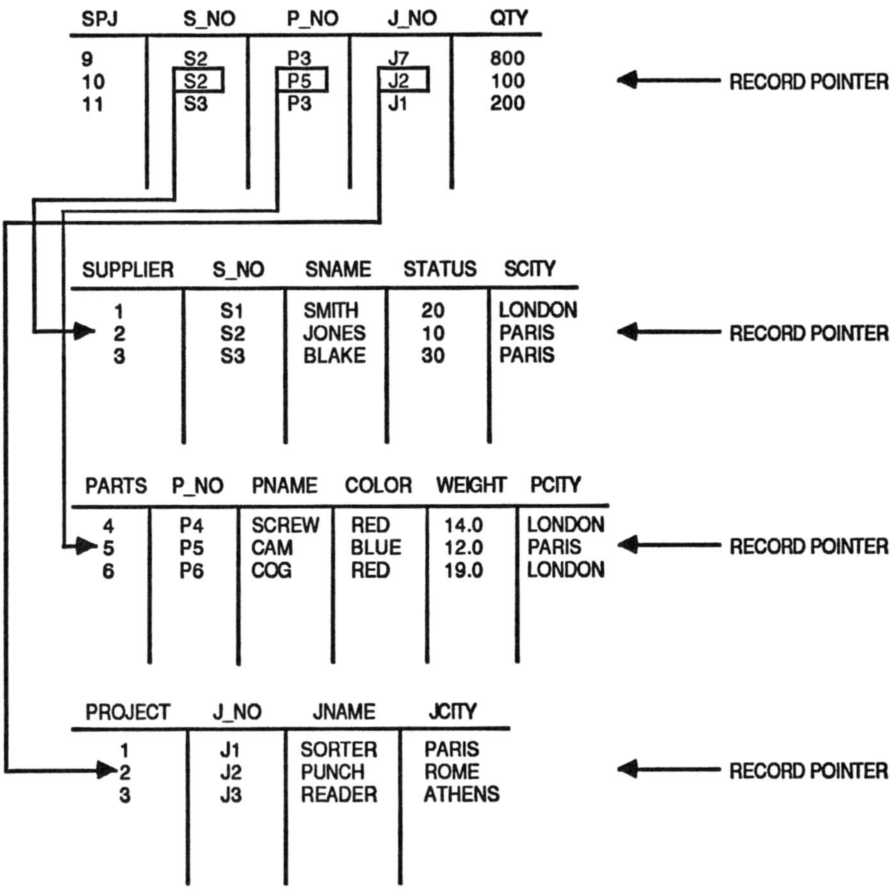

SPJ	S_NO	P_NO	J_NO	QTY
9	S2	P3	J7	800
10	S2	P5	J2	100
11	S3	P3	J1	200

← RECORD POINTER

SUPPLIER	S_NO	SNAME	STATUS	SCITY
1	S1	SMITH	20	LONDON
2	S2	JONES	10	PARIS
3	S3	BLAKE	30	PARIS

← RECORD POINTER

PARTS	P_NO	PNAME	COLOR	WEIGHT	PCITY
4	P4	SCREW	RED	14.0	LONDON
5	P5	CAM	BLUE	12.0	PARIS
6	P6	COG	RED	19.0	LONDON

← RECORD POINTER

PROJECT	J_NO	JNAME	JCITY
1	J1	SORTER	PARIS
2	J2	PUNCH	ROME
3	J3	READER	ATHENS

← RECORD POINTER

Once the relationship is defined, the program examines the key field in the parent database. The record pointer in the child database moves to the first occurrence of this value. Subsequently, whenever the pointer in the parent database moves, the one in the child database moves to the first record with a corresponding key field value. Since the child database is indexed on this field, a fast internal SEEK moves the pointer. Note that the parent database's pointer can be moved either explicitly with a statement such as

GOTO, SEEK, or SKIP, or implicitly with a database operation such as LIST, JOIN, or REPORT.

In the preceding example, every time the LIST command changes the current record of the SPJ database, the pointer in the SUPPLIER database moves to the first occurrence of the new key field value (S_NO). The value of supplier->sname is thus the name of the supplier defined by the S_NO field in the current record of the SUPPLIER database.

Multiple Relations

Now suppose we also want to print both the project name and the part name. We must set a relation into the two databases from the SPJ database. This is where compatibility with dBASE ends. The following code does the job in Clipper:

```
SELECT 0
USE supplier
INDEX ON s_no TO s_no

SELECT 0
USE parts
INDEX ON p_no TO p_no

SELECT 0
USE project
INDEX ON j_no TO j_no

SELECT 0
USE spj
SET RELATION TO s_no INTO supplier, TO p_no INTO parts, ;
                    TO j_no INTO project

LIST s_no, supplier->sname, p_no, parts->pname, j_no, project->jname, qty
```

There are now three relations set from the parent. Once again, every time the pointer in the parent database moves, the pointers in the child databases move according to the key field values. Note that each relation has its own key field.

If there is no match for the key field in the child database, its pointer moves to the end of file, and the fields are blank. You can test for end of file by using the alias functions described previously, as in:

```
child -> (eof())
```

If the child database contains several matching records, its pointer will be at the first one. You can use the SKIP ALIAS command to advance the pointer through all such records. For example, the following code lists all SPJ records with the supplier's name alphabetized:

```
SELECT 0
USE spj
INDEX ON s_no TO s_no

SELECT 0
USE supplier
INDEX ON sname TO sname

GOTO TOP
SET RELATION TO s_no INTO spj
DO WHILE !eof()             && in supplier

     * while relation is maintained ...
     DO WHILE s_no = spj -> s_no .AND. !spj -> (eof())

          ? sname, spj -> s_no, spj -> p_no, spj -> j_no, spj -> qty

          SKIP ALIAS spj

     ENDDO

     SKIP   && supplier database

ENDDO
```

Here the SUPPLIER database is primary. For each record in it, the program lists all matching records in the SPJ database. If the SPJ database has records with a S_NO field not present in the SUPPLIER database, they are not listed (spj -> eof = .T.).

A relation is "bound" to the database and area for which it is defined. You can thus have different relations set in different areas. If you select a new area and then return to the original, its relation(s) will still be in effect. The examples show this in practice.

You can add to a currently active relation with the "additive" option of the SET RELATION TO command. For example, assume that we establish a relation with the following command:

```
SET RELATION TO s_no INTO supplier
```

Later, we want to add a relation from both the P_NO field and the J_NO field to give the three child relationship in the previous example. The following statement would do the job:

```
SET RELATION ADDITIVE TO p_no INTO parts, TO j_no INTO project
```

The Summer '87 release also introduced the DBRELATION function. It returns the "TO" part of the passed relation number.

A relation need not be just a field. It can involve any valid expression, as long as the child database is indexed on it. For example, the following code shows a relationship established between two copies of the SPJ database on a combination of two fields:

```
SELECT 0
USE spj ALIAS spj1
INDEX ON s_no + p_no TO sp_no

SELECT 0
USE spj

SET RELATION INTO spj1 TO s_no + p_no

LIST s_no, p_no, j_no, qty, spj1 -> (recno())
```

The output is:

```
 1 S01  P1  J1   200   1
 2 S01  P1  J4   700   1
 3 S02  P3  J3   400   3
 4 S02  P3  J2   200   3
 5 S02  P3  J1   200   3
 6 S02  P3  J4   600   3
 7 S02  P3  J5   600   3
 8 S02  P3  J6   400   3
 9 S02  P3  J7   800   3
10 S02  P5  J2   100  10
11 S03  P3  J1   200  11
12 S03  P4  J2   500  12
13 S04  P6  J3   300  13
14 S04  P6  J7   300  13
15 S05  P2  J2   200  15
16 S05  P2  J4   100  15
17 S05  P5  J5   500  17
18 S05  P5  J7   100  17
19 S05  P6  J2   200  19
20 S05  P1  J4  1000  20
21 S05  P3  J4  1200  21
22 S05  P4  J4   800  22
23 S05  P5  J4   400  17
24 S05  P6  J4   500  19
25 S06  P4  J2   400  25
26 S02  P7  J7   100  26
```

By studying this routine and its output, you can see that the child's record pointer only moves when the expression S_NO + P_NO changes. That is the basis of the relation. You can also see that when duplicates of the parent keys exist in the child, the pointer always ends up at the first occurrence.

Multiple Indexes

Clipper allows up to 15 indexes to be open concurrently on a database file. Initially, the file is processed in the order specified by the first index file. We call it the primary index. We call other open indexes secondary indexes. They do not affect the order in which database records are traversed, but they are updated according to changes made to a field that affects their keys.

To change the primary index, use the SET ORDER command. Invoke it with the number (in the index file list) of the new primary index. The old primary index now becomes secondary.

The programmer should use the SET ORDER TO command rather than reissuing the USE or SET INDEX command. SET ORDER maintains the current index and database buffers. Reissuing the USE or SET INDEX command reloads these buffers from disk. This can be time consuming.

> **TIP**
>
> Use SET ORDER to change primary indexes rather than reissuing a USE or SET INDEX.

Creating Databases

COPY STRUCTURE and CREATE FROM

We often want to create a database from within an application. An installation program, for example, must create empty database files for later use. The traditional approach is a COPY STRUCTURE EXTENDED command followed by a CREATE FROM command. COPY

STRUCTURE EXTENDED creates a new database file with four fields: "field_name", "field_type", "field_len", and "field_dec". Fields of the currently selected database become records in the new database. You can then modify its fields according to the format of the database to be created. If a different number of fields are required, we can APPEND or DELETE records. A later CREATE FROM command reads the STRUCTURE EXTENDED file and builds an empty database from it - the inverse of COPY STRUCTURE EXTENDED. With this method, you must have a database in order to create one.

CREATE

Clipper simplifies the process with the CREATE <file_name> command. It creates an EMPTY database with the same four fields as COPY STRUCTURE EXTENDED. Records are then simply appended to the file and assigned values as required to describe the structure of the new database. Using CREATE eliminates the need to have an open database before creating another one. Once we have created the extended database, we issue a CREATE FROM command to create the new database. The following example shows the creation of the SPJ database:

```
CREATE dummy

APPEND BLANK
REPLACE field_name WITH "s_no", field_type WITH "C", ;
            field_len WITH 4, field_dec WITH 0

APPEND BLANK
REPLACE field_name WITH "p_no", field_type WITH "C", ;
            field_len WITH 4, field_dec WITH 0

APPEND BLANK
REPLACE field_name WITH "j_no", field_type WITH "C", ;
            field_len WITH 300, field_dec WITH 0

APPEND BLANK
REPLACE field_name WITH "qty", field_type WITH "N", ;
            field_len WITH 5, field_dec WITH 0

CREATE newspj FROM dummy
```

CREATE dummy makes DUMMY the active database in the currently selected area. Similarly, "CREATE new_spj FROM dummy" makes NEW_SPJ the active database. If the routine selected a new area before creating the NEW_SPJ database, a run time error would occur. DUMMY would not be closed, and since we just created it, its records could not be seen. To create a new database in a different area, you must first explicitly close the DUMMY database. Note that, unlike USE, CREATE and CREATE FROM do not set up a default alias.

Even though the "field_dec" field is only strictly required for numerics, Clipper requires you to set it to zero for non-numeric fields. Clipper also requires a correct field_len field, even for types with a predefined length. These are:

- Logical (L) - 1
- Date (D) - 8
- Memo (M) - 10

Generic Create

Program 8-4 is a general purpose database create routine. It takes the file name and four arrays as parameters. The arrays are (in order): field names, field types, field lengths, and field decimal places.

Program 8-4. Clipper Database Creation Procedure

```
PROCEDURE create_dbf

PARAMETERS file_name, f_names, f_types, f_lens, f_decs
PRIVATE num_fields, i

    SELECT 0
    CREATE dummy
    num_fields = len(f_names)

    FOR i = 1 TO num_fields

        APPEND BLANK

        REPLACE field_name WITH f_names[i], field_type WITH f_types[i], ;
            field_len WITH f_lens[i], field_dec WITH f_decs[i]

    NEXT

    CREATE (file_name) FROM dummy   && dummy gets closed here

RETURN
```

The following call creates the SPJ database:

```
PRIVATE spj_names[4], spj_types[4], spj_lens[4], spj_decs[4]

spj_names[1] = "S_NO"
spj_types[1] = "C"
spj_lens[1] = 4
spj_decs[1] = 0

spj_names[2] = "P_NO"
spj_types[2] = "C"
spj_lens[2] = 4
spj_decs[2] = 0

spj_names[3] = "J_NO"
spj_types[3] = "C"
spj_lens[3] = 4
spj_decs[3] = 0

spj_names[4] = "QTY"
spj_types[4] = "N"
spj_lens[4] = 5
spj_decs[4] = 0

DO create_dbf WITH "SPJ", spj_names, spj_types, spj_lens, spj_decs
```

Character Fields Longer than 999

Both CREATE and COPY STRUCTURE EXTENDED create a database file with a numeric field, "field_len", of length 3. This effectively prohibits character fields with a length greater than 999. However, as you might expect, there is a way around the restriction. In the actual .DBF file, where the field sizes are defined, the byte used to store the number of decimal places is the more significant part of a word value for character fields. This is why we clear it even when it is not used. By setting the "field_dec" field in the database created by CREATE or COPY STRUCTURE EXTENDED, we can manipulate this byte in the DBF file. The "field_dec" field should be set to the integral value of the required size divided by 256 (use the INT function). The "field_len" field should be the remainder. The following call to create_dbf (Program 8-4) creates a database "test" with a character field "names" of length 1024.

```
PRIVATE f_names[1], f_types[1], f_lens[1], f_decs[1]

f_names[1] = "names"
f_types[1] = "C"
f_lens[1] = 1024 % 256
```

```
f_decs[1] = INT(1024 / 256)

DO create_dbf WITH "test", f_names, f_types, f_lens, f_decs
```

Clipper CREATE code provides two ways to create character fields with lengths between 256 and 999. For example, the following two calls create the same structure:

```
f_type = "C"
f_name = "chars"
f_lens[1] = 256
f_decs[1] = 0

DO create_dbf WITH "test", f_names, f_types, f_lens, f_decs


f_type = "C"
f_name = "chars"
f_lens[1] = 0
f_decs[1] = 1

DO create_dbf WITH "test", f_names, f_types, f_lens, f_decs
```

The reason for the equivalence is that the Clipper CREATE code basically does the following function:

```
IF field type == CHAR
      field len = field len + (field dec * 256);
```

Chapter 12 contains a C routine, callable from Clipper, that creates a database, given the same four arrays.

JOIN

The JOIN command creates a new database by combining fields from two open databases according to some condition. Although it is a standard dBASE command, we describe it here because of a useful trick that applies in Clipper but not in dBASE.

The JOIN command works as follows. For each record in the currently selected database, it looks at every record in the "alias" database and applies the condition. If the condition holds, JOIN creates a new record in the destination database with a structure determined by the field list.

Study the following example:

```
SELECT 0
```

```
USE parts

SELECT 0
USE supplier

JOIN WITH parts TO samecity FOR scity = parts->pcity
```

This code produces a new database SAMECITY, describing parts and suppliers located in the same city. SAMECITY contains all fields from both databases. Its structure is:

SAMECITY.DBF

Field	Field Name	Type	Width	Dec
1	S_NO	Character	4	
2	SNAME	Character	10	
3	STATUS	Numeric	3	
4	SCITY	Character	15	
5	P_NO	Character	4	
6	PNAME	Character	15	
7	COLOR	Character	10	
8	WEIGHT	Numeric	5	1
9	PCITY	Character	15	
	** Total **		82	

It contains the following records:

RECORD#	S_NO	SNAME	STATUS	SCITY	P_NO	PNAME	COLOR	WEIGHT	PCITY
1	S01	SMITH	20	LONDON	P1	NUT	RED	12.0	LONDON
2	S01	SMITH	20	LONDON	P4	SCREW	RED	14.0	LONDON
3	S01	SMITH	20	LONDON	P6	COG	RED	19.0	LONDON
4	S02	JONES	10	PARIS	P2	BOLT	GREEN	17.0	PARIS
5	S02	JONES	10	PARIS	P5	CAM	BLUE	12.0	PARIS
6	S03	BLAKE	30	PARIS	P2	BOLT	GREEN	17.0	PARIS
7	S03	BLAKE	30	PARIS	P5	CAM	BLUE	12.0	PARIS
8	S04	CLARK	20	LONDON	P1	NUT	RED	12.0	LONDON
9	S04	CLARK	20	LONDON	P4	SCREW	RED	14.0	LONDON
10	S04	CLARK	20	LONDON	P6	COG	RED	19.0	LONDON
11	S08	THOMAS	20	LONDON	P1	NUT	RED	12.0	LONDON
12	S08	THOMAS	20	LONDON	P4	SCRE	RED	14.0	LONDON
13	S08	THOMAS	20	LONDON	P6	COG	RED	19.0	LONDON
14	S12	SPENCE	40	LONDON	P1	NUT	RED	12.0	LONDON
15	S12	SPENCE	40	LONDON	P4	SCREW	RED	14.0	LONDON
16	S12	SPENCE	40	LONDON	P6	COG	RED	19.0	LONDON

You can see how JOIN works by studying the result. It starts with the first record in the SUPPLIER database (S1, SMITH, 20, LONDON) and compares its city field to every record in the PARTS database. It finds that parts p1, p4, and p6 match, and so it puts them in the SAMECITY database. Once it has processed the entire PARTS database, it then advances the record pointer in the

SUPPLIER database to record 2 (S2, JONES, 10, PARIS) and processes the entire PARTS database again. It repeats this until it reaches end of file in the SUPPLIER database.

The destination database is thus ordered in the same way as the source database. Within this order, it is ordered in the same way as the alias database. Since the source database is ordered by ascending supplier code, the destination database is, too. Within this order, records appear in order of ascending part codes, as in the alias database.

If you execute a JOIN command without a condition clause (which Clipper allows), the destination database contains a number of records given by the product of the number in the currently selected database times the number in the alias database. This could be enormous. For example, applying the following JOIN command:

```
SELECT 0
USE parts

SELECT 0
USE supplier

JOIN WITH parts TO example
```

would produce 102 records (17 * 6). Joining two databases with 100 and 1000 records, respectively, produces a 100,000 record destination database. Join with care!

JOIN commands do not duplicate field names in the destination database. For example:

```
SELECT 0
USE spj

SELECT 0
USE supplier

JOIN WITH spj TO example FOR s_no = spj->s_no
```

produces the following database structure:

EXAMPLE.DBF

Field	Field Name	Type	Width	Dec
1	S_NO	Character	4	
2	SNAME	Character	10	
3	STATUS	Numeric	3	
4	SCITY	Character	15	
5	P_NO	Character	4	
6	J_NO	Character	4	
7	QTY	Numeric	5	
	**Total **		46	

and the following contents:

Record#	S_NO	SNAME	STATUS	SCITY	P_NO	J_NO	QTY
1	S01	SMITH	20	LONDON	P1	J1	200
2	S01	SMITH	20	LONDON	P1	J4	700
3	S02	JONES	10	PARIS	P3	J3	400
4	S02	JONES	10	PARIS	P3	J2	200
5	S02	JONES	10	PARIS	P3	J1	200
6	S02	JONES	10	PARIS	P3	J4	600
7	S02	JONES	10	PARIS	P3	J5	600
8	S02	JONES	10	PARIS	P3	J6	400
9	S02	JONES	10	PARIS	P3	J7	800
10	S02	JONES	10	PARIS	P5	J2	100
11	S02	JONES	10	PARIS	P7	J7	100
12	S03	BLAKE	30	PARIS	P3	J1	200
13	S03	BLAKE	30	PARIS	P4	J2	500
14	S04	CLARK	20	LONDON	P6	J3	300
15	S04	CLARK	20	LONDON	P6	J7	300
16	S05	ADAMS	30	ATHENS	P2	J2	200
17	S05	ADAMS	30	ATHENS	P2	J4	100
18	S05	ADAMS	30	ATHENS	P5	J5	500
19	S05	ADAMS	30	ATHENS	P5	J7	100
20	S05	ADAMS	30	ATHENS	P6	J2	200
21	S05	ADAMS	30	ATHENS	P1	J4	1000
22	S05	ADAMS	30	ATHENS	P3	J4	1200
23	S05	ADAMS	30	ATHENS	P4	J4	800
24	S05	ADAMS	30	ATHENS	P5	J4	400
25	S05	ADAMS	30	ATHENS	P6	J4	500
26	S06	PLATT	20	CHICAGO	P4	J2	400

Although the S_NO field appears in both the SPJ and SUPPLIER databases, it appears only once in the EXAMPLE database.

JOINing More than 2 Databases

JOIN can only work on two databases. You must apply it iteratively to JOIN more. For example, Program 8-5 lists the names of suppliers, parts, and projects located in the same city.

Program 8-5. Applying JOIN Iteratively

```
SELECT 0
USE supplier

SELECT 0
USE parts

JOIN WITH supplier TO temp FOR pcity = supplier->scity ;
     FIELDS pcity, pname, supplier->sname
```

```
SELECT supplier                 && re-use this area
USE project

SELECT parts                    && re-use this area
USE temp

JOIN WITH project TO samecity FOR pcity = project->jcity ;
      FIELDS pname, sname, project->jname
```

The intermediate file temp has the following structure:

TEMP.DBF:

Field	Field Name	Type	Width	Dec
1	PCITY	Character	15	
2	PNAME	Character	15	
3	SNAME	Character	10	
	** Total **		41	

and the following contents:

RECORD#	PCITY	PNAME	SNAME
1	LONDON	NUT	SMITH
2	LONDON	NUT	CLARK
3	LONDON	NUT	THOMAS
4	LONDON	NUT	SPENCE
5	PARIS	BOLT	JONES
6	PARIS	BOLT	BLAKE
7	LONDON	SCREW	SMITH
8	LONDON	SCREW	CLARK
9	LONDON	SCREW	THOMAS
10	LONDON	SCREW	SPENCE
11	PARIS	CAM	JONES
12	PARIS	CAM	BLAKE
13	LONDON	COG	SMITH
14	LONDON	COG	CLARK
15	LONDON	COG	THOMAS
16	LONDON	COG	SPENCE

Note that we had to save the city field for use in the next JOIN. The samecity database has the following structure:

SAMECITY.DBF:

Field	Field Name	Type	Width	Dec
1	PNAME	Character	15	
2	SNAME	Character	10	
3	JNAME	Character	15	
	** Total **		41	

and the following contents:

RECORD#	PNAME	SNAME	JNAME
1	NUT	SMITH	COLLATOR
2	NUT	SMITH	TAPE
3	NUT	CLARK	COLLATOR
4	NUT	CLARK	TAPE
5	NUT	THOMAS	COLLATOR
6	NUT	THOMAS	TAPE
7	NUT	SPENCE	COLLATOR
8	NUT	SPENCE	TAPE
9	BOLT	JONES	SORTER
10	BOLT	BLAKE	SORTER
11	SCREW	SMITH	COLLATOR
12	SCREW	SMITH	TAPE
13	SCREW	CLARK	COLLATOR
14	SCREW	CLARK	TAPE
15	SCREW	THOMAS	COLLATOR
16	SCREW	THOMAS	TAPE
17	SCREW	SPENCE	COLLATOR
18	SCREW	SPENCE	TAPE
19	CAM	JONES	SORTER
20	CAM	BLAKE	SORTER
21	COG	SMITH	COLLATOR
22	COG	SMITH	TAPE
23	COG	CLARK	COLLATOR
24	COG	CLARK	TAPE
25	COG	THOMAS	COLLATOR
26	COG	THOMAS	TAPE
27	COG	SPENCE	COLLATOR
28	COG	SPENCE	TAPE

JOINing a Database to Itself

Sometimes we want to join a table to itself. Unfortunately, dBASE does not allow this, as it does not let the same database be open in two different areas. Clipper does. Assume for example, you wanted to retrieve from the SUPPLIER database all pairs of suppliers located in the same city. The following Clipper code would do this:

```
SELECT 0
USE supplier ALIAS supp1

SELECT 0
USE supplier

JOIN WITH supp1 TO newsupp FOR scity = supp1->scity ;
      FIELDS s_no, supp1->s_no
```

The NEWSUPP database has the following structure:

NEWSUPP.DBF :

Field	Field Name	Type	Width	Dec
1	S_NO	Character	4	
2	S_NO	Character	4	
	** Total **		9	

Note that the two fields have the same name! As we noted, Clipper will not duplicate names if no field list is specified. However, here we explicitly told it to generate a database with two fields of the same name using the FIELDS option. LISTing this database in dBASE without a field list would produce:

RECORD#	S_NO	S_NO
1	S01	S01
2	S01	S04
3	S01	S08
4	S01	S12
5	S02	S02
6	S02	S03
7	S03	S02
8	S03	S03
9	S04	S01
10	S04	S04
11	S04	S08
12	S04	S12
13	S05	S05
14	S06	S06
15	S06	S14
16	S07	S07
17	S08	S01
18	S08	S04
19	S08	S08
20	S08	S12
21	S09	S09
22	S10	S10
23	S11	S11
24	S12	S01
25	S12	S04
26	S12	S08
27	S12	S12
28	S14	S06
29	S14	S14
30	S15	S15
31	S16	S16
32	S17	S17
33	S18	S18

You can see that the command works correctly. However, you cannot use Clipper's LIST command to display the database, as it requires a field list. The value of S_NO would always be that of the first field. For example, the following LIST command:

```
LIST s_no, s_no
```

displays two identical columns. This is because it associates the name S_NO with one field, and just lists it twice.

The only way to access the second field (other than with a dBASE "MODIFY STRUCTURE" command) is to use the field rename function developed in Chapter 12. Examples appear at the end of this chapter.

> **NOTE**
>
> Clipper allows a database to be joined to itself.

Before we finish with JOIN, a warning is in order. JOIN is powerful and does a complex task. It is also rather slow. Furthermore, it will create a huge database if applied to a large source database without a scope. You must take care when using JOIN. The following section shows alternative approaches using custom written routines.

Simulating JOIN

As noted, JOIN is slow for large databases. There is no way around this - it does a complex operation and caters to the general, rather than the specific case. In some cases, however, JOIN does a lot of redundant processing. We can do better with a custom routine.

When JOIN operates without a scope, you cannot increase its speed. With a scope, however, you may be able to reduce the number of records that it must process in the alias database. Study the first JOIN example from the previous section:

```
SELECT 0
USE parts

SELECT 0
USE supplier

JOIN WITH parts TO samecity FOR scity = parts -> pcity
```

This produces a database of parts and suppliers in the same city. Now assume that the PARTS database is indexed on PCITY, so that it logically appears as:

PARTS.DBF :

RECORD#	P_NO	PNAME	COLOR	WEIGHT	PCITY
1	P1	NUT	RED	12.0	LONDON
4	P4	SCREW	RED	14.0	LONDON
6	P6	COG	RED	19.0	LONDON
2	P2	BOLT	GREEN	17.0	PARIS
5	P5	CAM	BLUE	12.0	PARIS
3	P3	SCREW	BLUE	17.0	ROME

Now consider how JOIN works. It starts at record 1 in the SUPPLIER database, which has LONDON in the SCITY field. It scans every record in the PARTS database looking for PCITY fields containing LONDON. It does not know, as we do, that the PARTS database is ordered on PCITY, and there is no way to inform it. So, even though the command could stop scanning the alias database after record 6, the last one with LONDON in PCITY, it continues through end of file.

A custom version (Program 8-6) could consider the ordering of the alias database, and proceed to the next record in the source database. Applying this technique to an alias database of a few hundred records, with only one or two matches for each scan, produces a huge speed increase.

Program 8-6. Custom JOIN Routine

```
* Custom JOIN of PARTS and SUPPLIER on city
*
* 1 - Create empty destination database as combination of PARTS and
*       SUPPLIER
*
* 2 - Index parts database (in practice, it would already
*       be indexed so this step is redundant)
*
* 3 - For every record in SUPPLIER
*
*       3.1 - Select parts and go top
*
*       3.2 - For each PARTS record with city matching SUPPLIER's city
*
*             3.2.1 - Add record to destination database
*

* first create destination database with correct format :
SELECT 0
USE parts

COPY STRUCTURE EXTENDED TO examp
```

```
USE supplier
COPY STRUCTURE EXTENDED TO examp1

* want to "join" these two databases ...
USE examp1
APPEND FROM examp

CREATE example FROM examp1

* now do join simulation:

USE example

SELECT 0
USE parts
INDEX ON pcity TO pcity

SELECT 0
USE supplier

* for every record in source database
DO WHILE !eof()

    SELECT parts
    GOTO TOP

    * scan only records in destination with same city
    SEEK supplier -> scity

    DO WHILE pcity = supplier -> scity .AND. !eof()

        SELECT example
        APPEND BLANK

        REPLACE s_no WITH supplier -> s_no
        REPLACE sname  WITH supplier -> sname
        REPLACE status WITH supplier -> status
        REPLACE scity  WITH supplier -> scity
        REPLACE p_no WITH parts -> p_no
        REPLACE pname  WITH parts -> pname
        REPLACE color  WITH parts -> color
        REPLACE weight WITH parts -> weight
        REPLACE pcity  WITH parts -> pcity

        SELECT parts
        SKIP

    ENDDO

    * advance to next record in source database ...
    SELECT supplier
    SKIP

ENDDO
```

Program 8-6 shows the destination database being created and records being added to it. In practice, you would probably display the records on the screen or the printer, or save them in an array.

> **TIP**
>
> When a JOIN command operates without a scope on an indexed database, a custom routine will usually run much faster.

REPLACE

The only difference between the Clipper and dBASE REPLACE commands is Clipper's ability to REPLACE to an unselected area. This is useful when updating one database, depending on the contents of another. For example, suppose we wanted to increase a supplier's status by 10 for every project in LONDON it supplies with either part P1 or part P3. The following routine does the job:

```
SELECT 0
USE project
INDEX ON j_no TO j_no

SELECT 0
USE supplier

SELECT 0
USE spj
SET RELATION TO j_no INTO project

REPLACE supplier->status WITH supplier->status + 10 ;
            FOR project->jcity = "LONDON" .AND. p_no = "P1"
```

We can also update several databases with one REPLACE statement. The following example shows this:

```
SELECT 0
USE supplier
LOCATE FOR sname = "JONES"

SELECT 0
USE parts
LOCATE FOR p_no = "P4"

SELECT 0
```

```
USE project
LOCATE FOR j_no = "J2"

REPLACE project->jcity  WITH "ATHENS", ;
          parts->pcity   WITH "LISBON", ;
          supplier->scity WITH "NICE"
```

Note that when the database being REPLACEd into has open index files, keys are added in accordance with the current setting of SET UNIQUE.

Editing Records in a Database

Simulating EDIT

Since Clipper has neither EDIT nor BROWSE commands (the traditional method of editing records in a dBASE program), the programmer must write editing routines. This is fairly simple. Assuming the database is open and the pointer is at the required record, Program 8-7 permits editing, skipping records as required.

Program 8-7. Custom Editing Routine

```
* EDIT simulation
*
*     1 - Save state of READEXIT, set it to .T.
*
*     2 - DO UNTIL BOF, EOF, or user exits
*
*          2.1 - For each field
*
*               2.1.1 - Save value, place GET on screen
*
*          2.2 - Do READ
*
*          2.3 - Move database pointer according to key used to exit
*
*  3 - Restore READEXIT state

FUNCTION do_edit

PRIVATE i, num_fields, save_rexit, fname, edit_more
```

```
CLEAR

save_rexit = readexit()
readexit(.T.)
num_fields = fcount()

PRIVATE save_fields[num_fields]

edit_more = .T.
DO WHILE .NOT. eof() .AND. .NOT. bof() .AND. edit_more

     * position GETs

     FOR i = 1 TO num_fields
          fname = fieldname(i)
          save_fields[i] = &fname
          @ 3 + i, 10 GET &fname
     NEXT

     READ

     key = lastkey()
     DO CASE
          CASE key = UP_ARROW .OR. key = PG_UP .OR. key = LT_ARROW
               SKIP -1

          CASE key = CTRL_W
               edit_more = .F.

          CASE key = ESC
               * restore original values
               edit_more = .F.
               FOR i = 1 TO num_fields

                    fname = fieldname(i)
                    REPLACE &fname WITH save_fields[i]

               NEXT

          OTHERWISE
               SKIP

     ENDCASE
ENDDO

readexit(save_rexit)
RETURN (.T.)
```

Program 8-7 displays the GETs and issues a READ. On exiting from the READ, it uses LASTKEY to determine how the READ ended. An up arrow, page up, or left arrow moves the database pointer back one record. Ctrl-w or Esc cause the edit to exit; Escape does not save the current read. Any other key moves the database pointer forward one record. You call do_edit as follows:

```
init_consts()
CLEAR

USE spj
do_edit()
```

Note that Program 8-7 cannot handle more than one column of GETs. However, you can extend it by changing the code that positions the GETs.

DBEDIT

Another way to do interactive editing is with the DBEDIT function in the extend library. In its native state, DBEDIT does not allow editing, but we can easily tailor its user defined function to do so. DBEDIT is like BROWSE. It devotes one line to each record in the database, scrolling as required both vertically (for new records) and horizontally (for new fields within a same record). It takes the following 12 parameters:

1) Top left row of editing window.
2) Top left column of window.
3) Bottom right row of window.
4) Bottom right column of window.
5) Array containing either field names or expressions to be browsed or edited.
6) User defined function to call at every keystroke.
7) An array of picture strings, corresponding to the field array, used for column formatting.
8) An array of column headings, corresponding to the field array.
9) An array of characters, corresponding to the field array, used to draw the lines separating the headings from the field display area.
10) An array of characters, corresponding to the field array, used to draw lines separating the columns.

11) An array of characters, used to draw lines separating the footings from the display area.

12) An array of characters for column footings.

Parameters 9 through 12 can be a single character to be used everywhere.

Simply invoking DBEDIT with:

```
USE spj

dbedit()
```

makes it operate with its default values. In this mode, it devotes the entire screen to browsing (no editing is allowed), and all fields are displayed.

As described previously, we can allow editing through the user defined function. Called after each keystroke, it gets two parameters: a mode, indicating the state of DBEDIT when the key was pressed, and the array element number of the field currently selected. The mode parameter has one of the following values:

0 - indicates that DBEDIT was in an "idle" state. This mode is generated by cursor movement keys, with the exception of those defined below. Note (very important!) that the keys have already been processed and their default actions performed, before the function is called with 0 mode.

1 - indicates that the user tried to move the cursor past the beginning of file.

2 - indicates that the user tried to move the cursor past the end of file.

3 - indicates that the database file is empty.

4 - indicates a keystroke exception, such as Enter or an Escape being pressed.

The function must return a value to DBEDIT. The defined values are:

0 - forces DBEDIT to quit.

1 - forces DBEDIT to continue.

2 - forces DBEDIT to reread the database and repaint the screen.

A simple trial user defined function simply returns a default value and prints the parameters. You should define the seven "constants" in the "init_consts" routine, described in Chapters 3 and 5, as in:

```
PUBLIC DBE_QUIT, DBE_CONT, DBE_REPAINT
PUBLIC DBE_IDLE, DBE_PAST_BOF, DBE_PAST_EOF, DBE_EXCEP

        DBE_QUIT = 0
        DBE_CONT = 1
        DBE_REPAINT = 2

        DBE_IDLE = 0
        DBE_PAST_BOF = 1
        DBE_PAST_EOF = 2

        DBE_EXCEP = 4
```

The following code displays the user function's parameters:

```
init_consts() && make constants available
USE spj

ufunc_count = 0

CLEAR
? dbedit(10, 10, 20, 20, "", "ufunc")

FUNCTION ufunc

PARAMETERS mode, fld_ptr

        ufunc_count = ufunc_count + 1

        @ 24, 10 SAY mode
        @ 24, 20 SAY fld_ptr
        @ 24, 30 SAY ufunc_count

RETURN DBE_CONT
```

Note that the user function is passed without the parenthetical suffix. This code can verify the mode values. Note that the user cannot now exit with either the Enter or the Escape keys, as DBEDIT does in its native state. That is because the function returns 1, forcing DBEDIT to continue, regardless of which key was pressed. To have Enter or Escape force an exit, we must rewrite the function as:

```
FUNCTION ufunc

PARAMETERS mode, fld_ptr
PRIVATE ret_val

        DO CASE
                CASE mode = DBE_EXCEP
                        IF lastkey() = ESC .OR. lastkey() = ENTER
                                ret_val = DBE_QUIT
```

```
            ENDIF

        OTHERWISE
            ret_val = DBE_CONT

    ENDCASE

RETURN ret_val
```

We use LASTKEY to determine the cause of the exception. If it was the pressing of either the Enter or the Escape key, we force DBEDIT to exit by returning a zero. Otherwise, we return a 1, forcing it to continue.

Within this framework, we can easily allow editing. We will use the Enter key to indicate that the currently selected field needs to be edited. When the key is detected, the routine (Program 8-8) uses the cur_field parameter to determine which field to GET, and the ROW and COL functions to determine the location of the GET.

Program 8-8. DBEDIT User Function Allowing Editing

```
FUNCTION ufunc

PARAMETERS mode, fld_ptr
PRIVATE ret_val, cur_field

    cur_field = fnames[fld_ptr]

    DO CASE
        CASE mode = DBE_EXCEP
            IF lastkey() = ESC
                ret_val = DBE_QUIT
            ELSEIF lastkey() = ENTER
                @ row(), col() GET &cur_field

                SET CURSOR ON
                READ
                SET CURSOR OFF

                ret_val = DBE_CONT
            ELSE
                ret_val = DBE_CONT
            ENDIF

        OTHERWISE
            ret_val = DBE_CONT

    ENDCASE

RETURN ret_val
```

Program 8-8 relies on DBEDIT maintaining the record pointer at the currently highlighted record. It also relies on the availability of a global array "fnames", containing the names of the fields. You can easily create fnames with:

```
PRIVATE fnames[fcount()]
afields(fnames)
```

> **NOTE**
>
> DBEDIT maintains the record pointer at the highlighted record.

Since DBEDIT operates without a visible cursor, the routine should turn the cursor on before issuing the READ, and then off when the READ ends. You can use the cursor save and restore routines we show in Chapter 11 to do this.

We can easily modify the routine to allow appending of records. Program 8-9 appends a record when it detects that the user tried to move the cursor past the end of the file.

Program 8-9. DBEDIT User Function Allowing Editing and Appending

```
FUNCTION ufunc

PARAMETERS mode, fld_ptr
PRIVATE ret_val, cur_field

     DO CASE
          CASE mode = DBE_EXCEP
               IF lastkey() = ESC
                    ret_val = DBE_QUIT
               ELSEIF lastkey() = ENTER
                    cur_field = fnames[fld_ptr]
                    @ row(), col() GET &cur_field

                    SET CURSOR ON
                    READ
                    SET CURSOR OFF

                    ret_val = DBE_CONT
               ELSE
                    ret_val = DBE_CONT
               ENDIF
```

```
        CASE mode = DBE_PAST_EOF
             APPEND BLANK
             ret_val = DBE_CONT

        OTHERWISE
             ret_val = DBE_CONT

    ENDCASE

RETURN ret_val
```

Although DBEDIT allows horizontal "panning" of fields too large to fit on one line, it does not allow fields to be locked. However, a technique like that used with ACHOICE in Chapter 3 lets us simulate locking with the user defined function. You may want to review the discussion of ACHOICE and Program 3-9 before proceeding.

To simulate scrolling, we build arrays with sets of fields. When the user function detects the need for a horizontal scroll, it forces DBEDIT to terminate. The calling function detects that DBEDIT terminated, and reinvokes it with another array. All we then must do is put fields in the same positions in all arrays, and they appear to be locked.

Here we have two problems that do not occur in the ACHOICE version. First, whereas ACHOICE lets you define both the initial element to select and its offset in the window, DBEDIT allows only the former to be simulated by starting the display at the current record number. This means that when DBEDIT is re-invoked, the record selected when the function caused the exit is displayed at offset 0 in the window. Second, a left scroll occurs when the user presses the left arrow key with the highlight bar on the first field. When the function is re-invoked, the highlight bar should be on the last field of the new array. However, it is actually on the first field, and there is no way to force DBEDIT to behave otherwise.

Program 8-10 illustrates these two problems. We use the "merchant - distributor" database from Chapter 3. Its structure is repeated here for convenience:

```
*** structure of database merch_dis.dbf ***

Last update 88 1 7

Data offset 641
Record size 100
Number of records 4
```

NAME	TYPE	LEN	DEC
DIST_ID	N	3	0
MERCH1_ID	N	2	0
MERCH1_86	N	7	2
MERCH1_87	N	7	2
MERCH2_ID	N	2	0
MERCH2_86	N	7	2
MERCH2_87	N	7	2
MERCH3_ID	N	2	0
MERCH3_86	N	7	2
MERCH3_87	N	7	2
MERCH4_ID	N	2	0
MERCH4_86	N	7	2
MERCH4_87	N	7	2
MERCH5_ID	N	2	0
MERCH5_86	N	7	2
MERCH5_87	N	7	2
MERCH6_ID	N	2	0
MERCH6_86	N	7	2
MERCH6_87	N	7	2

This database contains a distributor identification code and information concerning six merchants. For each merchant, the database has an identification code and the 1986 and 1987 total sales figures. Now, assume we must pan between the following views:

view 1: distributor id, + id, 86, and 87 fields of merchants 1 and 2.

view 2: distributor id, + id, 86, and 87 fields of merchants 3 and 4.

view 3: distributor id, + id, 86, and 87 fields of merchants 5 and 6.

We must declare and initialize the arrays as:

```
PRIVATE pan1[7]
PRIVATE pan2[7]
PRIVATE pan3[7]

* fields for first view ...

pan1[1] = "dist_id"
pan1[2] = "merch1_id"
pan1[3] = "merch1_86"
pan1[4] = "merch1_87"
pan1[5] = "merch2_id"
pan1[6] = "merch2_86"
pan1[7] = "merch2_87"
```

```
* fields for second view

pan2[1] = "dist_id"
pan2[2] = "merch3_id"
pan2[3] = "merch3_86"
pan2[4] = "merch3_87"
pan2[5] = "merch4_id"
pan2[6] = "merch4_86"
pan2[7] = "merch4_87"

* fields for third view

pan3[1] = "dist_id"
pan3[2] = "merch5_id"
pan3[3] = "merch5_86"
pan3[4] = "merch5_87"
pan3[5] = "merch6_id"
pan3[6] = "merch6_86"
pan3[7] = "merch6_87"
```

and call DBEDIT as follows:

```
init_consts()

USE merch_dis

PRIVATE fnames[fcount()]

afields(fnames)

CLEAR

view = 1
DO WHILE lastkey() != ESC

    cview = ltrim(str(view))

    * To prevent repetitive left scroll ...
    last_field = 0

    dbedit(10, 0, 20, 79, pan&cview, "ufunc")

    * if last key was right arrow, view was either 1 or 2
    IF lastkey() = RT_ARROW
        view = view + 1
    ELSEIF lastkey() = LT_ARROW
        view = view - 1
    ENDIF

ENDDO
```

We define the user function as shown in Program 8-10.

Program 8-10. DBEDIT with Locked Fields, Part I

```
FUNCTION ufunc

PARAMETERS mode, fld_ptr
PRIVATE ret_val, cur_field

    DO CASE
        CASE mode = DBE_EXCEP
            IF lastkey() = ESC
                ret_val = DBE_QUIT
            ELSEIF lastkey() = ENTER

                cur_field = fnames[fld_ptr]
                @ row(), col() GET &cur_field

                SET CURSOR ON
                READ
                SET CURSOR OFF

                ret_val = DBE_CONT
            ELSE
                ret_val = DBE_CONT
            ENDIF

        CASE mode = DBE_PAST_EOF
            APPEND BLANK
                ret_val = DBE_CONT

        CASE mode = DBE_IDLE

            IF lastkey() = RT_ARROW .AND. view < 3 .AND. last_field = 7
                ret_val = DBE_QUIT
            ELSEIF lastkey() = LT_ARROW .AND. view > 1 .AND. last_field = 1
                ret_val = DBE_QUIT
            ELSE
                ret_val = DBE_CONT
            ENDIF

        OTHERWISE
            ret_val = DBE_CONT

    ENDCASE

    last_field = fld_ptr
RETURN ret_val
```

We initially invoke DBEDIT with the first view, given by array pan1. The user function returns the quit value to scroll, when it detects that either a left arrow key was pressed with the first field highlighted, or a right arrow with the last field (in this case, field 7) highlighted. Exceptions occur at boundaries where there is nowhere to scroll.

Now, because DBEDIT processes "idle" keys before the function is called, we cannot use the fld_ptr parameter to check the position of the highlight bar. fld_ptr gives its CURRENT position. For an idle mode, it includes cursor movement produced by the key just pressed. To detect that scrolling is necessary, the function must know where the highlight bar was BEFORE the arrow key was processed. The variable last_field holds this value. The user function updates it to the value of fld_ptr before exiting.

You may have noticed from the user function that printed its parameters that DBEDIT invokes the function once before a key is pressed. That is why we reset last_field to 0, rather than 1, before invoking DBEDIT. If it were set to 1, when DBEDIT was invoked as a result of a left scroll, say from view 3 to view 2, the first call to the user function (before a key was pressed) would cause an immediate exit. LASTKEY would still return a LT_ARROW value, last_field would be 1, and view would be 2. An initial value of 0 for last_field stops this from happening.

Finally, note that if the arrays do not all have the same number of fields, we would have to modify the user function code that checks for the last field number. You would switch on the view number to do this.

> **TIP**
>
> Simulate locking of fields by forcing DBEDIT to quit, and then reinvoking it.

We can position the highlight bar correctly after a left scroll by using the KEYBOARD command (described in Chapter 5) to stuff right arrow keys into the keyboard buffer. The following code shows this (the array initialization and the user function are the same as in the previous version).

```
init_consts()

USE merch_dis

PRIVATE fnames[fcount()]
```

```
afields(fnames)

CLEAR
view = 1
DO WHILE lastkey() != ESC

      cview = ltrim(str(view))

      * To prevent repetitive left scroll ...
      last_field = 0

      dbedit(10, 0, 20, 79, pan&cview, "ufunc")

      * if last key was right arrow, view was either 1 or 2
      IF lastkey() = RT_ARROW
            view = view + 1
      ELSEIF lastkey() = LT_ARROW  && if left arrow, either 2 or 3
            view = view - 1
            KEYBOARD replicate(chr(RT_ARROW), 6)  && size of array - 1
      ENDIF

ENDDO
```

A similar approach solves the problem of the highlighted record always being at offset 0 inside the window following a scroll. Stuffing the keyboard buffer with enough up arrow keys scrolls the record to the desired position. Then stuffing the same number of down arrow keys to re-select the record will achieve the desired result. To calculate the number to stuff, we must first determine the offset of the selected field within the window. You cannot do this with record number arithmetic since the database could be indexed, have a filter set, etc. You must do it by determining the current row (the row number of the selected record), and subtracting the row number of the first record in the DBEDIT window. You must determine these values before reinvoking DBEDIT, as shown in Program 8-11.

Program 8-11. DBEDIT with Locked Fields, Part II

```
init_consts()

USE merch_dis

PRIVATE fnames[fcount()]

afields(fnames)

CLEAR
```

```
view = 1
DO WHILE lastkey() != ESC

        cview = ltrim(str(view))

        * To prevent repetitive left scroll ...
        last_field = 0

        dbedit(10, 0, 20, 79, pan&cview, "ufunc")
        num_scroll = row() - 12       && 12 is row of first record

        * if last key was right arrow, view was either 1 or 2
        IF lastkey() = RT_ARROW
                view = view + 1
                KEYBOARD replicate(chr(UP_ARROW), num_scroll) + ;
                                replicate(chr(DOWN_ARROW), num_scroll)

        ELSEIF lastkey() = LT_ARROW  && if left arrow, either 2 or 3
                view = view - 1
                KEYBOARD replicate(chr(RT_ARROW), 6) + ;
                                replicate(chr(UP_ARROW), num_scroll) + ;
                                replicate(chr(DOWN_ARROW), num_scroll)
        ENDIF

ENDDO
```

Again, you need not change the user function or the array declaration. The code determines the number of lines needed to scroll with:

```
num_scroll = row() - 12       && 12 is row of first record
```

DBEDIT is invoked in a window starting at row 10. That row contains the headings. Row 11 has the separator lines, and so row 12 is the first line for records. We subtract 12 from the current row position to compute the number of rows to scroll. Note that we could not use a separate KEYBOARD command to scroll, as it would cancel the effect of the previous KEYBOARD command.

> **TIP**
>
> Use the KEYBOARD command to correctly position DBEDIT after a horizontal scroll with locked fields.

DBEDIT with a WHILE Scope

You can restrict the records displayed by DBEDIT by setting a filter condition. It acts like a FOR condition on a LIST command. However, there is no simple way to restrict the view with a WHILE condition. To see why this is a problem, imagine using DBEDIT on an unindexed database. Assume we only want to view records with a name field of "Spence". We are currently positioned at the first of these records, record number 750. The next ten records have the name "Spence". We can restrict the scope by setting the filter to "name = 'Spence'". Now, if the database contains 10,000 records, it will take a long time to skip past the last record in the scope, number 759. Clipper has to skip the next 9,240 records to ensure no more matches.

If we could specify a WHILE scope to DBEDIT, the problem would be solved. As soon as the user tried to skip past record 759, Clipper would recognize the end of the WHILE scope and stop. Although DBEDIT does not allow a WHILE scope, you can simulate it with a SET FILTER.

What you must do is set a filter to a user defined function. The function is called every time a SKIP is performed. As soon as the function determines that the WHILE scope is FALSE, it forces either an end of file, or a beginning of file, depending on the direction. Program 8-12 shows a general purpose function to implement a WHILE clause for DBEDIT, and a sample call.

Program 8-12. DBEDIT with a WHILE Scope

```
* Sample code to use DBEDIT with a WHILE clause
*
* 1 - Use database
*
* 2 - Seek to start of records we want to view WHILE condition is .T.
*
* 3 - Set filter condition to user defined function
*
* 4 - Call DBEDIT if we found at least one record

init_consts()

USE test1

@ 0, 0 TO 24, 79

* Must locate to start of records (WHILE scope) ...
LOCATE FOR name = 'Spence'
```

```
* Only turn filter on AFTER initial locate.
* If you need a FOR condition as well, combine with .AND.
SET FILTER TO db_while("name = 'Spence'")

* If we found at least one, view them with DBEDIT
IF found()
	* use default fields, but specify user function
	dbedit(1, 1, 23, 78, "", "ufunc")
ENDIF

* This is the filter function that forces the WHILE.
* Pass it a scope.

FUNCTION db_while
PARAM cond

PRIVATE key, save_filter

	IF !&cond
		* We are past scope (WHILE would return .F.)
		* Force to either BOF or EOF, depending on which
		* way user was travelling

		* turn filter off before SKIP, else the routine recurses
		* first save it, so we can restore it

		save_filter = dbfilter()
		SET FILTER TO

		key = lastkey()
		IF key = UP_ARROW .OR. key = PG_UP
			* user was going up, so force BOF
			GOTO TOP
			SKIP -1
		ELSE
			* user was going down, so force EOF
			GOTO BOTTOM
			SKIP
		ENDIF
		SET FILTER TO &save_filter
	ENDIF

RETURN .T.

* This is the DBEDIT user function. It allows escape with Enter
* or Escape, and displays EOF / BOF message on line 24

FUNCTION ufunc

PARAMETERS mode, fld_ptr
PRIVATE ret_val
```

```
        DO CASE
            CASE mode = DBE_EXCEP
                IF lastkey() = ESC .OR. lastkey() = ENTER
                    ret_val = DBE_QUIT
                ENDIF

            CASE mode = DBE_PAST_BOF
                @ 24, 0 SAY "bof"
                inkey(0)
                @ 24, 0
                ret_val = DBE_CONT

            CASE mode = DBE_PAST_EOF
                @ 24, 0 SAY "eof"

                inkey(0)
                @ 24, 0
                ret_val = DBE_CONT

            OTHERWISE
                ret_val = DBE_CONT

        ENDCASE

    RETURN ret_val
```

Note that the routine saves the filter and then restores it. It cannot just set it to the cond parameter, as the filter could have been combined with another expression to implement a FOR scope as well.

> **TIP**
>
> You can use DBEDIT with a WHILE scope by setting the filter to a user defined function that simulates it.

DBEDIT is a powerful function that allows browsing, appending, and editing of database records. You should master its use. Simulating the WHILE scope makes it more efficient for large databases.

Adding Records to a Database File

Interactive Appending

Since Clipper has no interactive APPEND command, the programmer must develop appending routines. To do this, you use the APPEND BLANK command to add an empty record at the end of a database, and then the REPLACE command to assign data to each field. Chapter 6 contains the source code for a routine that appends records to the SPJ database. We repeat it here for convenience.

```
USE spj

ESC = 27
key = 0
changed = .T.

CLEAR

DO WHILE changed

    APPEND BLANK

    m_s_no = s_no
    m_p_no = p_no
    m_j_no = j_no
    m_qty = qty

    changed = .F.

    @ 10, 10 SAY "S_NO " GET m_s_no
    @ 11, 10 SAY "P_NO " GET m_p_no
    @ 12, 10 SAY "J_NO " GET m_j_no
    @ 13, 10 SAY "QTY  " GET m_qty

    READ

    IF updated()

        changed = .T.
        REPLACE s_no WITH m_s_no
        REPLACE p_no WITH m_p_no
        REPLACE j_no WITH m_j_no
        REPLACE qty  WITH m_qty

    ENDIF
ENDDO
```

As noted in Chapter 6, this routine has the unfortunate side effect of adding an extra blank record to the database. We add the record to get blank memory variable copies of each field with the correct size and type. One sure way to remove it is to delete it and PACK the database. However, this is usually impractical. The solution lies in the "ghost" record at end of file. A GOTO BOTTOM followed by a SKIP moves the pointer to end of file. The fields in the "ghost" record have the empty values we need.

We can now write the APPEND code (Program 8-13) by initially saving the fields from the "ghost" record in memory variables. They are copied to the variables we GET before the GETs are issued. We thus have two sets of memory variables, one for the GETs and the other to save the blank fields.

Program 8-13. Using the "Ghost" Record in a Custom APPEND Routine

```
* Custom APPEND
*
*     1 - GET "ghost" fields as memory variables
*
*     2 - DO UNTIL not appending anymore
*
*          2.1 - Set memvars to "ghost" memvars

*
*          2.2 - Do READ
*
*               2.2.1 - if updated, append blank record and replace
*                            memvars into it
*
*               2.2.2 - not appending anymore = .F.

SELECT 0
USE spj

GOTO BOTTOM
SKIP

empty_s_no = s_no
empty_p_no = p_no
empty_j_no = j_no
empty_qty = qty

ESC = 27
key = 0
changed = .T.
```

```
CLEAR

DO WHILE changed

     m_s_no = empty_s_no
     m_p_no = empty_p_no
     m_j_no = empty_j_no
     m_qty = empty_qty

     changed = .F.

     @ 10, 10 SAY "S_NO " GET m_s_no
     @ 11, 10 SAY "P_NO " GET m_p_no
     @ 12, 10 SAY "J_NO " GET m_j_no
     @ 13, 10 SAY "QTY  " GET m_qty

     READ

     IF updated()

          APPEND BLANK

          changed = .T.

          REPLACE s_no WITH m_s_no
          REPLACE p_no WITH m_p_no
          REPLACE j_no WITH m_j_no
          REPLACE qty  WITH m_qty

     ENDIF
ENDDO
```

We can make Program 8-13 into a general-purpose routine to append records to the currently open database, using an array to save the empty values of the fields. Program 8-14 shows this.

Program 8-14. Using the "Ghost" Record in a General Purpose Append Routine

```
* General purpose APPEND
*
*      1 - GET "ghost" fields into array
*
*      2 - DO UNTIL not appending any more
*
*           2.1 - Copy "ghost" array to empty data array
*
*           2.2 - Do READ
*
```

```
*                    2.2.1 - if updated, append blank record and replace
*                              array elements into it
*
*                    2.2.2 - not appending anymore = .F.

FUNCTION app

PARAMETER fname
PRIVATE num_fields, i, ESC, key, changed, field_name

     GOTO BOTT
     SKIP

     num_fields = FCOUNT()

     PRIVATE empty_data[num_fields]
     PRIVATE field_data[num_fields]

     FOR i = 1 TO num_fields

          field_name = fieldname(i)
          empty_data[i] = &field_name

     NEXT

     ESC = 27
     key = 0
     changed = .T.

     CLEAR

     DO WHILE changed

          acopy(empty_data, field_data, 1, num_fields)

          changed = .F.

          FOR i = 1 TO num_fields

               @ 5 + i, 0  SAY fieldname(i)
               @ 5 + i, 12 GET field_data[i]

          NEXT

          READ

          IF updated()

               APPEND BLANK

               changed = .T.
               FOR i = 1 TO num_fields
```

```
                    field_name = fieldname(i)
                    REPLACE &field_name WITH field_data[i]

                NEXT

            ENDIF
        ENDDO

    RETURN (.F.)
```

We can invoke Program 8-14 (the app function) with a call such as:

```
USE spj
app()
```

We save the field names in a memory variable only because Clipper does not allow a macro to be applied to a function result. For example, the following is incorrect:

```
REPLACE &fieldname(i) WITH field_data[i]
```

Use Program 8-14 as the basis for any APPEND routines you need to write.

Appending from Another Database

An APPEND FROM command can append a series of records from one database to the currently selected one. The command allows WHILE and FOR clauses and a field list (dBASE does not allow the field list).

For example, assume we want to create a database containing just the part codes of the nuts. The following routine would do the job:

```
SELECT 0
CREATE temp

APPEND BLANK
REPLACE field_name WITH "P_NO", field_type WITH "C" ;
        field_len WITH 5, field_dec WITH 0

CREATE nuts FROM temp

APPEND FROM parts FIELD p_no FOR parts -> pname = "NUT"
```

Unfortunately, we cannot use the APPEND FROM command to

add records to a database based on fields from different databases (using a SET RELATION, for example). The APPEND FROM command can only add records to a database whose fields are a subset of those of the source database. Similarly, the COPY TO command only creates a database with a subset of the structure of the original database. We would prefer to have these commands operate on databases linked by a SET RELATION. To show how this inadequacy creates a problem, assume we want to create a SPJ type database using names rather than codes. The logical way to program this would be:

```
SELECT 0
USE project
INDEX ON j_no TO j_no

SELECT 0
USE parts
INDEX ON p_no TO p_no

SELECT 0
USE supplier
INDEX ON s_no TO s_no

SELECT 0
USE spj

SET RELATION TO j_no INTO project, ;
             TO p_no INTO parts, ;
             TO s_no INTO supplier

COPY TO newspj FIELDS supplier -> sname, parts -> pname, ;
                        project -> jname, qty
```

However, although Clipper does not report an error in the COPY command, it produces a database with just the qty field, and copies only its values. To get the correct result, we must create the database manually (using CREATE or CREATE FROM), and append the records individually by SKIPping through the SPJ database.

Deleting Records from a Database File

If you delete a record from a database, it does not disappear until you PACK it. If SET DELETED is OFF, the record is still visible. However, PACK is time consuming and dangerous. It operates on one copy of the database, and a power loss could cause the database to be destroyed. A common technique that avoids PACK but reclaims unused space is "record recycling". To delete a record, you set one of its fields to a predefined value, signifying that it is no longer in use. Later, before appending a blank, you look for "recycled" records. If the database is indexed on the field, you can find this quickly with a SEEK. If there is a recycled record, you use it.

> **TIP**
>
> Use "record recycling" rather than DELETE/PACK.

Deleting a series of key fields in a database poses an interesting problem. Assume you have a database with a character field, "line_num", of length 10. The database is indexed on it. Now, assume you want to recycle all records with line_num of "208", by setting the field to spaces. The most logical way to write this is:

```
SEEK "208"
DO WHILE line_num = "208"

    REPLACE line_num WITH space(10)
    SKIP

ENDDO
```

However, this is incorrect. The REPLACE logically moves the record to the start of the database. The next SKIP then takes place from there, not from the previous record where line_num was "208".

Program 8-15 is an elegant solution to this problem. We do a SKIP before the record is recycled, save the record number, and then SKIP back to the previous record. After recycling it, instead of doing a SKIP to get to the next record, we do a GOTO.

Program 8-15. Recycling a Series of Key Fields

```
* Recycle records for line_num 208. The database is indexed
 * on this field and the index is primary.

SEEK "208"

DO WHILE line_num = "208"
     SKIP

       save_rec = recno()
  SKIP -1
```

```
REPLACE line_num WITH space(10)

GOTO save_rec

ENDDO
```

Database SETs

UNIQUE

SET UNIQUE ON prevents duplicate keys from being added to a database. An INDEX ON command executed with UNIQUE ON adds only new keys. When a database contains records with identical keys, only the lowest numbered ones appear in the index. UNIQUE affects commands that add or modify a database record similarly. A REPLACE command, or a GET to a field name, will add only new keys to the index if it was created with UNIQUE ON. Changing a duplicate key does NOT cause the duplicate to be added to the database. Of course, a REINDEX would do this.

The UNIQUE flag is "bound" to an index file. When one created with UNIQUE ON is re-opened, its UNIQUE status remains as it was originally.

The UNIQUE flag is a "system wide" setting. When it is ON, all index files are created with unique keys only.

Here is an example use of the SET UNIQUE ON command. Assume we want to list the codes of all suppliers who provide at least one part. Duplicates should not be listed. The following code does the job.

```
SELECT 0
USE spj
SET UNIQUE ON
INDEX ON s_no TO s_no
LIST s_no
```

It produces the following result:

```
RECORD#  s_no
     1    S1
     3    S2
    11    S3
    13    S4
```

```
15      S5
25      S6
```

The examples at the end of this chapter show another way to create unique data sets without creating a new index.

DELETED

The SET DELETED command is system wide. It affects all open databases, even those opened after the command is issued. To operate concurrently on two databases, one with deleted on and one with it off, we must continually change the state of SET DELETED.

The default state of the flag is off, i.e., deleted records are visible.

FILTER

The SET FILTER command restricts the view of the database to records matching the filter condition. Clipper has one incompatibility with dBASE here - the execution of a SET FILTER such as:

```
filt = ""
SET FILTER TO &filt
```

causes a run time error at the next statement that moves the database pointer (this is when the filter condition is processed). dBASE allows a null filter.

A common error in applying SET FILTER is to use RECCOUNT to determine how many records an operation will process. This does not work unless all records in the database satisfy the filter condition. Another error is not issuing a SKIP or GOTO TOP after setting the filter. Unlike SET RELATION, SET FILTER does not reposition the database pointer. The pointer could therefore be at a record that does not satisfy the filter.

A SET FILTER command applies only to a specified area and database. It is not system - wide like SET DELETED. DBFILTER returns the contents of the current filter.

Examples

This section uses the commands and functions to program sample database operations. The examples show reasonable methods but not the only possible ones. In practice, where alternatives exist, the best choice depends on the size of the databases, the scope of the records, and the indexes that exist. The examples start with simple operations, but increase in complexity. Refer to Figures 8-1 through 8-4 to view the sample databases.

1) Get codes and names for suppliers in LONDON with status > 20.

```
USE suppliers
LIST s_no, sname FOR scity = "LONDON" .AND. status > 20
```

Result:

```
RECORD # S_NO  SNAME
   12    S12   SPENCE
```

2) Get codes and status for suppliers in LONDON with status > 20, in descending order of status.

```
USE suppliers

SORT TO temp ON status/D FOR status > 20 .AND. scity = "LONDON"

USE temp
LIST s_no, status
```

or

```
USE suppliers

SET FILTER TO scity = "LONDON" .AND. status > 20
GOTO TOP
SORT TO temp ON status/D

USE temp
LIST s_no, status
```

Result:

```
RECORD #   S_NO    STATUS
    1      S12     40
```

3) Get the names of suppliers for part P2.

```
SELECT 0
USE supplier
INDEX ON s_no TO s_no

SELECT 0
USE spj
SET RELATION INTO supplier TO s_no

LIST supplier->sname FOR p_no = "P2"
```

This is an interesting example. It sets a relation from the "parent" database SPJ into the SUPPLIER database. It then scans the parent database for records with part code P2. For each one found, it prints the supplier name from the child database. INDEX ON is necessary only if the index file does not already exist, or is out of date. In this example, and in many that follow it, we show the INDEX ON command explicitly for clarity.

If SPJ were indexed on the P_NO field, we could change the FOR scope on the LIST command to a WHILE scope. As described in Chapter 2, the WHILE scope causes the command to terminate as soon as the condition is not met. On a large database, the time saving is tremendous. Here is the code for the routine:

```
SELECT 0
USE supplier
INDEX ON s_no TO s_no

SELECT 0
USE spj
INDEX ON p_no TO p_no
SET RELATION INTO supplier TO s_no

SEEK "P2"
LIST supplier->sname WHILE p_no = "P2"
```

The routine SEEKs to the first SPJ record with P_NO equal to P2. It then processes only records with the same P_NO value. As soon as it finds a record with a non-matching value, the LIST command terminates. This technique processes only records matching the scope.

4) Get all combinations of supplier and part information in which the supplier city is alphabetically larger than the part city.

```
SELECT 0
USE supplier

SELECT 0
USE parts

JOIN WITH supplier TO bigcity FOR supplier -> scity > pcity

USE bigcity
LIST s_no, sname, status, scity, p_no, pname, color, weight, pcity
```

Result:

RECORD#	S_NO	SNAME	STATUS	SCITY	P_NO	PNAME	COLOR	WEIGHT	PCITY
1	S02	JONES	10	PARIS	P1	NUT	RED	12.0	LONDON
2	S03	BLAKE	30	PARIS	P1	NUT	RED	12.0	LONDON
3	S07	BAKER	40	L.A.	P1	NUT	RED	12.0	LONDON
4	S11	BROWN	30	MEMPHIS	P1	NUT	RED	12.0	LONDON
5	S15	CHILES	30	RENO	P1	NUT	RED	12.0	LONDON
6	S16	SMYTH	40	WICHITA	P1	NUT	RED	12.0	LONDON
7	S17	ABBOTT	30	NEW YORK	P1	NUT	RED	12.0	LONDON
8	S15	CHILES	30	RENO	P2	BOLT	GREEN	17.0	PARIS
9	S16	SMYTH	40	WICHITA	P2	BOLT	GREEN	17.0	PARIS
10	S16	SMYTH	40	WICHITA	P3	SCREW	BLUE	17.0	ROME
11	S02	JONES	10	PARIS	P4	SCREW	RED	14.0	LONDON
12	S03	BLAKE	30	PARIS	P4	SCREW	RED	14.0	LONDON
13	S07	BAKER	40	L.A.	P4	SCREW	RED	14.0	LONDON
14	S11	BROWN	30	MEMPHIS	P4	SCREW	RED	14.0	LONDON
15	S15	CHILES	30	RENO	P4	SCREW	RED	14.0	LONDON
16	S16	SMYTH	40	WICHITA	P4	SCREW	RED	14.0	LONDON
17	S17	ABBOTT	30	NEW YORK	P4	SCREW	RED	14.0	LONDON
18	S15	CHILES	30	RENO	P5	CAM	BLUE	12.0	PARIS
19	S16	SMYTH	40	WICHITA	P5	CAM	BLUE	12.0	PARIS
20	S02	JONES	10	PARIS	P6	COG	RED	19.0	LONDON
21	S03	BLAKE	30	PARIS	P6	COG	RED	19.0	LONDON
22	S07	BAKER	40	L.A.	P6	COG	RED	19.0	LONDON
23	S11	BROWN	30	MEMPHIS	P6	COG	RED	19.0	LONDON
24	S15	CHILES	30	RENO	P6	COG	RED	19.0	LONDON
25	S16	SMYTH	40	WICHITA	P6	COG	RED	19.0	LONDON
26	S17	ABBOTT	30	NEW YORK	P6	COG	RED	19.0	LONDON

The results appear in order of ascending P_NO, the "native" order of the PARTS database.

In this case, a custom version of the JOIN command will definitely save database comparisons, and probably time as well. If the PARTS database is indexed on PCITY, we can restrict the processing to records with PCITY fields less than the current value of SCITY. The following routine shows this:

```
SELECT 0
USE supplier

SELECT 0
USE parts

INDEX ON pcity TO PCITY

DO WHILE !supplier -> (eof())

    GOTO TOP

    DO WHILE pcity < supplier -> scity .AND. !eof()
```

```
            ? supplier -> s_no, supplier -> sname, supplier -> status, ;
              supplier -> scity, p_no, pname, color, weight, pcity
            SKIP

        ENDDO
        SKIP ALIAS supplier

    ENDDO
```

Here is the output:

```
S02  JONES    10  PARIS     P1  NUT    RED    12.0  LONDON
S02  JONES    10  PARIS     P4  SCREW  RED    14.0  LONDON
S02  JONES    10  PARIS     P6  COG    RED    19.0  LONDON
S03  BLAKE    30  PARIS     P1  NUT    RED    12.0  LONDON
S03  BLAKE    30  PARIS     P4  SCREW  RED    14.0  LONDON
S03  BLAKE    30  PARIS     P6  COG    RED    19.0  LONDON
S07  BAKER    40  L.A.      P1  NUT    RED    12.0  LONDON
S07  BAKER    40  L.A.      P4  SCREW  RED    14.0  LONDON
S07  BAKER    40  L.A.      P6  COG    RED    19.0  LONDON
S11  BROWN    30  MEMPHIS   P1  NUT    RED    12.0  LONDON
S11  BROWN    30  MEMPHIS   P4  SCREW  RED    14.0  LONDON
S11  BROWN    30  MEMPHIS   P6  COG    RED    19.0  LONDON
S15  CHILES   30  RENO      P1  NUT    RED    12.0  LONDON
S15  CHILES   30  RENO      P4  SCREW  RED    14.0  LONDON
S15  CHILES   30  RENO      P6  COG    RED    19.0  LONDON
S15  CHILES   30  RENO      P2  BOLT   GREEN  17.0  PARIS
S15  CHILES   30  RENO      P5  CAM    BLUE   12.0  PARIS
S16  SMYTH    40  WICHITA   P1  NUT    RED    12.0  LONDON
S16  SMYTH    40  WICHITA   P4  SCREW  RED    14.0  LONDON
S16  SMYTH    40  WICHITA   P6  COG    RED    19.0  LONDON
S16  SMYTH    40  WICHITA   P2  BOLT   GREEN  17.0  PARIS
S16  SMYTH    40  WICHITA   P5  CAM    BLUE   12.0  PARIS
S16  SMYTH    40  WICHITA   P3  SCREW  BLUE   17.0  ROME
S17  ABBOTT   30  NEW YORK  P1  NUT    RED    12.0  LONDON
S17  ABBOTT   30  NEW YORK  P4  SCREW  RED    14.0  LONDON
S17  ABBOTT   30  NEW YORK  P6  COG    RED    19.0  LONDON
```

If you have trouble understanding the routine, draw a diagram of the databases and step through the code line by line, noting the processing and the results.

Although the results are the same, the JOIN command orders them by ascending part code, whereas this routine orders them by ascending supplier code. You can easily change the routine to order its output by PART code:

```
SELECT 0
USE parts

SELECT 0
USE supplier
```

```
INDEX ON scity TO scity

SET SOFTSEEK ON

DO WHILE !parts -> (eof())

     * seek to scity immediately following this pcity
     seeker = parts -> pcity
     seeker = substr(seeker, 1, 3) + chr(asc(substr(seeker, 4, 1)) + 1)

     SEEK seeker

     DO WHILE !eof()

          ? s_no, sname, status, scity, parts -> p_no, parts -> pname, ;
          parts -> color, parts -> weight, parts -> pcity
          SKIP

     ENDDO

     SKIP ALIAS parts

ENDDO
```

However, the sequence is still not the same as the JOIN. The records are ordered first by ascending PART code, but the next ordering is by supplier city, since the database was indexed on that field. The original JOIN made the secondary order ascending SUPPLIER code. To write a custom routine that takes advantage of the supplier city ordering, we must append the records, as processed, to a database indexed on a combination of the two fields.

5) Get all pairs of codes for suppliers located in the same city. Do not include pairs such as (S1, S1)

```
SELECT 0
USE supplier ALIAS supp1

SELECT 0
USE supplier

JOIN WITH supp1 TO samecity FOR scity = supp1->scity ;
                    .AND. s_no != supp1->s_no FIELDS s_no, supp1->s_no

newname("samecity.dbf", 2, "s_no1")

USE samecity        && re-use area
LIST s_no, s_no1
```

Here, the JOIN command joins a database to itself. Since the

S_NO field appears twice, we use the "newname" function (see Program 12-7) to rename the second one as S_NO1. We must link the OBJ file, supplied on the sample disk or created from the source code in Chapter 12, with the routine.

The second condition on the join command, "s_no != suppl->s_no", prevents the addition of records such as (S_NO, S_NO).

Result:

Record#	S_NO	S_NO1
1	S01	S04
2	S01	S08
3	S01	S12
4	S02	S03
5	S03	S02
6	S04	S01
7	S04	S08
8	S04	S12
9	S06	S13
10	S08	S01
11	S08	S04
12	S08	S12
13	S12	S01
14	S12	S04
15	S12	S08
16	S13	S06

Once again, by relying on the ordering of one field, we can improve performance with a custom JOIN. In this case, we will open the same database in two areas, indexing one on the SCITY field so we can stop the comparisons when the fields do not match. The following code shows this:

```
SELECT 0
USE supplier

SELECT 0
USE supplier ALIAS supp
INDEX ON scity TO scity

DO WHILE !supplier -> (eof())

    SEEK supplier -> scity

    * For every supplier with this city ...
    DO WHILE scity = supplier -> scity .AND. !eof()

        IF s_no != supplier -> s_no
            ? supplier -> s_no, s_no
        ENDIF
```

```
            SKIP
        ENDDO

        SKIP ALIAS supplier

    ENDDO
```

We can avoid the initial SEEK by setting a relation from one database to the other (even though it is the same database). The following code shows this:

```
    SELECT 0
    USE supplier ALIAS supp1
    INDEX ON scity TO scity

    SELECT 0
    USE supplier

    SET RELATION INTO supp1 TO scity

    DO WHILE !eof()

        DO WHILE scity = supp1 -> scity .AND. !supp1 -> (eof())
            IF s_no != supp1 -> s_no
                ? supp1 -> s_no, s_no
            ENDIF
            SKIP ALIAS supp1
        ENDDO

    ENDDO
```

6) Get a list of all part color/part city combinations with duplicate pairs eliminated.

```
    USE parts

    SET UNIQUE ON
    INDEX ON color + pcity TO pno_city

    LIST color, pcity
```

Result:

```
    5      BLUE      PARIS
    3      BLUE      ROME
    2      GREEN     PARIS
    1      RED       LONDON
```

Since the INDEX ON command is very fast, this solution is acceptable. The alternative is to process the database manually, storing the results in an array used to check for uniqueness. The following code shows this:

```
USE parts
PRIVATE already_seen[reccount()]

num_found = 0

DO WHILE !eof()

     * Already processed?
     IF ascan(already_seen, color + pcity, 1, num_found) = 0

          ? p_no, pcity
          num_found = num_found + 1
          already_seen[num_found] = color + pcity

     ENDIF

     SKIP
ENDDO
```

We declare the size of the already seen array as the number of records in the database. This allows for the worst case in which all records are unique.

7) Get unique part codes for parts provided by a supplier in London to a project in London.

```
SELECT 0
USE project
INDEX ON j_no TO j_no

SELECT 0
USE suppliers
INDEX ON s_no TO s_no

SELECT 0
USE spj

SET RELATION INTO project TO j_no, ;
                INTO suppliers TO s_no

COPY TO temp FOR supplier->scity = "LONDON" .AND. ;
                    project->jcity = "LONDON" FIELDS p_no

USE temp
SET UNIQUE ON
INDEX ON p_no TO p_no
LIST p_no
```

Result:

```
1    P6
```

We use COPY rather than LIST so that we can then do an INDEX to remove the duplicates. Again, we can write a custom routine to handle the UNIQUE values with an array, as the previous example did. Here, this is definitely preferable as it saves a COPY, INDEX, and LIST command. The following code shows this:

```
SELECT 0
USE parts

PRIVATE already_seen[reccount()]

num_found = 0

USE project                    && reuse this area
INDEX ON j_no TO j_no

SELECT 0
USE supplier
INDEX ON s_no TO s_no

SELECT 0
USE spj

SET RELATION INTO project TO j_no, ;
                    INTO supplier TO s_no

DO WHILE !eof()

     IF supplier -> scity = "LONDON" .AND. project -> jcity = "LONDON"

          * If this part code has already been processed, don't output
          * again
          IF ascan(already_seen, p_no, 1, num_found) = 0

               ? p_no
               num_found = num_found + 1
               already_seen[num_found] = p_no

          ENDIF
     ENDIF

     SKIP
ENDDO
```

8) Get all pairs of part codes with no duplicates that have a common supplier. Also, do not include duplicate pairs such as (P1, P1).

```
SELECT 0
USE spj ALIAS spj1

SELECT 0
USE spj

JOIN WITH spj1 TO temp FOR s_no = spj1->s_no .AND. p_no > spj1->p_no ;
      FIELDS p_no, spj1->p_no

newname("temp.dbf", 2, "p_no1")

USE temp
SET UNIQUE ON

INDEX ON p_no1 + p_no TO p_no

LIST p_no1, p_no
```

Result:

```
  9     P1     P2
 57     P1     P2
 31     P1     P3
 34     P1     P4
 13     P1     P5
 25     P1     P6
 29     P2     P3
 32     P2     P4
 11     P2     P5
 21     P2     P6
  8     P3     P4
  1     P3     P5
 26     P3     P6
 49     P3     P7
 15     P4     P5
 27     P4     P6
 23     P5     P6
 56     P5     P7
```

The second condition on the JOIN command prevents pairs such as (P1, P1) from appearing in the destination database. It also prevents transposed pairs such as (P1, P2) and (P2, P1) from appearing by requiring the part code in the source database to be greater than the one in the alias database.

However, the JOIN command does not prevent duplicate pairs such as (P1, P2) and (P1, P2) from appearing. We handle this by creating the index with UNIQUE on.

Once again, we can improve the query's performance by ordering the database on P_NO within S_NO and using SOFTSEEK to do relative seeks. We guarantee uniqueness by saving the resulting pairs in an array, and only printing different ones. The following code does this:

```
SELECT 0
USE spj

PRIVATE already_seen[reccount()]              && assume worst case size
num_found = 0

INDEX ON s_no + p_no TO sp_no
SET SOFTSEEK ON

GOTO TOP
DO WHILE !eof()
        save_p_no = p_no
        save_s_no = s_no

        SEEK s_no + substr(p_no, 1, 3) + chr(asc(substr(p_no, 4, 1)) + 1)

        save_recno = recno()  && this is where we will start next time ...

        DO WHILE s_no = save_s_no .AND. !eof()

                IF ascan(already_seen, save_p_no + p_no, 1, num_found) = 0
                        ? save_p_no, p_no
                        num_found = num_found + 1
                        already_seen[num_found] = save_p_no + p_no
                ENDIF

                SEEK save_s_no + substr(p_no, 1, 3) + ;
                         chr(asc(substr(p_no, 4, 1)) + 1)
        ENDDO
        GOTO save_recno
ENDDO
```

9) Get the codes of suppliers providing part P1 in a quantity greater than the average shipment for a particular project.

```
SELECT 0
USE spj

LIST s_no FOR p_no = "P1" .AND. qty > avg(j_no)

FUNCTION avg

PARAMETERS job_no

PRIVATE save_sel, aver

        IF p_no != "P1"
                aver = 0
        ELSE
```

```
        save_sel = select()
        SELECT 0

        USE spj

        AVERAGE qty TO aver FOR p_no = "P1" .AND. j_no = job_no

        USE

        SELECT (save_sel)
    ENDIF

    RETURN (aver)
```

Result:

```
20    S05
```

Note that because of the way Clipper handles logical functions (see Chapter 2), the AVG user defined function is called regardless of whether p_no = P1. AVG therefore includes a test to avoid unnecessary calculations. A more efficient solution would be to use the SET FILTER command, as shown below:

```
SELECT 0
USE spj
SET FILTER TO p_no = "P1"

LIST s_no FOR qty > avg(j_no)

FUNCTION avg

PARAMETERS job_no
PRIVATE save_sel, aver

    save_sel = select()
    SELECT 0

    USE spj

    AVERAGE qty TO aver FOR p_no = "P1" .AND. j_no = job_no

    save_sel = str(save_sel)
    SELECT &save_sel

RETURN (aver)
```

Note that SET FILTER is "bound" to an area, not to a database (although executing a new USE in an area cancels any active SET FILTER). Therefore, we must include the p_no = "P1" condition in the AVERAGE command. Of course, we could issue another SET FILTER command instead.

We can improve this initial solution considerably. It calls the AVG function repeatedly with the same values. Look at the following fragment of the SPJ database showing all records containing J1:

```
 1   S01   P1   J1   200
 •
 •
 5   S02   P3   J1   200
 •
 •
11   S03   P3   J1   200
```

These records cause the AVG function to be called three times for this project. There are eight records containing J4, which would cause the function to be called eight times. Obviously, each call returns the same value. A better solution is to initially calculate the average shipments of P1 to each project, and save the values in an array, indexed by project code. Since project code is not a numeric field, we cannot use it directly as an index. However, assuming that a project code always consists of the letter "J" followed by digits (as it does in this database), we can extract an array subscript from the field by applying the function:

```
int(val(substr(j_no, 2)))
```

The following code builds the array.

```
SELECT 0
USE project

num_recs = reccount()
PRIVATE avgs[num_recs]

SELECT 0
USE spj          && in same area, don't need

FOR i = 1 TO num_recs
     GOTO TOP              && of spj

     AVERAGE qty TO aver FOR p_no = P1" .AND. j_no = project -> j_no
     avgs[int(val(substr(j_no, 2)))] = aver

     SKIP ALIAS project
NEXT
```

We would then recode the query as:

```
SELECT spj
GOTO top

LIST s_no FOR p_no = "P1" .AND. qty > avgs[int(val(substr(j_no, 2)))]
```

10) Get project codes for projects using at least one part available from supplier S1. Note that this supplier need not actually supply that part.

```
SELECT 0
USE spj ALIAS spj

SELECT 0
USE spj ALIAS spj1

LIST j_no FOR exists("SPJ", "spj1->p_no = p_no .AND. s_no = 'S01'")

FUNCTION exists

PARAMETERS sel_name, cond
PRIVATE save_sel, save_fnd

        save_sel = select()

        select &sel_name

        LOCATE FOR &cond

        save_fnd = found()

        SELECT (save_sel)

RETURN (save_fnd)
```

Result:

```
 1    J1
 2    J4
20    J4
```

This is a complex example worthy of study. The EXISTS function is very powerful. It uses a LOCATE to check for the existence of a record. If the database were indexed on the required key, we could have passed the index file name and done a SEEK. The ability to call a user defined function as a condition on a database operation is one of Clipper's outstanding features. It allows database operations with arbitrarily complex matching conditions.

To remove duplicates from the above query, we would recode it as:

```
SELECT 0
USE spj ALIAS spj

SELECT 0
USE spj ALIAS spj1

COPY TO temp FIELD j_no ;
        FOR exists("SPJ", "spj1->p_no = p_no .AND. s_no = 'S01'")

USE temp
SET UNIQUE ON
INDEX ON j_no TO j_no

LIST j_no

FUNCTION exists

PARAMETERS sel_name, cond
PRIVATE save_sel, save_fnd

        save_sel = select()

        SELECT &sel_name

        LOCATE FOR &cond

        save_fnd = found()

        SELECT (save_sel)

RETURN (save_fnd)
```

An alternative approach uses the array method to eliminate duplicates.

```
SELECT 0
USE project

PRIVATE j_nos[reccount()]

num_found = 0

USE spj ALIAS spj

SELECT 0
USE spj ALIAS spj1

DO WHILE !eof()

        IF exists("SPJ", "spj1->p_no = p_no .AND. s_no = 'S01'")

                IF ascan(j_nos, j_no, 1, num_found) = 0
```

```
                    ? j_no
                    num_found = num_found + 1
                    j_nos[num_found] = j_no
                ENDIF

        ENDIF
        SKIP

ENDDO

FUNCTION exists

PARAMETERS sel_name, cond
PRIVATE save_sel, save_fnd

        save_sel = select()

        SELECT &sel_name

        LOCATE FOR &cond

        save_fnd = found()

        SELECT (save_sel)

RETURN (save_fnd)
```

By studying this example, you will see that for each record in the SPJ database, it searches SPJ in a different area. A more efficient solution would be to find what parts are available from supplier S1, as in:

```
USE parts

PRIVATE p_nos[reccount()]
num_p_nos = 0

USE spj
INDEX ON s_no TO s_no

SEEK "S01"
DO WHILE s_no = "S01" .AND. !eof()

        IF ascan(p_nos, p_no, 1, num_p_nos) = 0

                num_p_nos = num_p_nos + 1
                p_nos[num_p_nos] = p_no

        ENDIF
        SKIP

ENDDO
```

Then, for each SPJ record having a part code in the array we just created, we print the project code.

```
SELECT 0
USE project

DECLARE j_nos[reccount()]
num_j_nos = 0

SELECT spj

GOTO TOP

DO WHILE !eof()

     IF ascan(p_nos, p_no, 1, num_p_nos) = 0

          IF ascan(j_nos ,  j_no, 1, num_j_nos) = 0

               ? j_no
               num_j_nos = num_j_nos + 1
               j_nos[num_j_nos] = j_no

          ENDIF

     ENDIF
     SKIP

ENDDO
```

11) Get project codes for projects not supplied with any red part by any London supplier.

```
SELECT 0
USE supplier
INDEX ON s_no TO s_no

SELECT 0
USE parts
INDEX ON p_no TO p_no

SELECT 0
USE spj

SET RELATION TO p_no INTO parts, ;
                TO s_no INTO supplier

SELECT 0
USE project

LIST j_no FOR !exists("spj", "project->j_no = j_no .AND. " + ;
                   "parts->color = 'RED' .AND. supplier->scity = 'LONDON'")
```

```
FUNCTION exists

PARAMETERS sel_name, cond
PRIVATE save_sel, save_fnd

        save_sel = select()
        SELECT &sel_name

        LOCATE FOR &cond

        save_fnd = found()

        SELECT (save_sel)

RETURN (save_fnd)
```

Result:

```
2     J2
5     J5
6     J6
8     J8
9     J9
```

In this solution, every record in the PROJECT database causes a sequential scan of the SPJ database. A more efficient solution would be to build an array of suppliers located in London who provide red parts, and then use it to determine whether one of them supplies a particular project. The following code shows this:

```
SELECT 0
USE supplier
PRIVATE s_nos[reccount()]
num_s_nos = 0

INDEX ON s_no TO s_no

SELECT 0
USE parts
INDEX ON p_no TO p_no

SELECT 0
USE spj

SET RELATION TO p_no INTO parts, ;
                         TO s_no INTO supplier

* find (unique) suppliers in London who supply a RED part
DO WHILE !eof()

        IF parts -> color = "RED" .AND. supplier -> scity = "LONDON"
```

```
            IF ascan(s_nos, s_no, 1, num_s_nos) = 0

                  num_s_nos = num_s_nos + 1
                  s_nos[num_s_nos] = s_no

            ENDIF

      ENDIF
      SKIP

ENDDO

SELECT spj
INDEX ON j_no TO j_no

SET SOFTSEEK ON

GOTO TOP

DO WHILE !eof()

      save_j_no = j_no
      good_j_no = .T.
      DO WHILE  j_no = save_j_no .AND. !eof() .AND.  good_j_no

            * is this a bad supplier?
            good_j_no = ascan(s_nos, s_no, 1, num_s_nos) = 0
            IF good_j_no
                  SKIP
            ENDIF

      ENDDO
      IF good_j_no
            ? save_j_no
      ENDIF

      * go to start of next set of j_nos
      SEEK substr(save_j_no, 1, 3) + chr(asc(substr(save_j_no, 4, 1))
      + 1)

ENDDO
```

Result:

```
J2
J5
J6
```

As you can see from the result, the solution does not show J8 and J9, as they are not yet supplied. To produce these two values, we must set a relation from the PROJECT database into the SPJ database and the required subset in the SPJ database. The following code shows this:

```
SELECT 0
USE supplier

DECLARE s_nos[reccount()]
num_s_nos = 0

INDEX ON s_no TO s_no

SELECT 0
USE parts
INDEX ON p_no TO p_no

SELECT 0
USE spj

SET RELATION TO p_no INTO parts, ;
                TO s_no INTO supplier

* find (unique) suppliers in London who supply a red part
DO WHILE !eof()

     IF parts -> color = "RED" .AND. supplier -> scity = "LONDON"

          IF ascan(s_nos, s_no, 1, num_s_nos) = 0

               num_s_nos = num_s_nos + 1
               s_nos[num_s_nos] = s_no

          ENDIF
     ENDIF
     SKIP

ENDDO

SELECT spj
INDEX ON j_no TO j_no

SELECT 0
USE project
SET RELATION TO j_no INTO spj

DO WHILE !eof()

     save_j_no = j_no
     good_j_no = .T.
     DO WHILE j_no = spj->j_no .AND. !spj -> (eof()) .AND. good_j_no

          * is this a bad supplier?
          good_j_no = ascan(s_nos, spj -> s_no, 1, num_s_nos) = 0
```

```
			IF good_j_no
				SKIP ALIAS spj
			ENDIF

		ENDDO

		IF good_j_no
			? j_no
		ENDIF

		SKIP
	ENDDO
```

12) Get the codes of projects supplied entirely by supplier S1.

```
	SELECT 0
	USE spj

	SELECT 0
	USE project

	LIST j_no FOR !exists("spj", "project- >j_no = j_no .AND. s_no != 'S01'") ;
			.AND. exists("spj", "project-> j_no = j_no")

	FUNCTION exists

	PARAMETERS sel_name, cond
	PRIVATE save_sel, save_fnd

		save_sel = select()
		SELECT &sel_name

		LOCATE FOR &cond

		save_fnd = found()

		SELECT (save_sel)

	RETURN (save_fnd)
```

Result: (nothing found)

No project satisfies this condition. Supplier S01 only supplies projects J1 and J4, and others also supply them.

This solution, albeit correct, is inefficient. For each record in the PROJECT database, it does two searches in the SPJ database. The first ensures that no other supplier supplies this project, the second that the result does not include projects not yet supplied. A better solution is to order the SPJ database by supplier code within project code, and use SOFTSEEK to sequentially search the database. The following code shows this:

```
SELECT 0
USE spj

INDEX ON j_no + s_no TO s_no

SET SOFTSEEK ON
GOTO TOP

DO WHILE !eof()

    save_j_no = j_no
    SEEK save_j_no + 'S01'

    IF found()
        * Now try to find same project with a different supplier
        SEEK save_j_no + substr(s_no, 1, 3) ;
            + chr(asc(substr(s_no, 4, 1)) + 1)
        IF j_no != save_j_no
            * Didn't find one, so this is a good project ...
            ? save_j_no
            * goto next project
            SEEK substr(save_j_no, 1, 3) + ;
                + chr(asc(substr(save_j_no, 4, 1)) + 1)
        ELSE
            SEEK substr(save_j_no, 1, 3) + ;
                + chr(asc(substr(save_j_no, 4, 1)) + 1)
        ENDIF
    ELSE   && it is not supplied by S01 .. go to next project
        SEEK substr(save_j_no, 1, 3) + ;
            + chr(asc(substr(save_j_no, 4, 1)) + 1)
    ENDIF

ENDDO
```

The reader should trace this code line by line to see how it works.

13) Delete all shipments for suppliers in London.

```
SELECT 0
USE supplier
INDEX ON s_no TO s_no

SELECT 0
USE spj
SET RELATION TO s_no INTO supplier

DELETE FOR supplier->scity = "LONDON"
```

Resulting database:

RECORD#	S_NO	P_NO	J_NO	QTY
1	S01	P1	J1	200
2	S01	P1	J4	700
3	S02	P3	J3	400
4	S02	P3	J2	200
5	S02	P3	J1	200
6	S02	P3	J4	600
7	S02	P3	J5	600
8	S02	P3	J6	400
9	S02	P3	J7	800
10	S02	P5	J2	100
11	S03	P3	J1	200
12	S03	P4	J2	500
13	S04	P6	J3	300
14	S04	P6	J7	300
15	S05	P2	J2	200
16	S05	P2	J4	100
17	S05	P5	J5	500
18	S05	P5	J7	100
19	S05	P6	J2	200
20	S05	P1	J4	1000
21	S05	P3	J4	1200
22	S05	P4	J4	800
23	S05	P5	J4	400
24	S05	P6	J4	500
25	S06	P4	J2	400
26	S02	P7	J7	100

14) Delete all projects with no shipments.

```
SELECT 0
USE spj

SELECT 0
USE project

DELETE FOR !exists("spj", "project->j_no = j_no")

FUNCTION exists

PARAMETERS sel_name, cond
PRIVATE save_sel, save_fnd

        save_sel = select()
        SELECT &sel_name

        LOCATE FOR &cond

        save_fnd = found()
        SELECT (save_sel)

RETURN (save_fnd)
```

Resulting database:

RECORD#	J_NO	JNAME	JCITY
1	J1	SORTER	PARIS
2	J2	PUNCH	ROME
3	J3	READER	ATHENS
4	J4	CONSOLE	ATHENS
5	J5	COLLATOR	LONDON
6	J6	TERMINAL	OSLO
7	J7	TAPE	LONDON
8	J8	REEL	ST.LOUIS
9	J9	CRT	DENVER

An elegant, more efficient alternative is to set a relation from the PROJECT database into the SPJ database. If there are no records in the SPJ database, then there are no shipments for the project. We can detect this by examining EOF on the child database. The following code does the job:

```
SELECT 0

USE spj

INDEX ON j_no TO j_no

SELECT 0
USE project

SET RELATION TO j_no INTO spj

DELETE FOR spj -> (eof())
```

15) Increase the quantity by 10 percent for all shipments by suppliers who provide a red part.

```
SELECT 0
USE supplier

SELECT 0
USE parts
INDEX ON p_no TO p_no

SELECT 0
USE spj
SET RELATION TO p_no INTO parts

DO WHILE !supplier -> (eof())

    LOCATE FOR s_no = supplier->s_no .AND. parts->color = "RED"

    IF found()
```

```
            REPLACE qty WITH qty * 1.1 FOR s_no = supplier->s_no
        ENDIF

        SKIP ALIAS supplier

    ENDDO
```

Resulting database:

```
 1  S01  P1  J1   220
 2  S01  P1  J4   770
 3  S02  P3  J3   400
 4  S02  P3  J2   200
 5  S02  P3  J1   200
 6  S02  P3  J4   600
 7  S02  P3  J5   600
 8  S02  P3  J6   400
 9  S02  P3  J7   800
10  S02  P5  J2   100
11  S03  P3  J1   220
12  S03  P4  J2   550
13  S04  P6  J3   330
14  S04  P6  J7   330
15  S05  P2  J2   220
16  S05  P2  J4   110
17  S05  P5  J5   550
18  S05  P5  J7   110
19  S05  P6  J2   220
20  S05  P1  J4  1100
21  S05  P3  J4  1320
22  S05  P4  J4   880
23  S05  P5  J4   440
24  S05  P6  J4   550
25  S06  P4  J2   440
26  S02  P7  J7   100
```

For every record in the supplier database, this routine issues a SEEK in the SPJ database, possibly followed by a global REPLACE statement. We can improve its performance substantially by first determining which suppliers supply a red part, and then scanning the database, updating the QTY field of all records containing a supplier code saved on the first pass. The following code shows this:

```
    SELECT 0
    USE supplier

    PRIVATE s_nos[reccount()]
    num_s_nos = 0
```

```
SELECT 0
USE parts
INDEX ON p_no TO p_no

SELECT 0
USE spj
SET RELATION TO p_no INTO parts

* first build array of suppliers who provide a red part
DO WHILE !eof()

	IF parts -> color = "RED"
		IF ascan(s_nos, s_no, 1, num_s_nos) = 0
			num_s_nos = num_s_nos + 1
			s_nos[num_s_nos] = s_no
		ENDIF
	ENDIF

	SKIP
ENDDO

GOTO TOP

* now re-process record by record ...

DO WHILE !eof()

	* if this supplier supplies a red part ...
	IF ascan(s_nos, s_no, 1, num_s_nos) != 0
		REPLACE qty WITH qty * 1.1
	ENDIF

	SKIP
ENDDO
```

16) Construct a database containing a list of part codes that are supplied either by a London supplier or to a London project.

```
SELECT 1		&& perform absolute select because Clipper does not
			&& assign an alias to a newly created database ..
CREATE temp
APPEND BLANK
REPLACE field_name WITH "p_no"
REPLACE field_type WITH "C"
REPLACE field_len  WITH 4
REPLACE field_dec  WITH 0

CREATE new_parts FROM temp

SELECT 0
```

```
USE parts

PRIVATE new_parts[reccount()]
num_new_parts = 0

SELECT 0
USE supplier
INDEX ON s_no TO s_no

SELECT 0
USE project
INDEX ON j_no TO j_no

SELECT 0
USE spj

SET RELATION TO s_no INTO supplier, TO j_no INTO project

DO WHILE ! EOF()

    IF project -> jcity = "LONDON" .OR. supplier -> scity = "LONDON"

        IF ascan(new_parts, p_no, 1, num_new_parts) = 0

            num_new_parts = num_new_parts + 1
            new_parts[num_new_parts] = p_no
            SELECT 1                    && new_parts
            APPEND BLANK
            REPLACE p_no WITH spj -> p_no

            SELECT spj

        ENDIF

    ENDIF

    SKIP

ENDDO
```

Result:

RECORD#	P_NO
1	P1
2	P3
3	P6
4	P5
5	P7
6	P4

If Clipper had an APPEND INTO <alias> command, we could simplify the code.

Hints and Warnings

- Use SELECT 0 to get the next unused area, then refer to it only by its alias.
- Use the alias functions such as spj -> (eof()) to avoid having to continually select different databases.
- When using the same database in more than one area, only do read operations. Although Clipper will not report an error if you try to write, the results are not guaranteed to be correct.
- Be sure you understand how and when to use SOFTSEEK. It provides relative seeking of records.
- Use SET ORDER when changing indexes rather than reissuing the USE or SET INDEX command. It maintains the index and database buffers. The other two do not.
- Question all JOINs in your program. See if you can write a custom routine that runs faster. You usually can except in the rare case in which JOIN is used without a scope or condition.
- Study the examples to see how to improve query performance. If you are having difficulty programming a query, see if a similar situation is solved in the examples and analyze its approach.

References

1. Date, C.J. *A Guide to DB2.* Reading, MA: Addison-Wesley, 1984.
2. Date, C.J. *An Introduction to Database Systems, Vol. I,* 4th ed. Reading, MA: Addison-Wesley, 1986.

9

Direct File Access

Clipper has functions for low level file and device access. You can use them to access any type of file, not just the types that are intrinsic to dBASE, such as databases and indexes. C programmers should already be familiar with the concepts behind these functions. Basically, they let you open any file and do anything you want to it (including destroy it). Since DOS treats devices such as printers and communication ports as files, you may also access them in the same way. This chapter describes the functions, extends them, and gives examples of their use in applications. The functions are in the extend.lib file. You must make it available to the linker when you use them.

Low-Level File and Device Access

Table 9-1. Clipper File Functions

FUNCTION NAME	PURPOSE
FCLOSE	Closes a file opened with FOPEN or FCREATE
FCREATE	Creates a new file and opens it
FERROR	Returns an error code set by a previous file operation
FOPEN	Opens a file
FREAD	Reads bytes from a file
FREADSTR	Reads a string from a file
FSEEK	Moves the file pointer
FWRITE	Writes bytes to a file

Table 9-1 lists the Clipper file functions. We will now describe them in detail.

- FCLOSE closes an open file. You should close files as soon as you are finished with them.
- FCREATE creates and opens a file. If a file by the given name already exists, all information in it is lost and a new file of length 0 is created. FCREATE returns a number called a *handle*. It identifies the file in later processing code. FCREATE takes two parameters. The first is the file name, the second its DOS attribute (a numeric). The attribute appears in the file's directory entry. It indicates what type the file is and what operations you may do on it.

  The Nantucket documentation defines the following attribute values:

  0 - read/write, the default value.

  1 - read-only.

2 - hidden, the file is invisible to standard DOS commands such as DIR.

4 - system, a relic from CP/M. It has no significance under DOS.

The values refer to specific bits of a byte that is simply passed to DOS. Some combinations are meaningful, such as the hidden bit and either the read-only or the read/write bit. Figure 9-1 shows the structure of the attribute byte.

Figure 9-1. File Attribute Byte

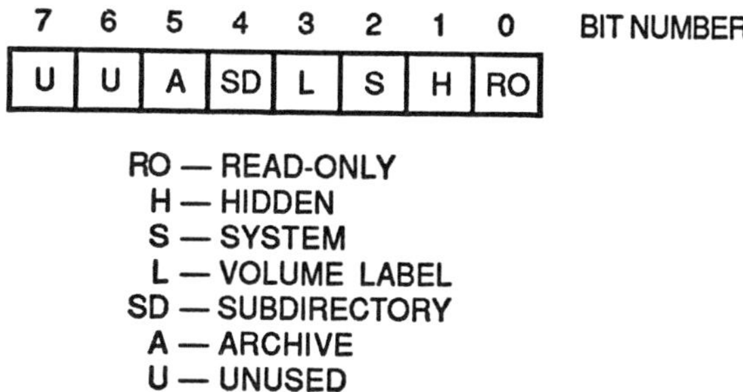

You might think that you could create a subdirectory by calling FCREATE with the subdirectory bit set. However, this is not the case. Subdirectory creation requires a different DOS call that Clipper does not provide. Setting the subdirectory bit on an FCREATE call will, in fact, cause the function to fail.

You can create a file as both read-only and hidden by adding the bit values to get 3. The usual way of combining bits is with a bitwise OR operation (| in C). Clipper does not allow bitwise OR but since every value is a single bit, an addition is equivalent. To create a file as both read-only and hidden, you would use the following code:

```
* define the attributes as pseudo-constants
CREAT_RD_ONLY = 1
CREAT_HIDDEN = 2

handle = fcreate("security", CREAT_RD_ONLY + CREAT_HIDDEN)
```

Now DOS commands such as DEL and DIR cannot see the file, but FOPEN can open it under program control. You can use this as a simple form of copy protection. When you install your application, create a hidden file. On loading, the application ensures that the file is present. If not, it refuses to load. Someone who copies your program cannot run it unless he or she understands hidden files. The file's presence must be detected by opening it - the FILE function will not find it if it is hidden. Refer to the DOS Technical Reference Manual for a thorough discussion of file attributes.

- FERROR returns 0 or a DOS error number after any other function is executed. Refer to the DOS Technical Reference Manual for a list of error codes and their meanings.
- FOPEN opens an existing file. It takes two parameters - the file name and the DOS open mode (a numeric). The following modes are defined (again, refer to the DOS manual for more details):

  0 - read-only, the default mode.

  1 - write-only.

  2 - read/write.

FOPEN returns a numeric, the DOS file handle. It identifies the file in subsequent processing.

Note the relationship between a file's attributes and the mode in which it is opened. The attribute setting is more permanent. It determines whether the open mode is valid. For example, if you try to open a file created with a read-only attribute, it will fail with any mode other than read-only. For an open file, the mode determines how you can access it. For example, a write will fail if the file was opened in read-only mode.

The Nantucket documentation states that files are opened in compatibility mode. This determines how other users may open them. Of course, it is only relevant on a network. You can change modes, although the documentation does not say so. Other users' rights are determined by the sharing mode (valid only in DOS 3.0 and later), which is part of the open mode. It occupies bits 4 through 6. They are zero in all values defined in this chapter, indicating compatibility mode. For more information on the values, refer to the DOS Technical Reference Manual.

- FREAD reads characters from a file into a character memory variable. It takes three parameters. The first, a numeric, is a file handle returned by a previous FCREATE or FOPEN. The second is a character memory variable, into which the file contents will go. You must pass it by reference. If you do not understand call by reference, refer to Chapter 2. The third parameter is the number of bytes to read. It is critical to check whether the variable is large enough to hold all requested bytes. If not, memory corruption will occur and the program will surely fail disastrously. Not assigning a large enough variable is probably the most common mistake made when using low-level I/O functions.

  One guaranteed approach is to use the length of the memory variable as the third parameter, as in:

  ```
  buffer = space(512)

  handle = fopen("file1.txt")  && open in read-only (default)
  .
  .
  .
  fread(handle, @buffer, len(buffer))
  ```

  FREAD returns the actual number of bytes read. If the read succeeded, it will be the number asked for, the third parameter. If the two numbers differ, it usually means that FREAD reached the end of file before reading all the bytes. Another possibility is a disk error. Programmers generally use a short count with no error (see the FERROR function) to detect end of file. We will show this later.

  FREAD reads all characters, including control characters and nulls. It does not stop reading after receiving a null.

- FREADSTR reads characters from a file. It differs from FREAD in two ways. First, it returns a string rather than taking one as a reference parameter. Second, it stops reading if it encounters a null (ASCII 0). FREADSTR returns a null string ("") if it encounters end of file. It takes two parameters, the file handle and the maximum number of characters to read.

- FSEEK moves the file pointer. Every read and write operation starts at the pointer. It is set to the beginning of a newly opened file, and it is advanced automatically following a read or write operation by the number of bytes transferred. You can use FSEEK to move the file pointer anywhere in the file.

It takes up to three parameters: the file handle, the number of bytes to move the pointer, and the seek mode. The mode defines the origin of the movement. It can have the following values:

0 - Beginning of file. The second parameter is an absolute position.

1 - Current pointer position. The second parameter is an offset. The file pointer is moved by this many bytes (positive or negative).

2 - End of file. The second parameter is an offset.

FSEEK returns the current file pointer.

When using the beginning of file (0) mode, remember that the first byte is at position 1, not zero.

Figure 9-2 shows how the file pointer moves after both an FREAD and an FSEEK function call.

Figure 9-2. File Pointer Movement

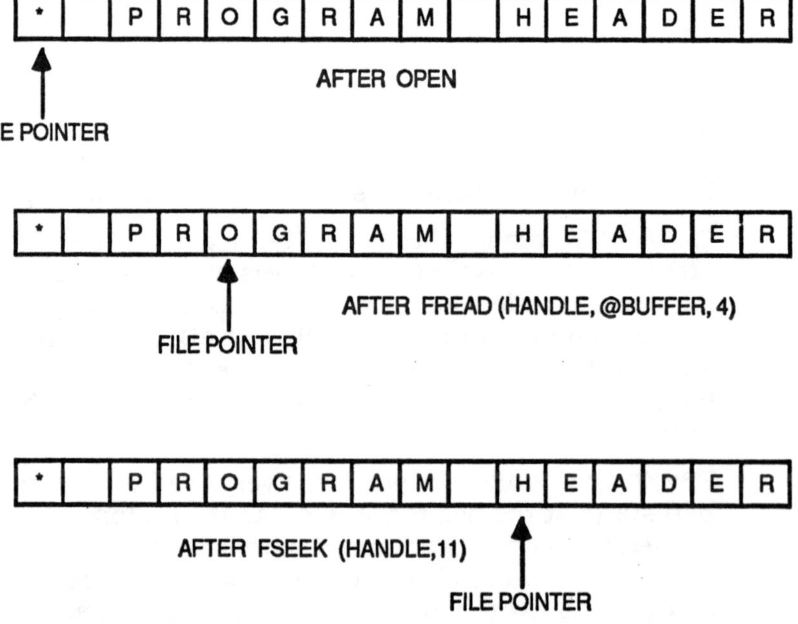

- FWRITE writes a character expression to a file. It takes three parameters: the file handle, the character expression, and the number of characters to write. If you omit the last parameter, FWRITE writes the entire string.

Clipper doesn't provide an FTELL function that returns the current file position. However, you can easily implement it by doing an FSEEK with 0 bytes and a seek mode of 1. Since FSEEK returns the current file position and no movement occurred, its return value is the required file position. The following function does this:

```
FUNCTION ftell

PARAM handle

RETURN fseek(handle, 0, 1)
```

The low-level file functions have many uses, since they provide complete control over all DOS files and devices. Previously, you could only get such control by programming in another language, such as C. Indeed, this was one of the main reasons programmers used C with Clipper. With the arrival of these functions, however, we recommend that you use them instead of C unless you need to do intricate, time consuming processing. A later section presents two file copy routines, one written in C, the other in Clipper. Our tests show them to be almost equivalent in performance.

We now present some practical uses of these functions.

File Copy

Program 9-1 copies a file.

Program 9-1. File Copy Using Low-Level Clipper I/O

```
SIZE = 512
buffer = space(SIZE)

ACCEPT "Source file: " TO source
ACCEPT "Target file: " TO target
?

* Try to open source file in read-only mode, the default
ifile = FOPEN(source)
```

```
IF ferror() != 0
        ? source, " could not be opened"
        QUIT
ENDIF

* Try to create output file with read/write attributes
ofile = FCREATE(target)

IF ferror() != 0
        ? target, " Could not be created"
        QUIT
ENDIF

num_read = fread(ifile, @buffer, SIZE)

* while read a buffer full ... (!eof())
DO WHILE num_read = SIZE

        fwrite(ofile, buffer, SIZE)
        num_read = fread(ifile, @buffer, SIZE)

ENDDO

* write final partial buffer
fwrite(ofile, buffer, num_read)

* finally, close the two files

fclose(ifile)
fclose(ofile)
```

The program detects an end of file by determining that not all the requested bytes were transferred. C programmers often use this technique, and Clipper programmers should also. The last write to the output file handles the smaller buffer by writing the same number of bytes that were read.

> **TIP**
>
> Detect end of file with FREAD by comparing the number of bytes read with the number requested.

The buffer's size is very important. It determines the speed of the routine. The larger the buffer, the faster it runs. Fewer calls are made to DOS, less disk head activity occurs as there are fewer reads and writes, and the loop executes fewer times. In the example, we used a buffer size of 512. This is the minimum size you should use. By changing the pseudo constant SIZE in Program 9-1, you can experiment with different sizes. Later in the chapter, we compare the speed of a C routine against the Clipper version for various buffer sizes.

File Security

A simple way of protecting a DBF file is to change its first byte. If someone tries to access it using dBASE, they will get only the message "Not a dBASE III file".

The first byte of every dBASE III file is either 03 if it has no memo fields, or 83 hex if it has some. Program 9-2 uses low level Clipper file functions to overwrite the first byte so that dBASE no longer recognizes the file.

Program 9-2. Simple File Protection Function

```
* Function writes FFh in the first byte of a .DBF file
* if it has no associated .DBT file and FEh if it has.
* If the bytes have already been written, it
* returns them to their proper values of 03h and 83h. If it
* finds unspecified values, it leaves them as is.

READ_WRITE = 2

FUNCTION protect

PARAMETERS fname
PRIVATE handle, firstbyte, putchar

        *Open the file and get DOS handle
        *Open file in read/write mode

        handle = fopen(fname, READ_WRITE)
        IF ferror() <> 0
                ? "Open file error, DOS error: ", ferror()
                RETURN .F.
        ENDIF

        * Read first byte from target file
        firstbyte = freadstr(handle, 1)
        IF ferror() <> 0
                ? "Read file error, DOS error: ", ferror()
                RETURN .F.
        ENDIF
```

```
        DO CASE
              CASE firstbyte = chr(255)  && protected file without DBT
                    putchar = chr(3)     && restore it to regular dbf

              CASE firstbyte = chr(254)  && protected file with DBT
                    putchar = chr(131)   && restore it to dbf with dbt

              CASE firstbyte = CHR(3)    && unprotected without DBT
                    putchar = chr(255)   && protect it

              CASE firstbyte = chr(131)  && unprotected with DBT
                    putchar = chr(254)   && protect it

              OTHERWISE                  && unrecognized, so complain
                    RETURN .F.
        ENDCASE

        * Move pointer to beginning of file
        fseek(handle, 0, 0)

        * Write new (un)protect character at beginning of file.
        fwrite(handle, putchar, 1)

        IF ferror() <> 0
              ? "Write file error, DOS error: ",FERROR()
              RETURN .F.
        ENDIF

        fclose(handle)
        IF ferror() <> 0
              ? "Close file error, DOS error: ", ferror()
              RETURN .F.
        ENDIF

RETURN .T.
```

Here is a sample call of Program 9-2:

```
CLEAR
ACCEPT "Filename " TO filename
protect(filename)
```

Note that the routine requires a complete file name. It does not add the DBF extension. The function returns .T. if it executed successfully, and .F. otherwise. You may want to remove the error display code when you link it into an application.

We chose the values used to protect the file (255 and 254) arbitrarily. They can be anything you like as long as they differ from the usual Clipper values.

In applications that require all database files to be unprotected initially and protected at termination, use the following skeleton:

```
* start of application, unprotect files
DO file_prot

•
•
•
•

* end of application, protect them
DO file_prot


PROCEDURE file_prot

      FOR each dbf ...

            protect(this dbf))

      NEXT

RETURN
```

File Size

Clipper's DISKSPACE function indicates how much space remains on disk. If your DBF file has no memo fields, you can also figure its size from (reccount() * recsize()) + header(). However, if it has memo fields, RECSIZE returns only 10 bytes for each. There is no built-in function to determine the combined size of the DBF and DBT file, or the size of another file, such as an index. The low level file functions, however, make it easy to write your own FILESIZE function. FSEEK moves the file pointer relative to the beginning of the file. Therefore, if you open a file, and use FSEEK to move the pointer to the end of file, the result is the file length. Program 9-3 uses this approach.

Program 9-3. Generalized File Size Function

```
ACCEPT "File: " TO filename
? filesize(filename)

SEEK_EOF = 2
```

```
FUNCTION filesize

PARAMETER fname
PRIVATE ret_val, handle

      handle = fopen(fname)
      IF FERROR() = 0
            ret_val = fseek(handle, 0, SEEK_EOF)
            fclose(handle)
      ELSE
            ? "File error, DOS error ", ferror()
            ret_val = -1
      ENDIF

      fclose(handle)
RETURN (ret_val)
```

To return the combined length of the DBF and DBT files, you must call Program 9-3 twice, once for each file. This routine also requires the full file name; it does not assume any extension. It returns a value of -1 if an error occurs. Again, you may want to remove the error display code in a real application.

Device Control

DOS defines the following handles:

0 - Standard input

1 - Standard output

2 - Standard error

3 - Standard AUX (COM1), unless re-assigned

4 - Standard PRN (LPT1), unless re-assigned

You can address the devices directly by using the handles. The first three are not of much use to Clipper programmers. Clipper does not do I/O through DOS, and using these handles directly causes conflict. However, you can access the serial and parallel devices directly. You can program printer escape sequences using FWRITE. You can also send data directly to the serial port. However, reading directly from the serial port is more difficult. If you ask for 20 bytes, for example, DOS will wait until 20 characters have been received, or a timeout occurs. Unfortunately, FREAD returns the number of characters requested, even if a timeout occurred. To be sure of getting a character, we must first read the port's status to see whether one is available. If so, the code can go ahead and read. If not, it must do something else, or reissue the read status command. Characters are thus processed one by one. The routine that checks status must be written in C or assembly language (see Chapter 11).

Reading Lines

Another useful function lacking in Clipper is one that reads a line from the input file. Luckily, we can easily write it (Program 9-4) using the FREAD function. FREADLN reads the input file a line at a time until it encounters a carriage return/line feed sequence or an end of file, or the maximum line length is exceeded. It returns a logical, indicating whether it encountered end of file. The function takes three parameters: a file handle, a buffer (must be passed by reference), and the maximum line length. The buffer must be large enough for the length.

Program 9-4. Read a Line from the Input File Unbuffered

```
FUNCTION freadln

PARAM handle, buffer, max_line
PRIVATE ch, line_size, num_read, save_pos

    ch = " "
    buffer = ""
    line_size = 0

    num_read = fread(handle, @ch, 1)

    DO WHILE num_read = 1 .AND. ch != chr(13) .AND. line_size < max_line

        buffer = buffer + ch
        line_size = line_size + 1

        num_read = fread(handle, @ch, 1)

    ENDDO

    * if we terminated on CR, skip (assumed) lf
    IF ch = chr(13)
        num_read = fread(handle, @ch, 1)
    ENDIF

RETURN num_read != 0          && If last read failed, eof
```

Program 9-4 assumes that a CR/LF pair terminates a line. Note that we initialize the memory variable ch to " ", not "". It must have a size of at least one, to give FREAD somewhere to place its value.

Using FREADLN, Program 9-5 lists a file with line numbers down the left side.

Program 9-5. Unbuffered File List Routine

```
* flist.prg

LINE_SIZE = 512
line = space(LINE_SIZE)

ACCEPT "File: " TO filename

* Try to open file in read-only mode ...

handle = fopen(filename)

IF ferror() != 0
        ? filename, " could not be opened"
        QUIT
ENDIF

line_num = 1

DO WHILE freadln(handle, @line, LINE_SIZE)

        ? str(line_num, 4)
        ?? "├" + substr(line, 1, 74)
        line_num= line_num + 1

ENDDO

* print last line
? str(line_num, 4)
?? "├ " + substr(line, 1, 74)
line_num= line_num + 1
```

Unfortunately, Program 9-5 is slow. Very slow, in fact. The reason is that it calls DOS for every character read. It does no buffering. As a first stage in improving its performance, we will implement a simple readahead buffer (Program 9-6). It reads the number of characters specified by the maximum line size parameter into a string. It then searches the string with the AT function to determine where the line ends.

Program 9-6. Buffered Line Reading Routine

```
FUNCTION freadln

PARAM handle, buffer, max_line
PRIVATE line, BUF_SIZE, eol, num_read, SEEK_BOF, save_pos

      * seek mode, absolute position
      SEEK_BOF = 0

      line = SPACE(max_line)
      buffer = ""

      * save current file position for later seek
      save_pos = ftell(handle)

      num_read = fread(handle, @line, max_line)

      eol = AT(chr(13), substr(line, 1, num_read))

      IF eol = 0
            buffer = line                   && line overflow or eof
      ELSE
            buffer = substr(line, 1, eol) && copy up to eol

            * now position file to next line (skip lf) ...
            fseek(handle, save_pos + eol + 1, SEEK_BOF)

      ENDIF

RETURN num_read != 0          && If last read didn't succeed, eof
```

The flist code remains the same, except that the last line need not be printed separately. The main loop can handle it because of the readahead. In the single character version, there would still be characters in the buffer when the read failed; they must be flushed.

> **NOTE**
>
> Reading characters one at a time is slow. You must implement a simple buffer to speed things up.

We can improve this program further. After the readahead, the file pointer is at the start of the next line. The next read starts there. However, as many as several lines may already be in the buffer. Program 9-6 does not take advantage of this. The next section describes a general purpose buffering system that does.

General-Purpose Read Buffering

Program 9-6 uses a special purpose buffering scheme to improve the performance of line reading. This section develops a more general read-buffering system that allows for many files, and for reads of any size. The latter feature is very important. It allows character by character processing, but buffers the underlying reads, giving performance similar to routines that do their own buffering (such as the FCOPY and FREADLN routines we already presented).

The system includes the following functions:

1) **BINIT.** Its parameters are the number of files and the buffer size. It is the initialization code. It must be called before any other functions are used. It allocates structures needed for read buffering. The number of files parameter specifies the maximum number of files to be buffered. The buffer size parameter specifies the amount of memory to allocate to each buffer.

2) **BEOF.** Its parameter is a file handle. It returns end of file status.

3) **BEND.** It has no parameters. It is the inverse of BINIT. It should be called when the buffering system is no longer required. It releases the memory allocated by BINIT.

4) **BOPEN.** Its parameters are a file spec and an open mode. Use it in place of FOPEN when you are using buffering. It sets up the buffer structures needed for the file. Like FOPEN, it returns a file handle.

5) **BCLOSE.** Its parameter is a file handle. It replaces FCLOSE when you are using buffering. It releases the buffer space used by the file handle.

6) **BREAD.** Its parameters are a buffer to receive data (passed by reference), and the size to read. It returns the actual number of bytes read. It replaces FREAD when you are using buffering.

The functions BREAD, BOPEN, and BCLOSE (Program 9-7) emulate the Clipper functions FREAD, FCLOSE, and FOPEN.

Program 9-7. General-Purpose Buffered I/O Routines

```
***
* bfiles.prg
*
* Buffered I/O for Clipper files
*
*
* First call BINIT with the number of files to buffer, and the size of
* each buffer. Call BEND when finished to release memory. BOPEN opens
* a file in buffered mode, BCLOSE closes it. BREAD reads from it.

***
* binit(num_handles, buffer_size)
*
*       Initialize buffering system, return .T. for success,
*       .F. for failure
*

FUNCTION binit

PARAM num_handles, buffer_size

PUBLIC buffers[num_handles]
PUBLIC BUFF_SIZE
PUBLIC next_char[num_handles]
PUBLIC num_in_buff[num_handles]
PUBLIC more_to_read[num_handles]
PUBLIC handles[num_handles]

        BUFF_SIZE = buffer_size
        afill(handles, 0)

RETURN .T.

***
*  Return end of file status for this file
*

FUNCTION beof

PARAM handle
PRIVATE buff_no

        buff_no = ascan(handles, handle)

RETURN !more_to_read[buff_no] .AND. ;
          next_char[buff_no] = num_in_buff[buff_no] + 1

***
* bend()
```

```
*
*       Terminate the buffering system.

FUNCTION bend

        RELEASE buffers
        RELEASE BUFF_SIZE
        RELEASE next_char
        RELEASE num_in_buff
        RELEASE more_to_read
        RELEASE handles

RETURN .T.

***
* bopen(file_spec, open_mode)
*
*       Open file_spec with open_mode. Return file handle. -1 if error.
*

FUNCTION bopen

PARAM file_spec, open_mode
PRIVATE handle, buff_no

        handle = fopen(file_spec, open_mode)

        IF handle != (-1)

                * allocate a buffer number for it ...
                buff_no = ascan(handles, 0)

                IF buff_no != 0

                        * set up structure

                        handles[buff_no] = handle
                        buffers[buff_no] = space(BUFF_SIZE)
                        next_char[buff_no] = 1
                        num_in_buff[buff_no] = 0
                        more_to_read[buff_no] = .T.

                ELSE

                        * no room for buffer, so close file and return -1

                        fclose(handle)
                        handle = -1

                ENDIF
        ENDIF
```

```
RETURN handle

***
* bclose(handle)
*
*       Close handle.

FUNCTION bclose

PARAM handle
PRIVATE buff_no

        buff_no = ascan(handles, handle)

        buffers  [buff_no] = .T.       && cannot release
                                       && array elements
        handles[buff_no] = 0
        fclose(handle)

RETURN .T.

***
* bread(handle, buffer, size)
*
*       Buffered read from handle for size bytes. Buffer must be passed by
*       reference. Returns number of bytes read.
*

FUNCTION bread

PARAM handle, buffer, size
PRIVATE remain, tbuffer, buff_no

        buff_no = ascan(handles, handle)
        tbuffer = space(BUFF_SIZE)

        * Can the entire read be satisfied from the buffer?
        remain = num_in_buff[buff_no] - next_char[buff_no] + 1

        IF remain >= size
                * yes, it can, so simply return it

                buffer = substr(buffers[buff_no], next_char[buff_no], size)
                next_char[buff_no] = next_char[buff_no] + size

        ELSE
                * no, it can't, so get what is required from this buffer, then
                * refill repeatedly until bread is satisfied
                IF remain > 0
                        buffer = substr(buffers[buff_no], next_char[buff_no], remain)
                        size = size - remain
                        next_char[buff_no] = next_char[buff_no] + remain
                ELSE
```

```
            buffer = ""
        ENDIF

        DO WHILE size > 0 .AND. more_to_read[buff_no]
            * refill buffer, or best we can ...
            num_in_buff[buff_no] = fread(handle, @tbuffer, BUFF_SIZE)
            buffers[buff_no] = tbuffer
            more_to_read[buff_no] = IIF(num_in_buff[buff_no] = BUFF_SIZE,;
                                                   .T.,.F.)

            * can it now be satisfied from buffer?
            IF size <= num_in_buff[buff_no]
                * yes, so finish off ...

                buffer = buffer + substr(buffers[buff_no], 1, size)
                next_char[buff_no] = size + 1
                size = 0
            ELSE
                buffer = buffer + substr(buffers[buff_no], 1, ;
                                                  num_in_buff[buff_no])
                next_char[buff_no] = num_in_buff[buff_no] + 1
                size = size - num_in_buff[buff_no]
            ENDIF
        ENDDO
    ENDIF

RETURN len(buffer)
```

Program 9-7 maintains the following data for each open file:

1) buffers
2) next_char (an offset into the buffer)
3) num_in_buff
4) more_to_read, a logical indicating whether there is more to read from the file

The handles array maps a file handle onto a buffer number. We cannot use handles directly since they may not be consecutive (databases and indexes use a file handle), and they do not start at 1.

Program 9-8 uses the buffering routines to dump the contents of a file on the screen. It displays the contents in both hex and ASCII.

Program 9-8. Buffered Dump Utility

```
************
*
* Program....: CLIPDUMP
* Filename...: CLIPDUMP.PRG
* Author......: Jon P. Rognerud
* Date..........: 01/23/88
* Purpose.....: Dump a file in hex and ASCII to the standard output
*                       device.
*
*               Usage:  CLIPDUMP <file.ext>
*               Compile: Clipper, Summer '87
*               Link:  LINK clipdump bfiles,,,clipper extend
*
*
************

PARAMETERS fname

IF type("fname") == "U"
        ? "CLIPDUMP: No filename given."
        ?
        QUIT
ENDIF

* initialize buffering system for 1 buffer, 2K
binit(1, 2048)

* try to open a file read-only, return handle
fhandle = bopen(fname, 0)

IF ferror() != 0
        ? "CLIPDUMP: Open error on file " + fname + " DOS error", FERROR()
        ERRORLEVEL (1)          && set new errorlevel (optional)
        QUIT
ENDIF

size = 16
buffer = SPACE(size)            && initialize buffer

? "Clipper Binary File Dump Utility, Version 1.0"
? "Written By Jon P. Rognerud, Copyright (c) 1988."
?
? SPACE(15) + "Dump of file", UPPER(fname)
?
?

fline = 0
```

```
status = bread(fhandle, @buffer, size)

DO WHILE status != 0

        DUMPCHARS(fline,buffer)
        status = bread(fhandle, @buffer, size)
        fline = fline + size

ENDDO

bclose(fhandle)

* terminate buffer system
bend()

***
* dumpchars
***

FUNCTION DUMPCHARS
PARAMETERS frec, buff

PRIVATE frec, buff, byte
PRIVATE local_char[size]

        @ ROW(),COL() SAY transform(frec,"####") + ":"

        col = 6
        FOR n = 1 to size
                byte = substr(buff,n,1)
                @ ROW(), col SAY dec2hex(asc(byte))
                local_char[n] = byte
                col = col + 3           && a space
        NEXT

        @ ROW(),COL() SAY space(5)

        FOR n = 1 to size

                * if not printable, show .

                IF (ASC(local_char[n]) < 32 .OR. ASC(local_char[n]) > 126)
                        local_char[n] = '.'
                ENDIF

                @ ROW(),COL() SAY local_char[n]

        NEXT
        ?
RETURN ("")

* Handles numbers from 0-255 (in hex) only
```

```
FUNCTION DEC2HEX
PARAMETERS decnum

PRIVATE hexnum, remainder, answer

        remainder = INT(decnum % 16)
        answer = INT(decnum / 16)
        t = SUBSTR("0123456789ABCDEF", remainder+1, 1)
        hexnum = t
        again = .T.

        DO WHILE again

                remainder = INT(answer % 16)
                answer = INT(answer / 16)
                t = SUBSTR("0123456789ABCDEF", remainder+1, 1)
                hexnum = t + hexnum
                again = .F.

        ENDDO

RETURN (hexnum)

* EOF: CLIPDUMP.PRG
```

We suggest you use Program 9-7 instead of your own specialized buffering routines. You can easily extend it to incorporate versions of FSEEK and FWRITE.

Searching Files

To search through a file, you can use a buffered FREADLN to retrieve lines, and the AT function to search the lines. Program 9-9 searches the file specified by the handle from the current position for the specified string. It returns the first line in which it found the string, or a null string indicating a failure.

Program 9-9. Search for a String

```
FUNCTION fsearch

PARAM handle, string
PRIVATE line, LINE_SIZE, found_yet, read_ok

        LINE_SIZE = 512
```

```
          line = space(LINE_SIZE)

          found_yet = .F.
          read_ok = .T.
          DO WHILE !found_yet .AND. read_ok

                read_ok = freadln(handle, @line, LINE_SIZE)
                IF read_ok
                      found_yet = AT(string, line) != 0
                ENDIF
          ENDDO

    RETURN IIF(found_yet, line, "")
```

Note that we cannot write the WHILE loop as:

```
DO WHILE !found_yet .AND. freadln(handle, @line, LINE_SIZE)
```

because Clipper evaluates the entire WHILE condition even when an early term settles the outcome (see Chapter 2). Here, when a string is found, found_yet is set to .T.. When the condition is re-evaluated, FREADLN re-executes (unnecessarily), and the line variable we required is overwritten with the new line.

The following sample routine drives Program 9-9:

```
ACCEPT "File to search:            " TO file_name
ACCEPT "String to search for : " TO search_for

handle = fopen(file_name)
IF handle = -1

      ? "Error opening ", file_name
      QUIT

ENDIF

line = fsearch(handle, search_for)

IF line == ""
      ? "Not found"
ELSE
      ? line
ENDIF
```

If it finds the string, it displays the line that contains it. Otherwise, it displays the message "Not found".

To show all occurrences of the chosen string, we would change the driver routine to:

```
ACCEPT "File to search:              " TO file_name
ACCEPT "String to search for : " TO search_for

handle = fopen(file_name)
IF handle = -1

        ? "Error opening ", file_name
        QUIT

ENDIF

line = fsearch(handle, search_for)

num_found = 0
DO WHILE "" != line
        num_found = num_found + 1
        ? line
        line = fsearch(handle, search_for)
ENDDO

?
? str(num_found, 4), " Occurrences of ", search_for, " found"
```

This works since the FSEARCH function starts from the current position. To show the line numbers as well as the line, change the driver to:

```
ACCEPT "File to search:              " TO file_name
ACCEPT "String to search for : " TO search_for

handle = fopen(file_name)
IF handle = -1

        ? "Error opening ", file_name
        QUIT

ENDIF

line_no = 0
line = fsearch(handle, search_for)

num_found = 0
DO WHILE "" != line
        num_found = num_found + 1
        ? str(line_no, 4)
        ?? line
        line = fsearch(handle, search_for)
ENDDO
?
? str(num_found, 4), " Occurrences of ", search_for, " found"
```

Then in the FREADLN routine, increment line_no.

A simple change allows the routine to search any number of files. Instead of reading just a file name, it now reads a file spec which may contain the wildcard characters ? and *. Specifying *.prg would then cause all prg files to be searched. The following is the driver code.

```
ACCEPT "File spec to search: " TO file_spec
ACCEPT "String to search for: " TO search_for

* load target files into an array
num_files = adir(file_spec)
PRIVATE fnames[num_files]
adir(file_spec, fnames)

* now search each file
FOR i = 1 TO num_files

    handle = fopen(fnames[i])
    IF handle = -1

        ? "Error opening ", fnames[i]
        QUIT

    ENDIF

    ? fnames[i]
    line_no = 0
    line = fsearch(handle, search_for)

    * find every occurrence
    num_found = 0
    DO WHILE "" != line
        num_found = num_found + 1
        ? str(line_no, 4)
        ?? line
        line = fsearch(handle, search_for)
    ENDDO

    ?
    ? str(num_found, 4), " Occurrences of ", search_for, " found"

    fclose(handle)          && make sure we close it so we don't
                            && run out of file handles

NEXT
```

We need not change either FREADLN or FSEARCH. This routine can search all source files for a given string, such as a procedure definition or a function call.

Comparison to C

Table 9-2 shows the relationships between C functions and the new Clipper functions:

Table 9-2. Clipper and C Function Relationships

Clipper	C
fcreate	creat
fopen	open
fread	read
freadstr	
fclose	close
fseek	seek
fwrite	write

These C functions are the level 1 functions. They are most like the Clipper functions. We discuss the level 2 functions later.

There are differences in the parameters for the create and open routines. C's open function supports modes not implemented in the Clipper FOPEN function. For example, Clipper has no equivalent of C's text mode which translates between internal carriage returns and external carriage return/line feed pairs. Clipper's input works like C's binary mode. The C open function allows a file to be created, whereas Clipper's does not. When this is specified in the open mode flag, an extra parameter is passed that specifies the file's attribute. This is what is passed to the CREAT function.

We can emulate the other open modes that C supports by performing an FSEEK immediately after the open.

If you are familiar with C, you will know that it also offers functions with the same names as the Clipper functions. They are called the level 2 I/O functions. The C routine FREAD, for example, does buffered, formatted I/O. An extra parameter gives the number of elements of a given size to return. However, the level 2 functions are difficult to use for most purposes. Programmers usually prefer the level 1 functions. The one advantage of the level 2 functions is buffering. The C library routines do readahead buffering for level 2, but not for level 1. If the programmer does not perform his or her own buffering for level 1 files, byte by byte processing of level 2 files is faster. A simple level 1 buffering system, however, will produce much faster results. A major reason why the Summer '87 version compiles so much faster is the change from level 2 to level 1 functions with a simple buffer.

So, the Clipper functions are equivalent to level 1 C functions, even though they have the same names as level 2 C functions. To further complicate matters, C code used with Clipper may still use the level 2 functions, even though the names are the same as the Clipper functions. This is because the Microsoft C 5.00 compiler adds an underscore ahead of global variables or routines that the code accesses. If the application uses FREAD in its Clipper code and FREAD in its C code, at run time there will be both an FREAD symbol and an _FREAD symbol. Examining the map file after a link will confirm this. Refer to Chapter 11 for more details.

To compare the speed of Clipper's and C's level 1 I/O system, we use Program 9-10, a file copy routine, equivalent in function to the Clipper version.

Program 9-10. C File Copy

```
/***
* FCOPY1.C
*/

#include "stdio.h"
#include "stdlib.h"

#include "fcntl.h"

#include "\mc\include\sys\types.h"
#include "\mc\include\sys\stat.h"

#include "io.h"

#define BUF_SIZE 32768

main(argc, argv)

int argc;
char *argv[];

{
        int ihandle, ohandle;

        unsigned num_read;
        char *buffer;

        buffer = malloc(BUF_SIZE);

        if ((ihandle = open(argv[1], O_RDONLY | O_BINARY)) == -1)
```

```
    {
        printf("Error opening file %s\n", argv[1]);
        exit(1);
    }

    if ((ohandle = open(argv[2], O_CREAT | O_RDWR | O_BINARY,
            S_IREAD | S_IWRITE)) == -1)
    {
        printf("Error creating file %s\n", argv[2]);
        exit(1);
    }

    while ((num_read = read(ihandle, buffer, BUF_SIZE)) == BUF_SIZE)

        write(ohandle, buffer, BUF_SIZE);

    write(ohandle, buffer, num_read);

    close(ihandle);
    close(ohandle);
}
```

Table 9-3 shows our results from copying a 500K file.

Table 9-3. Execution Times for Clipper and C Copy Routines (500K File, in Seconds)

Buffer Size	Clipper (Program 9-1)	C (Program 9-10)
512	1:12	1:03
1024 (1K)	39	35
4096 (4K)	13	13
16384 (16K)	10	8

As you can see, there is little difference between the versions. We therefore recommend that you use the Clipper functions for convenience. If you need to do a lot of data processing, however, C may be the better choice.

Hints and Warnings

- Buffer all I/O. The larger the buffer, the better. The general purpose routines presented allow character by character processing with transparent buffering. This gives the speed of a special purpose buffering system, but the flexibility of direct DOS calls. Extend the routines to allow writing (BWRITE) and seeking (BSEEK).

- Use pseudo constants to define the buffer size, open modes, and other standard parameters.
- If you must import data from a foreign source and it is not available in SDF or DELIMITED format, use the file I/O functions to convert it.
- Remember that FREAD requires its parameter to be passed by reference. Failing to do this is probably the most common mistake made when using low level I/O.
- Use Clipper's low level I/O functions rather than C's when you do not need to do much processing.

10

Networking

Clipper's Autumn '86 release was the first one to support local area networks. It provided commands and functions for sharing files and networked printers. Programmers new to local area networks are often overwhelmed at the prospect of writing network applications. Don't be. To gain familiarity and confidence with a network, first convert an application to use files on a server in single user mode. As you gain confidence, use this chapter to identify parts of your program that require special attention on a network. Then approach them one at a time.

Clipper and Local Area Networks

Before proceeding, we must define two terms:

- A *server* is a networked computer that lets other computers access its files and peripherals.
- A *client* is a networked computer that does not let others share its files and peripherals, but uses those provided by a server.

Different networks allow different combinations of servers and clients. Some require a dedicated server, whereas others allow the server to be a client as well (*non-dedicated server*). Some allow only one server, others allow several.

Clipper does not address the idiosyncrasies of different networks. It simply uses the functions in MS-DOS 3.1 (or later) to implement network commands. If a particular network does not support those commands, Clipper does not run on it. Fortunately, most do.

Unlike dBASE, Clipper does not require software to be installed on the server. A Clipper compiled application simply runs on the client, relying on the operating system to direct file and peripheral accesses. Typically, the same application will run on all clients attached to the network, but this is not mandatory. Clipper shares files and peripherals in a "well behaved" way, and should coexist with any other network application, including another Clipper application running on another client.

To show how Clipper works with a network, consider the implementation of an INDEX ON command for a database resident on a server. The remote database is first USEd according to the file naming conventions specified by the network vendor. The INDEX ON command is then executed. It reads every record in the database and creates the index file. When the database file resides on a server, every record is transferred from server to client, and every index page is transferred back from client to server. Obviously, this is time consuming, and the programmer must minimize the number of database wide commands. The difference in execution speed between an operation performed on a server database and one performed on a local database is significant.

Any command that applies to a single-user database also applies to one residing on a server. Clipper imposes certain requirements that we discuss later in this chapter.

Network Programming Problems

The fact that more than one user can access a file simultaneously causes programming problems that do not occur on a single user system. Two common ones are:

- Lost update.

  Without concern for syntax, assume the following pieces of code are running on two networked computers. The file they are both using (file1) resides on the server:

COMPUTER A	COMPUTER B
USE z:file1	USE z:file1
REPLACE field1 WITH field1 - 10	REPLACE field1 WITH field1 - 5

  Assuming that field1's initial value is 100, what is its value after both programs run? There are three possible results. Consider how REPLACE works. It first reads the value of field1 from the database, modifies it, and then writes it back. The results depend on the sequencing of the commands.

  - If one machine finishes its REPLACE command before the other begins, the result will be 85 (100 - 15).
  - If computer A reads field1, then computer B performs its entire REPLACE operation before A writes its result, the answer will be 90. Computer B's update is simply lost.
  - Similarly, if computer B reads field1, then computer A performs its entire update operation before B writes its results, the answer will be 95. Computer A's update is lost.

- Inconsistent analysis.

  Again, study the following two pieces of code:

COMPUTER A	COMPUTER B
USE z:file1	USE z:file1
GOTO 10 REPLACE field1 WITH field1 - 10	TOTAL field1 TO mfield1

The result depends on whether computer A executes the REPLACE statement before computer B processes record 10.

These problems arise because data accesses are not synchronized. Although we know the order of execution of each computer's instructions, we do not know which one's will execute first. Just looking at the shared data accesses, for example, does not let us determine the order in which they will occur.

When analyzing network programs, you should take the worst case approach. Assume the worst possible timing of instructions and guard against it. Only in this way can you assure that your application will work under any circumstances.

We refer to the two problems just described throughout this chapter. It is essential that the reader understand them thoroughly.

> **NOTE**
>
> Inconsistent analysis and lost updates can occur in network programs if data accesses are not synchronized.

Clipper Network Commands

To solve these problems, the programmer must control the data to be shared. He or she can either open the file in a mode that provides exclusive access, or, working in a shared mode, use a lock function to provide for exclusive access temporarily.

Opening Files

There are two ways to open a file in exclusive mode. Either issue the SET EXCLUSIVE ON command before issuing the USE, or add the EXCLUSIVE option to the USE. The SET EXCLUSIVE command determines how USE will open database files subsequently. SET EXCLUSIVE ON means that only one user can open the file - he or she has EXCLUSIVE use of it. Other users' attempts to open the file will fail. The EXCLUSIVE option of the USE command only affects a particular USE, and only is meaningful if SET EXCLUSIVE is off.

The default mode of SET EXCLUSIVE is on. To open a file in shared mode, issue a SET EXCLUSIVE OFF command.

The way you refer to a file on the server varies among networks. For IBM Token-Ring, you issue a NET USE command either from the command line or from the menus, and associate a drive letter with a server directory. When you later refer to a file on that drive, the network operating system recognizes it as a server file, and redirects the reference.

If the directory on our server is drive z, then a USE command such as:

```
USE z:test1
```

will use server database test1.

The following example illustrates open modes:

```
* open telefon in exclusive mode
SELECT 0
USE z:telefon

SET EXCLUSIVE OFF

* open wakeups in shared mode
SELECT 0
USE z:wakeups

* open calls in exclusive mode
SELECT 0
USE z:calls EXCLUSIVE
```

To test your network application in single user mode, simply USE the files on the server with SET EXCLUSIVE off. The program will work just as it would if the files were local.

> Network databases can be opened in either SHARED or EXCLUSIVE mode.

NETERR

If one user tries to open a file that another already has open in EXCLUSIVE mode, his or her USE will fail. The same thing happens if one user tries to open a file in EXCLUSIVE mode that someone else has open in shared mode. Since USE does not return any indication of whether it succeeded, a new function, NETERR, is provided. It returns .T. or .F. according to the status of the previous USE or APPEND BLANK command. A .T. value indicates that the command failed, an .F. that it succeeded. We should then rewrite our code as:

```
* open telefon in exclusive mode
SELECT 0
USE z:telefon
IF neterr()
        ? "open telefon failed, leaving"
        quit
ENDIF

SET EXCLUSIVE OFF

* open wakeups in shared mode
SELECT 0
USE z:wakeups

IF neterr()
        ? "open wakeups failed, leaving"
        quit
ENDIF

* open calls in exclusive mode
SELECT 0
USE z:calls EXCLUSIVE

IF neterr()
        ? "open calls failed, leaving"
        quit
ENDIF
```

Of course, simply terminating the program when it detects a USE error is rarely the correct action. We discuss error handling later in this chapter.

The value returned by NETERR is reset only after another USE, or APPEND BLANK command. It is initially .F..

Appending

Like USE, APPEND BLANK may also fail when applied to a shared file. Someone else may be trying an APPEND BLANK at the same time, or may have the file locked. Since APPEND BLANK does not return anything, we use NETERR to determine whether it succeeded. A .F. value indicates success, a .T. value indicates an error.

Note that Clipper, unlike other dBASE language products, does not require a file lock to be in effect for APPEND BLANK.

After a successful APPEND BLANK, the record is locked.

> The NETERR function checks whether a database USE or APPEND BLANK succeeded.

Locking

For a shared database, we can use the lock functions to provide exclusive access temporarily. The functions are:

- RLOCK tries to lock the current record in the file open in the currently selected area. It returns .T. or .F., depending on whether the lock succeeds. If it succeeds, it prevents others from locking the record. However, it does not stop them from locking another record in the same file.

  An RLOCK will fail if someone else has either the record or the file locked.

- FLOCK tries to lock the entire file in the currently selected area. It returns .T. or .F., depending on whether the lock succeeds. If it succeeds, it prevents others from locking the file or any record in it. It does not stop others from reading the file, just from locking and therefore writing.

  FLOCK fails if another user has a record locked in the file, or has the file locked.

- UNLOCK [ALL] releases the file or record lock in the currently selected work area. The ALL option releases all current locks in all work areas. The UNLOCK and UNLOCK ALL commands remove only locks placed by the current user.

Once issued, a lock remains in effect until its owner issues one of the following commands:

- UNLOCK in the locked area, or UNLOCK ALL.
- USE in the locked area.
- RLOCK on a different record in the same file.

or the program terminates.

The lock functions thus allow a file to be locked in each area, but only allow one record to be locked per file. When you try to RLOCK a record, any previously existing record lock in the file is first released. Thus, the old record lock is lost, regardless of whether the new one succeeds.

RULES

- RLOCK locks the current record, but others can still read it.
- FLOCK locks the currently selected file, but others can still read it.

Naming

In some networks, each station has a unique user name. This is the case with IBM's Token-Ring. The Clipper function NETNAME returns the name of the station on which the program is running. We use it in an electronic mail system developed later in this chapter.

Printing

The SET PRINTER TO <destination> command specifies where subsequent printer output goes. <destination> can either be a network device name, or a file name. If it is not specified, the print spool file is emptied, and the default destination is reset.

Clipper Enforced Rules

Clipper imposes networking rules. To execute a command that writes to a shared database, either the entire file or the destination record must be locked, or the file must be open in exclusive mode. Table 10-1 shows the commands and their requirements.

RULE

To write to a shared database, you must have the record or file locked.

Table 10-1. Locking Requirements

COMMAND	MINIMUM REQUIREMENT
APPEND FROM	FLOCK
REPLACE <single record>	RLOCK
REPLACE <multiple records>	FLOCK
DELETE <single record>	RLOCK
DELETE <multiple records>	FLOCK
RECALL <single record>	RLOCK
RECALL <multiple records>	FLOCK
GET <fieldname>	RLOCK
UPDATE ON	FLOCK

If you violate the rules, Clipper objects with a sullen "System error not locked" message. The specified requirement is only a minimum. A command that requires a RLOCK will also work if the file is FLOCKed or open in EXCLUSIVE mode. Clipper thus has a locking hierarchy, as described in Table 10-2.

Clipper also requires a database to be open in exclusive mode to execute the following commands:

```
PACK
REINDEX
ZAP
```

If it is not, Clipper will report "System error not exclusive".

The combination of these rules, and the protocol enforced by the locking commands, ensure that only one user at a time (the lock's owner) may write to the database. They do allow many users to read at one time, even though someone may have the database locked (the only way to prevent this is to open the database in exclusive mode).

TABLE 10-2. Locking Hierarchy

COMMAND	YOU CAN	OTHERS CAN	REQUIREMENTS
OPEN - EXCLUSIVE	Do anything	Not open file	File cannot be open in either mode
FLOCK	Do anything except PACK, REINDEX, ZAP	Not RLOCK any record in file or FLOCK it. Cannot write therefore but can still read	No one else can have an RLOCK in file or have it FLOCKed
RLOCK	Write to record	Read it, but not lock it.	No one else can have it RLOCKed, or file FLOCKed.

At the top of Table 10-2, OPEN EXCLUSIVE gives the owner the most power. Conversely, it restricts other users the most. At the bottom of the table, RLOCK gives the owner the least power. It restricts other users the least. The requirements specify what is necessary for the commands to succeed.

Making a single user application conform to Clipper's rules is a straightforward task. There are even program generators that will do it for you. You insert file and record locks at the appropriate places and open the databases in the required mode. For example, review the two problems presented in the first part of this

this chapter. Study the "lost update" problem, repeated here for convenience.

```
COMPUTER A                          COMPUTER B

USE z:file1                         USE z:file1

REPLACE field1 WITH field1 - 10     REPLACE field1 WITH field1 - 5
```

Assume we compile and run this code as is. We know that Clipper requires either file1 or record1 in file1 (the current record) to be locked before the REPLACE command is executed (Table 10-1 shows this). Since neither program issues locks, they would both fail with "system error, not locked" messages. We would therefore probably recode them as:

```
COMPUTER A                          COMPUTER B

SET EXCLUSIVE OFF                   SET EXCLUSIVE OFF
USE z:file1                         USE z:file1
IF neterr()                         IF neterr()
      ? "Cannot open file1"               ? "Cannot open file1"
      quit                                quit
ENDIF                               ENDIF

WHILE !rlock()                      WHILE !rlock()

ENDDO                               ENDDO

REPLACE field1 WITH field1 - 10     REPLACE field1 WITH field1 - 5

UNLOCK                              UNLOCK
```

Neither computer can execute the replace until it has the record locked. Once one machine successfully locks a record, it then updates it and releases the lock. The other machine's lock then succeeds, and it too can proceed with its update.

This guarantees that neither update is lost. However, simply placing a lock command around the REPLACE command is not the entire solution to the "lost update" problem, as we will see later.

Now consider the "inconsistent analysis" problem again, repeated here for convenience:

```
COMPUTER A                          COMPUTER B

USE z:file1                         USE z:file1

GOTO 10
REPLACE field1 WITH field1 - 10     TOTAL field1 TO mfield1
```

We know that computer A must issue a lock command before it can execute the REPLACE statement, and so we would probably rewrite the code as:

COMPUTER A	COMPUTER B
USE z:file1	USE z:file1
GOTO 10 WHILE !rlock()	
ENDDO	
REPLACE field1 WITH field1 - 10	TOTAL field1 TO mfield1

Although this code would execute without producing a run time error, the results are still unpredictable. Since the TOTAL command simply reads the database, it does not require a lock. Computer A's lock command will then succeed regardless of the current state of computer B's program. Once again, the result depends on whether computer A's REPLACE executes before computer B's TOTAL command reaches record 10. Here the programmer must determine exactly what is required. He or she may decide that the update may occur during the TOTAL command, or he or she may prefer to lock the database.

This section has described Clipper rules governing certain commands for shared databases. Conforming to these rules is trivial, but is only part of the problem. Although the rules help avoid some difficulties inherent in network programming (that is why they exist), they do not solve all "lost update" or "inconsistent analysis" problems. We will return to the problems later in this chapter, but first we must discuss error recovery techniques.

> Commands that write to a shared database require locks. Refer to Tables 10-1 and 10-2 for specifics.

Handling Errors

How should we respond to a failed use or lock? How long should we persist at repeating the commands? So far we have shown two extremes. One method simply tries forever, whereas the other gives up after the first attempt. As both methods are impractical in practice, a policy somewhere in-between is necessary.

Several alternatives exist, such as:

- Retrying for a fixed amount of time.
- Retrying until the user interrupts.
- Asking the user whether to retry.

We could also use a combination of methods.

Which alternative is best depends on the application, and in particular, on what the user who is restricting us is doing. It makes a big difference whether he or she has a record locked during a replacement, or a 100,000 record file locked during a PACK. We cannot generalize about which method is best. In practice, we prefer a combination of retrying for a fixed amount of time and a user option.

Nantucket supplies routines (see Table 10-3) that extend the basic locking commands. The file locks.prg, supplied on the Clipper release disks, provides the source code to user defined functions that help the programmer retry and wait for a lock or use.

Table 10-3. Nantucket's Network Functions

FUNCTION	PURPOSE	PARAMETERS	RETURN VALUE
NET_USE	Open a file for shared or exclusive use	Filename Exclusive? Timeout	Success or failure of USE
FIL_LOCK	Lock current shared file	Timeout	Success or failure of FLOCK
REC_LOCK	Lock current record	Timeout	Success or failure of RLOCK
ADD_REC	Append record to shared database	Timeout	Success or failure of APPEND BLANK

Program 10-1 is the source code for the "NET_USE" function.

Program 10-1. Network USE Function

```
****
* NET_USE function
*
* Tries to open a file for exclusive or shared use.
* SET INDEXes in calling procedure if successful.
* Pass the following parameters
```

```
*       1. Character - name of the DBF file to open
*       2. Logical - mode of open (exclusive/.NOT. exclusive)
*       3. Numeric - seconds to wait (0 = wait forever)
*

* Example:
*       IF NET_USE("Accounts", .T., 5)
*         SET INDEX TO Name
*       ELSE
*         ? "Account file not available"
*       ENDIF

FUNCTION NET_USE
PARAMETERS file, ex_use, wait
PRIVATE forever

forever = (wait = 0)
DO WHILE (forever .OR. wait > 0)

        IF ex_use                            && exclusive
                USE &file EXCLUSIVE
        ELSE
                USE &file                    && shared
        ENDIF

        IF .NOT. NETERR()                    && USE succeeds
                RETURN (.T.)
        ENDIF

        INKEY(1)                             && wait 1 second
        wait = wait - 1
ENDDO

RETURN (.F.)                                 && USE fails
* End - NET_USE
```

Reprinted by Permission of Nantucket Corp.

Program 10-1 tries to USE a file in the specified mode. It returns a logical value indicating whether the USE succeeded. The routine takes a timeout value as a parameter. It is the length of time, in seconds, that the routine will wait if it cannot open the file, retrying once a second. The one second delay is important - it avoids excessive repetition of the USE command that could cause a bottleneck.

The sample call in the comment at the head of the routine retries an unsuccessful open five times in five seconds before reporting a failure. The required area must be selected before the routine is called. A common mistake is to issue a series of calls to NET_USE without selecting different areas.

> You must select an area before calling NET_USE.

Program 10-2. File Lock Function

```
****
* FIL_LOCK function
*
* Tries to lock the current shared file
* Pass the following parameter
*       1. Numeric - seconds to wait (0 = wait forever)
*
* Example:
*       IF FIL_LOCK(5)
*         REPLACE ALL Price WITH Price * 1.1
*       ELSE
*         ? "File not available"
*       ENDIF

FUNCTION FIL_LOCK
PARAMETERS wait
PRIVATE forever

IF FLOCK()
       RETURN (.T.)                  && locked
ENDIF

forever = (wait = 0)
DO WHILE (forever .OR. wait > 0)

       INKEY(.5)                     && wait 1/2 second
       wait = wait - .5

       IF FLOCK()
              RETURN (.T.)           && locked
       ENDIF

ENDDO

RETURN (.F.)                         && not locked
* End - FIL_LOCK
```

Reprinted by Permission of Nantucket Corp.

Program 10-2 is the source code for the "FIL_LOCK" function. It tries to lock the database file in the currently selected area. It also takes a timeout value in seconds. Since it calls FLOCK every 1/2 second (as compared to every second in NET_USE), it will try to lock the file a maximum number of times given by twice the time period. The sample call, for example, will try 10 times in 5 seconds.

Program 10-3. Record Lock

```
****
* REC_LOCK function
*
* Tries to lock the current record
* Pass the following parameter
*       1. Numeric - seconds to wait (0 = wait forever)
*
* Example:
*  IF REC_LOCK(5)
*        REPLACE Price WITH newprice
*  ELSE
*        ? "Record not available"
*  ENDIF

FUNCTION REC_LOCK
PARAMETERS wait
PRIVATE forever

IF RLOCK()
      RETURN (.T.)                          && locked
ENDIF

forever = (wait = 0)
DO WHILE (forever .OR. wait > 0)

      IF RLOCK()
            RETURN (.T.)                    && locked
      ENDIF

      INKEY(.5)                             && wait 1/2 second
      wait = wait - .5

ENDDO

RETURN (.F.)                                && not locked
* End - REC_LOCK
```

Reprinted by Permission of Nantucket Corp.

Program 10-3 is the source code for the "REC_LOCK" function.

It tries to lock the current record in the current area. It retries for a period of time specified by its parameter. Like FIL_LOCK, it retries twice a second.

Program 10-4. Add Record

```
****
*  ADD_REC function
*
* Returns true if record appended. The new record is current
* and locked.

* Pass the following parameter
*       1. Numeric - seconds to wait (0 = wait forever)
*

FUNCTION ADD_REC
PARAMETERS wait
PRIVATE forever

APPEND BLANK
IF .NOT. NETERR()
        RETURN (.T.)
ENDIF

forever = (wait = 0)
DO WHILE (forever .OR. wait > 0)

        APPEND BLANK
        IF .NOT. NETERR()
                RETURN .T.
        ENDIF

        INKEY(.5)                               && wait 1/2 second
        wait = wait - .5

ENDDO

RETURN (.F.)                                    && not locked
* End ADD_REC
```

Reprinted by Permission of Nantucket Corp.

Program 10-4 is the source code for the ADD_REC function. It tries to APPEND a record to the database file. As we previously described, it can fail if someone else is APPENDing or has the file FLOCKed. Note that you cannot lock a nonexistent record.

ADD_REC works like the other routines. It takes a timeout value as a parameter, retrying twice a second.

These functions use the basic network commands and functions to implement a higher level interface for the programmer. We prefer to take the abstraction a level further, and incorporate user interaction as well. Table 10-4 lists the extended functions.

Table 10-4. Extended Network Functions

FUNCTION	PURPOSE	PARAMETERS	RETURN VALUE
E_NET_USE	Open file with user interaction	file alias exclusive? timeout message message row message column	Success or failure of use
E_FIL_LOCK	Lock file with user interaction	timeout message message row message column	Success or failure of FLOCK
E_REC_LOCK	Lock record with user interaction	timeout message message row message column	Success or failure of RLOCK
E_ADD_REC	Append record with user interaction	timeout message message row message column	Success or failure of APPEND BLANK

All the functions ask the user how to proceed in the event of failure. If the user agrees to retry, the process is applied again. If he or she decides to quit, the routine exits, returning .F..

We now describe the functions. The first one, "E_NET_USE" (Program 10-5), is an alternative to "NET_USE".

Program 10-5. Network USE with User Interaction

```
***
* Logical E_NET_USE(file, alias, ex_use, wait, error_message, error_row,
*                             error_col)
*

* Character file
```

```
* Character alias
* Logical ex_use
* Numeric wait
* Character error_message
* Numeric error_row
* Numeric error_col
*
*
* NET_USE with user interaction if USE fails. Calls E_NET_USE1,
* modified NET_USE (with alias) to do actual USE.
*
* Sample call:
*
* IF e_net_use("calls", "calls", .F., 5, "Retry Calls open? ", 10 , 10)
*
FUNCTION e_net_use

PARAMETERS file, alias, ex_use, wait, error_message, error_row, error_col

PRIVATE success, retry, key, retry_win

    retry = .T.
    success = .F.

    * Save three lines
    retry_win = savescreen(error_row - 1, error_col - 1, ;
                        error_row + 1, error_col + len(error_message) + 1)

    DO WHILE retry .AND. !success

        success = e_net_use1(file, alias, ex_use, wait)

        IF !success
            @ error_row - 1, error_col - 1, error_row +1, ;
             error_col + len(error_message) + 1 BOX singbox

            @ error_row, error_col SAY error_message

            key = inkey(0)
            retry = (key = ASC('Y')) .OR. (key = ASC('y'))

        ENDIF

        restscreen(error_row - 1, error_col - 1, ;
            error_row + 1, error_col + len(error_message) + 1, retry_win)

    ENDDO

RETURN (success)
```

Program 10-5 takes the three parameters in Program 10-1, plus four others. The first extra parameter, "alias", is the alias for the database. We had to modify Nantucket's "NET_USE" to take this new field as a parameter and use it in the "USE" statement. Program 10-6 shows the code, in a function we have named "E_NET_USE1".

Program 10-6. Modified Network USE with Alias Capability

```
FUNCTION E_NET_USE1

PARAMETERS file, alias, ex_use, wait
PRIVATE forever

     forever = (wait = 0)
     DO WHILE (forever .OR. wait > 0)
          IF ex_use                          && exclusive
               USE &file EXCLUSIVE ALIAS &alias
          ELSE
               USE &file ALIAS &alias  && shared
          ENDIF

          IF .NOT. NETERR()          && USE succeeds
               RETURN (.T.)
          ENDIF

          INKEY(1)                           && wait 1 second
          wait = wait - 1

     ENDDO

RETURN (.F.)                             && USE fails
```

While in most cases, the ability to open a shared file with an alias is not important, it is useful for testing in a single user environment. A later section discusses this.

Now back to Program 10-5. Its second new parameter, "error_message", is a character string for display in the event of a failure. The other two parameters, "error_row" and "error_col", are the coordinates of the display. The message should contain text such as:

"Use of SPJ database failed, retry (Y, N)?"

as the function reads a key, and retries if the user presses "y" or "Y".

Program 10-5 first uses SAVESCREEN to save the area where the message is displayed. It restores the area after receiving the response. It frames the message with a box, so the coordinates should not be at a screen boundary. There must be at least one row above and below them, and one column to the left and right.

Program 10-7 is the source code to the "E_FIL_LOCK" function, an alternative to "FIL_LOCK".

Program 10-7. File Lock with an Error Message

```
***
* Logical E_FIL_LOCK(wait, error_message, error_row, error_col)
*
* Numeric wait

* Character error_message
* Numeric error_row
* Numeric error_col
*
* File lock routine with user interaction if lock fails
*
* Sample call:
*
* IF e_fil_lock(5, "Lock of calls failed, retry?", 10, 10)
*


FUNCTION e_fil_lock

PARAMETERS wait, error_message, error_row, error_col

PRIVATE success, retry, key, retry_win

        retry = .T.
        success = .F.

        * three lines
        retry_win = savescreen(error_row - 1, error_col - 1, ;
                              error_row + 1, error_col + len(error_message) + 1)

        DO WHILE retry .AND. !success

                success = fil_lock(wait)

                IF !success
                        @ error_row - 1, error_col - 1, error_row + 1, ;
                          error_col + len(error_message) + 1 BOX singbox

                        @ error_row, error_col SAY error_message

                        key = inkey(0)
                        retry = (key = ASC('Y')) .OR. (key = ASC('y'))
```

```
        ENDIF
        restscreen(error_row - 1, error_col - 1, ;
                error_row + 1, error_col + len(error_message) + 1, retry_win)
    ENDDO

RETURN (success)
```

Program 10-7 takes the same timeout parameter as "FIL_LOCK" (Program 10-2), and the same extra three parameters as "E_NET_USE" (Program 10-5). It works like E_NET_USE, trying to lock the file within the specified time period, displaying the message if necessary, and waiting for the key.

Program 10-8 is the source for the "E_REC_LOCK" function, an alternative to "REC_LOCK".

Program 10-8. Record Lock with an Error Message

```
***
* Logical E_REC_LOCK(wait, error_message, error_row, error_col)
*
* Numeric wait
* Character error_message
* Numeric error_row
* Numeric error_col
*
*
* Record lock function with user interaction if lock fails
*
* Sample call:
*
* IF e_rec_lock(5, "record lock failed, retry? ", 10, 10)
*


FUNCTION e_rec_lock

PARAMETERS wait, error_message, error_row, error_col

PRIVATE success, retry, key, retry_win

    retry = .T.
    success = .F.

    * three lines
    retry_win = savescreen(error_row - 1, error_col - 1, ;
                    error_row + 1, error_col + len(error_message) + 1)

    DO WHILE retry .AND. !success
```

```
            success = rec_lock(wait)
            IF !success
                @ error_row - 1, error_col - 1, error_row +1, ;
                  error_col + len(error_message) BOX singbox

                @ error_row, error_col SAY error_message

                key = inkey(0)
                retry = (key = ASC('Y')) .OR. (key = ASC('y'))

            ENDIF

            restscreen(error_row - 1, error_col - 1, ;
                error_row + 1, error_col + len(error_message) + 1, retry_win)

        ENDDO

    RETURN (success)
```

Program 10-8 takes the same timeout parameter as REC_LOCK (Program 10-3). In the event of failure, it displays the message at the specified coordinates and waits for the user to respond. If he or she agrees to retry, the process is repeated. If not, the routine exits, returning .F..

Program 10-9 is the source for the "E_ADD_REC" function, an alternative to "ADD_REC" (Program 10-4).

Program 10-9. Add Record with an Error Message

```
***
* Logical E_ADD_REC(wait, error_message, error_row, error_col)
*
* Numeric wait
* Character error_message
* Numeric error_row
* Numeric error_col
*
*
* APPEND BLANK function with user interaction in event of failure
*
* Sample call:
*
* IF e_add_rec(5, "Could not add record, retry?", 10, 10)
*

FUNCTION e_add_rec

PARAMETERS wait, error_message, error_row, error_col
```

```
PRIVATE success, retry, key, retry_win

    retry = .T.
    success = .F.

    * save three lines
    retry_win = savescreen(error_row - 1, error_col - 1, ;
                error_row + 1, error_col + len(error_message) + 1)

    DO WHILE retry .AND. !success

        success = add_rec(wait)

        IF !success
            @ error_row - 1, error_col - 1, error_row + 1, ;
             error_col + len(error_message) BOX sing_box

            @ error_row, error_col SAY error_message

            key = inkey(0)
            retry = (key = ASC('Y')) .OR. (key = ASC('y'))

        ENDIF

        restscreen(error_row - 1, error_col - 1, ;
            error_row + 1, error_col + len(error_message) + 1, retry_win)

    ENDDO

RETURN (success)
```

Program 10-9 takes the same parameters as Programs 10-7 and 10-8 and operates similarly.

Use these routines rather than the ones Nantucket supplies. They offer a high level interface to the low level locking functions. They combine a periodic retry with user interaction.

So far we have discussed how to open, lock, and append to networked databases. We now need to look at index files.

Index Files

An index file used with a database inherits its open mode. If, for example, the database is opened in shared mode, the index file is, too. The same holds for exclusive mode.

There are two ways to associate an index file with a database. The first is to use the index option of the USE command, as in:

```
USE test INDEX testname, testcity, testzip
```

The second is to use the SET INDEX TO command after opening the database, as in:

```
USE test

SET INDEX TO testname, testcity, testzip
```

The two methods are equivalent on a single user system. On a network, however, they have a fundamental difference. If the "USE test" command fails because someone has the database open in exclusive mode, NETERR is set to true. If the "USE test INDEX ...." command fails, Clipper responds with a disruptive run time error message. For this reason, you should separate the index use from the database use with the SET INDEX command. Since the open mode of the index file is inherited from the database, the SET INDEX TO command is guaranteed to succeed if the USE did. If our USE command succeeded, anyone else using the database must be doing so in shared mode. Since the mode extends to index files, our index file open must succeed.

> **TIP**
>
> Open network index files with SET INDEX TO.

Other Types of Files

Some Clipper commands open files implicitly. On a single user system, the programmer need not be concerned with how this happens since there is no "competition" for them. However, when the files reside on a server, the programmer must know how they are opened. Table 10-5 lists the modes for various commands.

Table 10-5. Implicit Open Modes for Clipper Commands

COMMAND	OPEN MODE	FILE TYPE
APPEND FROM <file>	Shared	database (.DBF)
COPY STRUCTURE TO <file>	Exclusive	database (.DBF)
COPY TO <file>	Exclusive	database (.DBF)
CREATE <file>	Exclusive	database (.DBF)
CREATE <file1> FROM <file>	Shared	database (.DBF) (file1 EXCLUSIVE)

INDEX ON ... TO <file>	Exclusive	index (.NTX / .NDX)
JOIN ... TO <file>	Exclusive	database (.DBF)
LABEL FORM <file>	Shared	label (.LBL)
REPORT FORM <file>	Shared	report (.FRM)
RESTORE FROM <file>	Shared	memory (.MEM)
SAVE TO <file>	Exclusive	memory (.MEM)
SET ALTERNATE TO <file>	Exclusive	text (.TXT)
SORT ... TO <file>	Exclusive	database (.DBF)
TOTAL ... TO <file>	Exclusive	database (.DBF)
TYPE <file>	Shared	text (.TXT)
UPDATE ... FROM <file>	Shared	database (.DBF)

The modes refer only to <file>. If the command uses another file, it must have been opened explicitly with a USE command and its mode explicitly specified. Note that if the command merely reads <file>, then it is opened in a shared mode. If the command writes to <file>, then it is opened in exclusive mode.

These commands fail if <file> (or <file1> in the case of CREATE FROM), cannot be opened in the correct mode. In the EXCLUSIVE case, this occurs if another user has the file open in any mode. In the SHARED case, this occurs if another user has it open EXCLUSIVE. Note that since both CREATE and CREATE FROM create the new file in exclusive mode, it can immediately be REPLACEd into without being locked first.

These commands do not affect the value returned by NETERR. The network operating system will report the error directly. For example, in the case of IBM Token-Ring, the message is:

"Sharing Violation error reading drive Z: A/R/I ?"

The user may retry, abort, or ignore.

The operating system message is usually unacceptable. We prefer to avoid the error altogether. We can do this by defining an "operational protocol" using a shared database, say "semaphores", as an intermediary. The protocol defines what "system wide" operations must be performed, and assigns a record number in the "semaphore" database to each one. Before a program can do an operation, it must first gain control of the corresponding records. The protocol must define how to do this. In the simplest case, just lock the record. However, this uses an extra file handle (at a premium in DOS versions before 3.3) and a selection area. Another way is to have the record contain a logical field that is set to .T. to indicate that a program is, or is about to, perform the operation. Once the operation is finished, the program resets the value to .F.. This protocol essentially implements a semaphore system. An elegant extension is to have a name field that contains the "netname" of the user currently performing the operation.

For example, assume that the "system" consists of the following operations:

- INDEX of shared database, "z:file1", to shared index "file1".
- SORT of shared database, "z:file2", to shared database "file2".
- REPORT FORM of shared FRM file "file3". Since other users periodically change the FRM file with RL, which opens the file in EXCLUSIVE mode, the program must ensure that its REPORT FORM will succeed.

We assign record numbers in the semephore database according to the preceding operations. INDEX is 1, SORT is 2, and REPORT FORM is 3. We use the following structure for the semaphore database:

```
NAME      TYPE LEN  DEC

LOCKED    L     1
USER      C     15
```

We need a routine (Program 10-10) that tries to gain control of the record, and returns a logical indicating its success or failure.

Program 10-10. Lock a Semaphore

```
* Lock a semaphore - operational protocol routine
*
* Tries to lock specified record in semaphore database
*
* Returns its status

FUNCTION lock_for_op

PARAM operation, file_name
PRIVATE sel, ret_val

     * save current selection
     sel = select()

     SELECT 0
     USE (file_name)
     ret_val = neterr()

     IF !ret_val
          GOTO operation
```

```
        ret_val = e_rec_lock(5, "Cannot lock semaphore, retry? ", 23, 10)

        IF ret_val
            ret_val = !locked
            IF ret_val
                REPLACE locked WITH .T.

                REPLACE name WITH netname()
            ENDIF
            UNLOCK
        ENDIF

        USE
    ENDIF

    SELECT (sel)

RETURN (ret_val)
```

To perform operation 1 according to the protocol, we first try to lock "semaphore" record 1 with:

```
file_name = "z:semaphore"
IF lock_for_op(1, file_name)
    * Do the index
ELSE
    * do some error recovery
ENDIF
```

A good idea is to define the operation numbers as memory variables, and then only refer to the operations by name, as in:

```
OP_INDEX = 1
OP_SORT = 2
OP_REPORT = 3

file_name = "z:semaphore"
IF lock_for_op(OP_INDEX, file_name)
    * do the index
ELSE
    * error handling code goes here
ENDIF
```

Once the operation is complete, we must unlock the semaphore (Program 10-11).

Program 10-11. Unlock a Semaphore

```
* Unlock a semaphore - operational protocol routine
*
* Tries to unlock specified record in semaphore database
*
```

```
* Returns its status

FUNCTION op_unlock

PARAM operation, file_name
PRIVATE sel, ret_val

    sel = select()

    SELECT 0
    USE (file_name)
    ret_val = neterr()
    IF !ret_val
        GOTO operation

        ret_val = e_rec_lock(5, "Cannot lock semaphore, retry? ", 23, 10)

        IF ret_val
            REPLACE locked WITH .F.
            REPLACE name WITH ""

            UNLOCK
        ENDIF
        USE
    ENDIF

    SELECT (sel)

RETURN (ret_val)
```

Use these routines to ensure the success of commands that use more than one file on a network.

> **NOTE**
>
> Files opened implicitly (see Table 10-5) do not set NETERR. If they fail, the operating system reports an error. You can guard against this by defining an operational protocol.

Read/Modify/Write Cycles

The Clipper enforced rule that a shared database can be written only when the record is locked ensures that the REPLACE statement does not cause a lost update. However, REPLACE is just one of a class of programming operations known as read/modify/write cycles. They read data, modify it, and write it back.

We showed the problems that could occur as a result of unsynchronized data accesses. Our solution was to lock the data during the read/modify/write cycle, in that case just the REPLACE command. Clipper requires a lock for exactly this reason.

However, the read/modify/write cycle may span many commands over which Clipper cannot exercise any control. After all, it does not understand the intricacies of your program. For example, study Program 10-12.

Program 10-12. Example Read/Modify/Write Cycle

COMPUTER A

```
USE z:file1
IF neterr()
	? "Cannot open file1"
	quit
ENDIF

afield1 = field1

afield1 = afield1 - 10
WHILE !rlock()

ENDDO

REPLACE field1 WITH afield1
```

COMPUTER B

```
USE z:file1
IF neterr()
	? "Cannot open file1"
		quit
ENDIF

bfield1 = field1

bfield1 = bfield1 - 5
WHILE !rlock()

ENDDO

REPLACE field1 WITH bfield1
```

This is the "lost update" program recoded to spread the updating over several instructions. Although the record locks satisfy Clipper's requirement that a database be locked before being changed, the original problem has resurfaced. Once again, field1 has three possible values upon termination of the programs, depending on the order of execution of the statements. In this case, the read/modify/write cycle consists of the assignment of the field to the memory variable, the updating of the memory variable, and the replacement of the field.

To solve the problem, we could take the same approach as with the REPLACE command and lock the data during the cycle, as in Program 10-13.

Program 10-13. Lock for Duration of Read/Modify/Write Cycle

COMPUTER A

```
USE z:file1
IF neterr()
```

COMPUTER B

```
USE z:file1
IF neterr()
```

```
        ? "Cannot open file1"                ? "Cannot open file1"
        QUIT                                 QUIT
ENDIF                                ENDIF

WHILE !rlock()                       WHILE !rlock()

ENDDO                                ENDDO

afield1 = field1                     bfield1 = field1

afield1 = afield1 - 10               bfield1 = bfield1 - 5

REPLACE field1 WITH afield1          REPLACE field1 WITH bfield1
```

This satisfies Clipper's requirement, and handles the lost update problem. The data is not read until the record is locked.

Although this solution is satisfactory here, there are cases where it is not - when user interaction is involved. Let us study a typical edit operation on a simple shared database as shown in Program 10-14.

Program 10-14. Simple Shared Database Edit

```
IF !e_net_use("z:test1", test1, .F., 10, "retry? ", 24, 10)
        ? "Error, could not open file"
        QUIT
ENDIF

GOTO 23

mfield1 = field1
mfield2 = field2

@ 10, 10 SAY "field1" GET mfield1
@ 10, 10 SAY "field1" GET mfield1

READ

REPLACE field1 WITH mfield1
REPLACE field2 WITH mfield2
```

Program 10-14's read/modify/write cycle consists of assigning the fields to the memory variables, the GET/READ, and the REPLACE. If we lock the data during the cycle, we would code the example as Program 10-15.

Program 10-15. Simple Shared Database Edit with Lock for Cycle

```
IF !e_net_use("z:test1", "test1", .F., 10, "retry? ", 24, 10)
        ? "Error, could not open file"
        QUIT
ENDIF

GOTO 23

IF !e_rec_lock(10, "Could not lock, retry? ", 24, 10)
        mfield1 = field1
        mfield2 = field2

        @ 10, 10 SAY "field1" GET mfield1
        @ 10, 10 SAY "field1" GET mfield1

        READ

        REPLACE field1 WITH mfield1
        REPLACE field2 WITH mfield2
        UNLOCK
ELSE
        * could not lock ...
ENDIF
```

Once the record is locked, we read the data, let the user change it, and then unlock it. The problem is the lack of control over how long the user has the record locked, thereby preventing others from changing it. It also prevents others from performing an operation that requires the database to be open in exclusive mode, since their USE .. EXCLUSIVE will fail. Even if the user edits the record immediately, the delay is still long in "computer" time.

> **TIP**
>
> Lock data for as short a time as possible.

We can lock the record just before the REPLACE command as Program 10-16 shows.

Program 10-16. Simple Shared Database Edit with Lock before Update

```
USE z:test
IF !e_net_use("z:test1", "test1", .F., 10, "retry lock? ", 24, 10)
	? "Error, could not open file"
	QUIT
ENDIF
GOTO 23

mfield1 = field1
mfield2 = field2

@ 10, 10 SAY "field1" GET mfield1
@ 10, 10 SAY "field1" GET mfield1

READ

IF e_rec_lock(10, "retry lock? ", 24, 10)
	REPLACE field1 WITH mfield1
	REPLACE field2 WITH mfield2
ELSE
	* lock failed ..
ENDIF
```

This minimizes the length of the lock, but could cause a lost update as in Program 10-12. Since the record is not locked while the user is editing, there is nothing to stop someone else from locking the same record, changing it, and rewriting it before the first user finishes. The first user is then examining outdated information (the inconsistent analysis problem). If he or she goes ahead and writes the changed records, the second user's update will be lost (the lost update problem).

There are two ways to handle the problem. The first is to save a copy of the original record which will remain unedited. After locking the record, but before writing the new data, compare the current data with the original record. If there are differences, we know someone has changed the record. If they are the same, we know we can go ahead and safely write. Program 10-17 is a typical implementation of this method.

Program 10-17. Comparing All Edit Fields to Detect Changes

```
IF !e_net_use("z:test1", "test1", .F., 10, "retry use? ", 24, 10)
	? "Error, cannot open file"
	QUIT
ENDIF
```

```
GOTO 23

mfield1 = field1
mfield2 = field2

save_field1 = mfield1
save_field2 = mfield2

@ 10, 10 SAY "field1" GET mfield1
@ 10, 10 SAY "field1" GET mfield1

READ

IF e_rec_lock(10, "retry lock? ", 24, 10)
        IF save_field1 = field1 .AND. save_field2 = field2

                REPLACE field1 WITH mfield1
                REPLACE field2 WITH mfield2

        ELSE
                * Data was changed ..
        ENDIF
        UNLOCK

ELSE
        * lock failed ..
ENDIF
```

We must make two points about Program 10-17. First, it is important to lock the record before making the comparison. Otherwise, another user could change the record after the comparison is made, undermining the validity of the check. Second, we must retrieve the saved values from the memory variables, not from the fields themselves. Otherwise, the values in the field could be changed between getting the memory variables and getting the saved values, again undermining the validity of the check. Remember, worst case analysis!

Saving the contents of the entire record and comparing each field can be time consuming. A better method is to have an extra field for a "signature" or update marker. The user would not edit this field. The programmer would simply use it internally to avoid inconsistent analysis. Typically, it would be a numeric, and its value would be incremented every time a record is updated. Before a field in the record is read (in preparation for an update), its value would be saved. After the lock, but before the update occurs, its value is reread and compared with the saved value. If they differ, we know that another user changed the field. If they are the same, we know we can safely go ahead and write, incrementing the marker field.

The second method is a variation of the first - in both we save a value, make local changes, lock, and then compare two values. The difference between the two methods is that the second compares only one field. Program 10-18 is a typical implementation of the second method.

Program 10-18. Using a Signature Field to Detect Changes

```
IF !e_net_use("z:test1", "test1", .F., 10, "retry use? ", 24, 10)
        ? "Error, cannot open file"
        quit
ENDIF

GOTO 23

e_rec_lock(0, "", 0, 0)  && this simply waits forever, no message required

mfield1 = field1
mfield2 = field2

mmarker = marker

UNLOCK

@ 10, 10 SAY "field1" GET mfield1
@ 10, 10 SAY "field1" GET mfield1

READ

IF e_rec_lock(10, "retry lock? ", 24, 10)
        IF marker = mmarker

                REPLACE field1 WITH mfield1
                REPLACE field2 WITH mfield2
                REPLACE marker WITH mmarker + 1

        ELSE
                * was changed ...
        ENDIF
        UNLOCK
ELSE
        * lock failed ..
ENDIF
```

Note that Program 10-18 locks the record while we are saving the marker and the fields in memory variables. Otherwise, someone could change a value between readings, and we would end up with a mixed set. Once again, and we cannot emphasize this enough, perform worst case analysis on your network application.

The second method requires all database users to follow the protocol defined on the marker field, whereas the first method is more general.

This section has discussed read/modify/write cycles. It pointed out the problems that can occur if you program these cycles incorrectly. When designing a network application, or converting a single user application to a network, identify all read/modify/write cycles and use one of the techniques discussed here to avoid problems.

> **TIP**
>
> Use a signature field to detect inconsistent analysis in read/modify/write cycles involving user interaction.

File Snapshot Commands

Commands that read from an entire database, such as SUM, TOTAL, and REPORT, require special care on a network. While they do not require the database to be locked, a lock does avoid inconsistent analysis. We have already shown how one user's REPLACE command could cause another's TOTAL command to produce inconsistent results.

Before issuing an FLOCK (a sure way to avoid the problem), the programmer should carefully consider the consequences. The file lock prohibits others from updating records. While this is exactly what is required to overcome the problem, the database-wide operation could take a long time.

The programmer must decide whether the results of the database-wide operation are actually inconsistent because of another user's update, or whether the updates would just create a different, but still valid, result. It depends on the meaning of the data and on the effect of the update. An example where the update would produce a different, but still valid, result is the counting of available seats on an aircraft. Updating the status of one seat would produce a different but valid result. Howerver, a seat reassignment made during the counting procedure may produce an inconsistent result. For example, Program 10-19 shows a transaction moving the occupant of seat 10 to seat 7.

Program 10-19. Changing a Passenger's Seat Assignment

Computer A	**Computer B**
USE z:test	USE z:test

IF neterr()
    * Error handling ...
ENDIF
	IF neterr()
	    * Error handling ...
	ENDIF

num_seats = 0	
DO WHILE !eof()	GOTO 10 IF rlock() REPLACE reserved WITH .F.

IF reserved
        num_seats = num_seats + 1
    ENDIF
	GOTO 7
	    IF rlock()
	        REPLACE reserved WITH .T.
	    ENDIF

ENDDO	ENDIF

If computer A has processed record 7, but not record 10, by the time computer B updates 10, the counting routine would show 1 less seat reserved than actually existed. The only solution is for computer A to lock the file before starting the operation. Again, the key to success in writing stable network applications is to recognize ambiguous sequences and code against them.

Transactions

Program 10-19 assumed that seat 7 was available, would stay that way, and that the record locks would succeed. In the real world, of course, we must assume the worst, and program accordingly. It is possible that after relinquishing seat 10, seat 7 is not available, or its record could not be locked. In this case, we are performing one transaction that cannot be interrupted. It consists of checking the availability of seat 7, releasing seat 10, and reserving seat 7.

This is a complex read/modify/write cycle. In the previous examples, we updated only one record. We overcame the inconsistency problem by issuing a record lock in the simple case, and by using a record lock and a marker field in the more complex case. In this case, we would have to lock two records in the same file, which Clipper does not allow. The only solution then is to lock the database during the transaction.

When a transaction involves several records, each in a separate file, the RLOCK method works and is preferable. For a transaction involving several databases, the programmer must ensure that each is updated successfully. This is a real problem in both dBASE and Clipper. The only way to ensure success is to lock all the records before starting the transaction. When two records in the same file must be locked, lock the file instead.

This restrictive technique is necessary because Clipper does not allow "rollback". What would help is a pair of statements such as

```
BEGIN TRANSACTION
```

and

```
END TRANSACTION
```

to delimit the transaction's scope. Then if during it the program cannot proceed (for example, it could not lock a file or record), a ROLLBACK command would 'undo' all updates since the transaction started. Look for a feature like this in a future version of Clipper.

Deadlock

Deadlock is another network problem you will eventually face. Study the following two pieces of code:

Computer A	**Computer B**
SET EXCLUSIVE OFF	SET EXCLUSIVE OFF
SELECT 0 USE z:test1 ALIAS test1	SELECT 0 USE z:test1 ALIAS test1
SELECT 0 USE z:test2 ALIAS test2	SELECT 0 USE z:test2 ALIAS test2
SELECT test1	SELECT test2

DO WHILE !flock()
    inkey(0.5)
ENDDO
	DO WHILE !flock()
	    inkey(0.5)
	ENDDO

* line 15	
SELECT test2	SELECT test1

DO WHILE !flock()
    inkey(0.5)
ENDDO
	DO WHILE !flock()
	    inkey(0.5)
	ENDDO

Assume that both programs reach line 15, i.e., each has successfully executed its first lock. Now, computer A requests a lock on test2. It will be denied since computer B has test2 locked. Similarly, computer B requests a lock on test1. This will also be denied since computer A has it locked. Since neither user will relinquish the first file before locking the second one, neither can proceed.

This situation is deadlock, or the "deadly embrace". It has been the subject of much operating systems research. A simple system such as MS-DOS does not try to handle the problem; it leaves the programmer to his or her own devices. There are several ways to handle deadlock. The techniques we discussed for handling a failed lock are relevant here. We could simply inform the user of the failure and give him or her the option of retrying or abandoning. Fortunately, there is a better solution. We are concerned here with the failure of two well-behaved programs that have conflicting resource requirements. The problem is that they require multiple file locks.

The solution is for each user to release the first lock when the second one fails, and then retry the first one. Program 10-20 shows the code for this.

Program 10-20. Overcoming Deadlock by Relinquishing Resources

Computer A

```
SET EXCLUSIVE OFF

SELECT 0
USE z:test1 ALIAS test1

SELECT 0
USE z:test2 ALIAS test2

lock1 = .F.
lock2 = .F.

DO WHILE !lock1 .AND. !lock2
    SELECT test1

    lock1 = flock()
    IF lock1

        SELECT test2

        lock2 = flock()
        IF !lock2
            SELECT test1
            UNLOCK
        ENDIF
    ENDIF
ENDDO
```

Computer B

```
SET EXCLUSIVE OFF

SELECT 0
USE z:test1 ALIAS test1

SELECT 0
USE z:test2 ALIAS test2

lock1 = .F.
lock2 = .F.

DO WHILE !lock1 .AND. !lock2
    SELECT test2

    lock2 = flock()
    IF lock2

        SELECT test1

        lock2 = flock()
        IF !lock2
            SELECT test2
            UNLOCK
        ENDIF
    ENDIF
ENDDO
```

We can extend this method to any number of files. You should try to write a three file version.

This section has discussed transactions and deadlock. The programmer must carefully analyze his or her code and identify all transactions and potential deadlock problems. Then use the techniques discussed here to solve them.

Electronic Mail

Using the routines we have developed, an electronic mail system becomes a simple task. It will serve as a practical application of techniques discussed in this chapter. The system uses two shared databases. The first, "NETNAMES", has a record for each user. It contains the user's name, as returned by the "netname" function, and a logical value indicating whether he or she is currently using the system. Its structure is:

NAME	TYPE	LEN	DEC
NAME	C	15	
ON_LINE	L	1	

The second database, "MESSAGES", contains the messages sent. It has the following structure:

NAME	TYPE	LEN	DEC
MEMO	M	10	
TIME_SENT	C	8	
DATE_SENT	D	8	
FROM	C	15	
TO	C	15	
SUBJECT	C	20	

The field MEMO contains the text. The field SUBJECT contains a brief summary. Fields TO and FROM specify the addressee and sender, respectively.

We will allow the following commands:

- **VIEW** - View messages sent to the current user.
- **SEND** - Send a message to another user.
- **DELETE** - Delete a message sent to the current user.
- **MAINTENANCE** - Maintain the database, doing tasks such as packing deleted records.

Program 10-21 shows the source code for the main routine.

Program 10-21. Basic Electronic Mail System

```
* Simple electronic mail system
*
* Allows
*
*       VIEW
*
*       SEND
*
*       DELETE
*
*       MAINTENANCE
*
*
* 1 - Verify that user's name is in database
*
* 2 - Update on_line flag
*
* 3 - Open messages database
*
* 4 - Load all users' names into nnames array
*
* 5 - Issue MENU
*
* 6 - Switch on selection
*
*
* 6.1  VIEW -
*
*               Use dbibrows routine (Chapter 6) to view this user's messages
*
*
* 6.2  SEND -
*
*               Select destination using abrowse (Chapter 6) to scroll
*               nnames array
*
*
* 6.3  DELETE -
*
*               Scroll messages with dbibrows routine. DELETE selected
*               message.
*
*
* 6.4  MAINTENANCE -
*
*               Pack messages database
```

```
SET EXCLUSIVE OFF

init_consts()

CLEAR

myname = trim(netname())
SELECT 0
IF !e_net_use("z:netnames", "netnames", .F., 10, ;
  "Cannot open netnames, retry (y/n)? ", 23, 10)
        QUIT
ENDIF

* make sure this user is in the database

LOCATE FOR name = myname

IF !found()
        ? "Cannot find your name in database"
        QUIT
ENDIF

* lock this record to update on_line flag

IF !e_rec_lock(20, "Cannot lock record, retry (y/n)? ", 23, 10)
        QUIT
ENDIF

REPLACE on_line WITH .T.
UNLOCK

num_names = reccount()

PRIVATE nnames[num_names]

GOTO TOP

* load names of all users into array

FOR i = 1 TO num_names
        nnames[i] = name
        SKIP
NEXT

SELECT 0
IF !e_net_use("z:messages", "messages", .F., 10, ;
        "Cannot open messages, retry (y/n)? ", 23, 10)
        QUIT
ENDIF

* do not see deleted messages (this SET is system-wide)
SET DELETED ON
```

```
* Just my messages ... (this SET is just for the active database)
SET FILTER TO to = myname

C_VIEW = 1
C_SEND = 2

C_DEL  = 3
C_MAIN = 4

@ 0, 10 PROMPT "VIEW"
@ 0, 20 PROMPT "SEND"
@ 0, 30 PROMPT "DELETE"
@ 0, 40 PROMPT "MAINTENANCE"

i = C_VIEW
MENU TO i

DO WHILE i != 0
        DO CASE

                CASE i = C_VIEW
                        DO view

                CASE i = C_SEND
                        DO send

                CASE i = C_DEL
                        DO del

                CASE i = C_MAIN
                        DO main

        ENDCASE

        CLEAR
        @ 0, 10 PROMPT "VIEW"
        @ 0, 20 PROMPT "SEND"
        @ 0, 30 PROMPT "DELETE"
        @ 0, 40 PROMPT "MAINTENANCE"

        i = C_VIEW
        MENU TO i
ENDDO

* View messages

PROCEDURE view

PRIVATE expr, sel

        SELECT messages
        GOTO TOP
```

```
        * view time, date, subject, and from fields

        expr = "time_sent + ' ' + dtoc(date_sent) + ' ' + subject + " + ;
                "' ' + from"
        sel = dbibrows(expr, 10, 10, 20, 60)

        IF sel != 0
                GOTO sel
                @ 10, 10, 20, 60 BOX singbox
                memoedit(memo, 11, 11, 19, 59, .T.)
        ENDIF

RETURN

* Send messages

PROCEDURE send

PRIVATE sel, who_to, subj, mess

        IF num_names > 0
                @ 8, 10 SAY "Whom to?"
                sel = abrowse(nnames, num_names, 10, 10, 20, 22)

                IF sel != 0

                        @ 10, 10, 20, 22 BOX ""

                        who_to = nnames[sel]
                        @ 8, 20 SAY who_to

                        subj = SPACE(20)
                        @ 9, 10 SAY "Subject " GET subj
                        READ

                        @ 10, 10, 20, 60 BOX singbox

                        mess = memoedit("", 11, 11, 19, 59, .T.)

                        SELECT messages

                        IF e_add_rec(5, "Could not add record, retry?", 10, 10)

                                REPLACE memo WITH mess
                                REPLACE time_sent WITH time()
                                REPLACE subject WITH subj
                                REPLACE from WITH myname
                                REPLACE date_sent WITH date()
                                REPLACE to WITH who_to

                                UNLOCK
```

```
                ENDIF
            ENDIF
        ENDIF

    RETURN

    * Delete a message
    PROCEDURE del

    PRIVATE expr, sel

        SELECT messages
        GOTO TOP

        expr = "time_sent + ' ' + dtoc(date_sent) + ' ' + subject + " + ;
                "' ' + from"

        sel = dbibrows(expr, 10, 10, 20, 60)
        IF sel != 0
            GOTO sel

            IF e_rec_lock(20, "Cannot lock record, retry (y/n)? ", 23, 10)
                DELETE
                UNLOCK
            ENDIF
        ENDIF

    RETURN

    PROCEDURE main

        SELECT messages

        * Open exclusively to PACK
        IF e_net_use("z:messages", "messages", .T., 10, ;
            "Cannot open messages exclusively, retry (y/n)? ", 23, 10)
            PACK
        ENDIF

        IF !e_net_use("z:messages", "messages", .F., 10, ;
            "Cannot open messages, retry (y/n)? ", 23, 10)
            QUIT
        ENDIF

        * Re-issue since lost after re-use
        SET FILTER TO to = myname

    RETURN
```

Program 10-21 uses the browse routines developed in Chapter 6 to let the user select the destination and the message to view. Note that to PACK the messages database, we must re-open the file in EXCLUSIVE mode to conform to Clipper's rule.

The names of all users are loaded into an array nnames. The send routine uses it with the abrowse function to select a destination. MEMOEDIT is used to construct the message. Finally, the e_add_rec function is used to append the record in preparation for the subsequent REPLACE.

The SET FILTER statement in the initialization limits viewing to messages intended for this user.

We could expand the system in many ways. We could use the "on_line" flag to list current users. An option could allow printing of a message. Another option could forward a message. We leave these as exercises for the reader.

The delete and view code uses the "dbibrows" routine to browse the messages database. It operates rather slowly for databases on a server. A common way to speed up network operations is to load required records into an array, then operate on it. In the electronic mail system, we cannot simply do this on startup, since new messages are arriving continually. The "del" and "send" routines in Program 10-22 read the records into an array every time the function is invoked.

Program 10-22. Delete and Send Routines Using an Array

```
PROCEDURE send

PRIVATE sel, who_to, subj, mess

    IF num_names > 0
        @ 8, 10 SAY "Who to?"
        sel = abrowse(nnames, num_names, 10, 10, 20, 22)

        IF sel != 0

            @ 10, 10, 20, 22 BOX ""

            who_to = nnames[sel]
            @ 8, 20 SAY who_to

            subj = SPACE(20)
            @ 9, 10 SAY "Subject " GET subj
            READ

            @ 10, 10, 20, 60 BOX singbox

            mess = memoedit("", 11, 11, 19, 59, .T.)

            SELECT messages
```

```
                        IF e_add_rec(5, "Could not add record, retry?", 10, 10)

                              REPLACE memo WITH mess
                              REPLACE time_sent WITH time()
                              REPLACE subject WITH subj
                              REPLACE from WITH myname
                              REPLACE date_sent WITH date()

                              REPLACE to WITH who_to

                              UNLOCK

                        ENDIF
                  ENDIF
            ENDIF

      RETURN

      PROCEDURE del

      PRIVATE sel, num_messages, max_messages

            SELECT messages
            GOTO TOP

            IF e_fil_lock(20, "Cannot lock file, retry (y/n)? ", 23, 10)

                  max_messages = reccount()
                  PRIVATE mess[max_messages]
                  PRIVATE recs[max_messages]

                  num_messages = 0
                  DO WHILE !eof()
                        num_messages = num_messages + 1

                        mess[num_messages] = time_sent + ' ' + dtoc(date_sent) + ;
                                                            ' ' + subject + ' ' + from
                        recs[num_messages] = recno()
                        SKIP
                  ENDDO

                  UNLOCK

                  * this returns element number, of course ...
                  sel = abrowse(mess, num_messages, 10, 10, 20, 60)

                  IF sel != 0
                        GOTO recs[sel]

                        IF e_rec_lock(20, "Cannot lock record, retry (y/n)? ", 23, 10 )
                              DELETE
                              UNLOCK
```

```
                ENDIF
            ENDIF

        ENDIF

    RETURN
```

Program 10-22 applies the functions developed in this chapter. It can serve as the basis for any electronic mail system. It is also a good place to start your local area network efforts. The code is simple and easy to modify. Furthermore, errors in it cannot cause much damage.

Disclaimer: The author does not accept any legal, financial, ethical, or moral responsibility for anything, much less anyone's network. He will, however, consider accepting generous consulting fees paid in unmarked gold bars. Swiss bank account number available on request!

Single User Testing

Clipper lets you test network programs on a single user system. You can test file and record locks, error recovery schemes, message positioning, and screen layout without running on a network. The key here is Clipper's ability to open the same file in different areas.

Even though the file is local to the application, we must run the network software. For IBM's Token-Ring, running the SHARE.EXE terminate and stay resident program is sufficient. It runs automatically when you start the network, either from the NET menus or by using the NET START command. This is necessary to ensure the correct operation of the USE ... EXCLUSIVE and record and file lock commands and functions.

Study the following code:

```
SET EXCLUSIVE ON

SELECT 0
USE test2 ALIAS test21

IF neterr()
    ? "Error, first open of test2 failed"
ENDIF

* USE should fail because the file was opened in exclusive mode
SELECT 0
```

```
USE test2 ALIAS test22

IF neterr()
        ? "Error, second open of test2 failed"
ENDIF

* close first file opened
SELECT test21

USE

SET EXCLUSIVE OFF

* open original file in shared mode
SELECT 0
USE test2 ALIAS test21

IF neterr()
        ? "Error, third open of test2 failed"
ENDIF

* This open will succeed because file was opened in shared mode
SELECT 0
USE test2 ALIAS test22

* Try to lock this file, this will succeed
IF !flock()
        ? "First File lock failed"
ENDIF

* Try to lock the first file, this will fail since already locked.
SELECT test21
IF !flock()
        ? "Second File lock failed"
ENDIF

* Now unlock locked file
SELECT test22
UNLOCK

* Now lock first record in this file, this will succeed
IF !rlock()
        ? "First record lock failed"
ENDIF

* Now lock record in other file, this will fail since already locked
SELECT test21
IF !rlock()
        ? "Second rlock failed"
ENDIF

* advance to next record (# 2), and lock it. This will succeed
```

```
SKIP
IF !rlock()
        ? "Third rlock failed"
ENDIF
```

The comments describe the actions and expected results. Run the program. If the results do not agree with the comments, you probably did not run the software (or SHARE in the Token-Ring case). If you did, Clipper must have problems running on your network, and you should contact Nantucket technical support.

In the preceding example, we USE a database with an alias and then check for NETERR. The alias is necessary since we are opening the file in two different areas. An alternative is the user defined function. We could use E_NET_USE, since it accepts an alias. Note that we could NOT use Nantucket's NET_USE. This is the primary reason why we modified "NET_USE" to "E_NET_USE1" (Program 10-6).

Non-Dedicated Servers

Some networks allow applications to run on the server. There are two issues Clipper programmers should consider when writing applications for a non-dedicated server. First, memory will be at a premium, as the network software will use a large amount of it. Second, the files will be named differently. Whereas an application running on a client machine refers to a file with a network drive name, the application running on the server will refer to it as a local file.

You can overcome the memory shortage either by careful use of the SET CLIPPER environment variable, or with overlays. If overlays are necessary, leave the source code the same for the server, and just change the linking instructions.

The different names cause a more serious problem. The solution lies in the program recognizing that it is running on the server. It can then use the appropriate names. You can do this with the FILE function. If the application uses a file "test" on network drive z: (one that is always present), then the following call to FILE will fail if the program is running on the server:

```
file("z:test")
```

Summary

This is a long chapter. We have discussed many problems related to programming for local area networks. We have provided suggestions on how to overcome them. If you run across a problem in a network application, classify it in one of the categories we discussed, and apply the appropriate techniques. Here are some key points:

- To start, use an existing application with file names referring to the server.
- Once you are confident about a network, modify the electronic mail system.
- Apply worst case analysis to all code.
- Use the routines given in this chapter to use, lock, and append to databases.
- Watch for the following problems and write your code to avoid them:
  - Deadlock
  - Interrupted read/modify/write cycles
  - Uncompleted transactions
  - Lost updates
  - Inconsistent analysis

11

Using C with Clipper

This Chapter describes how to use C with Clipper. We show how to transfer data between the two languages. We emphasize the Microsoft C 5.00 compiler. It is the most compatible compiler, as it is the one used to compile Clipper. One section also discusses the use of Microsoft's QuickC, Borland's Turbo C, and Lattice C. For a complete list of topics in this chapter, turn the page.

Overview

C is useful for doing tasks that are difficult or impossible in Clipper. Although it is a high-level language, C provides almost complete machine control through direct pointer addressing and library functions that access DOS, the ROM BIOS, and the I/O ports. If your program cannot do its tasks using C, they probably cannot be done. One of Clipper's biggest advantages is its C interface. If you reach Clipper's limits, write the functions you need in C. This chapter shows you how.

We cover the following topics:

- Accessing C from Clipper
- Transferring data to and from Clipper
- Call by value and call by reference
- Compiling and linking
- Accessing Clipper internal values
- Cursor handling
- Mouse interface
- Debugging
- Serial communications
- Windowing

The first sections cover background material. We then present a series of practical examples.

Accessing C from Clipper

You can access C in two ways from Clipper, either through user defined functions or with the CALL statement. You call a C user defined function in the same way you call a Clipper function. There is no difference in the Clipper code. You pass parameters in the same way, and the function returns its value in the same manner. The interface is elegant and consistent.

A CALL statement, on the other hand, uses a different syntax. It takes the form:

```
CALL <proc> WITH <param1>, <param2> ...
```

A typical example is the use of CALL in the Autumn '86 release to turn the cursor on or off. A CALL _SETCTYP WITH 0 simply calls a procedure written in another language. In fact, _SETCTYP is an assembly language routine located in the Clipper drivers. The syntax and parameters are the same, however, regardless of whether you call C or assembly language routines.

Nantucket openly discourages the use of the CALL command. Its syntax does not even appear in the Summer '87 documentation. Its description is relegated to the end of the addendum.doc file under the heading 'Undocumented features'. There is good reason for this discouragement. The command's syntax is clumsy, and its implementation is machine-dependent. User defined functions, on the other hand, meld nicely into the Clipper language. You interface them through the Clipper-defined extend system. The approach is portable, and upward-compatible, regardless of machine or language.

The author agrees with Nantucket's philosophy with one exception. CALL is useful because its parameters are passed by reference and can therefore be changed. Although you can pass parameters by reference to user defined functions, the extend system does not provide sufficient tools to implement it. Until we can pass parameters successfully by reference to user defined functions written in C or assembly language, CALL has its place.

This chapter concentrates on the user defined function interface, although we use CALL in the section on windowing.

Getting Data From Clipper

If you are familiar with C, you know that its functions have their parameters specified in parentheses following the function name, and then listed separately defining their types, as in:

```
void func1(param1, param2, param3)

int param1;
char *param2;
double param3;
```

```
{
        •
        •
        •
}
```

This is NOT the correct approach when you call the function from Clipper. Instead, you must call a function from the extend library to get each parameter. The function retrieves the value from Clipper's internal stack, and converts it to a C data type. The actual function you call depends on the types of the Clipper memory variable and the C variable. Table 11-1 lists the routines that do the translations.

Table 11-1. Clipper Extend Functions for Converting C Parameters

Clipper	C	Extend Function
character	char *	_parc()
		_parclen()
date	char *	_pards()
logical	int	_parl()
numeric	int	_parni()
	long	_parnl()
	double	_parnd()

For example, to transform a Clipper logical into a C int, call the _parl function. To convert a Clipper character string into a C character pointer, call the _parc function.

It is good C programming practice to define prototypes for all functions used by a module. They specify the function's return type, and the types of its parameters. The compiler can then perform type checking at compile time. Even though a function may be defined in another module, the prototype allows the compiler to check its parameters and return value. It can thus identify problems at compile time, rather than at run time, when they are more difficult to detect and diagnose.

The function prototypes for the extend functions are in the include file 'extend.h'. You should include it in any C code that interfaces to Clipper. Here are the prototypes for the _par routines:

```
extern char *_parc(int, ...);
extern int _parclen(int, ...);

extern char *_pards(int, ...);
```

```
extern int _parl(int, ...);

extern int _parni(int, ...);
extern long _parnl(int, ...);
extern double _parnd(int, ...);
```

Look at the definition for _parc. It defines the function as returning a pointer to a character. It also defines the first parameter as an integer and an optional second parameter (...). If you use the function in a manner inconsistent with its definition, the compiler will report an error.

Note that all functions require an integer as their first parameter. It is the parameter's number in the actual parameter list. For example, if a function takes three parameters, you retrieve the first with a call to _par?(1), the second with a call to _par?(2), and the third with a call to _par?(3). The actual function (indicated by a ?) depends on the type. For example, if the first parameter is a logical, the second a character, and the third a number, you would retrieve them with calls to _parl(1), _parc(2), and _parni(3). The following code fragment shows this:

```
•
•
•

CLIPPER cfunc()

{
        int param1;
        char *param2;
        int param3;

        param1 = _parl(1);
        param2 = _parc(2);
        param3 = _parni(3);

        •
        •
        •
}
```

You can use either _parnl(3) or _parnd(3) instead of _parni(3). The choice depends on which C data type you want. Here we used an int. If the parameter were greater than 64K, we would have to make it either a long or a double.

You use the second parameter when passing an array. It specifies the element number. For example, assume that parameter 3 is an array, and that its fifth element is a logical. You would get it with a call to _parl(3, 5).

You use _parclen to get the length of a character parameter. You cannot use the conventional C routine 'strlen'. It determines the length of a string by looking for a terminator byte (0 or CHR(0) in Clipper). Since Clipper allows CHR(0) inside a string, strlen will not work.

Two other functions in extend.h allow for type checking. They are:

```
extern int _parinfo(int);
extern int _parinfa(int, int);
```

The _parinfo function returns the parameter's type. _parinfa does the same for an array, assuming that the second parameter specifies the element. If you pass a zero to _parinfo, it returns the number of parameters. If you pass a zero as the second parameter to _parinfa, it returns the number of elements in the array.

You can use the type checking functions at the start of a function to verify the number of parameters and their types. Each type has a specific value, as listed in Table 11-2 (these are defined in extend.h).

Table 11-2. Type Definitions and Values in extend.h.

#define	UNDEF	0
#define	CHARACTER	1
#define	NUMERIC	2
#define	LOGICAL	4
#define	DATE	8
#define	ALIAS	16
#define	MPTR	32
#define	MEMO	65
#define	WORD	128
#define	ARRAY	512

Clipper uses these values internally to represent the types. Although not indicated in the Nantucket documentation, they are actually separate bits in a 16-bit word. Figure 11-1 shows the word's structure.

Figure 11-1. Clipper Data Type Indicators

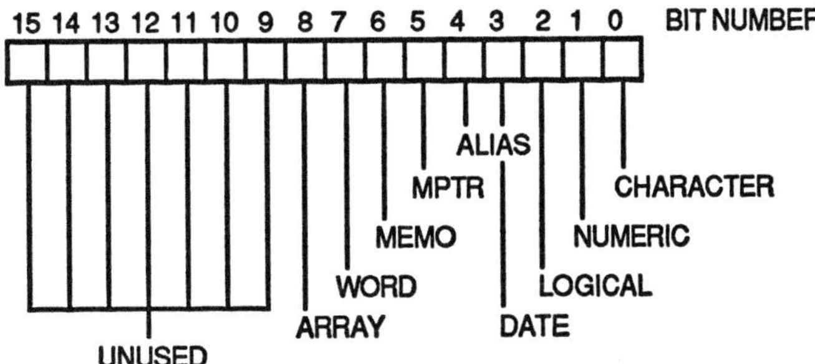

Figure 11-1 shows the bit used for memo fields as bit 6 (value 64 decimal or 40 hex), but the value defined in the extend.h file is 65. The 65 value combines the MEMO bit and the CHARACTER bit, so memo fields can be processed as character fields.

The MPTR bit indicates (with a 1) a parameter passed by reference. The value returned from parinfo depends on whether the parameter was passed by value or by reference. For example, a character field passed by value has a value of 1 (bit 0 set), whereas one passed by reference has a value of 33 (bits 0 and 5 set). Figure 11-2 shows this.

Figure 11-2. Character Type Values

15	14	13	12	11	10	9	8	7	6	5	4	3	2	1	0	BIT NUMBER
0	0	0	0	0	0	0	0	0	0	0	0	0	0	0	1	

PASSED BY VALUE = 1

15	14	13	12	11	10	9	8	7	6	5	4	3	2	1	0	BIT NUMBER
0	0	0	0	0	0	0	0	0	0	1	0	0	0	0	1	
										32		+			1	

PASSED BY REFERENCE = 33

_parinfo returns a type ARRAY when the parameter is an array. To find the value of a particular element, use the parinfa function.

Nantucket defines compiler macros that you can use to check a parameter's type. Here is how they appear in the extend.h file:

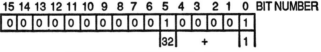

```
#define ISCHAR(n)     (_parinfo(n) & CHARACTER)
#define ISNUM(n)      (_parinfo(n) & NUMERIC)
#define ISLOG(n)      (_parinfo(n) & LOGICAL)
#define ISDATE(n)     (_parinfo(n) & DATE)
```

```
#define ISMEMO(n)        (_parinfo(n) & MEMO)
#define ISBYREF(n )      (_parinfo(n) & MPTR)
#define ISARRAY(n)       (_parinfo(n) & ARRAY)
```

The macros are logical expressions. You can thus use them in sequences such as:

```
if (ISCHAR(1))
{
    /* parameter 1 is a character */
  •
  •
  •
}
```

Note that they check a bit, rather than looking for a specific absolute value. This allows them to return the correct logical value regardless of whether the parameter was passed by reference.

Two other macros (PCOUNT and ALENGTH) return the number of parameters passed and the length of an array, as in:

```
#define ALENGTH(n)       (_parinfa(n, 0))

#define PCOUNT           (_parinfo(0))
```

You should use the macros to simplify code and make it more readable. They are preferable to a 'hard-coded' _parinfo call.

> **RULE**
>
> To transfer data to C from Clipper, you must call one of the _par functions in the extend library.

Returning Data to Clipper

A similar set of functions allows C code to return a value to Clipper. Again, the particular routine to be called depends on the type to be returned. Table 11-3 lists the functions.

Table 11-3. Clipper Extend Functions for C Return Values

C	Clipper	Extend Function
char *	character	_retc()
		_retclen()
	date	_retds()
int	logical	_retl()
	numeric	_retni()
long	numeric	_retnl()
double	numeric	_retnd()

You call the function with the value to be returned. For example, to return a logical to Clipper, call the _retl function with a C integer (a logical .F. is defined as 0, a .T. as any non-zero value, although 1 is common). To return a C string (represented by char *) as a Clipper character type, pass the _retc function a string.

The value is the result of the user defined function. You access it from Clipper as a function return value in the same way as built-in functions such as CTOD and STR, and user defined functions written in Clipper. Make sure you call the correct _ret function. Clipper does not know what type should be returned. It will create a variable of whatever type you specify. If this is wrong, a type error will occur when the data is processed.

The _retclen function is basically the inverse of the _parclen function. It takes a string and a length as parameters, and returns them to Clipper. The length is used to correctly return a string with embedded CHR(0)'s, or to return part of a larger string.

Just as Clipper user defined functions must return a value regardless of whether it is used, so must functions written in C. They must call one of the _ret functions. The extend system conveniently provides a function _ret() to handle a 'null value' return. You should use it if the function does not return a value.

The _ret? function prototypes are defined in extend.h as:

```
extern void _retc(char *);
extern void _retclen(char *, int);
extern void _retni(int);
extern void _retnl(long);
extern void _retnd(double);
extern void _retl(int);
extern void _retds(char *);
extern void _ret(void);
```

Nantucket defines the functions as returning a void because

they do not return a value to C. Instead, they manipulate Clipper's internal stack directly. You will notice from Table 11-3 that a parameter type for a return function corresponds to the type returned by the function.

> **RULE**
>
> To return a value from C to Clipper, you must call one of the _ret functions in the extend library. Call _ret to return a null value.

Call by Value and Call by Reference

This section discusses call by value and call by reference. If you do not understand the terms, refer to Chapter 2. As you know, unless instructed otherwise, Clipper passes parameters to functions by value. Any changes the function makes to the parameters are only local. They are not reflected on return. Array parameters are an exception. They are passed by reference.

You can override the default rules by preceding the actual parameter with the @ symbol, indicating a call by reference. (This does not work with array elements, see Chapter 3).

In C, you can use the ISBYREF macro to determine whether a parameter has been passed by reference. It checks the bit in the word returned from the _parinfo function.

Unfortunately, the extend system does not allow correct processing of variables passed by reference. The whole point of call by reference is to allow parameters to be changed, but how can we access them? For example, the _parni function returns an integer, not a pointer to an integer. Since we do not have access to its address, we cannot change it. The same applies to logicals and dates. Dates are passed as strings, but internally they are represented as doubles, which cannot be accessed.

Character strings, on the other hand, can be changed since the _parc function returns a pointer. Incidentally, it does this regardless of whether the parameter is passed by reference.

User defined functions in C (or in assembly language for that matter) thus differ from their Clipper counterparts in that they cannot modify parameters passed by reference. A new set of _par functions is required that returns pointers to the actual types (pointer to logical, int, etc), or a set of _sto functions (_stoc, _stoin) that store the value back into the parameter. Later in this Chapter we show a technique that overcomes this limitation.

> **NOTE**
>
> There is no way to change a parameter passed by reference to C.

Compiling and Linking

Before proceeding to meaningful examples, we must first show how to compile and link a C function.

Microsoft C

To compile a Microsoft C program to run with Clipper, you must use the following flags:

1) /c - Compile only, do not automatically invoke the linker (the default).

2) /AL - Use the "large model". This is a requirement for all routines linked with Clipper. Clipper itself is compiled in the large model.

3) /Gs - Do not generate stack probes. Again, this is necessary since Clipper is compiled with the flag.

4) /Zl - Do not place the names of the default libraries in the object file.

5) /FPa - Do not generate floating point calls. Select the alternate mathematical package. Necessary because Clipper uses this library.

Subsequent sections show the use of the flags.

We have already discussed the include file "extend.h". You must include it in any C code that interfaces with Clipper. The file relies on definitions in the other header file Nantucket supplies, "nandef.h". You must also include it in the C code before extend.h.

By default, the Microsoft compiler inserts an underscore ahead of function names it places in the OBJ file. For example, a function defined as "test" appears in the OBJ file as "_test". Now, Clipper does not add this leading underscore, so a call to "test" appears in the Clipper produced OBJ file as "test". When the two routines are linked, the linker will complain - it cannot find the function test.

You can stop the Microsoft compiler from adding the leading underscore by declaring the function as type 'pascal'. The new type also affects the way the routine receives parameters. However, this does not matter as Clipper called C routines receive their parameters with the _par routines anyway.

Since the routines do not return a C value (they use _ret routines), they must also be declared as void. For example, you must define a function "test" with:

```
#include "nandef.h"

#include "extend.h"

•
•
•

void pascal test()

{
        •
        •
        •
}
```

If you look at the extend.h file, you will see that it defines the symbol CLIPPER as "void pascal", so the following is equivalent and preferred:

```
#include "nandef.h"
#include "extend.h"

•
•
•

CLIPPER test()

{
        •
        •
        •
}
```

This is the general form of all C user defined functions.

When linking the Microsoft libraries, you must use the /NOE option to suppress duplicate symbol warnings. Some symbols are defined in both the Clipper and Microsoft libraries. Without the flag, the linker produces a series of irritating warnings.

Tlink, the linker supplied with Borland's Turbo C, does not always link OBJ modules produced with the Microsoft compiler. Microsoft has introduced new record types into the OBJ file format. Currently, Tlink does not support them. However, the DOS linker and PLINK86 both work.

This section has discussed Microsoft C 5.00. To summarize:

- You must always include nandef.h and extend.h.
- You should define Clipper callable functions as CLIPPER.
- You must call one of the ret functions. Call _ret if the function does not return an actual value.
- Compile with: CL /c /AL /Gs /Zl /FPa.
- Link with /NOE when using the Microsoft Library.

Other Compilers

This section shows how to use compilers other than Microsoft C 5.00.

The Clipper library and the Clipper compiler are written in Microsoft C. The OBJ files Clipper produces are compatible with those produced by Microsoft - they must be since they are linked with the Clipper library to produce the EXE file.

To link OBJ files produced with other compilers, you must ensure that they are compatible with Microsoft files. This section discusses just what compatibility means, and how Lattice C 3.2, Borland's Turbo C, and Microsoft's QuickC measure up.

An OBJ file consists of a number of sections called segments. Different segments hold different things. One holds the program code, another the data, still another constants. Each segment has a name, a class, and a set of attributes. Run-time code uses the segment's name to find its starting point. The class of a segment controls the order in which it appears at run time. Segments with different names, but the same class, are ordered consecutively, regardless of their positions in the OBJ file. The attributes specify, among other things, how the linker should combine the segment with others of the same name. An attribute PUBLIC means that segments of the same name and class should be combined into one larger segment. An attribute PRIVATE means that they should be kept separate.

The order in which segments are defined in the OBJ file is important. This, and the class, defines the order in which they are placed in the EXE file, and thus loaded into memory. Run-time code resident in the Clipper library depends on a strict segment ordering. The first OBJ file specified on the link line defines this, so it must be Clipper-produced.

All Microsoft OBJ files conform to a segment architecture called DOSSEG. It defines the names, classes, attributes, and order of an OBJ file's segments. The Clipper produced OBJ file is actually a superset of the DOSSEG architecture. It adds segments Clipper needs in a way that is compatible with the basic DOSSEG architecture.

You can use other compilers only if they produce OBJ files with the DOSSEG architecture. Borland's Turbo C does by default. So does Microsoft's QuickC. Lattice C, on the other hand, does not. The 3.2 release, however, allows you to produce such files by using the -cx flag.

Another factor to consider is how the compiler uses the machine registers at run time. For example, say a linked C routine calls the extend functions written in Microsoft C. If the calling routine expects the return value in certain registers but Microsoft C returns them in others, you will have problems. Only Lattice C fails here, but again, by using the -cx flag, it can produce return values compatible with Microsoft.

Using a compiler's library functions causes another problem. The Microsoft libraries, of course, can be used freely. The Lattice library cannot be used. It is compiled with Lattice's default segment architecture and function return values, incompatible with Microsoft as already discussed. The Microsoft library, however, can be linked successfully with Lattice OBJs. Add an underscore at the beginning of any library routine called. The Turbo C library can be used, because its default architecture and function return values are compatible with Microsoft. QuickC's library cannot be used. Its floating point routines conflict with Clipper's, causing the program to crash on startup.

All these libraries, however, present a problem with floating point numbers. Whenever you use a C double or float, the compiler generates calls to run-time routines to do type conversion and arithmetic. These are implicit. The programmer does not explicitly call the routines; the compiler does it automatically. The Lattice compiler produces calls to its own routines, and since we cannot link its library, they will not work. Linking a Turbo C routine with implicit floating point calls produces unresolved external messages. They presumably refer to data resident in its startup code.

Here is how to invoke the Lattice compiler to produce OBJs for use with Clipper:

```
lc -ml -ccdmsuw -v -cx test
```

The -ml, -ccdmsuw and -v flags are the same as for use with the Autumn '86 release. The -cx is the Microsoft compatibility option we discussed.

Here is how to invoke the Turbo C compiler to produce OBJs for use with Clipper:

```
tcc -c -ml test.c
```

The -ml indicates the large model, and the -c instructs it to compile only (it links as well by default).

To use QuickC, compile with:

```
qcl /c /AL /Zl /Olt /Gs testc.c
```

This ends our discussion of specific compilers. The rest of the Chapter concentrates on using the C language, regardless of the compiler.

So far we have shown how to transfer data to and from C, and how to compile and link C routines. With this background information in place, we now present our first example.

Cursor Control

In Chapter 7 we used a routine "setcurs" to control the cursor's shape. It took two numeric parameters, the start and end lines of the cursor. Program 11-1 is the source for "setcurs".

Program 11-1. Cursor Shape Control

```
/***
* cursset.c
*
*       Use int86 function to invoke ROM BIOS to set cursor shape. Clipper
* callable.
*/

#include "nandef.h"
#include "extend.h"

#include "dos.h"

#define SET_CTYPE 1
#define VIDEO 0x10
```

```
CLIPPER setcurs()

{
        union REGS inregs;
        union REGS outregs;

        inregs.h.ah = SET_CTYPE;

        inregs.h.ch = _parni(1);     /* start line */
        inregs.h.cl = _parni(2);     /* end line */

        int86(VIDEO, &inregs, &outregs);

        _ret();
}
```

Using Microsoft C, we would compile Program 11-1 with:

```
cl /c /AL /Oalt /FPa /Gs cursset.c
```

The trailing .c on the file name is mandatory. If it is missing, the compiler simply exits without compiling. It does not even report an error!

You call the function as follows:

```
* ctest.prg

setcurs(4, 7)  && set half-height
wait           && pause to view display
setcurs(7, 7)  && reset underscore cursor
wait           && pause to view display
```

The above calls are for a color screen. See Chapter 7 for details.

You link the function with

```
link ctest curset,,,\clipper\clipper \clipper\extend \mc\lib\llibca /noe
```

We use the library function int86 to call the ROM BIOS. The routine uses interrupt 10 (hex), the video interrupt, with function 1, set cursor type. It requires the start line in register CH, and the end line in CL. See the appropriate technical reference manual or Peter Norton's book (*Programmer's Guide to the IBM PC*, Redmond, WA: Microsoft Press, 1985) for details.

The Microsoft library documentation describes the int86 function. It takes three parameters:

1. The interrupt number.
2. A memory copy of the machine registers to load before making the interrupt call.
3. A memory copy of the machine registers set on return from the interrupt.

You cause the registers to be loaded by assigning values to the structure. We set the values to the parameters passed from Clipper, retrieved with _parni. Before making the interrupt call, the function loads the registers from the structure. On return from the interrupt, it saves the registers in the second structure. The calling function can then access the return value from the output structure.

Program 11-1 shows just how easy it is to interface C routines to Clipper. By using the library functions such as int86 for ROM BIOS and DOS interrupts, and the in and out functions to directly control the I/O ports, you can gain almost complete machine control.

> **TIP**
>
> Use the INT86 library routine to interface to DOS and the ROM BIOS.

Accessing Clipper Internal Variables

SET Functions

Clipper provides functions that check the current state of some SETs. setcolor(), dbrelation(), etc., return their current assignments. For most SETs, however, programmers are left to their own devices. As discussed in Chapter 4, a common way to check states is to write a function for each SET. It assigns the value to a public variable, and then does the actual SET. Whenever the program must determine the state, it simply examines the global variable.

However, there is a better way. Here we develop C routines that directly access Clipper internal values.

The first step in developing the functions is to determine the variables' names. We do this by generating a detailed map file. You can use a simple one line program without any C code to do this.

Take any Clipper-compiled program, such as maptest, and link it with:

```
link maptest,maptest/m,,\clipper\clipper
```

The option maptest/m makes the linker produce a file maptest.map. It shows the segment structure of the EXE file, and lists all public symbols defined in all linked OBJs. They include all public symbols contained in Clipper.lib, so by examining the map file, we can see the names of all public internal variables! Since the names are public, we can develop C code to use them. The trick lies in knowing which variables do what. Here is where a symbolic debugger such as Lattice's C-Sprite or Microsoft's CodeView comes into play. If you perform a SET and then cause a breakpoint, you can examine the public symbols and determine which ones have changed.

We discuss the use of symbolic debuggers later in this chapter. Now, unless you know the names of the internal variables, or which module in Clipper.lib they come from, you are in for a lot of work. However, we have done the analysis and present the results here.

Look at the map file. It consists of three sections. The first shows the run-time segment structure. The second lists all public symbols by name, the third lists them in order of ascending address. Now, consider the names of the SETs for which Clipper does not provide status functions. We have alternate, cursor, bell, century, exact, etc. You might guess that the internal names for these SETs would resemble their external names. You would be correct. If you look in the list that shows the symbols ordered by name, you will see names such as __alternate_on, __curs_on, __bell_on, __century_on, __exact_on, etc. They are the variables that maintain the states of the SETs. The only ones whose variables are not public are those affected by SET MESSAGE TO and SET TYPEAHEAD TO. It is thus impossible to access them.

To access the SETs from C, you must define the names as external and assign them types. For SET CURSOR, we would define the name as:

```
extern Boolean _curs_on;
```

Note that we use only one underscore, even though the name appears in the map file with two. The compiler adds the other one.

We can now write a function to return the value of _curs_on as:

```
#include "nandef.h"
#include "extend.h"

/***
* LOGICAL curs_on()
*
*        Return current state of SET CURSOR
*/
CLIPPER curs_on()

{
        _retl(_curs_on);
}
```

The routine returns a logical, as the comment at the head states. We would access it from a Clipper routine as:

```
cur_cursor = curs_on();
```

A better form (Program 11-2) allows an optional parameter. If it exists, the routine sets the internal variable to it. In any case, the routine returns the variable's original value.

Program 11-2. Get/Set State of SET CURSOR

```
/***
* LOGICAL curs_on()
*
*        Get/set state of SET CURSOR. If parameter, set to its value.
* Return previous value.
*/

CLIPPER curs_on()

{
        _retl(_curs_on);

        if (PCOUNT)
                _curs_on = _parl(1);
}
```

The PCOUNT macro determines whether the routine received any parameters. If it did, _parl retrieves the value. The routine then assigns the value to _curs_on.

Let's look at another example. Program 11-3 handles SET EXACT. As in the previous routine, if a parameter is passed, SET EXACT is set to its value. In either case, the routine returns the current value (before the possible assignment occurs).

Program 11-3. Get/Set State of EXACT ON

```
/***
* LOGICAL exact_on()
*
* Get/set current state of EXACT ON. If parameter, set to its
* value. Return previous value.

*/

CLIPPER exact_on()

{
        _retl(_exact_on);

        if (PCOUNT)
                _exact_on = _parl(1);
}
```

The variable _exact_on maintains the state of the EXACT flag internally. A call to _retl returns its value.

This function has the same structure as Program 11-2. The required value is returned, PCOUNT determines whether a parameter was passed and, if one was, its value is retrieved with a '_par' function. The internal Clipper variable is then set to the value.

Appendix B contains the source code for functions that get/set the states of the following SETs, all written using the same structure:

- SET ALTERNATE ON/OFF
- SET ALTERNATE TO (including its file handle)
- SET BELL
- SET CENTURY
- SET CONFIRM
- SET CONSOLE
- SET CURSOR
- SET DATE
- SET DECIMALS
- SET DEFAULT TO
- SET DELETED

- SET DELIMITERS (ON/OFF and left and right delimiters)
- SET DEVICE TO
- SET ESCAPE
- SET EXACT
- SET EXCLUSIVE
- SET FUNCTION TO
- SET FORMAT TO
- SET FIXED
- SET INTENSITY
- SET MARGIN
- SET PATH
- SET PRINT ON
- SET PRINTER TO
- SET SCOREBOARD
- SET SOFTSEEK
- SET UNIQUE
- SET WRAP

Note that the functions depend on Clipper maintaining its internal naming conventions. They are correct for the Summer '87 release. If you have problems linking the routines with a future release, either scan the map file for a similar name and use the debugger to verify your guess, or discontinue their use. Admittedly this is a dangerous practice, and we would prefer to have Nantucket provide similar functions. Until then, however, the functions are too useful to give up.

We will now show functions that manipulate the internal representations of the keys set by a SET KEY TO statement.

Hot Key Table

In the map file, you will see a public symbol named _keyset. This is the start of an array of structures, one for each key set. The structure contains a two byte value giving the key number, and a pointer to the internal symbol representing the routine to be called. A pointer occupies four bytes since we are using the large model. Each element of the structure thus contains six bytes.

Clipper lets the programmer assign 32 keys, and it reserves space for the F1 default "HELP". The array thus contains 33 entries. The following C data structure defines it:

```
typedef struct
{
        quant key_val;
        char *key_routine;
} KEY_SET;                    /* 6 bytes */

/* number of keys that can be set, 32 + help */
#define KEY_SET_COUNT 33

extern KEY_SET _keyset[KEY_SET_COUNT];
```

_keyset is defined as an external array of structures with 33 entries. External means that the structure is defined elsewhere. We give the structure the name KEY_SET, and its elements are key_val and key_routine.

The most useful functions to process the structures are ones that push and pop the entire array on and off a stack. Another useful one saves the array, and then clears it so that no function keys are set. Program 11-4 contains all three functions.

Program 11-4. Hot Key Manager

```
/***
* hotkeys.c
*
*       Routines to push, push and clear, and pop the hot keys.
*/

/* maximum depth of stack */
#define STACK_DEPTH 10

char *set_key_stack[STACK_DEPTH];
unsigned sk_ptr = 0;

/***
* LOGICAL push_keys
*
*        Push the current state of the hot keys
*
*       1 - Verify that room exists on stack.
*
*       2 - Allocate memory for key save.
```

```
*
*       3 - Push onto stack.
*
*/
CLIPPER push_keys()

{
        Boolean ret_val;

        /* If no stack overflow ... */
        if (sk_ptr < STACK_DEPTH)
        {
                if (set_key_stack[sk_ptr] = malloc(sizeof(_keyset)))
                {
                        /* push onto stack by copying and incrementing pointer */
                        memcpy(set_key_stack[sk_ptr], (char *) _keyset,
                                sizeof(_keyset));
                        sk_ptr++;
                        ret_val = TRUE;
                }
                else  /* couldn't allocate memory - complain */
                        ret_val = FALSE;
        }
        else
                /* stack would overflow, so complain */
        ret_val = FALSE;

        _retl(ret_val);
}

/***
*       LOGICAL push_ckeys()
*
*         Push the current state of the hot keys, then clear them.
*
*       1 - Verify that room exists on stack.
*
*       2 - Allocate memory for key save.
*
*       3 - Push onto stack.
*
*       4 - Clear current keys.
*/

CLIPPER push_ckeys()

{
        Boolean ret_val;

        /* if no stack overflow */
        if (sk_ptr < STACK_DEPTH)
        {
```

```
                if (set_key_stack[sk_ptr] = malloc(sizeof(_keyset)))
                {
                        /* save them */
                        memcpy(set_key_stack[sk_ptr], (char *) _keyset,

                                sizeof(_keyset));
                        sk_ptr++;

                        /* now clear them */
                        memset((char *) _keyset, 0, sizeof(_keyset));
                        ret_val = TRUE;
                }
                else    /* memory allocation failed, complain */
                        ret_val = FALSE;
        }
        else            /* stack would overflow, complain */
                ret_val = FALSE;

        _retl(ret_val);
}

/***
* LOGICAL pop_keys()
*
*         Restore keys from top of stack.
*
*       1 - Verify no underflow.
*
*       2 - Pop from stack into current keys.
*
*       3 - Free memory.
*/

CLIPPER pop_keys()

{
        Boolean ret_val;

        /* if stack not empty */
        if (sk_ptr > 0)
        {
                sk_ptr--;
                memcpy((char *) _keyset, set_key_stack[sk_ptr], sizeof(_keyset));

                /* return memory to free pool */
                free(set_key_stack[sk_ptr]);
                ret_val = TRUE;
        }
        else    /* stack was empty, so complain */
                ret_val = FALSE;

        _retl(ret_val);
}
```

We define an array of size STACK_DEPTH. Each element is a character pointer. We use the array as a stack. The push routines 'push' a pointer onto the stack, the pop routines 'pop' it off. The pointer points to dynamic memory which saves a copy of the hot key table. This allows the saves to be nested. Your routines can save the state of the keys, and then set any it requires. They can then call another routine that saves this new state, and sets some keys it requires. When the second routine finishes, it pops the stack, resetting the keys required by the first routine. When it finishes, it pops the stack, resetting the keys to the values they had when it was called.

The depth of the nesting depends on the size of the array, in this case 10 (STACK_DEPTH). The variable sk_ptr keeps track of the top of stack.

The push_keys routine allocates dynamic memory in the current top of stack with a call to the library routine malloc. The entire key_set structure is then copied into this memory with a call to memcpy. push_ckeys does the same thing except that after saving the keys, it sets them to 0 with a call to memset, thus disabling them. It is the same as performing a SET KEY TO <null> for each key.

The pop_keys routine restores the set keys from the preceding push. It copies the string pointed to by the top of stack pointer into the _keyset area.

You may sometimes need to determine the states of individual SET KEYs, rather than process them as a whole as the previous routines do. You may want to save the state of just one key, turn it off, do some processing, and then re-enable it. Program 11-5 does this. The key number is the first parameter. It is mandatory. An optional second parameter sets the hot key's value. The routine returns the key's previous value.

Program 11-5. Manage an Individual Hot Key

```
/***
* NUMERIC key_set()
*
*       Get/set state of a function key. If parameter, set to the
* value. Previous value returned. Value passed must be one returned
* from this function previously, or 0 to unset it.
*
* 1 - Search _keyset for key.
*
* 2 - IF found
*               return its pointer
```

```
*        ELSE
*              return 0
*        ENDIF
*
*        3 - If second parameter (set key to this value)
*
*              3.1 - Did Step 2 find it?
*
*                    3.1.1 - Yes, set it to this new value.
*
*                    3.1.2 - No,
*
*                          3.1.2.1 - Search for an empty one.
*
*                          3.1.2.2 - Set value and key (key_value = 0)
*/
CLIPPER key_set()

{
	Boolean ret_val;
	unsigned i, key_look;

	/* get key under consideration */
	key_look = _parni(1);

	/* search for the key */
	for (i = 0; i < KEY_SET_COUNT && _keyset[i].key_val != key_look; i++);

	if (i < KEY_SET_COUNT)
	{
		/* found, so return its pointer value */
		_retnl((long) _keyset[i].key_routine);
	}
	else
	{
		/* not found, return 0 */
		_retnl(0l);
	}

	/* if the key is to be set, set it */
	if (PCOUNT == 2)
	{
		/* if we found it before, overwrite the value */
		if (i < KEY_SET_COUNT)
			_keyset[i].key_routine = (char *) _parnl(2);
		else
		{
			/* didn't find it, so look for blank spot, 0 */
			for (i = 0; i < KEY_SET_COUNT &&
						_keyset[i].key_val != 0; i++);
```

```
                /* Was blank spot found? */
                        if (i < KEY_SET_COUNT)
                        {
                                /* yes, so set new key and pointer */
                                _keyset[i].key_val = key_look;
                                _keyset[i].key_routine = (char *) _parnl(2);
                        }
                        /* else can't do anything, table full */
                }
        }
}
```

We retrieve the first parameter from Clipper with a call to _parni. It is the value of the key under consideration. We then search the _keyset table for it. If it is found, this means it was set; we return what it points to with a _retnl call. This value is meaningless to the caller. You should not change it or process it in any way. You should only use it to save the current value, and to reset the key to it later. If the key is not found, a zero is returned.

If a second parameter is passed (PCOUNT = 2), then we must set the key to it. It must either be a zero to turn the key off, or a value previously returned by a call to this function. If the previous search code found the key, then its location is updated to the new value. If it did not, we search the _keyset array for an unused element, represented by a zero key_val value. If we find one, then we update the structure with the new values. If we do not, then the key cannot be set. 33 are already in use, the maximum Clipper allows.

> **TIP**
>
> Use the functions here and in Appendix B to make your routines more generic. On entry, save the states of any SETs you change; on exit, restore them.

Managing the Real Cursor

The previous section showed how to access the internal SET CURSOR setting. Although useful, this does not entirely solve the problem of managing the cursor. For example, assume that SET

CURSOR is currently ON, and that a MENU/PROMPT command is issued. The cursor is not displayed. Now, further assume that a hot key is pressed that saves the state of the SET CURSOR variable, turns the cursor on, and then invokes MEMOEDIT. Upon return from MEMOEDIT, the SET CURSOR variable is returned to its original state, but the cursor is left on. It remains on for the remainder of the MENU/PROMPT. This creates an untidy interface.

The problem arises because the SET CURSOR variable does not always reflect the state of the real cursor that appears on the screen. A command such as MENU/PROMPT overrides the setting. To overcome this, and allow the cursor to be restored exactly as it was, we must write another function to read and set the real cursor.

The read involves finding the state of the real cursor as indicated by the ROM BIOS. As you know, the cursor shape is determined by two byte values that specify its starting and ending lines. The ROM BIOS maintains them in its data area at segment 40 (hex), offset 60 (hex). We can use C's direct pointer addressing to return the value.

We must set the real cursor by calling the ROM BIOS. It is not sufficient to set the bytes at 40:60. The 6845 video chip must be told that a new cursor shape has been defined. We do this by calling function of ROM BIOS interrupt 10 hex (video).

Program 11-6 contains the code. It sets the real cursor to the value of the parameter, if passed. In either case, it returns the current (previous) value.

Program 11-6. Control the Real Cursor

```
/***
* NUMERIC real_curs()
*
*       Get/set the real cursor from BIOS data area. In a prompt, for
*       example, the cursor is off, regardless of the status of SET CURSOR.
*       If a parameter is passed, set real cursor to its value. Return
*       previous value.
*/

CLIPPER real_curs()

{
        union REGS inregs;
        union REGS outregs;
        int *cur_ptr;

        /* return state of real cursor */
        /* BIOS keeps two bytes at segment 40, offset 60 */
```

```
        cur_ptr = (int *) 0x460;
        _retni(*cur_ptr);

        /* if parameter was passed, set cursor to it */
        if (PCOUNT)
        {
            /* set to new value */

            /* CH and CL registers must have start and end lines */
            inregs.x.cx = _parni(1);

            /* Function 01 (AH = 01) */
            inregs.x.ax = 0x0100;

            /* make BIOS call */
            int86(0x10, &inregs, &outregs);
        }
    }
```

To save the cursor's state, you must make two calls. The first to real_curs retrieves the cursor shape, the second to curs_on saves Clipper's internal setting. Similarly, when resetting the state, you must call both routines with the values they previously returned. These routines solve an irritating problem. A 'dangling' cursor (one mistakenly left on) is an untidy interface.

> **TIP**
>
> Use the real_curs and curs_on routines to control the cursor.

Mouse Interface

The mouse is an increasingly popular peripheral. You can use the extend functions to interface it with Clipper. This section shows how. We develop basic mouse functions that detect movement and button presses. We use them to develop emulations of the MENU/PROMPT functions.

The mouse interface is defined by the manual *Microsoft Mouse Programmer's Reference Guide.* It defines functions that are used to detect the location of the mouse cursor, determine whether a button has been pressed, track mouse movement, etc. The functions are implemented by the mouse device driver MOUSE.SYS. It must be installed if you want to use the mouse, regardless of whether you use it from Clipper. A library mouse.lib comes with the reference guide. It provides an interface for C programmers. However, since few Clipper programmers have access to it, we do not use it in this section. Instead, we write a generic mouse interface routine in C that basically does the same functions.

Interrupt 33 (hex) is used to interface the mouse driver. Register AX specifies the function. The ones we use pass parameters in registers BX, CX, and DX. They return values in registers AX, BX, CX, and DX.

Program 11-7 is a general-purpose interface to the mouse driver. It accepts up to four parameters, although in most cases we will be passing fewer. We use the Microsoft library function 'int86' to invoke the mouse driver via interrupt 33 (hex). We load the parameters from Clipper into the structure passed to this function.

Some mouse functions return more than one value. Since Clipper cannot pass parameters by reference to C user defined functions, we must find a way to handle this. The solution lies in saving the required return values in C global variables, and then writing a separate function to return each of them. The routines result1 ... result4 in Program 11-7 do this with the variables res1 ... res4. You can use the technique in any function that must return more than one value.

> **TIP**
>
> When a C function needs to return multiple values, save them in global variables and write separate functions to return them one at a time.

Program 11-7. Mouse Driver Interface Routine

```
/***
* cmouse.c
*
*       Basic interface routine to mouse driver.
*
*       1 - Load parameters.
*
*       2 - Make interrupt call.
```

```
*
*       3 - Set globals so results can be returned.
*/

#include "nandef.h"
#include "extend.h"

#include "dos.h"

/* Globals to maintain AX - DX on return from int86 call */
int res1, res2, res3, res4;

CLIPPER result1()

{
        _retni(res1);
}

CLIPPER result2()

{
        _retni(res2);
}

CLIPPER result3()

{
        _retni(res3);
}

CLIPPER result4()
{
        _retni(res4);
}

CLIPPER cmouse()

{
        union REGS inregs;
        union REGS outregs;

        inregs.x.ax = _parni(1);
        inregs.x.bx = _parni(2);
        inregs.x.cx = _parni(3);
        inregs.x.dx = _parni(4);

        int86(0x33, &inregs, &outregs);

        res1 = outregs.x.ax;
        res2 = outregs.x.bx;
        res3 = outregs.x.cx;
        res4 = outregs.x.dx;
```

```
        _ret();
}
```

The main function cmouse does not return a value. The functions result1 through result4 must be called to obtain return values. Make sure you understand these functions. They are the basis for the rest of this section.

Using these C functions as a base, we will now define some higher-level Clipper functions. To begin, let's define some pseudo-constants.

```
* MCONST_INIT
* define useful pseudo-constants for mouse interface

FUNCTION mconst_init

PUBLIC M_RESET, M_SHOW, M_REMOVE, M_READ, M_SET_CURS
PUBLIC M_MOTION, DONT_CARE, M_CURS_WIDTH, M_CURS_HEIGHT
PUBLIC MOUSE_INT

    M_RESET = 0                 && Reset mouse driver and return status
                                && AX has status, -1 if hardware and software
                                && installed, 0 if not. BX has number of
                                && buttons.

    M_SHOW   = 1                && Make mouse cursor visible
    M_REMOVE = 2                && Hide mouse cursor

    M_READ = 3                  && Get button status and mouse position
                                && BX has button status, bit 0 left button,
                                && bit 1 right button. bits are 0 if
                                && corresponding button up, 1 if down

    M_SET_CURS = 4              && Set cursor position.

    M_MOTION = 11               && return horizontal and vertical movement
                                && since last call to this function.

    DONT_CARE = .T.

    M_CURS_WIDTH = 8            && number of 'mickeys' horizontally
                                && per text character

    M_CURS_HEIGHT = 8           && number of 'mickeys' vertically
                                && per text character

    MOUSE_INT = 51              && 0x33, mouse interrupt vector

RETURN DONT_CARE
```

The first six constants define mouse commands. The comment after each definition specifies the registers used for the function. In the cmouse function, parameter 1 corresponds to register AX, parameter 2 to BX, parameter 3 to CX, and parameter 4 to DX. A return value in AX is returned by result1, in BX by result2, in CX by result3, and in DX by result4.

We use the constants M_CURS_WIDTH and M_CURS_HEIGHT to translate between the coordinates the mouse driver returns (in mickeys, the unit of mouse movement), and those Clipper uses. In the text video modes that Clipper uses, characters consist of 8 by 8 boxes. The mouse driver, however, returns a pixel address of the top left hand corner of the mouse cursor (in graphics modes, the programmer can define the 'cursor hot spot'). In text modes, the coordinates are always a multiple of 8, the smallest distance the mouse can be moved. To convert from the pixel address to a character address, we divide the value returned by the mouse driver by these constants.

The following Clipper function uses the C functions to reset the mouse and determine its status.

```
* Reset the mouse - num_buttons pass by reference, return .T. if present
* and mouse driver installed, .F. otherwise.

FUNCTION mouse_init

PARAM num_buttons
PRIVATE result

PUBLIC _messages

      cmouse(M_RESET)
      num_buttons = result2()

RETURN result1() = -1
```

We call the cmouse function (Program 11-7) with the RESET value. As the comment in the pseudo-constant definition states, on return AX has the status and BX the number of buttons. BX is returned by the result2 routine, AX by result1. Mouse_init uses these two routines to return its values. The num_buttons variable (which must be passed by reference) is set to the number of buttons, as returned by result2. The function return value is set from result1. If the mouse is installed (a value of -1 from result1), the function returns .T.. If not, it returns .F.. Note how we call the basic cmouse routine, then the result routines to get the results.

We will now develop Clipper functions that use the basic cmouse routine. We need them for the mouse menu code.

The first task for any mouse handling routine is to make the cursor visible. To do this, we must call the cmouse function with M_SHOW. This is defined as 1 by the 'mconst_init' routine. The following function does the job:

```
* Make the mouse cursor visible - no return value

FUNCTION mouse_on

        cmouse(M_SHOW)

RETURN DONT_CARE
```

After the function shows the mouse cursor, the mouse driver tracks and displays it automatically. We do not need to intervene any further.

We turn the mouse cursor off with a call to the same function with M_REMOVE, as in:

```
* Hide the mouse cursor - no return value

FUNCTION mouse_off

        cmouse(M_REMOVE)

RETURN DONT_CARE
```

The most important function reads the status of the mouse buttons (up or down), and returns the current cursor position. The same basic driver function handles these functions. The following routine takes four parameters that must all be passed by reference. They will be set to:

1) The status of the left button. .T. if depressed, .F. if not.
2) The status of the right button. As above.
3) The current horizontal position.
4) The current vertical position.

Here is the code:

```
* Read button status and cursor position. Pass all four parameters
* by reference.
* No return value

FUNCTION mouse_read

PARAM left_pressed, right_pressed, horizontal, vertical
PRIVATE but_stat
```

```
        cmouse(M_READ)

        left_pressed = result2() = 1 .OR. result2() = 3
        right_pressed = result2() = 2 .OR. result2()= 3
        horizontal = result3() / M_CURS_WIDTH
        vertical = result4() / M_CURS_HEIGHT

RETURN DONT_CARE
```

The routine invokes the mouse M_READ function. As the comment in mconst_init describes, BX returns the button status, CX the horizontal position, and DX the vertical position. They are returned by calls to result2(), result3(), and result4(), respectively. The routine then converts the pixel coordinates to text coordinates, and assigns them to the parameters. Since they were passed by reference, the calling procedure reflects their values.

The last function we need sets the position of the mouse cursor. It takes two parameters; horizontal and vertical position. They are passed to the mouse driver function m_set_curs. Here is the source code:

```
* Set new mouse cursor position. Pass both parameters by value

FUNCTION mouse_set_curs

PARAM new_horz, new_vert

        cmouse(M_SET_CURS, 0, new_horz, new_vert)

RETURN DONT_CARE
```

MENU/PROMPT with the Mouse

We can use the mouse functions to develop an emulation of the MENU/PROMPT command. The code does not allow keys, but it is a simple matter to provide for them.

PROMPT

We need two functions, one to emulate the PROMPT command and the other to emulate MENU TO. The PROMPT function will be called repeatedly to set up the prompts. This is similar to the use of the standard PROMPT command. It needs the coordinate pair and the prompt string. It saves them in a set of arrays that the menu function uses.

The first version we will develop does not handle messages. A revision implements them.

The function does not know in advance how many prompts will be issued, so it cannot allocate the array. We need another function, an initialization routine that is passed the maximum number of prompts this MENU wil issue. It will declare the arrays we require. We need one array to save the columns, one to save the rows, and a third to save the actual prompts. We also need two global variables; the actual number of prompts issued, and the maximum that CAN be issued (the size of the array). We can then write the initialization routine as:

```
* initialize mouse MENU/PROMPT system. pmax_prompts determines maximum
* number of prompts to be used. Pass by value.

FUNCTION mmenu_init

PARAM pmax_prompts

PUBLIC menu_row[pmax_prompts + 1], menu_col[pmax_prompts + 1]
PUBLIC menu_txt[pmax_prompts + 1]
PUBLIC num_prompts
PUBLIC max_prompts

        max_prompts = pmax_prompts
        num_prompts = 0

RETURN DONT_CARE
```

The prompt routine simply fills the arrays and increments the prompt counter. Here is its source code.

```
* issue a prompt. Pass all parameters by value.

FUNCTION mprompt

PARAM row, col, txt

        num_prompts = num_prompts + 1
        IF num_prompts > max_prompts
                RETURN .F.
        ENDIF

        menu_row[num_prompts] = row
        menu_col[num_prompts] = col
        menu_txt[num_prompts] = txt

RETURN .T.
```

If there is no room for the prompt, mprompt returns .F.. Otherwise, it returns .T..

MENU

So far, everything is straightforward. To implement the actual menu command, we must decide how to use the mouse. We will use a single click to highlight a prompt, and a double click to select it. The double click will cause the prompt number to be returned as the function's value (we will discuss an 'escape' later). To allow the single click to highlight a prompt, the code must detect it within the prompt's text. For example, if a prompt starts at column 10 and extends to column 20 in row 10, the prompt is highlighted when the mouse is clicked between coordinates 10, 10 and 10, 20. We detect this in a loop such as:

```
* vert and horiz are coordinates returned from mouse
* read routine

i = 1
found = .F.
DO WHILE i <= num_prompts .AND. !found
        found = vert = menu_row[i] .AND. ;
                                horiz >= menu_col[i] .AND. ;
                                horiz < menu_col[i] + len(menu_txt[i])

        IF !found
                i = i + 1
        ENDIF
ENDDO
```

The current position is checked against the bounds of every prompt saved in the array. If this section of code ends with found set to .T., then i is the prompt number that was clicked on.

Detecting a double click is more difficult. After detecting a single click, the code must determine that another one occurred within a certain time period. For another click to occur, the first one must be released, and the mouse must be clicked again and then released once more. During all this, the mouse cannot move.

The following code does the job, allowing up to a half second for the second click to be completed:

```
* save where click occurred so can cancel countdown if moved
interval = 0.5
vert_click = vert
horiz_click = horiz

* start countdown, 1/2 second
start = seconds()
```

```
* make sure it is released first
DO WHILE (left_down .OR. right_down) ;
          .AND. seconds() - start < interval .AND. horiz = horiz_click ;
          .AND. vert = vert_click

     mouse_read(@left_down, @right_down, @horiz, @vert)

ENDDO

* now wait for second click
DO WHILE !left_down .AND. !right_down ;
          .AND. seconds() - start < interval .AND. horiz = horiz_click ;
          .AND. vert = vert_click

     mouse_read(@left_down, @right_down, @horiz, @vert)

ENDDO

* wait for second release
DO WHILE (left_down .OR. right_down) ;
          .AND. seconds() - start < interval .AND. horiz = horiz_click ;
          .AND. vert = vert_click

     mouse_read(@left_down, @right_down, @horiz, @vert)

ENDDO

double_clicked = seconds() - start < interval .AND. vert = vert_click ;
                    .AND. horiz = horiz_click
```

The program assumes that the logical variables left_down and right_down are initially set according to where the click occurred. It also assumes that the location of the previous click is in variables vert and horiz, the vertical and horizontal coordinates, respectively. The logical 'double_clicked' is set to .T. if a double click occurs.

We can now write the actual menu code (Program 11-8). It takes one parameter, the initial prompt to be highlighted. It terminates when a prompt is double-clicked, and returns its number.

Program 11-8. Mouse Menu

```
* mmenu - mouse menu code
*
*    1 - Initialize variables.
*
*    2 - Display all prompts.
*
```

```
*       3 - Highlight current prompt.
*
*       4 - Make mouse cursor visible.
*
*       5 - DO UNTIL double_clicked.
*
*               5.1 - Read position and button status.
*
*               5.2 - IF clicked
*
*                       5.2.1 - IF inside PROMPT
*
*                               5.2.1.1 - Remove highlight from previous selection,
*                                             highlight this one.
*
*                               5.2.1.2 - Double click timeout.

FUNCTION mmenu

PARAM start_pos

PRIVATE i, left_down, right_down, horiz, vert, start, double_clicked
PRIVATE vert_click, hor_click, cur_pos, key, mess
PRIVATE start_mess, interval

        * Change this value for a longer double click value
        interval = 0.5

        * this keeps track of the currently highlighted prompt
        cur_pos = start_pos

        * no 'text' cursor during mouse routines, only mouse cursor
        SET CURSOR OFF

        * initialize local variables
        left_down = .F.
        right_down = .F.
        horiz = 0
        vert = 0

        * display all prompts
        FOR i = 1 TO num_prompts

                @ menu_row[i], menu_col[i] SAY menu_txt[i]

        NEXT

        * set currently selected one to reverse - insert your
        * own colors here ...
        SET COLOR TO N/W
        @ menu_row[cur_pos], menu_col[cur_pos] SAY menu_txt[cur_pos]
        SET COLOR TO  && and reset them here ...
```

```
* make mouse cursor visible
mouse_on()

double_clicked = .F.

* loop until double-clicked ...
DO WHILE !double_clicked

     * get mouse position and button status
     mouse_read(@left_down, @right_down, @horiz, @vert)

     IF left_down .OR. right_down
          * mouse was clicked, see if within a prompt ...
          i = 1
          found = .F.
          DO WHILE i <= num_prompts .AND. !found
               found = vert = menu_row[i] .AND. ;
                         horiz >= menu_col[i] .AND. ;
                         horiz < menu_col[i] + len(menu_txt[i])

               IF !found
                    * look at next one ...
                    i = i + 1
               ENDIF
          ENDDO

          IF found
               * was inside prompt ...

               * if not already highlighted
               IF cur_pos != i
                    * move from previously highlighted prompt
                    * to new one
                    move_to(i)
               ENDIF

               * save where click occurred so can cancel
               * countdown if moved
               vert_hit = vert
               horiz_hit = horiz

               * start countdown, 1/2 second

               start = seconds()

               * make sure button is released first
               DO WHILE (left_down .OR. right_down) ;
                    .AND. seconds() - start <.5 .AND. horiz = horiz_hit;
                    .AND. vert = vert_hit

                    mouse_read(@left_down, @right_down, @horiz,;
                         @vert)
```

```
                    ENDDO

                    * now wait for second click
                    DO WHILE !left_down .AND. !right_down ;
                      .AND. seconds() - start < .5 .AND. horiz = horiz_hit;
                      .AND. vert = vert_hit

                          mouse_read(@left_down, @right_down, @horiz,;
                                @vert)

                    ENDDO

                    * wait for second release
                    DO WHILE (left_down .OR. right_down) ;
                      .AND. seconds() - start < .5 .AND. horiz = horiz_hit;
                      .AND. vert = vert_hit

                          mouse_read(@left_down, @right_down, @horiz,
                          @vert)

                    ENDDO

                    * If all this happened within 1/2 second and mouse
                    * did not move, then successful double click occurred
                    double_clicked = seconds() - start < .5 ;
                                              .AND. vert = vert_hit ;
                                              .AND. horiz = horiz_hit

                ENDIF
            ENDIF
        ENDDO

        * Turn off mouse cursor
        mouse_off()

RETURN cur_pos

* Utility routine, move highlight bar from cur_pos to parameter

PROCEDURE move_to
PARAM new_pos

        mouse_off()
        @ menu_row[cur_pos], menu_col[cur_pos] SAY menu_txt[cur_pos]

        cur_pos = new_pos
        SET COLOR TO N/W
        @ menu_row[cur_pos], menu_col[cur_pos] SAY menu_txt[cur_pos]
        SET COLOR TO

        mouse_on()
RETURN
```

The menu code first displays all prompts. It highlights the initially selected one. It then makes the mouse cursor visible and repeats the main loop until the mouse is double-clicked. This main loop is the double click detection code shown previously. A 'mouse_read' call precedes it.

The utility routine 'move_to' is called when a new menu item is selected with a single click. It turns off the mouse cursor, removes the highlight from the previously selected prompt, and highlights the new one. The mouse cursor is then made visible again.

We call the code within a framework such as:

```
* mtest.prg
num_buttons = 0

mconst_init()

IF !mouse_init(@num_buttons)
        ? "No mouse"
        QUIT
ENDIF

mmenu_init(5)

CLEAR

@ 9, 9 TO 15, 20
mprompt(10, 10, "Accounts ")
mprompt(11, 10, "Reports ")
mprompt(12, 10, "Screen 1")
mprompt(13, 10, "Screen 2")
mprompt(14, 10, "Screen 3")

? mmenu(1)
```

We first call the mconst_init routine to initialize the pseudo-constants. We then call mouse_init to reset the mouse, and check whether it is available. If not (an .F. is returned), an error message is displayed and the code exits. If the mouse is installed, the routine initializes the menu code with a call to 'mmenu_init'. It passes 5 as a parameter, indicating that the following code will issue 5 menu commands. The individual prompts are then issued with separate calls to mprompt. Finally the actual menu routine is invoked with a starting prompt of 1. The value returned from this routine, the selected prompt number, is displayed on the screen.

We suggest that you combine the functions mmenu, move_to, mprompt, mmenuinit, etc. into one PRG file, say 'mlib.prg'. It is good practice to separate the implementation of a function from its use. In this case, the implementation is of the mouse. To change it, you need to modify only one module. If the interface stays the same, no other code requires changes.

If the C code is in file 'cmouse.c' and the test program is in 'mtest.prg' (as the comments at the heads of the routines suggest), you can use the following make file to build the system:

```
# basic mouse driver interface
cmouse.obj: cmouse.c
        cl /c /AL /Oalt /FPa /Gs cmouse.c

# Higher level Clipper mouse code
mlib.obj: mlib.prg
        clipper mlib

# test program
mtest.obj: mtest.prg
        clipper mtest

mtest.exe: mtest.obj mlib.obj cmouse.obj
        link mtest mlib cmouse,,,\clipper\clipper\clipper\extend \mc\lib\llibca /noe
```

Adding Messages

The Clipper MENU/PROMPT command supports the MESSAGE option. It displays a message on a predefined line when the user moves to a new prompt. The SET MESSAGE TO command defines the text. It also lets the programmer specify whether to center the text. To implement this in our mouse version, we need another function, say mmessage_line. It takes two parameters: the first is a numeric specifying the line on which the messages should appear, the second a logical indicating whether to center the messages. The function will set three globals for use by other routines. _messages, indicating that messages are to be used, _centered, indicating that the messages should be centered, and mmes_line, to save the line number. Here is the source:

```
* set message line for mouse menu messages. Centered optional,
* default .F. Pass parameters by value.
*

FUNCTION mmessage_line
PARAM mes_line, centered

PUBLIC mmes_line
PUBLIC _centered
```

```
        _messages = .T.
        mmes_line = mes_line

        * set default for centered parameter

        centered = IIF(type([centered]) = 'U', .F., centered)
        _centered = centered

RETURN DONT_CARE
```

If the centered parameter exists (type([centered]) != 'U'), the routine sets the global _centered to its value. Otherwise, it sets _centered to .F., the default.

The _messages global must be initialized to .F. in case the routine is not called. The best place to initialize it is in the mouse_init routine, as in:

```
* Reset the mouse - num_buttons pass by reference, return .T. if present
* and mouse driver installed, .F. otherwise.

FUNCTION mouse_init

PARAM num_buttons
PRIVATE result
PUBLIC _messages

        _messages = .F.

        cmouse(M_RESET)
        num_buttons = result2()

RETURN result1() = -1
```

We added the PUBLIC declaration and set the global to .F.. We must modify mmenu_init to allow the message to be saved.

```
* Initialize mouse MENU/PROMPT system. pmax_prompts determines maximum
* number of prompts to be used, not including escape prompt.
* Pass by value.

FUNCTION mmenu_init

PARAM pmax_prompts

PUBLIC menu_row[pmax_prompts + 1], menu_col[pmax_prompts + 1]
PUBLIC menu_txt[pmax_prompts + 1], menu_messages[pmax_prompts + 1]
PUBLIC num_prompts
PUBLIC max_prompts

        max_prompts = pmax_prompts
        num_prompts = 0

RETURN DONT_CARE
```

We simply added the PUBLIC array declaration for menu_messages.

We must change the prompt routine to pass and save the message:

```
* Issue a prompt, message parameter optional. Pass all parameters by
* value.

FUNCTION mprompt

PARAM row, col, txt, message

        num_prompts = num_prompts + 1
        IF num_prompts > max_prompts
                RETURN .F.
        ENDIF

        menu_row[num_prompts] = row
        menu_col[num_prompts] = col
        menu_txt[num_prompts] = txt

        * set default ...
        message = IIF(type([message]) = 'U', "", message)

        menu_messages[num_prompts] = message

RETURN DONT_CARE
```

If no message parameter is passed, the routine puts an empty string in the menu_messages array.

Finally, we must change the mmenu routine to display messages. Program 11-9 shows this.

Program 11-9. Modified Mouse Menu with Messages

```
* mmenu - mouse menu code
*
*       1 - Initialize variables
*
*       2 - Display all prompts, determine longest message
*
*       3 - Highlight current one, show current message
*
*       4 - Make mouse visible
*
*       5 - DO UNTIL double_clicked
*
*               5.1 - Read position and button status
*
*               5.2 - IF clicked
```

```
*                    5.2.1 - IF inside PROMPT
*
*                         5.2.1.1 - Remove highlight from previous selection,
*                                   highlight this selection. Display message.
*
*                         5.2.1.2 - Double click timeout

FUNCTION mmenu

PARAM start_pos

PRIVATE i, left_down, right_down, horiz, vert, start, double_clicked
PRIVATE vert_hit, hor_hit, cur_pos, key, longest_message, mess
PRIVATE start_mess

     longest_message = 0
     cur_pos = start_pos

     SET CURSOR OFF
     left_down = .F.
     right_down = .F.
     horiz = 0
     vert = 0

     FOR i = 1 TO num_prompts

          * Determine longest message
          IF len(menu_messages[i]) > longest_message
               longest_message = len(menu_message[i])
          ENDIF

          @ menu_row[i], menu_col[i] SAY menu_txt[i]

     NEXT

     * display first message
     IF _messages
          lspaces = int((longest_message - len(menu_messages[cur_pos])) / 2)
          rspaces = lspaces
          IF rspaces + lspaces + len(menu_messages[cur_pos]) != ;
                                        longest_message
               lspaces = lspaces + 1
          ENDIF

          mess = space(lspaces) + menu_messages[cur_pos] + space(rspaces)
          IF _centered
               @ mmes_line, int((80 - longest_message) / 2) SAY mess
          ELSE
               @ mmes_line, 0 SAY mess
          ENDIF
     ENDIF
```

```
* set currently selected one to reverse
SET COLOR TO N/W
@ menu_row[cur_pos], menu_col[cur_pos] SAY menu_txt[cur_pos]
SET COLOR TO

mouse_on()

double_clicked = .F.

DO WHILE !double_clicked

    mouse_read(@left_down, @right_down, @horiz, @vert)

    IF left_down .OR. right_down
        i = 1
        found = .F.
        DO WHILE i <= num_prompts .AND. !found
            found = vert = menu_row[i] .AND. ;
                    horiz >= menu_col[i] .AND. ;
                    horiz < menu_col[i] + len(menu_txt[i])

            IF !found
                i = i + 1
            ENDIF
        ENDDO

        IF found

            IF cur_pos != i
                move_to(i)
            ENDIF

            * save where click occurred so we can cancel
            * countdown if mouse moves
            vert_hit = vert
            horiz_hit = horiz
            * start countdown, 1/2 second

            start = seconds()

            * make sure mouse button is released first
            DO WHILE (left_down .OR. right_down) ;
                .AND. seconds() - start <.5 .AND. horiz = horiz_hit;
                .AND. vert = vert_hit
                mouse_read(@left_down, @right_down, @horiz,;
                    @vert)

            ENDDO

            * now wait for second click
            DO WHILE !left_down .AND. !right_down ;
             .AND. seconds() - start < .5 .AND. horiz = horiz_hit;
```

```
                .AND. vert = vert_hit

                    mouse_read(@left_down, @right_down, @horiz,;
                        @vert)

               ENDDO

               * wait for second release
               DO WHILE (left_down .OR. right_down) ;
                .AND. seconds() - start < .5 .AND. horiz = horiz_hit;
                .AND. vert = vert_hit

                    mouse_read(@left_down, @right_down, @horiz,;
                        @vert)

               ENDDO

               double_clicked = seconds() - start < .5 ;
                                         .AND. vert = vert_hit ;
                                         .AND. horiz = horiz_hit

            ENDIF
        ENDIF
    ENDDO

    mouse_off()

RETURN cur_pos

* Utility routine

PROCEDURE move_to

PARAM new_pos

    mouse_off()
    @ menu_row[cur_pos], menu_col[cur_pos] SAY menu_txt[cur_pos]

    cur_pos = new_pos

    SET COLOR TO N/W
    @ menu_row[cur_pos], menu_col[cur_pos] SAY menu_txt[cur_pos]
    SET COLOR TO

    IF _messages
        lspaces = int((longest_message - len(menu_messages[cur_pos])) / 2)
        rspaces = lspaces
        IF rspaces + lspaces + len(menu_messages[cur_pos]) != ;
                        longest_message
            lspaces = lspaces + 1
        ENDIF
        mess = space(lspaces) + menu_messages[cur_pos] + space(rspaces)
```

```
                IF _centered
                        @ mmes_line, int((80 - longest_message) / 2) SAY mess
                ELSE
                        @ mmes_line, 0 SAY mess
                ENDIF
        ENDIF

        mouse_on()
RETURN
```

We changed Program 11-8 in several ways to incorporate messages. First, in the code that initially displays the prompts, we determine the length of the longest message. We need to know this to erase old messages. Second, the routine displays a message whenever the user selects a new prompt. The move_to routine does this. We pad all messages with spaces to the length of the longest one.

A typical call of Program 11-9 is:

```
num_buttons = 0

mconst_init()

IF !mouse_init(@num_buttons)
        ? "No mouse"
        QUIT
ENDIF

mmenu_init(5)

CLEAR

mmessage_line(24, .T.)

@ 9, 9 TO 15, 20

mprompt(10, 10, "Accounts ", "Choose this for Accounts")
mprompt(11, 10, "Reports ", "Choose this for Reports")
mprompt(12, 10, "Screen 1", "Choose this for Screen 1")
mprompt(13, 10, "Screen 2", "Choose this for Screen 2")
mprompt(14, 10, "Screen 3", "Choose this for Screen 3")

? mmenu(1)
```

We initially call mmessage_line with 24 and .T., indicating a centered message on line 24. The mprompt calls now contain messages. We can use the same make file as before to build the system.

Adding an Escape Option

In the regular keyboard-driven MENU/PROMPT code, pressing Escape causes an exit with a return value of zero. To implement this in our mouse version, we define the last prompt issued as the escape prompt. When it is double-clicked, the routine terminates and returns zero. You must add the following code to the mmenu code, immediately ahead of the return statement:

```
IF cur_pos = num_prompts
        cur_pos = 0
ENDIF
```

The routine now returns zero if the mouse is double-clicked on the last prompt. This is all we need to do. However, you should emphasize the special status of the escape prompt. Either change its message or its location. For example, the following code uses the ~ character in the top left-hand corner of the box as an escape prompt.

```
num_buttons = 0

mconst_init()

IF !mouse_init(@num_buttons)
        ? "No mouse"
        QUIT
ENDIF

* Add one to number of prompts
mmenu_init(6)

CLEAR

mmessage_line(24, .T.)

@ 9, 9 TO 15, 20

mprompt(10, 10, "Accounts ", "Choose this for Accounts")
mprompt(11, 10, "Reports ", "Choose this for Reports")
mprompt(12, 10, "Screen 1", "Choose this for Screen 1")
mprompt(13, 10, "Screen 2", "Choose this for Screen 2")
mprompt(14, 10, "Screen 3", "Choose this for Screen 3")

* Now put Escape prompt in top left-hand corner of box
mprompt(9, 9, chr(254), "Choose this to escape")

? mmenu(1)
```

This ends the discussion of the mouse interface. Most of the section has been Clipper code, interfacing to a general-purpose C routine. The C code is small, but it is the basis for the entire system. Without it, we could not write the program. This is an ideal use for C - performing a well-defined small function that serves as the basis for sophisticated Clipper code.

> **TIP**
>
> The mouse MENU/PROMPT/MESSAGE code does the same tasks as the regular keyboard code. Use it to incorporate the mouse in your user interfaces. Consider implementing a similar set of GET/READ functions. Allow a single click to select a GET, and a double click to read it. If you do the read with an actual READ command, the functions should behave exactly the same as the keyboard versions.

Debugging

Debugging C code linked to Clipper is straightforward. Microsoft's CodeView is a useful tool. It allows debugging at the source level; the actual C code remains resident. To use CodeView, you must add the flag /Zi to the compiler command line. It instructs the compiler to include line number and symbolic information in the OBJ file. When linking, you must use the /CO and /m flags. The result is an EXE file with symbol and line number information. The file will be larger, so remember to compile and link the final version without the extra flags. Refer to the CodeView manual for details on the actual commands.

You can also use Lattice's C-Sprite to provide symbolic debugging. By symbolic, we mean that variable and function names are visible, but source code is not. C-Sprite has an advantage over CodeView in that it works with overlays produced by Plink. Use Plink's SYMTABLE command to tell it to include symbol information in the EXE file. Use the /m option with the DOS linker or Tlink.

Since C-Sprite does not show the C source code, you need a basic understanding of assembly language to use it. You also must know what registers the compiler uses to return function values. The compiler documentation describes this.

Serial Communications

A computer's serial ports provide access to the outside world. The PC's ports conform to the RS-232 standard, so you can connect any RS-232 device to them. By controlling the serial ports from Clipper, you can open up a whole new world. Your database programs can directly interface devices such as electronic cash registers, PBXs, and other computers.

This section develops C routines to read, write, and check the status of a serial port. Using these basic routines, the building blocks of serial communications code, we develop a simple Clipper routine that allows two computers to converse. Readers with access to two computers can use it as a testbed to gain experience with serial communications.

The last part of this section contains a more detailed example of controlling a PBX. The code receives call records and performs wakeup calls. It is from actual installations at hotels in Zürich and Montreaux, Switzerland.

ROM BIOS INT 14 (Hex)

The complexity of serial communications has led to the development of special chips that do the basic tasks of timing and bit transmission and reception. The PC uses a National 8250 UART (universal asynchronous receiver/transmitter). Interrupt 14 (hex) of the ROM BIOS controls the UART, providing four functions:

0: Initialize the serial port. It selects the baud rate, number of data bits, number of stop bits, and parity.

1: Send a character to the serial port. If the routine cannot send the character because the previous one has not yet been sent, it returns a timeout error.

2: Read a character from the serial port. If a character is available, it is read. If not, the routine waits for a short time. If no character arrives, it returns a timeout error.

3: Read the status of the serial port.

We will develop C code, callable from Clipper, for the last three functions. The DOS MODE command can easily perform the initialization.

To write the functions, we must know where the BIOS expects

its input parameters, and where it returns the result. Armed with this information, we can use the int86 function to invoke the BIOS communications routines.

The required information is in the *DOS Technical Reference Manual.* It contains the complete source code for the BIOS. A comment at the start of each service routine documents the register conventions. We will examine them one at a time, but first let's define the required constants and include files. The following code must appear at the head of the C program that contains the routines developed in this section:

```
#include "nandef.h"
#include "extend.h"

#include "dos.h"
#define SEND_CHAR 1
#define READ_CHAR 2
#define READ_STAT 3

#define COMS_INT 0x14
```

The 'dos.h' include file is necessary, as we will use the register structures it defines. The constants specify the BIOS interrupt number for communications, and the function values.

Sending a Character

For the send routine, the character must be in register AL. The DX register selects the serial port (COM1 = 0, COM2 = 1). The AH register specifies the function, in this case send character (1). The function returns a value in AH. If bit 7 of AH is 1, a timeout error occurred and the character was not sent. Program 11-10 is the source for a C routine, ser_send, that receives a character from Clipper, sets up the registers, and calls the BIOS.

Program 11-10. Serial Output

```
/***
* ser_send
*
*       Clipper callable routine to send character to serial port.
*
*       1 - Load memory mapped registers.
*
*       2 - Make interrupt call.
*
```

```
*       3 - Return result to Clipper.
*/

CLIPPER ser_send()

{
        union REGS inregs;
        union REGS outregs;

        inregs.h.al = *_parc(1);
        inregs.h.ah = SEND_CHAR;
        inregs.x.dx = 0;            /* COM1 */

        int86(COMS_INT, &inregs, &outregs);
        _retni(outregs.h.ah);
}
```

The required register structures are defined. We get the character from Clipper with the *_parc(1) statement. It is stored in AL. We set AH to 1 (SEND_CHAR) and DX to 0 to select COM1. The routine returns the status returned from the BIOS.

To send the character 'a', we would call the routine with:

```
stat = ser_send('a')
```

To check for an error, we must examine bit 7 of stat. Since Clipper does not support bit manipulation, we cannot do this directly. However, since we know that the number returned is a byte value, we can simply check whether it is greater than or equal to 128 (bit 7 = 1).

Reading a Character

For the read character routine, we must set AH to the function number and DX to the port number. On return from the BIOS call, element AH has the status, and AL the character read. If AH is nonzero, an error occurred. Program 11-11, ser_read, loads the registers and invokes the BIOS. It returns the status of the operation. The character read is returned in the character parameter, which must be passed by reference.

Program 11-11. Serial Input

```
CLIPPER ser_read()

{
        union REGS inregs;
```

```
        union REGS outregs;
        char *ch;

        inregs.h.ah = READ_CHAR;
        inregs.x.dx = 0;            /* COM1 */

        int86(COMS_INT, &inregs, &outregs);

        *_parc(1) = outregs.h.al;

        _retni(outregs.h.ah);
}
```

To read a character into ch, you would call ser_read with:

```
ch = " "
stat = ser_read(@ch)
```

Error checking is simpler here, as the return value is non-zero if an error occurred.

Getting the Status

We also need a function that returns the status of the serial port. You would use it before a ser_read call to verify that a character is ready. Otherwise, ser_read times out if there is no character ready, wasting valuable processor time.

The most general way to implement a serial status check is to write a routine to return the status, and then let the Clipper routine decipher the bits it needs. However, as already mentioned, Clipper does not support bit manipulation. Here, the bit we must examine, the 'data ready' bit, is bit 0 of register AH, or bit 8 of AX. Not easy to access. So we define a ser_ready function that simply returns the bit's state. We can thus rapidly detect an incoming character. This is important since if the character is not read before another is received, the first one is overwritten and an overrun error occurs. Program 11-12 shows the function.

Program 11-12. Serial Status

```
/***
* ser_ready
*
*  Return true if serial port has data ready.
*
*       1 - Load memory mapped registers.
```

```
 *
 *      2 - Make read status interrupt call.
 *
 *      3 - Return logical indicating status of data ready bit.
 */

CLIPPER ser_ready()

{
        unsigned ser_status;

        union REGS inregs;
        union REGS outregs;

        inregs.h.ah = READ_STAT;
        inregs.x.dx = 0;                /* COM1 */
        int86(COMS_INT, &inregs, &outregs);

        /* check for data ready, bit 0 in AH */
        _retl(outregs.h.ah & 0x01);
}
```

Program 11-12 requires AH to be 3 and DX to be the port number. It returns the status in AH and AL. The Clipper function returns .T. if data is ready, and .F. otherwise. We do this by returning the state of the 'data ready' bit in AH.

Computer to Computer Communications

Using these routines, we can write a program that allows two computers connected by a serial cable to chat. Be sure to link them with a null modem cable. Program 11-13 simply alternates between seeing if a character is available from the serial port, reading and displaying it if so, and seeing if a character is available from the keyboard, displaying it and transmitting it if so.

Program 11-13. Serial I/O between Two Computers

```
CLEAR

ESC = 27
ENTER = 13
LINE_FEED = 10

key = 0
```

```
ch = " "

DO WHILE key != ESC

        * First check to see if incoming character is available
        IF ser_ready()
                * yes, so read it and echo it ...
                stat = ser_read(@ch)
                ?? ch
                IF ch = chr(ENTER)
                        ?? chr(LINE_FEED)
                ENDIF
        ENDIF

        * Now check to see if key to send
        key = inkey()
        IF key != 0 .AND. key != ESC
                * yes there is, so first echo it on own console ...
                ?? chr(key)

                * now send it
                ser_send(chr(key))
                IF key = ENTER
                        ?? chr(LINE_FEED)
                ENDIF
        ENDIF

ENDDO
```

Since pressing the Enter key generates only a carriage return character, the program adds a line feed.

Program 11-13 does not do anything fancy. It uses the basic routines we developed to show how simple serial communications can be. You can use it as a basis for experiments. The code does no error checking whatsoever. It relies on the simplistic assumption that, if a character ready status is received, the subsequent read call will work without any problems. No processing is done between the two calls for exactly this reason. The routine reads the data as quickly as possible to avoid overrun.

In more complex computer-computer communications such as file transfers, a higher level protocol than the parity checking done by the BIOS is essential. The protocol ensures the transfer of the correct number of bytes and verifies the checksum. The reader may want to write this code as an exercise.

PBX Control

Controlling a PBX is another typical serial I/O task. The controller reads bytes from the PBX, and sends others back to it. The PBX usually has both a high-level and a low-level protocol. The low-level protocol defines the baud rate, parity, number of stop bits, and number of data bits. The high-level protocol defines messages transmitted between the software on the PBX and that on the PC. It defines the exact layout, usually including a checksum field. The protocol defines two way communications. One side sends a message to the other, which then responds.

In our case, the low-level protocol is 1200 baud, odd parity, 7 data bits, and 2 stop bits. The high-level protocol defines a structure for each type of message, and the response it expects. Each message type has a unique identification code (incoming call, room status, lock phone, etc). Each message has a unique number. When one side responds to another's message, it uses the same type and identification numbers.

We will concentrate on two message formats here. The first is the 'incoming call', sent from the PBX when a guest terminates a call. It gives the number called, the length of the call, the number of units used, and the room number. The second structure is the 'wakeup call' record sent from the computer to the PBX. It contains the room number. The following C structure defines the message formats:

```
typedef struct
{
        byte f_stx;                 /* ASCII STX, 02 */
        byte f_job_code[2];         /* Message "10", outgoing call */
        byte f_space1[3];

        byte f_message_no[2];       /* Sequential message number */
        byte f_space2;
        byte room_no[4];            /* Room number making the call */
        byte f_space3;
        byte f_sort_char;           /* Call type, cabin, room, service, etc. */
        byte f_space4;
        byte f_date[6];             /* Date of call, format "yymmdd" */
        byte f_space5;
        byte f_time[5];             /* Time of call, format "hh:mm" */
        byte f_space6;
        byte f_call_duration[9];    /* Length of call, format "hhHmmMssS */
        byte f_space7;
        byte f_serial_no;           /* Consecutive number per user group */
        byte f_space8;
        byte f_trunk_no[3];         /* Outgoing line used */
        byte f_space9;
```

```
        byte f_call_no[20];         /* Number dialed */
        byte f_space10;
        byte f_tax[7];              /* Number of pulses */
        byte f_space11;
        byte f_id_num[9];
        byte f_checksum;            /* Checksum of data bytes */
        byte f_etx;                  /* ASCII ETX, 03 */
} CALL_REC;

typedef struct
{
        byte f_stx;                  /* ASCII STX, 02 */
        byte f_job_code[2];         /* Message "70", wakeup call */
        byte f_station_no[4];       /* Room number */
        byte f_checksum[2];
        byte f_etx;                  /* ASCII ETX, 03 */
} WAKEUP_REC;
```

Spaces separate the fields in the CALL_REC structure. When the PBX has no computer attached, it sends the fields directly to a printer. The spaces make the text more readable.

The checksum is the 'one byte negative sum' of all characters in the message's data area. The data area is the part of a message from (and including) the job_code field to (but not including) the checksum field. The 'one byte negative sum' is computed by summing bytes in a one byte field (ignoring overflow), and subtracting the result from 0. In the message, the number appears as two ASCII hex digits.

Program 11-14 calculates the checksum. You pass it the starting address of the data and its length.

Program 11-14. Negative Checksum

```
/***
* checksum

*
* Calculate negative checksum (sum all bytes in one byte, ignoring
* overflow, then subtract from 0), for number of bytes, from start.
*

*/

byte checksum(start, num)

byte *start;
byte num;

{
        byte sum, i;
```

```
        sum = 0;
        for (i = 0; i < num; i++)
                sum = sum + start[i];

        return 0 - sum;
}
```

You can use Program 11-14 for any message. Program 11-15 converts the byte value to a two hex digit ASCII string.

Program 11-15. Byte to Hex Conversion

```
/***
* C version of byte to hex
*
*       Convert byte value to two hex ASCII digits
*/

void cbytetohex(dec, ichars)

byte dec;
byte *ichars;

{
        int i;
        byte nib;

        /* for two digits */
        for (i = 1; i >= 0; i--)
        {
                nib = dec % 16;
                if (nib > 9)
                        nib = nib - 10 + 'A';
                else
                        nib = nib + '0';

                ichars[i] = nib;
                dec = dec / 16;

        }
}
```

When the computer receives a message from the PBX, it must verify the checksum. If the checksum is incorrect, it should ignore the message. When the computer sends a message to the PBX, it must calculate the checksum and include it in the message. If the checksum is incorrect, the PBX will ignore the message.

To initiate a wakeup call for a room, you must build a WAKE_UP record and send it to the serial port. Rather than calling ser_send for each character, we use a routine (Program 11-16) that sends a number of characters at one time. It is not callable from Clipper, but you can easily revise it. Just receive the string with _retc, determine its length with _parclen, and call _retni when finished.

Program 11-16. Send Serial Bytes

```
/***
* send_bytes
*
* Send a sequence of bytes to the serial port. Abort if timeout.
* Return last line status.
*/

byte send_bytes(bytes, num_bytes)
byte *bytes;
unsigned num_bytes;

{
        union REGS inregs;
        union REGS outregs;

        byte send_stat;
        unsigned bytes_index;

        bytes_index = 0;
        send_stat = 0;

        /* DO UNTIL all bytes sent, or timeout */
        while (bytes_index != num_bytes && !(send_stat & 0x80))
        {
                inregs.h.al = bytes[bytes_index];
                inregs.h.ah = SEND_CHAR;
                inregs.x.dx = 0;            /* COM1 */
                int86(COMS_INT, &inregs, &outregs);
                send_stat = outregs.h.ah;
                bytes_index = bytes_index + 1;
        }
        return(send_stat << 8);
}
```

send_bytes' parameters are a pointer to a series of bytes and a length. It sends the bytes to the serial port, terminating either when finished, or when a timeout error occurs.

Program 11-17 invokes the wakeup call. It gets the room number from Clipper with a call to _parc. The number is passed as a string.

Program 11-17. Invoke a Wakeup Call

```
/***
* wake_up
*
*       1 - Get room number from Clipper.
*
*       2 - Set up structure (STX, job, room #, checksum, ETX)
*
*       3 - Send to serial port.
*
*       4 - Return status.
*/

CLIPPER wake_up()

{
        char *room_no;
        WAKEUP_REC wakeup_rec;
        int i;
        byte c_sum;
        byte send_stat;

        room_no = _parc(1);

        wakeup_rec.f_stx = STX;
        wakeup_rec.f_job_code[0] = '7';
        wakeup_rec.f_job_code[1] = '0';

        memcpy(wakeup_rec.f_station_no, room_no, 4);

        /* set up checksum */
        c_sum = checksum(wakeup_rec.f_job_code, 6);
        cbytetohex(c_sum, wakeup_rec.f_checksum);

        wakeup_rec.f_etx = ETX;

        send_stat = send_bytes((char *) &wakeup_rec, sizeof(wakeup_rec));
        _retni(send_stat);
}
```

Program 11-17 puts the STX and ETX codes in the structure. It sets the job_code to '70', indicating a wakeup call. It then uses memcpy to move the room number into the structure. Finally, it computes the checksum, converts it to ASCII hex, and sends the bytes to the serial port.

To wake up the guest in room 1003, you would call the routine with:

```
wake_up("1003")
```

The PBX responds to the wakeup call with a message indicating whether the call was answered. We do not show this here.

To handle the incoming call records, the Clipper routine must determine whether a character is ready. We use the ser_ready routine to do this. It must then call a C routine to read the record. Here we are only concerned with the call record coming from the PBX to the computer. In practice, of course, we receive several different types of messages. However, we don't know until the job_code field is read what type is coming. The Clipper routine then must call a general routine that reads characters until it finds an ETX (all messages end with an ETX character). It can then determine what action to take based on the job_code field. The following Clipper code does the task:

```
* Check whether a character is ready
IF ser_ready()

        * Now read the data from serial port until ETX or error
        pbx_str = read_pbx()

        * Retrieve job code from record
        j_code = substr(pbx_str, 2, 2)
        DO CASE
                CASE j_code = "10"&& incoming call message

        •
        •
etc.
```

We can now write the read_pbx routine as Program 11-18.

Program 11-18. Read PBX Routine

```
/***
* read_pbx
*
* Read bytes from serial port until timeout or ETX
*/

CLIPPER read_pbx()

{
        byte ch;
        int i;
        byte ser_disp_stat[SIZE_PBX_STR]; /* Maximum message length */
```

```
        i = 0;
        last_stat = ser_read(&ser_disp_stat[i]);

        while (i < SIZE_PBX_STR && last_stat == 0 && ser_disp_stat[i] != ETX)
        {
                i = i + 1;
                last_stat = ser_read(&ser_disp_stat[i]);
        }

        /* only return as many characters as we read */
        _retclen(ser_disp_stat, i + 1);
}
```

The ser_read routine reads a character. Program 11-18 keeps calling it until it either reads an ETX character or returns a timeout value. _retclen ensures the correct length string is returned.

The computer must respond to the incoming call message. It sends a message with the following format:

```
typedef struct
{
        byte f_stx;                 /* ASCII STX code, 02 */
        byte f_job_code[2];         /* Message "10" */
        byte f_spaces[3];
        byte f_message_no[2];       /* Copy of message field received */
        byte f_result;              /* Response code to PBX. '1'-ok, '2'-bad */
        byte f_checksum[2];         /* Checksum of data bytes */
        byte f_etx;
} CALL_RESP;
```

The f_message_no field must have the value received from the PBX. It uniquely identifies the message. We will write a C routine, resp_call, to send the response message to the PBX. It will be passed the message number from Clipper.

```
* Check whether a character is ready
IF ser_ready()

        * Now read the data from serial port until ETX or error
        pbx_str = read_pbx()

        * Retrieve job code from record
        j_code = substr(pbx_str, 2, 2)
        DO CASE
                CASE j_code = "10"&& incoming call message
                        resp_call(substr(pbx_str, 7, 2))
```

On detecting the incoming call message, the code calls the resp_call routine with the f_message_no field. Program 11-19 is the source for the resp_call routine.

Program 11-19. Respond to a Call Record

```
/***
* resp_call
*
* Respond to a call record
*
*       1 - Get message number from Clipper.
*
*       2 - Set up structure.
*
*       3 - Calculate checksum and convert to ASCII hex.
*
*       4 - Send to serial port.
*/

CLIPPER resp_call()

{
        CALL_RESP call_resp;
        char *mess_no;
        byte c_sum, send_stat;

        mess_no = _parc(1);

        call_resp.f_stx = STX;
        call_resp.f_etx = ETX;
        call_resp.f_job_code[0] = '1';
        call_resp.f_job_code[1] = '0';

        memset((char *) call_resp.f_spaces, ' ',
                        sizeof(call_resp.f_spaces));
        memcpy((char *) call_resp.f_message_no, mess_no, 2);

        call_resp.f_result = '1';       /* accepted */

        /* set up checksum */
        c_sum = checksum(call_resp.f_job_code, 8);
        cbytetohex(c_sum, call_resp.f_checksum);
        send_stat = send_bytes((char *) &call_resp, sizeof(call_resp));
        _retni(send_stat);
}
```

In this section we developed basic serial communications routines. They provide direct access to the ROM BIOS serial interrupt handler. We used them to develop a simple computer to computer chat routine. Finally, we showed production code that uses the serial routines to control a PBX.

Windowing

An undocumented routine, _SETWIN, in the Clipper drivers module, allows for rudimentary windowing. It accepts four parameters defining the window's position. All subsequent screen output is then positioned relative to the window. For example, suppose we define the window from 10, 10 to 20, 20. An "@0,0 SAY " command would display output at an actual screen location of 10, 10. Similarly, an "@2,0 SAY " command would make text appear at an actual screen location of 12, 10. All CLEARs, BOXes, SCREENSAVEs, etc. are relative to the window. Text wraps in the window's width.

You can access _SETWIN directly from Clipper by CALLing it. Its parameters must be passed as WORDs. To set the window defined above, call it with:

```
CALL _setwin WITH WORD(10), WORD(10), WORD(20), WORD(20)
```

To go back to using the entire screen, redefine the window as:

```
CALL _setwin WITH WORD(0), WORD(0), WORD(24), WORD(79)
```

The biggest advantage of windowing functions is that you can write code without worrying about where the window is or how large it is. The code runs in a window, regardless of its position. You can then assign and move a window at run time, while the program is actually executing. Allowing the mouse to move the window produces a sophisticated user interface.

Hints and Warnings

- Save state functions are one of the highlights of this book. They make generic coding much easier.
- Use the mouse menu code. Implement equivalent GET/READ functions.
- Always return a value from a user defined function! Use _ret if the value is actually unnecessary.
- Use the extend compiler macros instead of coding your own versions.
- Use the serial communications functions to interface directly to RS232 serial devices.
- Use a symbolic debugger if you have problems (!). Microsoft's CodeView and Lattice's C-Sprite both work well.
- Build a windowing system around the _SETWIN routine.

12

File Structures

This chapter describes Clipper file structures and develops C code to handle them. It begins with a brief description of C data types, followed by a section on compiling and linking with Microsoft C. Readers who are not C programmers can still use the routines, even without understanding them in detail. The chapter shows a 'make' file to compile and link the routines and provides a sample call for each function.

You can link the routines directly with your applications to access the file structures. You can also use them as stand-alone utilities. Since they are written in C, they are much smaller than equivalents written directly in Clipper. For example, consider the simple task of listing a database's records or structure. A Clipper program to do this would occupy about 165K of disk space. The C equivalent takes 10K. The source code for both utilities is shown.

Overview

We develop routines to dump every type of file Clipper supports. This makes viewing them fast and simple. The alternative is to either use dBASE, a Nantucket application such as RL or DBU, or a custom Clipper program. The routines developed here are stand-alone utilities, invoked from the command line.

This chapter contains many example C programs. They illustrate tips and tricks of interest to the novice programmer. The routines that interface to Clipper show the use of the extend system. The section on memo fields explains how they can grow to enormous size, and develops a pack routine to solve this problem.

We discuss files in the following order:

- DBF
- DBT
- FRM
- LBL
- MEM
- NTX
- NDX

C Data Types

We use the following C types to describe file formats. Of course, their representation is compiler-dependent; we use Microsoft C, Version 5.00 for the IBM PC.

- **Int/short**. Shorts and ints are identical. They are represented by two bytes. In memory, the less significant byte is at the lower address, the more significant byte at the higher address. We call this *byte reversal*. For example,

  00 01 (two hex bytes)

  represents 256 decimal (0100 hex). Similarly,

  02 03 (two hex bytes)

  represents 770 decimal (0302 hex). Ints and shorts can be either signed or unsigned. The default is signed. An unsigned int is defined with "unsigned int", or simply "unsigned". Signed numbers are stored in two's complement form.

A signed int has a range from -32768 to +32767, an unsigned int from 0 to 65535.

- **Char.** It is represented by one byte, and can be either signed or unsigned. A signed character is stored in two's complement. It is declared simply with "char". An unsigned character is declared with "unsigned char".

  The range of a signed character is -128 to +127; that of an unsigned character is 0 to 255.

  Incorrect declaration of characters is a common source of errors. For example, the following code checks whether c is a graphics character (>127). If so, it calls proc_high_char. Otherwise, it calls proc_low_char.

```
char c;

/* assign graphics character for illustration */
c = 128;

if (c > 127)
        proc_high_char()
else
        proc_low_char();
```

  This routine calls proc_low_char incorrectly, if c is a graphics character. The compiler represents 128 internally as -128 (10000000 - reverse bits - 01111111 - add 1 - 10000000), so the else clause is executed.

- **Long.** A long is a 'qualified' int, qualified by the word long. It can be either signed or unsigned. An unsigned long is defined with "unsigned long", a signed long simply with "long." It is represented by four bytes stored in byte-reversed order. For example:

```
01 00 00 00 (four hex bytes)
```

  represents the number 1 (00000001 hex).

  The range of a signed long is -2,147,483,648 to +2,147,483,647. The range of an unsigned long is 0 to 4,294,987,295.

- **Double.** This is a floating point number represented by 64 bits (8 bytes), stored in IEEE format. Doubles are always signed.

Other C types consist of multiples of the basic types. An array consists of multiple variables (elements), all of the same type (contrast this with Clipper's arrays in which each element may be a different type). In C, the first element has index 0, and the last one has index n - 1, where n is the number of elements. Again, contrast this with Clipper arrays which start indexes at 1.

A structure is a collection of variables of any type, known as fields. It is like a RECORD in Pascal.

There is no way to tell whether a number is signed or unsigned. For example, the signed int -1 has the same physical representation as the unsigned int 65535. The distinction is important only in operations such as comparison and shifting. In many structures defined later, we do not care whether the fields are signed. No sign-dependent operations are performed.

An example is an ASCII character such as '+' (ASCII 246). If we declare it as a signed character, it is number -10; if we declare it as unsigned, however, it is number 246. However, unless we do comparisons or shifts on it, the destinction does not matter. In this case, we declare it as signed, the default.

This section described the representation of C data types in the Microsoft C 5.00 compiler. When studying file structures, remember that unsigneds, ints, and longs are byte-reversed.

Compiling and Linking

The make file in Figure 12-1 will compile and link all routines in this chapter. Refer to it when studying their code. If you are unfamiliar with MAKE, refer to Chapter 1 or review the Nantucket documentation.

Figure 12-1. Make File for Programs in Chapter 12

```
# all prgs are converted to objs by the following rule
.prg.obj:
        clipper $* -m

# all c files are converted to objs by the following rule
.c.obj:
        cl $**
```

```
# all objs are converted to exes by the following rule
.obj.exe:
        link $&,$&,$&/m,\mc\lib\llibca

#PRG file dependencies - if the file on the right hand side of the : is
#more recent than the one on the left, it is compiled according to the
#preceding rule for prg to obj
        mempak.obj:  mempak.prg

        mptest.obj: mptest.prg

        dbfctest.obj:  dbfctest.prg

#C file dependencies - if the file on the right hand side of the : is more
#recent than the one on the left, it is compiled according to the
#preceding rule for C to obj
        newtype.obj:  newtype.c

        newname.obj: newname.c

        cmemopak.obj: cmemopak.c

        dbflist.obj: dbflist.c

        list.obj:  list.c

        dbfstru.obj: dbfstru.c

        dbfcclip.obj: dbfcclip.c

        frmdump.obj: frmdump.c

        lbldump.obj: lbldump.c

                cl /c /AL /Gs /Zl /FPa /Zp1 lbldump.c

        ntxdump.obj:  ntxdump.c

        ndxdump.obj: ndxdump.c

        memopak1.obj: memopak1.c

        buff.obj: buff.c

        dbfhead.obj: dbfhead.c

        dbfcreat.obj: dbfcreat.c

#EXE file dependencies - if the file on the right hand side of the : is
#more recent than the one on the left, it is compiled according to the
#preceding rule for obj to exe
        ndxdump.exe:  ndxdump.obj
```

```
ntxdump.exe: ntxdump.obj

list.exe: list.obj

frmdump.exe: frmdump.obj

lbldump.exe: lbldump.obj

dbflist.exe: dbflist.obj

dbfstru.exe: dbfstru.obj

dbfhead.exe: dbfhead.obj

dbfcreat.exe: dbfcreat.obj

dbfctest.exe: dbfctest.obj dbfcclip.obj
        link $**,$&,$&/m,\summer\clipper \mc\lib\llibca /NOE

mptest.exe: mptest.obj mempak.obj cmemopak.obj newtype.obj
        link $**,$&,$&/m,\summer\clipper \mc\lib\llibca /NOE

mptest1.exe: mptest.obj mempak.obj memopak1.obj buff.obj newtype.obj
        link $**,$&,$&/m,\summer\clipper \mc\lib\llibca /NOE
```

The source files are identified by a comment at their heads. This make file assumes the following environment variables:

```
cl =/c /AL /Gs /Zl /FPa

include =\mc\include
```

The cl variable specifies default options for the cl.exe program, the Microsoft C 5.0 compiler driver. The options are:

- /c - Compile only without invoking the linker. This is necessary to link some routines with Clipper.
- /AL - Produce "large model" code. This is a requirement for all routines to be linked with Clipper. Some stand-alone routines developed in this chapter (those for which there is a link command) do not require the large model, but are compiled with it for consistency.
- /Gs - Do not generate stack probes. This is a requirement for Clipper-linked routines, but not for stand-alone routines.
- /Zl - Do not put the names of the default libraries in the object file.

- /FPa - Generate floating point calls and select the alternate math package. This is a requirement for Clipper-linked routines.

The include variable makes the compiler search the specified directory for include files not found in the current directory. We assume that the Microsoft compiler is installed in the conventional way, on drive C and in subdirectory \mc.

The make file further assumes that the files "nandef.h" and "extend.h", described in Chapter 11, are in the current directory.

We will now describe the file structures. In each case, we show a routine that simply displays the contents. These are stand-alone utilities. For some structures, we develop routines that you can link with your application.

DBF File Structure

This section describes the structure of a DBF file. We develop routines to display the database structure, list the records, create an empty database, and change fields' names and types.

We must consider two structures when describing a database file. The first is the header, which appears at the start of the file. The following C structure shows the header's format:

```
typedef struct
{
        char dbf_id;
        char last_update[3];
        long last_rec;          /* unsigned? */
        unsigned data_offset;
        unsigned rec_size;
        char filler[20];
} DBF_HEAD;
```

The first field, dbf_id, is a single byte that identifies the file type. A value of 03 indicates no memo fields. A value of 83 (hex) indicates a memo field. It is important to make this distinction, as memo fields are stored in a separate DBT file. Commands that process records in the DBF file must also process the corresponding records in the DBT file.

The second field, last_update, consists of three characters. It holds the date of the last update. The first character is the year number, the second the month number, and the third the day number.

The third field, last_rec, is a long containing the number of the last record. This is the value returned by the reccount function.

The fourth field, data_offset, gives the offset where the actual records start. Its value depends on the number of fields in a record.

The fifth field, rec_size, gives the size of each record. It is the sum of the field sizes plus one, to account for the delete character that starts each field.

The last field, filler, is 20 empty bytes, used to pad the structure to 32 bytes.

Using the C type information given earlier, we can define the field offsets as:

```
00    char dbf_id;
01    char last_update[3];
04    long last_rec;
08    unsigned data_offset;
0A    unsigned rec_size;
0C    char filler[20];
```

We can then easily dump the hexadecimal values of the start of a database file (with, for example, Debug on the DOS Supplemental Programs disk, or Phoenix's Dump) and match the values to the structure. For example, here are the first 16 bytes of a database file (in hex), displayed with the Dump utility:

Dump of SPJ.DBF

```
0: 03 57 0B 08 2C 00 00 00 A1 00 12 00 00 00 00 00 .W..,...;  ........
```

The field dbf_id is at offset 0. Here, its value is 03, indicating no memo fields.

The last_update array starts at offset 1. Here, its values are 57, 0B, and 08, or in decimal, 87, 11, and 08, indicating a last update on Nov. 8, 1987.

The last_rec field, starting at offset 4, contains the bytes 2C 00 00 00. The decimal value is 44 (remember the byte reversal), indicating 44 records in the database.

The data offset field, starting at offset 8, contains the bytes A1 00. The decimal value is 161 (again, remember the byte reversal). If we dump the spj database file starting at this offset, we would see its first record.

The rec_size field, starting at offset 0A, has the values 12 00, indicating a field size of 18 (decimal).

Program 12-1 reads a database header and displays it. This is the first stage of any file handling code - first dump the header and analyze the fields.

Program 12-1. Display a Database Header

```
/***
* dbfhead.c
*
*       Read database header and display it. First stage in database
*       processing code. Program takes one command line parameter:
*       the name of the DBF file. Include .dbf extension.
*
*        1 - Verify usage (1 parameter).
*
*        2 - Open the file.
*
*        3 - Read header.
*
*        4 - Display its fields.
*/

#include "stdio.h"

#include "stdlib.h"
#include "fcntl.h"
#include "io.h"

#include "dbf.h"

main(argc, argv)

int argc;
char *argv[]·

{
        int handle;

        /* define an instance of the DBF_HEAD structure */
        /* this is where header is read */
        DBF_HEAD dbf_head;

        /* verify usage - one parameter plus routine's name */
        if (argc != 2)
        {
                /* no file name, display error message and exit */
                printf("\nUsage : dbfhead <filename>\n");
                exit(1);
        }

        handle = open(argv[1], O_RDONLY | O_RAW);
```

```
        /* did open succeed? */
        if (handle == -1)
        {
                printf("\nError opening %s\n", argv[1]);
                exit(1);
        }

        /* read header into structure */
        if (read(handle, (char *) &dbf_head, sizeof(dbf_head))
                    != sizeof(DBF_HEAD))
        {
                printf("\nRead error\n");
                exit(1);
        }

        /* now display the fields */
        printf("\n*** database header %s ***\n\n", argv[1]);

        printf("Dbf id %d\n", dbf_head.dbf_id);
        printf("Last update %d %d %d\n\n", dbf_head.last_update[0],
              dbf_head.last_update[1], dbf_head.last_update[2]);

        printf("Data offset %d\n", dbf_head.data_offset);
        printf("Record size %d\n", dbf_head.rec_size);

        printf("Number of records %ld\n\n", dbf_head.last_rec);
        close(handle);
}
```

The include file "dbf.h" defines the structures.

The make file describes how to build the program. It shows that dbfhead.c depends on dbfhead.obj. The inference rule that describes how to convert C to OBJ files is:

```
.c.obj:
    cl $**
```

This specifies a compilation with cl. It uses the current setting of the CL environment variable (discussed previously) to invoke the C compiler.

The inference rule that specifies how to convert an OBJ file to a EXE is:

```
.obj.exe:
    link $&,$&,$&/m,\mc\lib\llibca
```

This links the OBJ file with the llibca library, resident in \mc\lib.

The routine introduces a technique used throughout the chapter.

The read statement reads 'sizeof(dbf_head)' bytes from the file directly into the dbf_head structure. The individual fields can then be processed independently. Reading the entire structure in this way is much faster than reading the fields independently. It uses less code and is easier to follow.

We must make one more point about the routine. We open the file with the "RAW" flag which directs the C library functions to do file I/O without text translation. Otherwise, the default mode translates carriage return characters into the pair carriage return/line feed. While this is usually necessary for text files, it is definitely NOT good for binary files.

The second structure we must examine, "FIELD_REC", defines the structure of a field in the database. Each field has a "FIELD_REC". The following C structure shows the format of a "FIELD_REC":

```
typedef struct
{
        char field_name[11];
        char field_type;
        char dummy[4];
        union
        {
                unsigned char_len;
                struct
                {
                        char len;
                        char dec;
                } num_size;
        } len_info;

        char filler[14];
} FIELD_REC;
```

This is a more complex structure than the header. The union statement defines a sequence of fields, only one of which is in use at a time. They can thus share an area of memory. This is the same as Pascal's variant record. The union variable may hold objects of different types and sizes at different times. So, the len_info union is either an unsigned, char_len, or another structure, num_size, which contains two character fields len and dec. The num_size structure is used when the field is numeric. It specifies the length and number of decimal places. The char_len field is used for all other types. It specifies the length. Only one byte is used unless the length is greater than 255.

The field_name field defines the field's name (strangely enough!). It has room for 10 characters and one null (a zero byte).

The field_type field defines the field's type (another imaginative name!). Its possible values are:

'C' (42 hex) - character

'D' (43 hex) - date

'L' (4C hex) - logical

'M' (4D hex) - memo

'N' (4E hex) - numeric

The filler fields simply pad the FIELD_REC structure to 32 bytes.

The first FIELD_REC appears immediately after the database header, at offset 20 hex, or 32 decimal. The last FIELD_REC is followed by a byte with the value 0D (hex), or 13 (decimal). Since the database header does not define the number of fields, we must keep reading FIELD_RECs until we find a 0D byte.

The offsets of each field in the "FIELD_REC" structure are as follows:

```
            typedef struct
            {
00          char field_name[11];
0B          char field_type;
0C          char dummy[4];
                union
                {
10              unsigned char_len;
                    struct
                    {
10                  char len;
11                  char dec;
                    } num_size;
                } len_info;

12          char filler[14];
            } FIELD_REC;
```

Note that the fields "char_len" and "len" start at the same offset because of the union. This structure is also defined in the 'dbf.h' file.

The following is a hex dump of the first part of a database file (the characters at the right are the ASCII representations):

Dump of SPJ.DBF

```
0:   03 57 0B 08 2C 00 00 00 A1 00 12 00 00 00 00 00 .W..,... ........
10:  00 00 00 00 00 00 00 00 00 00 00 00 00 00 00 00 ........ ........
20:  53 5F 4E 4F 00 20 31 00 00 00 00 43 0F 00 18 45 S_NO. 1. ...C...E
```

```
30:  04 00 00 00 01 00 00 00 00 00 00 00 00 00 00 00 ........ ........
40:  50 5F 4E 4F 00 20 32 00 00 00 00 43 13 00 18 45 P_NO. 2. ...C...E
50:  04 00 00 00 01 00 00 00 00 00 00 00 00 00 00 00 ........ ........
60:  4A 5F 4E 4F 00 20 33 00 00 00 00 43 17 00 18 45 J_NO. 3. ...C...E
70:  04 00 00 00 01 00 00 00 00 00 00 00 00 00 00 00 ........ ........
80:  51 54 59 00 64 20 34 00 00 00 00 4E 1B 00 18 45 QTY.d 4. ...N...E
90:  05 00 00 00 01 00 00 00 00 00 00 00 00 00 00 00 ........ ........
A0:  0D 20 53 31 20 20 50 31 20 20 4A 31 20 20 20 20 . S1 P1  J1
```

The first field record appears at offset 20. Using the offsets defined above, we can see that the first FIELD_REC has the following values:

```
field_name  S_NO
field_type  43 (C)
char_len    0004
```

defining a character field "S_NO" of length 4. Remember that the unsigned char_len is byte reversed.

The second FIELD_REC appears immediately afterward at offset 40. It has the following values:

```
field_name  P_NO
field_type  43 (C)
char_len    0004
```

This database file has four FIELD_RECS before the 0D terminator byte. The last two have the following values:

```
field_name  J_NO
field_type  43 (C)
char_len    0004

field_name  QTY
field_type  4E (N)
len         05
dec         00
```

The 0D FIELD_REC terminator byte is at offset A0. The next available byte is thus at offset A1, the start of the data records as specified by the header.

List Structure

Program 12-2 uses the structures just defined to display the structure of a database file, much like the dBASE "LIST STRU" command:

Program 12-2. C Version of the LIST STRU Command

```
/***
* dbfstru.c
*
*       Show structure of a database file directly from C. A stand-alone
* utility.
*
* 1 - Verify usage (one parameter).
*
* 2 - Open it.

*
* 3 - Read header.
*
* 4 - Display header.
*
* 5 - For each field
*
*               5.1 Display name, type, len, (and if numeric, number of
*                       decimal places)
*/

#include "stdio.h"
#include "stdlib.h"
#include "fcntl.h"
#include "io.h"
#include "nondef.h"
#include "dbf.h"

/* declare an instance of the DBF_HEAD structure */
DBF_HEAD dbf_head;

/* declare an instance of the FIELD_REC structure */
FIELD_REC field_rec;

main(argc, argv)

int argc;
char *argv[];

{
        int handle;
        int num_fields;
        Boolean more_fields;

        /* check for correct number of parameters (1) plus program name) */
        if (argc != 2)
        {
                printf("\nUsage : dbfstru <filename>\n");
                exit(1);
```

```
}

handle = open(argv[1], O_RDONLY | O_RAW);

/* did file open succeed? */
if (handle == -1)
{
        printf("\nError opening %s\n", argv[1]);
        exit(1);
}

/* read header */
if (read(handle, (char *) &dbf_head, sizeof(dbf_head)) !=
        sizeof(DBF_HEAD))
{

        printf("\nRead error\n");
        exit(1);
}

/* display header information */
printf("\n*** structure of database %s ***\n\n", argv[1]);
printf("Last update %d %d %d\n\n", dbf_head.last_update[0],
          dbf_head.last_update[1], dbf_head.last_update[2]);

printf("Data offset %d\n", dbf_head.data_offset);
printf("Record size %d\n", dbf_head.rec_size);

printf("Number of records %ld\n\n", dbf_head.last_rec);
printf("NAME          TYPE LEN DEC\n\n");

/* counter for number of fields */
num_fields = 0;

more_fields = TRUE;

/* for every field */
/* detect end of field list by read failing or 0D terminator */

while (more_fields)
{
        more_fields = (read(handle, (char *) &field_rec,
                                sizeof(FIELD_REC)) == sizeof(FIELD_REC));

        if (more_fields)
        {
                more_fields = (field_rec.field_name[0] != 0x0D);
                if (more_fields)
                {
                        /* display depends on field type */
                        switch(field_rec.field_type)
                        {
```

```
                        case 'N' :
                            /* numeric, so show decimal places */
                            printf("%-11s %-4c %3d %3d\n",
                                field_rec.field_name,
                                field_rec.field_type,
                                field_rec.len_info.num_size.len,
                                field_rec.len_info.num_size.dec);
                            break;

                        default :
                            /* not numeric, don't show decimal places */
                            printf("%-11s %-4c %3d\n",
                                field_rec.field_name,
                                field_rec.field_type,
                                field_rec.len_info.char_len);
                            break;
                    }

                }
            }
        }
        close(handle);
}
```

You must pass the name of the database (with the DBF extension) on the command line. Program 12-2 reads and displays the header just like Program 12-1. It determines that it has read all the FIELD_RECs in one of two ways. Either the read function fails to read a full 32 bytes (i.e., there are no records in the file), or the first byte it reads is 0D. Again, the make file specifies how to build the program.

Running Program 12-2 with the database dumped above produces the following output:

```
*** structure of database spj.dbf ***

Last update 87 11 08

Data offset 161
Record size 18
Number of records 44

NAME        TYPE LEN  DEC

S_NO        C      4
P_NO        C      4
J_NO        C      4
QTY         N      5    0
```

> **TIP**
>
> Use Program 12-2 to quickly display database structures. It is faster and smaller than a custom Clipper program, and faster and more flexible than loading dBASE.

Create Structure

Once we understand the structure of a database file, we can easily create one entirely from C. We will first show a stand-alone C routine to do this, then one that is callable from Clipper. Program 12-3 creates a database "SPJ1" with the same format as the "SPJ" database dumped above.

Program 12-3. Database Create in C

```
/***
* dbfcreat.c
*
*  Create database file directly from C. First stage toward a Clipper
* callable routine.
*
*       1 - Set up names, types, lens, and decs arrays.
*
*       2 - Call dbfcreate routine to do actual creation.
*
*       3 - dbfcreate:
*
*               3.1 - Open dbf file with CREAT mode.
*
*               3.2 - Get date from DOS
*
*               3.3 - Build header.
*
*               3.4 - Calculate record size and determine whether structure
*                       included a memo field.
*
*               3.5 - If memo field, create empty memo file.
*
*               3.6 - Write DBF header.
*
*               3.7 - For every field:
*
*                       3.7.1 - Build FIELD_REC structure.
*
```

```
*                          3.7.2 - Write it.
*
*                   3.8 - Write DBF tail.
*/

/* header files for library routines we use */
#include "stdio.h"
#include "stdlib.h"
#include "fcntl.h"
#include "string.h"
#include "io.h"
#include "malloc.h"
#include "\mc\include\sys\types.h"
#include "\mc\include\sys\stat.h"
#include "dos.h"
#include "handef.h"
#include "dbf.h"
/* main simply sets up arrays and calls dbfcreat */

main()
{
        /* reserve space for 4 fields */
        char *fnames[4];
        char ftypes[4];
        unsigned flens[4];
        unsigned fdecs[4];

        /* set up database structures */

        /* field 1 */
        fnames[0] = "S_NO";
        ftypes[0] = 'C';
        flens[0] = 4;

        /* field 2 */
        fnames[1] = "P_NO";
        ftypes[1] = 'C';
        flens[1] = 4;

        /* field 3 */
        fnames[2] = "J_NO";
        ftypes[2] = 'C';
        flens[2] = 4;

        /* field 4 */
        fnames[3] = "QTY";
        ftypes[3] = 'N';
        flens[3] = 5;
        fdecs[3] = 0;

        /* try to create this structure */
        if (dbfcreate("SPJ1.DBF", 4, fnames, ftypes, flens, fdecs))
```

```
                printf("%s successfully created\n", "SPJ1.DBF");
        else
                printf("%s could not be created\n", "SPJ1.DBF");
}

/***
* dbfcreat
*
* The actual creation routine. Creates dbf, sets up header.
* If memo field present, creates empty dbt file (just header)
*/

Boolean dbfcreate(filename, num_fields, fnames, ftypes, flens, fdecs)

char *filename;
unsigned num_fields;
char **fnames;

char ftypes[ ];
unsigned flens[ ];
unsigned fdecs[ ];

{
        int dbf_handle, dbt_handle;
        int i;
        unsigned rec_size;
        struct dosdate_t date;

        char *dbt_name;
        long dbt_head;
        char *dbt_data;

        Boolean is_memo;
        DBF_HEAD dbf_head;
        FIELD_REC field_rec;

        is_memo = FALSE;

        /* try to open file */
        dbf_handle = open(filename, O_CREAT | O_TRUNC | O_RDWR | O_BINARY,
                        S_I READ | S_I WRITE);
        if (dbf_handle == -1)
        {
                /* failed */
                printf("\nError creating %s\n", filename);
                return(FALSE);
        }

        /* get the current date so we can set dbf header */
        _dos_getdate(&date);

        /* build last_update field in header */
```

```
/* year */
dbf_head.last_update[0] = date.year - 1900;

/* month */
dbf_head.last_update[1] = date.month;

/* day */
dbf_head.last_update[2] = date.day;

/* reccount() = 0 */
dbf_head.last_rec = 0l;

/* set empty area to 0 */
memset(dbf_head.filler, 0, 20);

rec_size = 0;

/* This loop calculates record size by summing flens array */
/* It also determines whether a memo file is present */
for (i = 0; i < num_fields; i++)
{
        rec_size = rec_size + flens[i];
        if (ftypes[i] == 'M')
                is_memo = TRUE;
}

if (is_memo)
{
        /* memo field does exist, so create empty memo file */
        /* note id field is set to 83 */
        /* set count in header to 1, rest of header to 0 */
        /* write header, write eof marker */

        dbf_head.dbf_id = (char) 0x83;

        dbt_name = malloc(strlen(filename) + 1);

        /* make dbt file name */
        strcpy(dbt_name, filename);

        /* replace DBF with DBT */
        strcpy(&dbt_name[strlen(dbt_name) - 3], "DBT");

        /* create empty DBT file */
        dbt_handle = open(dbt_name, O_CREAT | O_TRUNC | O_RDWR
                                        | O_BINARY, S_IREAD | S_IWRITE);

        /* did memo file open succeed? */
        if (dbt_handle == -1)
        {
                /* no */
                printf("\nError creating %s\n", dbt_name);
```

```
            return(FALSE);
        }

        /* number of DBT records */
        dbt_head = 1l;

        /* write count at start of dbt header */
        if (write(dbt_handle, (char *) &dbt_head, sizeof(dbt_head))
                != sizeof(dbt_head))
        {
                /* write failed */
                printf("\nError writing %s\n", dbt_name);
                return(FALSE);
        }

        /* allocate rest of header */
        dbt_data = (char *) malloc(508);

        /* set to zero */
        memset(dbt_data, '\0', 508);

        /* write on disk */

        if (write(dbt_handle, (char *) dbt_data, 508) != 508)
        {
                /* error writing */
                printf("\nError writing %s\n", dbt_name);
                return(FALSE);
        }

        /* eof marker, (octal value), 1A hex */
        if (write(dbt_handle, "\032", 1) != 1)
        {
                printf("\nError writing %s\n", dbt_name);
                return(FALSE);
        }

        /* release allocated memory */
        free(dbt_name);
        free(dbt_data);
        close(dbt_handle);
}
else
        /* no memo fields in structure, id byte is 03 */
        dbf_head.dbf_id = (char) 3;

/* finish constructing header */
dbf_head.rec_size = rec_size + 1;

/* where data records start */
dbf_head.data_offset = sizeof(DBF_HEAD) +
                                num_fields * sizeof(FIELD_REC) + 1;
```

```
/* write header */
if (write(dbf_handle, (char *) &dbf_head, sizeof(DBF_HEAD))
                        != sizeof(dbf_head))
{
        /* error */
        printf("Error writing header\n");
        return(FALSE);
}

/* header is now written on disk, now write every field record */
for (i = 0; i < num_fields; i++)
{
        /* field name must be padded with zeros. Initially fill */
        memset(field_rec.field_name, 0, 11);

        /* copy field's name on top of zeros */
        strcpy(field_rec.field_name, fnames[i]);

        /* set field's type */
        field_rec.field_type = ftypes[i];

        /* unused space - set to zero */
        memset(field_rec.dummy, 0, 4);

        /* set up length and decimals information based on field's type */
        switch(ftypes[i])
        {
                case 'N':
                        /* numeric field */
                        field_rec.len_info.num_size.len = flens[i];
                        field_rec.len_info.num_size.dec = fdecs[i];
                        break;

                default:
                        /* all other types */
                        field_rec.len_info.char_len = flens[i];
                        break;
        }

        /* unused space, clear to zero */
        memset(field_rec.filler, 0, 14);

        /* write one field rec */
        if (write(dbf_handle, (char *) &field_rec, sizeof(FIELD_REC))
                                != sizeof(FIELD_REC))
        {
                /* error */
                printf("Error writing field\n");
                return(FALSE);
        }
}
```

```
        /* all field records written, write EOF marker */
        /* tail, these are octal, 1A hex */

        if (write(dbf_handle, "\015\032", 2) != 2)
        {
                printf("Error writing tail\n");
                return(FALSE);
        }

        close(dbf_handle);
        return(TRUE);
}
```

The main routine simply sets up the names, types, lens, and decs arrays, and calls the function "dbfcreat". You must specify field lengths even if they are predefined, as with:

- DATE - 8
- LOGICAL - 1
- MEMO - 10

The dbfcreat routine reads the current date with the library routine _dos_getdate. The values returned are stored in the header structure. The routine sets last_rec to 0 to indicate an empty file, and then checks the type of every field to see if any are memos. If so, it stores the value 83 (hex) in the "dbf_id" byte; otherwise, it stores 03 there. If it finds a memo field, it creates a DBT file with the same name as the DBF file. This is necessary, even though the database contains no records. An empty database with a memo field is incomplete without the corresponding (empty) memo file.

The first 512 bytes of a memo file are a header. The first four bytes are a long, the number of 512 byte records in the DBT file. Since this memo file has only a header, the count is set to 1. The other 508 bytes are filler. They are set to 0 and written to the DBT file. The eof marker (1A hex, 32 octal) is then written, and the DBT file is closed. We describe the structure of a memo file later in this chapter.

The size of the record is the sum of the lengths of the individual fields plus one. The extra byte holds the delete flag, the first byte of every record. The data offset field in the header (the offset where the data starts) is the number of fields multiplied by the size of each FIELD_REC, plus the size of the dbf header plus one. The last 1 accounts for the 0D terminator byte.

The header and the individual field records are written into the DBF file, followed by the 0D terminator and a 1A to mark the end of file. The empty file, SPJ1.DBF, would then appear as follows.

Dump of SPJ1.DBF

```
0:   03 57 0B 19 00 00 00 00 A1 00 12 00 00 00 00 00  .W...... ........
10:  00 00 00 00 00 00 00 00 00 00 00 00 00 00 00 00  ........ ........
20:  53 5F 4E 4F 00 00 00 00 00 00 00 43 00 00 00 00  S_NO.... ...C....
30:  04 00 00 00 00 00 00 00 00 00 00 00 00 00 00 00  ........ ........
40:  50 5F 4E 4F 00 00 00 00 00 00 00 43 00 00 00 00  P_NO.... ...C....
50:  04 00 00 00 00 00 00 00 00 00 00 00 00 00 00 00  ........ ........
60:  4A 5F 4E 4F 00 00 00 00 00 00 00 43 00 00 00 00  J_NO.... ...C....
70:  04 00 00 00 00 00 00 00 00 00 00 00 00 00 00 00  ........ ........
80:  51 54 59 00 00 00 00 00 00 00 00 4E 00 00 00 00  QTY..... ...N....
90:  05 00 00 00 00 00 00 00 00 00 00 00 00 00 00 00  ........ ........
A0:  0D 1A                                            ..
```

We can easily make the stand-alone create program callable from Clipper by using the extend functions. Program 12-4 shows the routine.

Program 12-4. Clipper Callable Code for Creating a Database

```
/***
* dbfcclip.c
*
*       Database create routine, callable from Clipper.
* Same as Program 12-3, except parameters are retrieved from Clipper with
* extend functions.
*/

/* header files for functions we use */

#include "stdio.h"
#include "stdlib.h"
#include "fcntl.h"
#include "string.h"
#include "io.h"
#include "malloc.h"
#include "sys\types.h"
#include "sys\stat.h"

#include "dos.h"

#include "nandef.h"
#include "extend.h"
#include "dbf.h"

CLIPPER dbfcreat()
```

```
int dbf_handle, dbt_handle, i;
unsigned rec_size;
struct dosdate_t date;

Boolean is_memo;
char *dbt_name;
long dbt_head;
char *dbt_data;

char *filename;
unsigned num_fields;
char **fnames;
char *ftypes;
unsigned *flens;
unsigned *fdecs;

DBF_HEAD dbf_head;

FIELD_REC field_rec;

is_memo = FALSE;

filename = _parc(1);
num_fields = _parni(2);
/* allocate space for arrays */
fnames = (char **) malloc(num_fields * sizeof(char *));
ftypes = (char *) malloc(num_fields * sizeof(char));
flens = (unsigned *) malloc(num_fields * sizeof(unsigned));
fdecs = (unsigned *) malloc(num_fields * sizeof(unsigned));

dbf_handle = open(filename, O_CREAT | O_TRUNC | O_RDWR | O_BINARY,
                  S_I READ | S_I WRITE );
if (dbf_handle == -1)
{
        /* error opening file */
        _retl(FALSE);
        return;
}

/* get current date so dbf header can be set */
_dos_getdate(&date);

/* set up last_update field */

/* year */
dbf_head.last_update[0] = date.year - 1900;

/* month */
dbf_head.last_update[1] = date.month;

/* day */
```

```
dbf_head.last_update[2] = date.day;

/* reccount() = 0 */
dbf_head.last_rec = 0l;

/* set unused area to zero */
memset(dbf_head.filler, 0, 20);

rec_size = 0;

/* get parameters from Clipper */
for (i = 1; i <= num_fields; i++)
{
        /* note C arrays are 0 based, Clipper arrays are 1 based */
        fnames[i - 1] = _parc(3, i);
        ftypes[i - 1] = *_parc(4, i);

        if (ftypes[i - 1] == 'M')
                is_memo = TRUE;

        flens[i - 1] = _parni(5, i);
        fdecs[i - 1] = _parni(6, i);

        rec_size = rec_size + flens[i - 1];
}

if (is_memo)
{
        /* create empty memo file */
        dbf_head.dbf_id = (char) 0x83;

        dbt_name = malloc(strlen(filename) + 1);

        /* make dbt file name */
        strcpy(dbt_name, filename);
        strcpy(&dbt_name[strlen(dbt_name) - 3], "DBT");

        /* create empty .DBT file */
        dbt_handle = open(dbt_name, O_CREAT | O_TRUNC | O_RDWR |
                        O_BINARY, S_I READ | S_I WRITE );

        if (dbt_handle == -1)
        {
                _retl(FALSE);
                return;
        }

        dbt_head = 1l;
        if (write(dbt_handle, (char *) &dbt_head, sizeof(dbt_head))
                != sizeof(dbt_head))
        {
                _retl(FALSE);
```

```
                return;
        }

        dbt_data = (char *) malloc(508);
        memset(dbt_data, '\0', 508);
        if (write(dbt_handle, (char *) dbt_data, 508) != 508)
        {
                _retl(FALSE);
                return;
        }

        /* eof marker (octal value) */
        if (write(dbt_handle, "\032", 1) != 1)
        {
                _retl(FALSE);
                return;
        }
        free(dbt_name);
        free(dbt_data);
        close(dbt_handle);
}
else
        dbf_head.dbf_id = (char) 3;

dbf_head.rec_size = rec_size + 1;

dbf_head.data_offset = sizeof(DBF_HEAD) +
                        num_fields * sizeof(FIELD_REC) + 1;
/* write dbf header */
if (write(dbf_handle, (char *) &dbf_head, sizeof(DBF_HEAD))
                != sizeof(dbf_head))
{
        _retl(FALSE);
        close(dbf_handle);
        return;
}

/* write every field record */
for (i = 0; i < num_fields; i++)
{
        memset(field_rec.field_name, 0, 11);
        strcpy(field_rec.field_name, fnames[i]);
        field_rec.field_type = ftypes[i];
        memset(field_rec.dummy, 0, 4);
        switch(ftypes[i])
        {
                case 'N':
                        field_rec.len_info.num_size.len = flens[i];
                        field_rec.len_info.num_size.dec = fdecs[i];
                        break;

                default:
```

```
                    field_rec.len_info.char_len = flens[i];
                    break;
            }

            memset(field_rec.filler, 0, 14);
            if (write(dbf_handle, (char *) &field_rec, sizeof(FIELD_REC))
                                != sizeof(FIELD_REC))
            {
                _retl(FALSE);
                close(dbf_handle);
                return;
            }
        }

        /* tail, the values are octal */

        if (write(dbf_handle, "\015\032", 2) != 2)
        {
            _retl(FALSE);
            close(dbf_handle);
            return;
        }

        free((char *) fnames);
        free(ftypes);
        free((char *) flens);
        free((char *) fdecs);

        close(dbf_handle);
        _retl(TRUE);

}
```

Program 12-4 is very similar to Program 12-3. We added code to retrieve the parameters from Clipper and save them in local arrays. Note one difference between the two languages - Clipper arrays start at 1, whereas C arrays start at 0. Also note that since the type requires only one character, the first character is simply taken from the string pointed to by the _parc function (*_parc(4, i)).

The routine reports its success or failure by returning a logical with the "retl" function.

Again the make file specifies how to build this routine. Note that only an .obj file is built, since it is to be linked with a Clipper routine.

To create the SPJ1 database, you call Program 12-4 with:

```
* dbfctest

num_fields = 4

DECLARE fnames[num_fields]
DECLARE ftypes[num_fields]
DECLARE flens[num_fields]
DECLARE fdecs[num_fields]

fnames[1] = "S_NO"
ftypes[1] = 'C'
flens[1] = 4
fdecs[1] = 0

fnames[2] = "P_NO"
ftypes[2] = "C"
flens[2] = 4
fdecs[2] = 0

fnames[3] = "J_NO'
ftypes[3] = "C"
flens[3] = 4
fdecs[3] = 0

fnames[4] = "QTY"
ftypes[4] = "N"
flens[4] = 5
fdecs[4] = 0

file = "spj1.dbf"

? dbfcreat(file, num_fields, fnames, ftypes, flens, fdecs)
```

TIP

Chapter 8 shows alternative ways to create dbf files. The method presented here is the fastest and easiest to use. Use it rather than CREATE or CREATE FROM.

Database List

The size and type dictate the representation of a field in a database record. The possibilities are:

- **Character** - A character field is represented by a sequence of ASCII characters, with the length specified. If a field is not full, it is padded with spaces.

- **Numeric** - A numeric field is represented by a sequence of ASCII characters, with the decimal point in the appropriate place. The number of decimal places is specified by the dec field in the FIELD_REC structure. It is padded with leading spaces if necessary. For example, a numeric field of size 10 with 2 decimal places is represented by a string with the following format:

  ```
  "9999999.99"
  ```

  Note that there are only seven digits ahead of the decimal point - the point itself takes one place.

- **Logical** - A logical field is represented by a byte containing either ASCII "F" or "T".

- **Memo** - A memo field is represented in the DBF file as a 10 digit numeric with no decimal places. This is the record number in the DBT file where the memo starts. The digits are simply ASCII. A record without an "active" memo field contains 10 spaces (hex 20).

- **Date** - A date field contains 8 ASCII characters in the format YYYYMMDD. For example, the string "19900301" represents March 1, 1990.

The first byte of each record is a delete flag. An ASCII space (20 hex) indicates that the record has not been marked for deletion, whereas ASCII * indicates that it has been.

Now that we know the structure of individual fields, we can develop a stand-alone program to list a database file. Program 12-5 is the source code for such a routine.

Program 12-5. List a Database

```
/***
* dbflist.c
*
*       Stand-alone code to list a database file.
* DBF file name is passed on command line, include dbf extension.
*
*       1 - Verify usage (one parameter).
*
*       2 - Open file.
*
*       3 - Read header.
*
```

```
*       4 - Build linked list of FIELD_RECs.
*
*       5 - Seek to start of data.
*
*       6 - For each record:
*
*               6.1 - Read it.
*
*               6.2 - Print delete flag (* or space)
*
*               6.3 - For each field:
*
*                       6.3.1 - Print it.
*/

/* headers for functions we use */
#include "stdio.h"
#include "stdlib.h"
#include "fcntl.h"
#include "string.h"
#include "io.h"
#include "malloc.h"
#include "nandef.h"
#include "dbf.h"

typedef struct fl_tag
{
        FIELD_REC field_rec;
        struct fl_tag *next_flist;
} FIELD_LIST;

main(argc, argv)

int argc;
char *argv[];

{
        FIELD_REC field_rec;
        FIELD_LIST *field_list, *flist_ptr, *last_flist;
        DBF_HEAD dbf_head;
        int handle;
        Boolean more_fields;
        unsigned rec_num, rec_offset, width, num_fields;
        char *record, *buffer;
        if (argc != 2)
        {
                printf("Usage : dbflist <filename>\n");
                exit(1);
        }

        handle = open(argv[1], O_RDONLY | O_RAW);
        if (handle == -1)
```

```
{
        printf("Error opening %s\n", argv[1]);
        exit(1);
}

if (read(handle, (char *) &dbf_head, sizeof(dbf_head))
        != sizeof(DBF_HEAD))
{
        printf("\nRead error\n");
        exit(1);
}

/* build dynamic field_list linked list */
last_flist = NULL;

more_fields = TRUE;
num_fields = 0;

/* for each field */
while (more_fields)
{
        more_fields = (read(handle, (char *) &field_rec,
                                sizeof(FIELD_REC)) == sizeof(FIELD_REC));

        if (more_fields)
        {
                /* is this last field ? */
                more_fields = (field_rec.field_name[0] != 0x0D);
                if (more_fields)
                {
                        /* no, add to list */
                        num_fields = num_fields + 1;
                        flist_ptr = (FIELD_LIST *) malloc(sizeof(FIELD_LIST));

                        memcpy((char *) &flist_ptr -> field_rec,
                                (char *) &field_rec, sizeof(FIELD_LIST));

                        flist_ptr -> next_flist = NULL;

                        /* is this the first entry in list?*/
                        if (last_flist)
                        {
                                /* no, add to list */
                                last_flist -> next_flist = flist_ptr;
                                last_flist = flist_ptr;
                        }
                        else
                        {
                                /* yes, start list */
                                field_list = flist_ptr;
                                last_flist = field_list;
                        }
```

```
            }
        }
    }

    /* Now that field list is built, list records */
    flist_ptr = field_list;

    /* position file to start of data */
    if (lseek(handle, (long) dbf_head.data_offset, 0) == -1l)
    {
        printf("Error seeking in database file\n");
        exit(1);
    }

    /* allocate space for 1 record */
    record = (char *) malloc(dbf_head.rec_size);

    /* This will cater to a record with 1 field */
    buffer = (char *) malloc(dbf_head.rec_size);

    printf("\n\n");

    /* for each record ... */
    for (rec_num = 1; rec_num <= dbf_head.last_rec; rec_num++)
    {
        read(handle, record, dbf_head.rec_size);
        printf("%4d", rec_num);

        /* for each field */
        flist_ptr = field_list;

        /* print deleted character */
        printf("%c", record[0]);

        rec_offset = 1;
        while (flist_ptr)
        {
            switch (flist_ptr -> field_rec.field_type)
            {
                case 'N':
                    width = flist_ptr ->
                            field_rec.len_info.num_size.len;
                    break;

                default:
                    width = flist_ptr -> field_rec.len_info.char_len;
            }

            strncpy(buffer, (char *) &record[rec_offset], width);
            buffer[width] = '\0';

            printf("%s ", buffer);
```

```
                rec_offset = rec_offset + width;
                flist_ptr = flist_ptr -> next_flist;
            }
            printf("\n");
        }
}
```

Program 12-5 builds a list of FIELD_LIST structures from the FIELD_REC structures located at the beginning of the database file. The list is simply a FIELD_REC with a pointer to the next "FIELD_LIST". It is necessary to provide the type and size of each database field when it is listed. The program positions the file at the start of the data (as specified by the header), and reads and displays each record. It extracts each field from the record and displays it separately.

This is for illustration only. As all types are represented by ASCII characters, we can display records without extracting the fields. However, the numeric types will not be aligned properly, and full fields will appear with no spaces between them. Program 12-6 shows the simpler LIST procedure.

Program 12-6. Simple Database List with No Formatting

```
/***
* list.c
*
*
*       Simpler list program without formatting
*
*       1 - Verify usage (one parameter).
*
*       2 - Open file.
*
*       3 - Read header.
*
*       4 - Seek to start of data.
*
*       5 - For each record:
*
*               5.1 - Read it.
*
*               5.2 - Print delete flag (* or space).
*
*               5.3 - Print record.
*/

#include "stdio.h"
```

```
#include "stdlib.h"
#include "fcntl.h"
#include "string.h"
#include "io.h"
#include "malloc.h"

#include "dbf.h"

main(argc, argv)

int argc;
char *argv[];

{
        DBF_HEAD dbf_head;
        int handle;
        unsigned rec_num;
        char *record;
        if (argc != 2)
        {
                printf("Usage : dbflist <filename>\n");
                exit(1);
        }

        handle = open(argv[1], O_RDONLY | O_RAW);
        if (handle == -1)
        {
                printf("Error opening %s\n", argv[1]);
                exit(1);
        }

        if (read(handle, (char *) &dbf_head, sizeof(dbf_head))
                 != sizeof(DBF_HEAD))
        {
                printf("\nRead error\n");
                exit(1);
        }

        /* position file to start of data */
        if (lseek(handle, (long) dbf_head.data_offset, 0) == -1l)
        {
                printf("Error seeking in database file\n");
                exit(1);
        }

        /* allocate space for 1 record */
        record = (char *) malloc(dbf_head.rec_size);

        printf("\n\n");

        /* for each record ... */
        for (rec_num = 1; rec_num <= dbf_head.last_rec; rec_num++)
```

```
        {
                read(handle, record, dbf_head.rec_size);

                printf("%4d ", rec_num);

                /* print delete character */
                printf("%c ", record[0]);

                printf("%.*s\n", dbf_head.rec_size, record);

        }
    }
```

Program 12-6 seeks to the start of the data and then simply reads a record and displays it. Note the * formatting character used in printf. It indicates that the size of the type is an argument (rather than an inline constant), and allows variable length strings to be printed.

> **TIP**
>
> To take a quick look at a database, use Program 12-5 or 12-6 as an alternative to either a custom Clipper program, or loading dBASE.

Changing Field Names

Knowing the structure of a database file makes it easy to change a field name. All you must do is read the appropriate FIELD_REC and change the field_name field. Program 12-7 contains the source code. It is callable from Clipper.

Program 12-7. Changing a Field's Name

```
/***
* newname.c
*
*       Clipper callable routine to change a field's name.
*/

#include "fcntl.h"
#include "string.h"
#include "io.h"

#include "dbf.h"
```

```
#include "nandef.h"
#include "extend.h"

/***
*  newname(file, field_no, new_name)
*
*  char *file
*  unsigned field_no
*  char *new_name
*
*        Change field in given file to this name
*
*  1 - Retrieve parameters from Clipper.
*
*  2 - Open file.
*
*  3 - Seek to required FIELD_REC.
*
*  4 - Read it.
*
*  5 - Change name.
*
*  6 - Reposition file to start of FIELD_REC.
*
*  7 - Write modified FIELD_REC.
*/

CLIPPER newname()

{
        char *file;
        unsigned  field_no;
        char *new_name;
        int handle;
        unsigned start_field;        /* offset into .dbf for this field */
        FIELD_REC field_rec;

        file = _parc(1);
        field_no = _parni(2);
        new_name = _parc(3);

        handle = open(file, O_RDWR | O_RAW);

        if (handle == -1)
        {
                _retl(FALSE);
                return;
        }

        start_field = sizeof(DBF_HEAD) + (sizeof(FIELD_REC)
                                * (field_no - 1));
```

```
        /* position file at start of required field ... */
        lseek(handle, (long) start_field, 0);

        /* read field */
        read(handle, (char *) &field_rec, sizeof(FIELD_REC));

        /* change name */
        strcpy(field_rec.field_name, new_name);

        /* reposition file */
        lseek(handle, (long) start_field, 0);

        /* write it out ... */
        write(handle, (char *) &field_rec, sizeof(FIELD_REC));
        close(handle);
        _retl(TRUE);
}
```

Program 12-7 takes the file name, the field number, and the new name as parameters. It positions the file at the start of the field, reads the FIELD_REC into a structure, changes the field name, and rewrites the FIELD_REC. The routine reports its success or failure by returning a logical.

The following call changes the name of field 3 in database SPJ1 to "JOB_NO", and displays the return code:

```
? newname("SPJ1.DBF", 3, "JOB_NO")
```

TIP

When you need to change a field's name, use Program 12-7 as an alternative to performing a MODI STRU command in dBASE or a Clipper equivalent. It allows you to change the name without copying the database.

Changing Field Types

It is equally simple to develop a routine to change a field's type. Although this may not appear to be useful, it is necessary for a routine developed later in this chapter. Program 12-8 shows the source for a routine callable from Clipper.

Program 12-8. Changing a Field's Type

```
/***
* newtype.c
```

```
*
* Change the type of the specified field.
*
*       1 - Retrieve parameters from Clipper.
*
*       2 - Open file.
*
*       3 - Seek to required FIELD_REC.
*
*       4 - Read it.
*
*       5 - Change type.
*
*       6 - Reposition file to start of FIELD_REC.
*
*       7 - Write modified FIELD_REC.
*/
#include "fcntl.h"
#include "io.h"

#include "dbf.h"

#include "nandef.h"
#include "extend.h"

/***
*  newtype(file, field_no, new_type)
*
* char *file
*  unsigned field_no
* char *new_type
*
*        Change field number in given file to this type
*/

CLIPPER newtype()

{
        char *file,
        unsigned field_no;
        char new_type;
        int handle;
        unsigned start_field;        /* offset into .dbf for this field */
        FIELD_REC field_rec;

        file = _parc(1);
        field_no = _parni(2);
        new_type = *_parc(3);

        handle = open(file, O_RDWR | O_RAW);

        if (handle == -1)
```

```
        {
                _retl(FALSE);
                return;
        }

        start_field = sizeof(DBF_HEAD) + (sizeof(FIELD_REC)
                                * (field_no - 1));

        /* position file at start of required field ... */
        lseek(handle, (long) start_field, 0);

        /* read field */
        read(handle, (char *) &field_rec, sizeof(FIELD_REC));

        /* change type */
        field_rec.field_type = new_type;

        /* reposition file */
        lseek(handle, (long) start_field, 0);

        /* write it out ... */
        write(handle, (char *) &field_rec, sizeof(FIELD_REC));
        close(handle);
        _retl(TRUE);
}
```

newtype takes three parameters: the file's name, the field number, and the new type. Like newname, newtype reads the field, changes the type byte, and rewrites the field. It also reports its success or failure by returning a logical. The following call changes the type of field 2 in database "MEMOS" to numeric, displaying its success or failure:

```
? newtype("MEMOS.DBF", 2, "N")
```

DBT File Structure

This section describes the structure of a DBT file. We show why they grow so large and develop a routine to pack them directly from C.

As discussed previously, the first 512 bytes of a memo file are a header. The first 4 bytes are a long, specifying the number of 512 byte records in the file, including the header. The rest of the header is unused. A memo field can be of any size, up to 64K. It consists of sequential 512 byte records. This allocation strategy may waste up to 511 bytes. (An exception is the last record, as it occupies only as many bytes as it needs. It is followed by the 1A end of file marker.)

Each memo field ends with a 1A character - it is padded with filler to the next 512 byte boundary, with the one exception noted above.

The memo field entry in the DBF file contains a record number in the DBT file where its data resides. For example, given d as the DBF entry, to find the data in the DBT file, we must seek to:

$$d \times 512$$

Since the DBT record numbers are stored as ASCII digits in the DBF file, both the DBFLIST and the LIST routines in the previous sections display the record number (whereas dBASE shows the word "memo"). For example, study the following database structure and program.

Program 12-9. Example Memo File Builder

```
*** structure of database memos.dbf ***
Last update 87 11 23

Data offset 65
Record size 11
Number of records 0

NAME       TYPE LEN DEC

MEMOS       M    10


USE memos
FOR i = 1 TO 10

      APPEND BLANK

NEXT

GOTO TOP

FOR i = 1 TO 10

      FOR j = 1 TO 10 * i

            mmemos = memos
            REPLACE memos WITH mmemos + "This is memo record " + str(i) ;
                                                  + chr(141) + chr(10)
```

```
        NEXT

        SKIP
    NEXT
```

Program 12-9 opens an empty database and appends 10 blank records. It then creates the memo field for each record by appending a string to it a variable number of times. The program creates a DBT file of size 710785. Running the DBFLIST program on the database would then produce:

```
  1     2
  2    12
  3    43
  4   102
  5   194
  6   327
  7   506
  8   736
  9  1027
 10  1382
```

The DBFLIST shows the record numbers in the DBT file where the records' memos starts. A dump at the appropriate locations would show the memo field's text. The reader should try this for practice.

Chapter 7 shows how quickly a memo field can consume disk space. Unused space, or fragmentation, occurs as a result of editing memo fields. Clipper does not reuse abandoned or empty space. Copying the database file will pack the memo file, but this is time consuming for a large database, and is inelegant to program as it involves new names, file deletion, etc.

If we copy the DBF file shown above, the new DBT file occupies only 21121 bytes. A DBFLIST of the database produces the following output:

```
  1   2
  2   3
  3   5
  4   7
  5  10
  6  14
  7  18
  8  23
  9  29
 10  35
```

By comparing this list with its predecessor, you can see just how much of the DBT file was unused. The new DBT file has no "holes", so by comparing adjacent record numbers, we can determine the size of each memo field. For example, the memo field in database record 8 uses six records.

Now that we know the structure of both a database file and a memo, we can write a function to pack the memo file without copying the database. To do this, we must move all memo file records to the start of the DBT file, reduce the file size, and then update the record numbers to point to the new locations. Figures 12-2 and 12-3 illustrate the process.

Figure 12-2. Unpacked DBT File Diagram

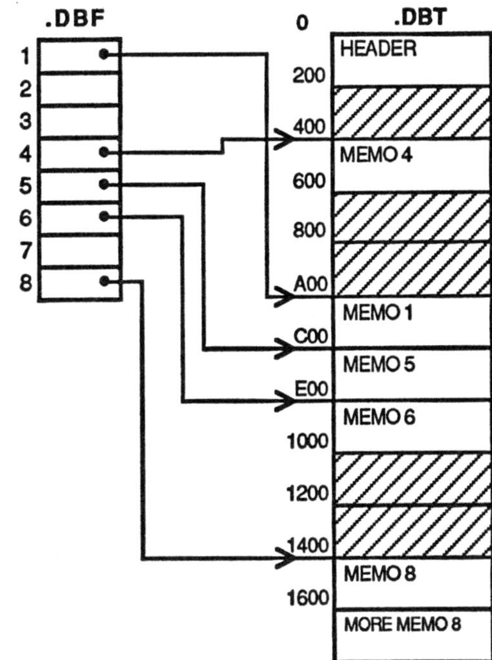

Figure 12-3. Packed DBT File Diagram

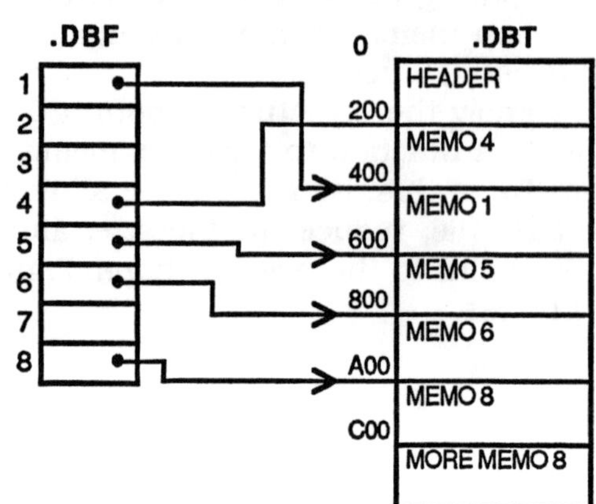

The biggest problem here is building an ordered list of the starting records. A trick can help.

We have noted that a memo field looks like a numeric of size 10. If we change its type to numeric (using the newtype function), we can index on its value. Skipping through this newly indexed database, we can save its record numbers and the dbt record numbers in two arrays, in order of ascending dbt record number. We can then pass the two arrays to a C function that moves the records in the DBT file (keeping track of where they go), then shrinks the file. The routine then goes back through the DBF file, updating the pointers to the memo fields. Program 12-10 shows the Clipper part of this process and a sample call to a function "mem_pak", which we will show shortly.

Program 12-10. Clipper Memo Pack

```
* MEMPAK.PRG
*
* 1 - Change type of memo field to numeric.
*
* 2 - Create index on the field.
*
* 3 - For each record, save DBT and DBF record numbers in parallel
*         arrays.
*
* 4 - Call mem_pack to do the pack.
```

```
*
* 5 - Change type back to memo.
*
* 6 - Delete index file.
*

FUNCTION memo_pack

PARAM file_name, field_num
PRIVATE field_name, num_recs, i

        * change memo field's type to numeric
        newtype(file_name + ".DBF", field_num, "N")

        * Now create the index ...
        USE &file_name

        field_name = fieldname(field_num)

        INDEX ON &field_name TO &field_name

        num_recs = reccount()

        * record numbers in dbf file
        PRIVATE dbfs[num_recs]

        * record numbers in dbt file
        PRIVATE dbts[num_recs]

        num_memos = 0
        GOTO TOP

        FOR i = 1 TO num_recs

                * Don't include unused memo fields ...
                IF memos != 0
                        num_memos = num_memos + 1
                        dbfs[num_memos] = recno()
                        dbts[num_memos] = &field_name
                ENDIF

                SKIP

        NEXT

        * Close the database ...
        USE

        * now do the pack ...
        mem_pak(file_name, field_num, num_memos, dbfs, dbts)

        * now change type back to memo
```

```
        newtype(file_name + ".DBF", field_num, "M")

        * Note extra . here, the macro processing consumes one of these ..
        DELETE FILE field_name..ntx

    RETURN (.T.)
```

The routine changes the memo field's type, does the indexing, builds the two arrays, and then calls the C function to pack the file. Upon return, the routine changes the type back to memo. When we change the type of the memo field to numeric, the empty field of 10 spaces appears as a 0, and is excluded from the list.

You call the Clipper function with:

```
* MPTEST.PRG
* call with base file name + field number that is memo.

? memo_pack("memos", 1)
```

Program 12-11 is the source for the C routine.

Program 12-11. Memo Pack

```
/***
* cmemopak.c
*
*       C code to do actual pack.
*
*       1 - Get parameters from Clipper and save them in local variables and arrays.
*
*       2 - Open memo and database files.
*
*       3 - For each memo record:
*
*               3.1 - Call move_memo to move it.
*
*                       3.1.1 - Seek to start of memo field record.
*
*                       3.1.2 - For each physical record occupied:
*
*                               3.1.2.1 - Copy it to new location.
*
*               3.2 - Save its new location.
*
*       4 - Shrink file by writing 0 bytes.
*
*       5 - Update DBT file header with new (smaller) number of records.
*
*       6 - Find offset of memo field into FIELD_REC
```

```
*
*       7 - For each memo field record:
*
*               7.1 - Update DBF record to point to new DBT record.
*/

#include "stdio.h"
#include "stdlib.h"
#include "fcntl.h"
#include "string.h"
#include "io.h"
#include "malloc.h"
#include "dos.h"

#include "dbf.n"
#include "nandef.h"
#include "extend.h"

#define MEMO_SIZE 512

unsigned move_memo(int, unsigned, unsigned);

CLIPPER mem_pak()

{
        unsigned *dbt_recs, *dbf_recs;
        unsigned i, num_memos, field_num, size_memo, next_memo;
        int dbt_handle, dbf_handle;
        char dbf_name[13], dbt_name[13];
        unsigned field_off;
        long num_mem_recs;
        unsigned n_written;

        DBF_HEAD dbf_head;
        FIELD_REC field_rec;

        /* get parameters from Clipper */
        strcpy(dbf_name, _parc(1));
        strcat(dbf_name, ".DBF");

        strcpy(dbt_name, _parc(1));
        strcat(dbt_name, ".DBT");

        field_num = _parni(2);
        num_memos = _parni(3);

        dbf_recs = (unsigned *) malloc(num_memos * sizeof(unsigned));
        dbt_recs = (unsigned *) malloc(num_memos * sizeof(unsigned));

        for (i = 1; i <= num_memos; i++)
        {
                dbf_recs[i - 1] = _parni(4, i);
```

```
        dbt_recs[i - 1] = _parni(5, i);
}

/* open memo file */
dbt_handle = open(dbt_name, O_RDWR | O_RAW);

if (dbt_handle == -1)
{
        _retl(FALSE);
        return;
}

/* open dbf file */
dbf_handle = open(dbf_name, O_RDWR | O_RAW);

if (dbf_handle == -1)
{
        _retl(FALSE);
        return;
}

/* move memo fields */
next_memo = 1;
for (i = 0; i < num_memos; i++)
{
        /* from, to */
        size_memo = move_memo(dbt_handle, dbt_recs[i], next_memo);

        /* where it is now (where it was moved to) ... */
        dbt_recs[i] = next_memo;

        /* where next one will go */
        next_memo = next_memo + size_memo;
}

/* shrink file */
_dos_write(dbt_handle, NULL, 0, &n_written);

lseek(dbt_handle, 0L, 0);

/* update header ... */
/* this is number of records in file (including header) */
num_mem_recs = next_memo;
write(dbt_handle, (char *) &num_mem_recs, 4);

close(dbt_handle);

dbf_handle = open(dbf_name, O_RDWR | O_RAW);

read(dbf_handle, (char *) &dbf_head, sizeof(dbf_head));

field_off = 1; /* skip delete flag */
```

```
        for (i = 0; i < field_num - 1; i++)
        {
                read(dbf_handle, (char *) &field_rec, sizeof(FIELD_REC));

                switch(field_rec.field_type)
                {
                        case 'N' :
                                field_off = field_off +
                                                        field_rec.len_info.num_size.len;
                                break;

                        default :
                                field_off = field_off + field_rec.len_info.char_len;
                                break;
                }
        }

        /* now update pointers to DBT in DBF */
        for (i = 0; i < num_memos; i++)
        {
                update_dbf(dbf_handle, dbf_recs[i], dbt_recs[i],
                                dbf_head.data_offset, field_off, dbf_head.rec_size);
        }

        close(dbt_handle);

        free((char *) dbf_recs);
        free((char *) dbt_recs);

        _retl(TRUE);
}

/***
* move_memo()
*
* Move entire memo field, handling those with more than one physical
* record, to new location further down in file.
*/

unsigned move_memo(handle, from, to)

int handle;
unsigned from, to;

{
        char *memo_rec;
        unsigned size_memo, num_memo_recs, i;
        Boolean eom;

        memo_rec = (char *) malloc(MEMO_SIZE);
        num_memo_recs = 1;
```

```
        lseek(handle, (long) from * (long) MEMO_SIZE, 0);

        eom = FALSE;
        size_memo = read(handle, memo_rec, MEMO_SIZE);

        while (!eom && size_memo == MEMO_SIZE)
        {
                i = 0;
                while (i < size_memo && memo_rec[i] != '\032')
                        i++;

                if (i == MEMO_SIZE)
                {
                        lseek(handle, (long) (to + num_memo_recs - 1) *
                                (long) MEMO_SIZE, 0);

                        write(handle, memo_rec, MEMO_SIZE);

                        num_memo_recs = num_memo_recs + 1;
                        lseek(handle, (long) (from + num_memo_recs - 1) *
                                (long) MEMO_SIZE, 0);

                        size_memo = read(handle, memo_rec, MEMO_SIZE);
                }
                else
                {
                        eom = TRUE;
                        size_memo = i + 1; /* to include 1A */
                }
        }

        lseek(handle, (long) (to + num_memo_recs - 1) *
                                        (long) MEMO_SIZE, 0);

        write(handle, memo_rec, size_memo);

        free(memo_rec);

        return(num_memo_recs);
}

/***
*       Set dbf field at record dbf_rec to point to new dbt_rec.
*
*/

update_dbf(handle, dbf_rec, dbt_rec, data_off, field_off, rec_size)

int handle;
unsigned dbf_rec, dbt_rec, data_off, field_off, rec_size;

{
```

```
        unsigned i, i1;
        char num_str[5];
        char num;

        lseek(handle, (long) (data_off + field_off +
                          (dbf_rec - 1L) * rec_size), 0);

        for (i = 0; i < 5; i++)
        {
                write(handle, " ", 1);
        }

        /* convert number to ASCII digit string */
        i = 10000;
        for (i1 = 0; i1 < 5; i1++)
        {
                num = dbt_rec / i;
                if (num > 0)
                {
                        dbt_rec = dbt_rec - num * i;
                        num_str[i1] = num + '0';
                }
                else
                        num_str[i1] = '0';

                i = i / 10;
        }

        write(handle, num_str, 5);
}
```

Program 12-11 retrieves the parameters from Clipper and saves them in local arrays. It then packs the memo file. It does this by starting with the lowest numbered record that has something in its memo field. This is shifted down to the start of the memo file. The next used memo record is then shifted down to the next unused space. This process repeats until all used memo fields have been moved. The move_memo routine does the move, given the source and destination record numbers. It handles memo fields that occupy more than one record, returning the number of records moved. The new location of the start of each memo field is then saved.

After all used records have been shifted down the file, it is shrunk through a direct call to MS-DOS. The call tells the operating system to write 0 bytes, which truncates the file to the current position.

The offset of the memo field in the record structure is then determined by reading all the FIELD_RECs and calculating the sum of their lengths, until one with field type "M" is found. Then the update_dbf routine updates the DBT record pointers in the DBF file to the new locations of their associated memo fields. Note that leading zero characters are added to the numeric string - both dBASE and Clipper allow this as an alternative to leading space characters.

When you apply Program 12-11 to the database shown above, it reduces the memo file to 20609 bytes. A DBFLIST of the file produces:

```
 1  00001
 2  00002
 3  00004
 4  00006
 5  00009
 6  00013
 7  00017
 8  00022
 9  00028
10  00034
```

The only difference between this list and the one produced from the "copied" database is that the first DBT record number used is 1, rather than 2. Clipper mistakenly fails to allocate this record, but will still function correctly if it is allocated (as dBASE does). This routine does not suffer from the problem, so the resulting DBT file is 512 bytes smaller.

Although Program 12-11 is elegant and does exactly what we want, it is quite slow. Introducing a simple buffering system improves its performance significantly. We now describe such a system, followed by its C implementation.

The routine allocates two buffer structures, one for reading and one for writing. Each contains the record number in the DBT file that is at the beginning of the buffer, a pointer to the buffer, its size, and the number of records it currently contains. The "init_buff" creates the structures.

When a DBT record is required, the "get_dbt_rec" routine is called. It handles read buffering. It first checks whether the required record is already in the read buffer. If it is, its address is simply returned with no disk read. If not, the routine positions the DBT file at the record, and fills the entire buffer with data. We refer to this as "reading ahead". As an example of how it improves performance, assume we need records in the following sequence: 1, 2, 4, 5, 6 and 7. The first call to get_dbt_rec with a 1 will read records 1 through 8 (as READ_RECS = 8). Subsequent calls with record numbers 2, 4, 5, 6 and 7 will not require disk accesses, since the records are already in the buffer.

The put_dbt_rec routine writes DBT records. It handles write buffering. The routine first determines whether there is room in the buffer for another record. If so, it puts it in the buffer at the next available spot; no disk access occurs. If there is no room, the routine writes the entire buffer to the file, adjusts its control structure (write_buff), and sets the pointer back to the now vacant first record.

The advantages of write buffering are obvious. Because of the way the pack algorithm operates, records are always written sequentially. Therefore, write buffering always saves disk writes. The sequential records are simply stored adjacently in the write buffer and are written with one command when either the buffer is full, or the program terminates. In the latter case, buff_end does the writing and also releases the allocated dynamic memory.

Figure 12-4 shows the read buffer after the first read when packing the memo file shown previously.

Figure 12-4. Memo Read Buffering

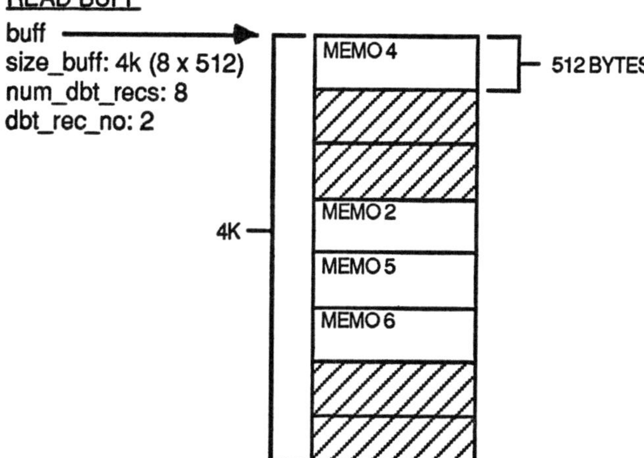

Figure 12-5 shows the state of the write buffer after 3 writes.

Figure 12-5. Memo Write Buffering

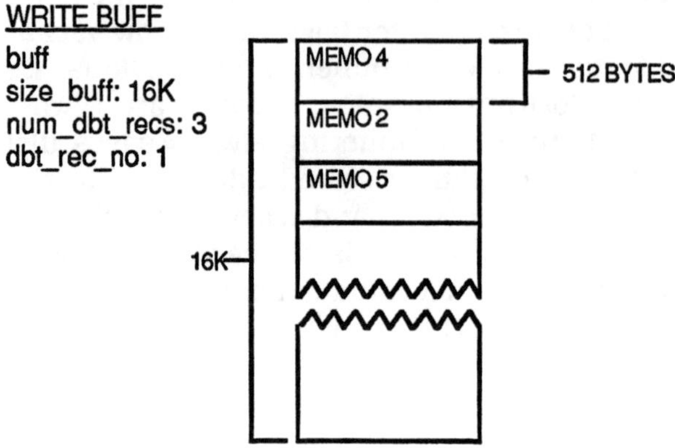

Because write buffering always improves performance, we give the write buffer more space than the read buffer.

Program 12-12 implements the buffering system.

Program 12-12. Memo Pack Buffering

```
/***
* buff.c
*
*       Buffering code for dbt files. Used with pack code.
*/

/* functions we are using */
#include "stdlib.h"
#include "string.h"
#include "fcntl.h"
#include "malloc.h"
#include "io.h"
#include "handef.h"
#include "dbf.h"

/* This is the buffer control structure */
typedef struct
{
        unsigned dbt_rec_no;
        char *buff;
        unsigned size_buff;
```

```
        unsigned num_dbt_recs;
} BUFFER;

/* here are two instances of it */
BUFFER read_buff;
BUFFER write_buff;

/* Required constants */
#define MEMO_SIZE 512
#define READ_RECS 8
#define WRITE_RECS 32
#define READ_BUFF_SIZE READ_RECS * MEMO_SIZE
#define WRITE_BUFF_SIZE WRITE_RECS * MEMO_SIZE

/***
* buff_init()
*
*       Initialize control structures, allocate buffers.
*/

Boolean buff_init()

{
        read_buff.size_buff = READ_BUFF_SIZE;
        read_buff.dbt_rec_no = 1;
        read_buff.num_dbt_recs = 0;

        read_buff.buff = (char *) malloc(READ_BUFF_SIZE);
        if (!read_buff.buff)
                return(FALSE);

        write_buff.size_buff = WRITE_BUFF_SIZE;
        write_buff.buff = (char *) malloc(WRITE_BUFF_SIZE);
        if (!write_buff.buff)
                return(FALSE);

        write_buff.dbt_rec_no = 1;
        write_buff.num_dbt_recs = 0;
}

/***
* buff_end()
*
*       Finished with buffers, release their memory, flush write buffer
*/

void buff_end(handle)

{
        lseek(handle, (long) write_buff.dbt_rec_no * MEMO_SIZE, 0);
        write(handle, write_buff.buff, write_buff.num_dbt_recs *
                MEMO_SIZE);
```

```
	free(write_buff.buff);
	free(read_buff.buff);
}

/***
* get_dbt_rec()
*
*	Return pointer to required dbt record. If record in buffer
* already, return it from there, saving disk reads. If not, read
* buffer full starting from this record (readahead).
*/

char *get_dbt_rec(handle, rec_no)

int handle;
unsigned rec_no;

{
	/* if requested record not in buffer, read it */
	if (rec_no < read_buff.dbt_rec_no ||
		rec_no > read_buff.dbt_rec_no + read_buff.num_dbt_recs - 1)
	{
		/* seek to start of record */
		lseek(handle, (long) rec_no * MEMO_SIZE, 0);

		/* read buffer full (readahead) */
		read_buff.num_dbt_recs =
			(read(handle, read_buff.buff, read_buff.size_buff) +
			MEMO_SIZE - 1) / MEMO_SIZE;
		read_buff.dbt_rec_no = rec_no;
	}

	/* return pointer to it */
	return((char *) &read_buff.buff[(rec_no - read_buff.dbt_rec_no) *
							MEMO_SIZE]);
}

/***
* put_dbt_rec()
*
*	Write specified record in buffer. If buffer is full, perform
* actual disk write to flush it first.
*/

void put_dbt_rec(handle, rec_no, rec)

int handle;
unsigned rec_no;
char *rec;
{
	/* flush buffer if full ... */
	if (write_buff.num_dbt_recs == write_buff.size_buff / MEMO_SIZE)
```

```
        {
                lseek(handle, (long) write_buff.dbt_rec_no * MEMO_SIZE, 0);
                write(handle, write_buff.buff, write_buff.size_buff);
                write_buff.dbt_rec_no = rec_no;
                write_buff.num_dbt_recs = 0;
        }

        /* place in buffer */
        memcpy(&write_buff.buff[(rec_no - write_buff.dbt_rec_no) * MEMO_SIZE],
                rec, MEMO_SIZE);

        /* increment count */
        write_buff.num_dbt_recs++;
}
```

Program 12-13 is the memo pack code of Program 12-11 with buffering.

Program 12-13. Memo Pack with Buffering

```
/***
* memopak1.c
*
*       Program 12-11 modified to use buffering routines. In move_memo,
* replace all reads with calls to get_dbt_rec, all writes with calls
* to put_dbt_rec. Include calls to buff_init and buff_end in mem_pak.
*/

#include "stdio.h"
#include "stdlib.h"
#include "fcntl.h"
#include "string.h"
#include "io.h"
#include "malloc.h"

#include "dbf.h"
#include "nandef.h"
#include "extend.h"

#define MEMO_SIZE 512

Boolean buff_init();

unsigned move_memo(int, unsigned, unsigned);

extern char *get_dbt_rec(int, unsigned);

CLIPPER mem_pak()
```

```
{
        unsigned *dbt_recs, *dbf_recs;
        unsigned i, num_memos, field_num, size_memo, next_memo;
        int dbt_handle, dbf_handle;
        char dbf_name[13], dbt_name[13];
        unsigned field_off;
        long num_mem_recs;
        unsigned n_written;

        DBF_HEAD dbf_head;
        FIELD_REC field_rec;

        /* get parameters from Clipper */
        strcpy(dbf_name, _parc(1));
        strcat(dbf_name, ".DBF");

        strcpy(dbt_name, _parc(1));
        strcat(dbt_name, ".DBT");

        field_num = _parni(2);
        num_memos = _parni(3);

        dbf_recs = (unsigned *) malloc(num_memos * sizeof(unsigned));
        dbt_recs = (unsigned *) malloc(num_memos * sizeof(unsigned));

        for (i = 1; i <= num_memos; i++)
        {
                dbf_recs[i - 1] = _parni(4, i);
                dbt_recs[i - 1] = _parni(5, i);
        }

        /* open memo file */
        dbt_handle = open(dbt_name, O_RDWR | O_RAW);

        if (dbt_handle == -1)
        {
                _retl(FALSE);
                return;
        }


        if (!buff_init())
        {
                _retl(FALSE);
                return;
        }

        /* open dbf file */
        dbf_handle = open(dbf_name, O_RDWR | O_RAW);

        if (dbf_handle == -1)
        {
```

```
        _retl(FALSE);
        return;
}

/* move memo fields */
next_memo = 1;
for (i = 0; i < num_memos; i++)
{
        /* from, to */
        size_memo = move_memo(dbt_handle, dbt_recs[i], next_memo);

        /* where it is now (where it was moved to) ... */
        dbt_recs[i] = next_memo;

        /* where next one will go */
        next_memo = next_memo + size_memo;
}

buff_end(dbt_handle);

/* shrink file */
_dos_write(dbt_handle, NULL, 0, &n_written);
lseek(dbt_handle, 0L, 0);

/* update header ... */
/* this is number of records in file (including header) */
num_mem_recs = next_memo;
write(dbt_handle, (char *) &num_mem_recs, 4);

close(dbt_handle);

dbf_handle = open(dbf_name, O_RDWR | O_RAW);

read(dbf_handle, (char *) &dbf_head, sizeof(dbf_head));

field_off = 1; /* skip delete flag */
for (i = 0; i < field_num - 1; i++)
{
        read(dbf_handle, (char *) &field_rec, sizeof(FIELD_REC));

        switch(field_rec.field_type)
        {
                case 'N' :
                        field_off = field_off +
                                        field_rec.len_info.num_size.len;
                        break;

                default :
                        field_off = field_off + field_rec.len_info.char_len;
                        break;
        }
}
```

```
        /* now update pointers to DBT in DBF */
        for (i = 0; i < num_memos; i++)
        {
                update_dbf(dbf_handle, dbf_recs[i], dbt_recs[i],
                                dbf_head.data_offset, field_off, dbf_head.rec_size);
        }

        close(dbf_handle);

        free((char *) dbf_recs);
        free((char *) dbt_recs);

        _retl(TRUE);
}

unsigned move_memo(handle, from, to)

int handle;
unsigned from, to;

{
        char *memo_rec;
        unsigned num_memo_recs, i;
        Boolean eom;

        memo_rec = get_dbt_rec(handle, from);
        num_memo_recs = 1;

        eom = FALSE;

        while (!eom)
        {
                i = 0;

                /* last record in memo field? */
                while (i < MEMO_SIZE && memo_rec[i] != '\032')
                        i++;

                if (i == MEMO_SIZE)
                {                               /* full record ... */
                        put_dbt_rec(handle, to + num_memo_recs - 1, memo_rec);

                        num_memo_recs = num_memo_recs + 1;

                        memo_rec = get_dbt_rec(handle, from + num_memo_recs - 1);
                }
                else
                {
                        eom = TRUE;
                }
        }

        put_dbt_rec(handle, to + num_memo_recs - 1, memo_rec);
```

```
        return(num_memo_recs);
}

/***
*       Set dbf field at record dbf_rec to point to new dbt_rec.
*
*/

update_dbf(handle, dbf_rec, dbt_rec, data_off, field_off, rec_size)

int handle;
unsigned dbf_rec, dbt_rec, data_off, field_off, rec_size;

{
        unsigned i, i1;
        char num_str[5];
        char num;

        lseek(handle, (long) (data_off + field_off + (dbf_rec - 1L) * rec_size), 0);

        for (i = 0; i < 5; i++)
        {
                write(handle, " ", 1);
        }

        /* convert number to ASCII digit string */
        i = 10000;
        for (i1 = 0; i1 < 5; i1++)
        {
                num = dbt_rec / i;
                if (num > 0)
                {
                        dbt_rec = dbt_rec - num * i;
                        num_str[i1] = num + '0';
                }
                else
                        num_str[i1] = '0';

                i = i / 10;
        }

        write(handle, num_str, 5);
}
```

Program 12-13 first calls buff_init to initialize the buffer structures. The move_memo routine now performs all its reads by calling the get_dbt_rec buffering routine. It does all its writes with calls to the put_dbt_rec routine. After moving the memos, the routine calls "buff_end" to terminate the buffering system.

Neither memo pack routine developed here will work for a database with more than one memo field per record. The problem is that records from both database files are stored in the same DBT file (the DBFLIST will show these). The pack code does not allow for this.

> **TIP**
>
> Use the pack routine with the buffering to pack your memo fields.

FRM File Structure

The following C structure defines a FRM file:

```
#define EXP_COUNT 55
#define MAX_EXPR 1440
#define MAX_FIELDS 25
typedef struct
{
        short sign1;
        short exp_end;
        short exp_length[EXP_COUNT];
        short exp_index[EXP_COUNT];
        char exp_area[MAX_EXPR];
        FRM_FIELD fields[MAX_FIELDS];
        short title_exp_num;
        short grp_on_exp_num;
        short sub_on_exp_num;
        short grp_head_exp_num;
        short sub_head_exp_num;
        short page_width;
        short line_per_page;
        short left_marg;
        short right_marg;
        short num_of_cols;
        char dbl_space;
        char summary;
        char eject;
        char plus_bytes;
        short sign2;
} FRM_STRUC;

typedef struct
{
        short width;
        short pad1;
        char pad2;
        char total;
        short dec;
        short exp_contents;
```

```
        short exp_header;
    } FRM_FIELD;
```

The fields are:

sign1 - a two byte integer, value 02, indicating a FRM file.

exp_end - the next free character in the exp_area, defined below.

exp_length[EXP_COUNT] - an array of expression lengths. The array index gives the expression number.

exp_index[EXP_COUNT] - an array of indexes into the exp_area where each expression starts. Once again, the array index gives the expression number.

exp_area[MAX_EXPR] - the area where the expressions reside, indexed by the above two arrays.

fields[MAX_FIELDS] - an array, size 25, of FRM_FIELDs. There is one entry for each field specified in the report. The first (indexed by 0) is not used.

title_exp_num - the expression number of the title string. Note that this is a string, not an expression.

grp_on_exp_num - the expression number of the GROUP ON expression.

sub_on_exp_num - the expression number of the SUB GROUP ON expression.

grp_head_exp_num - the expression number of the GROUP ON heading string. This is not an expression.

sub_head_exp_num - the expression number of the SUB GROUP ON heading string. This is not an expression.

page_width - page width (surprisingly enough!)

line_per_page - the number of lines per page.

left_marg - the size of the left margin.

right_marg - the size of the right margin.

num_of_cols - the number of columns (or fields) used in the report.

dbl_space - value "Y" or "N", signifying whether double spacing is required.

summary - value "Y" or "N", signifying whether a summary report is required

eject - value "Y" or "N", signifying whether to eject after each group.

plus_bytes - plain indicator in releases before dBASE III PLUS. It now contains three meaningful bits:

- PAGE EJECT AFTER PRINT, bit 1 is on (value 2).
- PAGE EJECT BEFORE PRINT, bit 0 is on (value 1).
- PLAIN report, bit 3 (value 4) is on.

There is a FRM_FIELD for each field specified in the report. The FRM_FIELDs are maintained in the fields array, described above. Each entry has the following format:

width - width in which the field is to be printed.

pad1 - two bytes of filler.

pad2 - one byte of filler

total - whether the (numeric) field is to be totalled.

dec - the number of decimal places for a numeric field.

exp_contents - expression number for this field's contents.

exp_header - expression number for this field's string. Note that it is a string - not an expression.

Strings and expressions are stored in the exp_area array. Each has an expression number. It is used as an index into the exp_index and exp_length arrays. They define the offset into the exp_area array where it starts, and its length, respectively.

Note the difference between strings and expressions. Expressions are evaluated at run time and may contain variables, etc., whereas strings are simply text.

The offsets into these structures for each field are as follows:

```
FRM_STRUC :

     00   short sign1;
     02   short exp_end;
     04   short exp_length[EXP_COUNT];
     72   short exp_index[EXP_COUNT];
     E0   char exp_area[MAX_EXPR];
    680   FRM_FIELD fields[MAX_FIELDS];
    7AC   short title_exp_num;
    7AE   short grp_on_exp_num;
    7B0   short sub_on_exp_num;
    7B2   short grp_head_exp_num;
```

```
7B4  short sub_head_exp_num;
7B6  short page_width;
7B8  short line_per_page;
7BA  short left_marg;
7BC  short right_marg;
7BE  short num_of_cols;
800  char dbl_space;
801  char summary;
802  char eject;
803  char plus_bytes;
804  short sign2;
```

FRM_FIELD:

```
00   short width;
02   short pad1;
04   char pad2;
05   char total;
07   short dec;
09   short exp_contents;
0B   short exp_header;
```

Here is a dump of a sample report:

Dump of REPTEST.FRM

```
0:   02 00 98 00 2E 00 11 00 06 00 10 00 06 00 06 00   ........ ........
10:  11 00 06 00 0C 00 05 00 0F 00 00 00 00 00 00 00   ........ ........
20:  00 00 00 00 00 00 00 00 00 00 00 00 00 00 00 00   ........ ........
30:  00 00 00 00 00 00 00 00 00 00 00 00 00 00 00 00   ........ ........
40:  00 00 00 00 00 00 00 00 00 00 00 00 00 00 00 00   ........ ........
50:  00 00 00 00 00 00 00 00 00 00 00 00 00 00 00 00   ........ ........
60:  00 00 00 00 00 00 00 00 00 00 00 00 00 00 00 00   ........ ........
70:  00 00 00 00 2E 00 3F 00 45 00 55 00 5B 00 61 00   ......?. E.U.[.a.
80:  72 00 78 00 84 00 89 00 00 00 00 00 00 00 00 00   r.x..... ........
90:  00 00 00 00 00 00 00 00 00 00 00 00 00 00 00 00   ........ ........
A0:  00 00 00 00 00 00 00 00 00 00 00 00 00 00 00 00   ........ ........
B0:  00 00 00 00 00 00 00 00 00 00 00 00 00 00 00 00   ........ ........
C0:  00 00 00 00 00 00 00 00 00 00 00 00 00 00 00 00   ........ ........
D0:  00 00 00 00 00 00 00 00 00 00 00 00 01 00 00 00   ........ ........
E0:  54 68 69 73 20 69 73 20 74 68 65 20 70 61 67 65   This is the page
F0:  20 74 69 74 6C 65 20 66 6F 72 20 74 68 65 20 72    title f or the r
100: 65 70 74 65 73 74 20 72 65 70 6F 72 74 00 63 68   eptest r eport.ch
110: 61 72 61 63 74 65 72 20 67 72 6F 75 70 73 00 63   aracter groups.c
120: 68 61 72 73 00 64 61 74 65 20 73 75 62 2D 67 72   hars.dat e sub-gr
130: 6F 75 70 73 00 64 61 74 65 73 00 63 68 61 72 73   oups.dat es.chars
140: 00 63 68 61 72 61 63 74 65 72 20 66 69 65 6C 64   .charact er field
150: 73 00 64 61 74 65 73 00 64 61 74 65 20 66 69 65   s.dates. date fie
160: 6C 64 73 00 6E 75 6D 73 00 6E 75 6D 65 72 69 63   lds.nums .numeric
170: 20 66 69 65 6C 64 73 00 00 00 00 00 00 00 00 00    fields. ........
```

```
680: 20 20 20 20 20 20 20 20 20 20 20 20 10 00 01 00  ....
690: 00 4E 00 00 05 00 06 00 0B 00 01 00 72 4E 00 00  .N...... ....rN..
6A0: 07 00 08 00 0E 00 01 00 20 59 02 00 09 00 0A 00  ........ Y......
6B0: 20 20 20 20 20 20 20 20 20 20 20 20 20 20 20 20
6C0: 20 20 20 20 20 20 20 20 20 20 20 20 20 20 20 20
6D0: 20 20 20 20 20 20 20 20 20 20 20 20 20 20 20 20
6E0: 20 20 20 20 20 20 20 20 20 20 20 20 20 20 20 20
6F0: 20 20 20 20 20 20 20 20 20 20 20 20 20 20 20 20
700: 20 20 20 20 20 20 20 20 20 20 20 20 20 20 20 20
710: 20 20 20 20 20 20 20 20 20 20 20 20 20 20 20 20
720: 20 20 20 20 20 20 20 20 20 20 20 20 20 20 20 20
730: 20 20 20 20 20 20 20 20 20 20 20 20 20 20 20 20
740: 20 20 20 20 20 20 20 20 20 20 20 20 20 20 20 20
750: 20 20 20 20 20 20 20 20 20 20 20 20 20 20 20 20
760: 20 20 20 20 20 20 20 20 20 20 20 20 20 20 20 20
770: 20 20 20 20 20 20 20 20 20 20 20 20 20 20 20 20
780: 20 20 20 20 20 20 20 20 20 20 20 20 20 20 20 20
790: 00 20 58 58 58 58 58 58 58 58 58 58 58 58 58 58  . XXXXXX XXXXXXXX
7A0: 58 58 58 58 58 58 58 58 58 58 58 58 00 00 02 00  XXXXXXXX XXXX....
7B0: 04 00 01 00 03 00 50 00 3A 00 08 00 00 00 03 00  ......P. :.......
7C0: 4E 4E 4E 00 02 00                                NNN...
```

By applying the field offsets to the dump, we can make out the report's structure as:

sign1 : 2
exp_end : 152
title expression : This is the page title for the reptest report
group on expression : chars
subgroup on expression : dates
group heading expression : character groups
subgroup heading : date subgroups
page width : 80
lines per page : 58
left margin : 8
right margin : 0
number of columns : 3
double space : N
summary : N
eject : N
page eject after print : N
page eject before print : Y
plain page : N
sign2 : 2

*** Field 1 ***
width : 16
total : N
dec : 0
exp_contents : chars
exp_header : character fields

```
*** Field 2 ***
width : 11
total : N
dec  : 0
exp_contents : dates
exp_header : date fields

*** Field 3 ***
width : 14
total : Y
dec  : 2
exp_contents : nums
exp_header : numeric fields
```

Program 12-14 reads a FRM file and displays its contents.

Program 12-14. Display a FRM File

```
/***
 * frmdump.c
 *
 *      Read FRM file and display its structure.
 *
 *      1 - Verify usage (one parameter).
 *
 *      2 - Open the file.
 *
 *      3 - Read file into structure.
 *
 *      4 - Display fields.
 */

#include "stdio.h"
#include "fcntl.h"
#include "stdlib.h"
#include "io.h"

#include "frmdump.h"

/* Global so doesn't occupy stack space */
FRM_STRUC frm_struc;

main(argc, argv)

int argc;
char *argv[];

{
        int i;
        int frm_handle;
```

```
if (argc != 2)
	{
		printf("Usage: frmdump file.frm\n\n");
		exit(1);
	}

	frm_handle = open(argv[1], O_RAW | O_RDONLY);

	if (frm_handle == -1)
	{
		printf("Error opening file %s\n", argv[1]);
		exit(1);
	}

	if (read(frm_handle, (char *) &frm_struc, sizeof(FRM_STRUC))
			!= sizeof(FRM_STRUC))
	{
		printf("Error reading %s\n", argv[1]);
		exit(1);
	}

	printf("\n\nsign1 %d\n", frm_struc.sign1);
	printf("exp_end %d\n", frm_struc.exp_end);

	if (frm_struc.title_exp_num != -1)
	{
		printf("title expression %s\n", &(frm_struc.exp_area
			[frm_struc.exp_index[frm_struc.title_exp_num]]));
	}

	if (frm_struc.grp_on_exp_num != -1)
	{
		printf("group on expression %s\n", &(frm_struc.exp_area
			[frm_struc.exp_index[frm_struc.grp_on_exp_num]]));
	}

	if (frm_struc.sub_on_exp_num != -1)
	{
		printf("subgroup on expression %s\n", &(frm_struc.exp_area
				[frm_struc.exp_index[frm_struc.sub_on_exp_num]]));
	}

	if (frm_struc.grp_head_exp_num != -1)
	{
		printf("group heading expression %s\n", &(frm_struc.exp_area
				[frm_struc.exp_index[frm_struc.grp_head_exp_num]]));
	}

	if (frm_struc.sub_head_exp_num != -1)
	{
		printf("subgroup heading %s\n", &(frm_struc.exp_area
			[frm_struc.exp_index[frm_struc.sub_head_exp_num]]));
```

```
    }

    printf("page width %d\n", frm_struc.page_width);
    printf("lines per page %d\n", frm_struc.line_per_page);

    printf("left margin %d\n", frm_struc.left_marg);
    printf("right margin %d\n", frm_struc.right_marg);
    printf("number of columns %d\n", frm_struc.num_of_cols);
    printf("double space %c\n", frm_struc.dbl_space);
    printf("summary %c\n", frm_struc.summary);
    printf("eject %c\n", frm_struc.eject);
    printf("page eject after print %c\n", (frm_struc.plus_bytes & 2) ?
            'Y' : 'N');

    printf("page eject before print %c\n", (frm_struc.plus_bytes & 1) ?
            'N' : 'Y');
    printf("plain page %c\n", (frm_struc.plus_bytes & 4) ? 'Y' : 'N');

    printf("sign2 %d\n", frm_struc.sign2);

    for (i = 1; i <= frm_struc.num_of_cols; i++)
    {
            printf("\n\n*** Field number %d ***\n", i);
            printf("width %d\n", frm_struc.fields[i].width);
            printf("total %c\n", frm_struc.fields[i].total);
            printf("dec  %d\n", frm_struc.fields[i].dec);
            printf("exp_contents %s\n", &(frm_struc.exp_area
                    [frm_struc.exp_index[frm_struc.fields[i].exp_contents]]));

            printf("exp_header %s\n", &(frm_struc.exp_area
                    [frm_struc.exp_index[frm_struc.fields[i].exp_header]]));
    }
}
```

The long expressions used in Program 12-14 require an explanation. The address of the start of expression "i" is:

```
&(frm_struc.exp_area[frm_struc.exp_index[i]])
```

This is used as an index in the exp_index array, contained in frm_struc. The array gives the offset inside frm_struc.exp_area where the string starts. If instead of i, the expression number is defined by a member of the structure, then the variable is substituted for it. For a field, this is defined by an array within the structure. The value is used instead of i. For example, study the following expression, which Program 12-11 uses to find the start of field i:

```
&(frm_struc.exp_area[frm_struc.exp_index
        [frm_struc.fields[i].exp_contents]]));
```

The inner expression "frm_struc.fields[i].exp_contents" gives the expression number for this field's contents. It is used instead of i. Its offset inside "exp_area" is then given by:

```
frm_struc.exp_index[frm_struc.fields[i].exp_contents]
```

To get the actual address, use the expression as the index into the "exp_area" array in the "frm_struc" structure.

> **TIP**
>
> Use FRMDUMP as an alternative to RL to view the contents of a FRM file.

LBL File Structure

The following C structure and constants define a LBL file:

```
#define INFO_COUNT 16
#define INFO_SIZE 60

/* .LBL file structure */
typedef struct
{
        char sign1;
        char remarks[60];
        short height;
        short width;
        short left_marg;
        short label_line;
        short label_space;
        short label_across;
        char info[INFO_COUNT][INFO_SIZE];
        char sign2;
} LABEL_STRUC;
```

sign1 - has the value 02, indicating a LBL file.

remarks - contains the message specifying a predefined size for the label.

height - contains the number of lines in the label.

width - contains the width of each label.

left_marg - contains the number of spaces in the left margin.

label_line - contains the number of lines between rows of labels.

label_space - contains the number of spaces between labels on the same line.

label_across - contains the number of labels per line.

info - can be considered as a two dimensional array, with dimensions 16 by 60, which contains 16 rows of 60-column text. It contains the expressions for each row of the label. Only "height" rows are used.

sign2 - has the value 02, indicating a LBL file.

The offsets of the fields in the structure are:

```
 00  char sign1;
 01  char remarks[60];
 3D  short height;
 3F  short width;
 41  short left_marg;
 43  short label_line;
 45  short label_space;
 47  short label_across;
 49  char info[INFO_COUNT][INFO_SIZE];
409  char sign2;
```

We must compile with the /Zl option to enforce byte alignment for structure members. Otherwise, the compiler would "pad" the structure to force even byte boundaries for certain fields. Since the code reads a file structure with a predefined format, this would cause errors.

Here is a dump of a sample LBL file:

Dump of LABTEST.LBL

```
0:    02 20 20 20 20 20 20 20 20 20 20 20 20 20 20 20  .
10:   20 20 20 20 20 20 20 20 20 20 20 20 20 20 20 20
20:   20 20 20 20 20 20 20 20 20 20 20 20 20 20 20 20
30:   20 20 20 20 20 20 20 20 20 20 20 20 20 05 00 23  ..#
40:   00 00 00 01 00 00 00 03 00 63 68 61 72 73 20 20  ........ .chars
50:   20 20 20 20 20 20 20 20 20 20 20 20 20 20 20 20
60:   20 20 20 20 20 20 20 20 20 20 20 20 20 20 20 20
70:   20 20 20 20 20 20 20 20 20 20 20 20 20 20 20 20
80:   20 20 20 20 20 64 61 74 65 73 20 20 20 20 20 20  dat es
90:   20 20 20 20 20 20 20 20 20 20 20 20 20 20 20 20
A0:   20 20 20 20 20 20 20 20 20 20 20 20 20 20 20 20
B0:   20 20 20 20 20 20 20 20 20 20 20 20 20 20 20 20
C0:   20 6E 75 6D 73 20 20 20 20 20 20 20 20 20 20 20  nums.
•
•
400:  20 20 20 20 20 20 20 20 20 02                    .
```

Applying the offsets to the dump gives the following label contents:

```
sign1 2
remarks < spaces >
height  5
width 35
left_marg 0
label_line  1
label_space 0
label_across 3
line 0   chars
line 1   dates
line 2   nums
line 3   <spaces>
line 4   <spaces>
sign2    2
```

We can readily develop a routine (Program 12-15) to read a LBL file and dump it.

Program 12-15. Display a LBL File

```
/***
* lbldump.c
*
*       Dump a LBL file.
*
*        1 - Verify usage (one parameter).
*
*        2 - Open the file.
*
*        3 - Read it into a structure.
*
*        4 - Display each field.
*/

#include "stdio.h"
#include "stdlib.h"
#include "fcntl.h"
#include "io.h"

#include "lbldump.h"

LABEL_STRUC lbl_struc;

int lbl_handle;

main(argc, argv)
```

```
int argc;
char *argv[];

{
        int i;

        if (argc != 2)
        {
                printf("Usage: lbldump file.lbl\n\n");
                exit(1);
        }

        lbl_handle = open(argv[1], O_RAW | O_RDONLY);

        if (read(lbl_handle, (char *) &lbl_struc, sizeof(LABEL_STRUC))
                        != sizeof(LABEL_STRUC))
        {
                printf("Error reading %s\n", argv[1]);
                exit(1);
        }

        printf("\n\nsign1 %d\n", lbl_struc.sign1);
        printf("remarks %.60s\n", lbl_struc.remarks);
        printf("height %d\n", lbl_struc.height);
        printf("width %d\n", lbl_struc.width);
        printf("left_marg %d\n", lbl_struc.left_marg);
        printf("label_line %d\n", lbl_struc.label_line);
        printf("label_space %d\n", lbl_struc.label_space);
        printf("label_across %d\n", lbl_struc.label_across);

        for (i = 0; i< lbl_struc.height; i++)
        {
                printf("line %d %.60s\n", i, (char *) &(lbl_struc.info[i][0]));
        }

        printf("sign2 %d \n", lbl_struc.sign2);
}
```

TIP

Use LBLDUMP as an alternative to RL to view the contents of a LBL file.

MEM File Structure

A save to command creates a MEM file. For each memory variable saved, the file contains a 32 byte header followed by the actual contents. The header has the following structure:

```
typedef struct
{
        char mname[11];             /* 10 + null */
        char mtype;
        char mfiller1[4];
        char mlen;
        char mdec;
        char mfiller2[14];
} MEM_REC;
```

mname is the variable's name.

mtype is the variable's type ("C", "D", "L" or "N") with the most significant bit set. For example, a character type is represented by "C" | 128 (i.e., ASCII C logically ORed with 128 decimal).

mfiller1 is 4 bytes of unused space.

mlen is the variable's length.

mdec is the number of decimal places for numeric variables, or the more significant byte of a word for character variables.

mfiller2 is 14 bytes of unused space.

Program 12-16 dumps a MEM file.

Program 12-16. Display a MEM File

```
/***
* memdump.c
*
*       Dump a MEM file.
*
*       1 - Verify usage (one parameter).
*
*       2 - Open file.
*
*       3 - While more MEM_RECs.
*
*               3.1 Read MEM_REC.
*
*               3.2 Display its fields.
*/

#include "stdio.h"
#include "fcntl.h"
#include "stdlib.h"
#include "io.h"
#include "malloc.h"
#include "memdump.h"

MEM_REC mem_rec;
```

```
main(argc, argv)

int argc;
char *argv[];

{
        int mem_handle;
        char *cstr;
        unsigned csize;
        double num;
        char log;

        if (argc != 2)
        {
                printf("Usage: memdump file.mem\n\n");
                exit(1);
        }

        mem_handle = open(argv[1], O_RAW | O_RDONLY);

        if (mem_handle == -1)
        {
                printf("Error opening file %s\n", argv[1]);
                exit(1);
        }

        while (read(mem_handle, (char *) &mem_rec, sizeof(MEM_REC))
            == sizeof(MEM_REC))
        {
                printf("\n\nname       : %s\n", mem_rec.mname);
                printf("type     : %c\n", mem_rec.mtype & 127);
                printf("len      : %d\n", mem_rec.mlen);
                printf("dec      : %d\n", mem_rec.mdec);

                switch(mem_rec.mtype & 127)
                {
                        case 'C' :
                                csize = mem_rec.mlen + mem_rec.mdec * 256;
                                cstr = malloc(csize);
                                read(mem_handle, cstr, csize);
                                printf("contents : %s\n", cstr);
                                free(cstr);
                                break;

                        case 'N' :
                                read(mem_handle, (char *)&num, 8);
                                printf("contents : %e\n", num);
                                break;

                        case 'D' :
                                read(mem_handle, (char *)&num, 8);
                                printf("contents : %e\n", num);
                                break;
```

```
                    case 'L' :
                        read(mem_handle, &log, 1);
                        printf("contents : %s\n", (log == 0) ? ".F." : ".T.");
                }
            }
    }
```

Program 12-16 reads a 32 byte header, then displays the memory variable that immediately follows it. The way in which the memory variable is retrieved and displayed depends on its representation, which in turn depends on its type. A character variable is simply represented as a sequence of characters with a length defined by the header. A numeric variable is an 8 byte C double. A date variable is also a C double. A logical variable is one byte, with 0 indicating false and 1 true.

> **TIP**
>
> Use MEMDUMP to view a MEM file. This is most useful when debugging a program where you may need to know the values saved to and restored from MEM files.

NTX File Structure

Theory

Clipper indexes use a modified B-tree system. (For a detailed description of B-Trees, see Wirth, N. *Algorithms + Data Structures = Programs*, Englewood Cliffs, NJ, Prentice-Hall, 1976.) Since their structure is not compatible with dBASE's, Clipper index files have an extension of NTX (although the Summer '87 release supports NDX files). An NTX file consists of 1024 byte (1K) pages. The first page is a header, the others contain the keys and pointers needed to implement the B-tree.

For those unfamiliar with B-trees, a little theory is in order. Let us start with a diagram.

Figure 12-6. NTX File Example

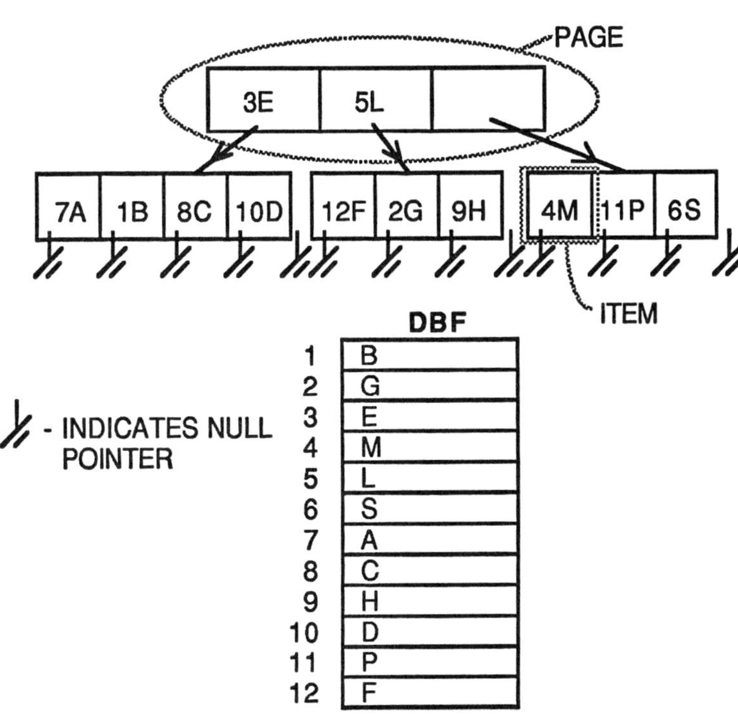

Figure 12-6 shows four "pages", each containing "ITEMs" consisting of a pointer, a record number, and the actual key. The record number is the origin of the key; it is represented by a long. The pointer is a long offset into the NTX file, indicating where a page at a lower level starts. Look at the page at the top of the diagram. Now look at the ITEM containing the key "E". The pointer to the left directs you to another PAGE consisting of keys preceding "E" alpabetically. The pointer to the right of "E" (also to the left of "L"), directs you to a page of keys after "E", but before "L". A pointer terminated by three horizontal lines is a NULL; the page is at the lowest level of the tree.

The diagram shows a tree with only two levels. In general, a tree consists of as many levels as needed to hold the keys in the index. There is always one more pointer than there are keys in every page. The extra pointer refers to a page containing keys greater than the one to the left of the pointer.

The keys in higher pages thus separate the pages indicated by the pointers at either side. Everything to the left of a key is less than it, and everything to its right is greater, according to the index expression. This allows a fast search.

The page at the top of the diagram is the "root" page, where the B-tree starts. This is the page to which the NTX file header points.

Header

The following C structure defines the header page:

```
#define MAX_KEY 256

typedef struct
{
        unsigned sign;
        unsigned version;
        long root;
        long next_page;
        unsigned item_size;
        unsigned key_size;
        unsigned key_dec;
        unsigned max_item;
        unsigned half_page;
        char key_expr[MAX_KEY];
        Boolean unique;
} NTX_HEADER;
```

The fields are:

sign - a two byte field with the value 03, indicating a dBASE/Clipper file.

version - a field Clipper uses to identify the version of the indexing system.

root - the offset in the file of the first index page.

next_page - the offset in the NTX file of the starting page of a list of unused index pages. The first 4 bytes of an unused page point to the next unused page. A zero value terminates the list. A value of 0 in this field indicates no more free pages in the index file. dBASE does not maintain such a free list, and thus abandoned pages are never reused.

item_size - is the size of the index key, plus the size of two longs. It is the distance between key records, and also the size of the "ITEM" type described subsequently.

key_size - is the size of the key on which the index is built. For example, the size is 10 if the index is built on a character field of size 10.

key_dec - the number of decimal places in the key, if it is numeric.

max_item - the maximum number of keys (with their pointers) that can fit in an index page.

half_page - the maximum number of keys that can fit in an index page, divided by two. This is an important value in a B-tree system as it is the minimum number of keys that must be in a page.

key_expr - the actual expression on which the index was built. It is a null terminated string with a maximum length of 256.

unique - a boolean containing the state of the unique flag when the index was created. A value of 1 indicates ON, a value of 0 OFF.

The rest of the 1024 bytes is filler.

The offsets of the fields into the NTX file are:

```
 00    unsigned sign;
 02    unsigned version;
 04    long root;
 08    long next_page;
 0C    unsigned item_size;
 0E    unsigned key_size;
 10    unsigned key_dec;
 12    unsigned max_item;
 14    unsigned half_page;
 16    char key_expr[MAX_KEY];
272    Boolean unique;
```

Program 12-17 reads an NTX file and dumps its header, assuming the definition of "NTX_HEADER" in "ntxdump.h".

Program 12-17. Display an NTX File Header

```
/***
* ntxhead.c
*
*     Dump ntx header. First stage in index processing code.
*
*     1 - Verify usage (one parameter).
*
*     2 - Open the file.
*
*     3 - Read into structure.
*
*     4 - Print fields.
```

```
*/

#include "stdio.h"
#include "stdlib.h"
#include "fcntl.h"
# include "nandef.h"
#include "ntxdump.h"

NTX_HEADER ntx_header;
int ntx_handle;

main(argc, argv)

int argc;
char *argv[];

{
        if (argc != 2)
        {
                printf("Usage: ntxhead file.ntx\n\n");
                exit(1);
        }


        /* file open mode incorrect */
        /* open the NTX file */
        ntx_handle = open(argv[1], 0x8000);

        if (ntx_handle == -1)
        {
                printf("Error opening %s\n", argv[1]);
                exit(1);
        }

        /* read the header */
        if (read(ntx_handle, &ntx_header, sizeof(NTX_HEADER))
                                        != sizeof(NTX_HEADER))
        {
                printf("Error reading header from %s\n", argv[1]);
                exit(1);
        }

        /* print the header information */
        printf("****** NTX HEADER *****\n");
        printf("Sign %x\n", ntx_header.sign);
        printf("Version %x\n", ntx_header.version);
        printf("Root %lx\n", ntx_header.root);
        printf("Next page %lx\n", ntx_header.next_page);
        printf("Item size %x\n", ntx_header.item_size);
        printf("Key size %x\n", ntx_header.key_size);
        printf("Key dec %x\n", ntx_header.key_dec);
        printf("Max item %x\n", ntx_header.max_item);
```

```
        printf("Half page %x\n", ntx_header.half_page);
        printf("Key expression : '%s'\n\n\n", &ntx_header.key_expr);
        printf("Unique : %d\n", ntx_header.unique);
}
```

Program 12-17 simply reads the header from the NTX file into an "NTX_HEADER" structure and displays its fields.

Each ITEM in an index file has the following format:

```
typedef struct
{
        long page;
        long rec_no;
        char key;
} ITEM;
```

The key field defines the start of the key. It is actually a character array with a size defined by the key_size field in the header, but C has no way to define such a data structure. Regardless of the key's type, it is stored as a character string. A date is stored in 8 characters, for example "19900301" is March 1, 1990. A numeric is stored in an array with a size dependent on the expression upon which it was indexed. It is padded with leading zeros if necessary.

The key_dec field in the header specifies the number of decimal places used in the key. For example, a numeric of size 10 with 2 decimal places would have the following format in an NTX file - "9999999.99". There are only seven digits ahead of the decimal point. This, of course, is the same as in a database file.

These "ITEM"s are accessed indirectly through an array located at offset 2 in the page. The array consists of max_item (as defined in the header) + 1 unsigneds, which are offsets into the page where the ITEM is located. The first two bytes in the page hold an unsigned specifying the number of ITEMs used. Because of the structure of a B-tree, this number is always between half_page and max_item, except in the root page, where it is between 1 and max_item. The following structure shows this:

```
typedef struct
{
        unsigned count;
        unsigned ref;
} BUFFER;
```

Again, the "ref" field is actually an array of unsigneds of size "max item". The ref field contains the address of the start of the array.

NTX Dump

Program 12-18 displays an NTX file, assuming the appropriate typedefs in "ntxdump.h".

Program 12-18. Display an NTX File

```
/***
* ntxdump.c
*
* 1 - Verify usage (one parameter).
*
* 2 - Open the file.
*
* 3 - Read header.
*
* 4 - Display header.
*
* 5 - dump_page (root).
*
*         5.1 - dump_page:
*
*                 5.1.1 - Allocate space for page.
*
*                 5.1.2 - Seek to it and read it.
*
*                 5.1.3 - For each ITEM.
*
*                         5.1.3.1 - If lower page, dump it (call dump_page
*                                           recursively).
*
*                         5.1.3.2 - Print dbf record number.
*
*                         5.1.3.3 - Print key.
*
*                 5.1.4 - Release memory.
*/

#include "stdio.h"
#include "fcntl.h"
#include "stdlib.h"
#include "io.h"
#include "malloc.h"

#include "nandef.h"
#include "ntxdump.h"

int ntx_handle;
```

```
main(argc, argv)
int argc;
char *argv[];

{
        NTX_HEADER ntx_header;

        if (argc != 2)
        {
                printf("Usage: ntxdump file.ntx\n\n");
                exit(1);
        }

        /* open the NTX file */
        ntx_handle = open(argv[1], O_RAW | O_RDONLY);

        if (ntx_handle == -1)
        {
                printf("Error opening %s\n", argv[1]);
                exit(1);
        }

        /* read the header */
        if (read(ntx_handle, (char *) &ntx_header, sizeof(NTX_HEADER))
                                        != sizeof(NTX_HEADER))
        {
                printf("Error reading header from %s\n", argv[1]);
                exit(1);
        }

        /* print the header information */
        printf("****** NTX HEADER *****\n");
        printf("Sign %x\n", ntx_header.sign);
        printf("Version %x\n", ntx_header.version);
        printf("Root %lx\n", ntx_header.root);
        printf("Next page %lx\n", ntx_header.next_page);
        printf("Item size %x\n", ntx_header.item_size);
        printf("Key size %x\n", ntx_header.key_size);
        printf("Key dec %x\n", ntx_header.key_dec);
        printf("Max item %x\n", ntx_header.max_item);
        printf("Half page %x\n", ntx_header.half_page);
        printf("Key expression : '%s'\n", ntx_header.key_expr);
        printf("Unique : %d \n\n\n", ntx_header.unique);

        /* start the traversal from root */
        dump_page(ntx_header.root);
}

/***
*       Traverse the tree, starting at this page, printing keys.
```

```
***/

dump_page(page_off)
long page_off;

{
        char *page;
        ITEM *item;
        BUFFER *buffer;
        unsigned i;
        unsigned *item_ref;

        /* allocate page dynamically to avoid using stack space */
        page = malloc(BUFF_SIZE);

        /* move to this position in the file */
        lseek(ntx_handle, page_off, 0);

        /* read the page */
        if (read(ntx_handle, page, BUFF_SIZE) != BUFF_SIZE)
        {
                printf("Error reading page %lx\n", page_off);
                exit(1);
        }

        /* do the pointer conversions to handle C's inadequacy */
        buffer = (BUFFER *) page;
        item_ref = &buffer -> ref;

        /* step through array printing items and traversing pages */
        for (i = 0; i < buffer -> count; i++)
        {
                item = (ITEM *) &page[item_ref[i]];
                if (item -> page)
                        dump_page(item -> page);

                printf("dbf rec num %lx\n", item -> rec_no);
                printf("key :     %.20s\n\n", &item -> key);
        }

        /* handle extra right pointer */
        item = (ITEM *) &page[item_ref[buffer -> count]];
        if (item -> page)
                dump_page(item -> page);

        free(page);
}
```

The dump_page routine takes the page's location as a parameter (the root page initially) and then traverses the tree, printing the keys and record numbers. It constructs a pointer to ITEM i with &page[item_ref[i]].

The routine calls itself recursively to dump other pages in the tree, an elegant solution since a tree is a recursive data structure.

> **TIP**
>
> Use NTXDUMP as a quick way to view the keys in an NTX file. This is useful in debugging where you may need to verify that keys are being updated correctly.

NDX File Structure

NDX files also use a modified B-tree system. They differ from NTX files as follows:

- NDX files have 512 byte pages.
- There is no pointer array at the beginning of each page.
- Pointers to other pages are in terms of record numbers and therefore must be multiplied by the record size to get the file offset. Contrast this with Clipper's absolute file offsets.
- Numeric and date indexes are represented as floating point numbers stored in IEEE format, occupying 8 bytes. Character indexes are simply ASCII characters, padded on the right with spaces if necessary.
- The keys in all pages not at the bottom of the tree are simply "direction pointers". They have a DBF record number of zero and are duplicated in the bottom pages. Figure 12-7 shows this. It uses the same keys as in the NTX file diagram (Figure 12-4).

Figure 12-7. Example NDX File Structure

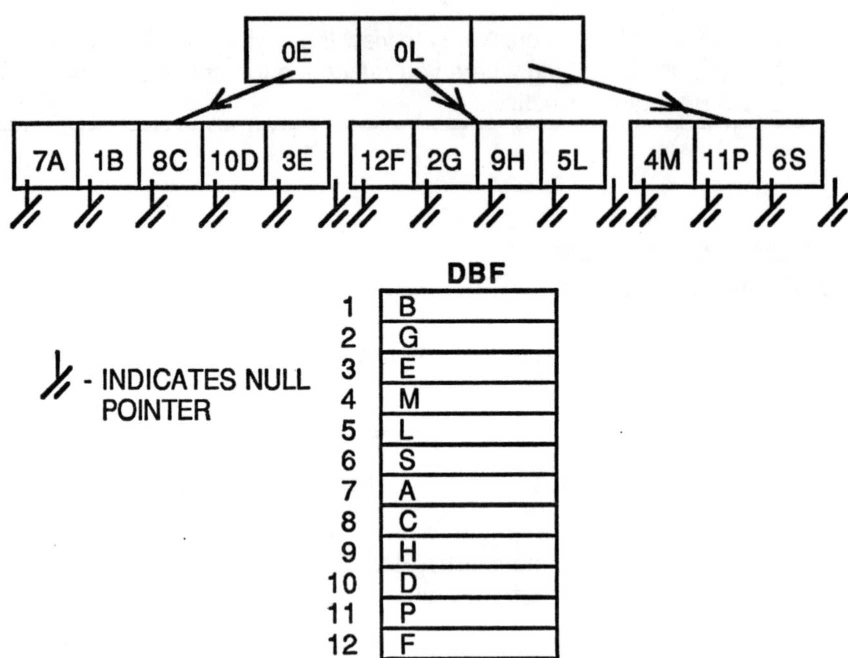

The following C structure defines the header of an NDX file:

```
typedef struct
{
        long start_key_page;
        long total_pages_in_file;
        long filler1;
        unsigned index_key_len;
        unsigned max_keys_page;
        unsigned ndx_key_type;
        long size_key_rec;
        char filler2;
        char unique;
        char key_name[488];
} NDX_HEADER;
```

The members are:

start_key_page - the record number of the root page.

total_pages_in_file - the number of 512 byte pages in the file.

filler1 - 4 bytes of unused space.

index_key_len - the size of the key.

max_keys_page - the maximum number of keys that can fit in one page.

ndx_key_type - the type of key on which the index was built. A value of 01 indicates numeric, 00 character. This is necessary because of the way different key types are represented in the NDX file (described later in this chapter).

size_key_rec - the size of a KEY_REC (subsequently described), and thus the distance between KEY_RECs.

filler2 - another byte of unused space.

unique - has a value of 1 if the index was created with UNIQUE on, and of 0 otherwise.

The offsets of the fields are:

```
00          long start_key_page;
04          long total_pages_in_file;
08          long filler1;
0C          unsigned index_key_len;
0E          unsigned max_keys_page;
10          unsigned ndx_key_type;
12          long size_key_rec;
16          char filler2;
17          char unique;
18          char key_name[488];
```

Each NDX page starts with a long specifying the number of KEY_RECs, followed by the KEY_RECs themselves. Once again, because of Cs limitations, we define a structure in which "first_key_rec" points to an array of KEY_RECs:

```
typedef struct
{
        long num_key_recs_this_page;
        KEY_REC first_key_rec;
} NDX_PAGE;
```

The following C structure defines a KEY_REC:

```
typedef struct
{
        long left_page_num;
        long dbf_rec_num;
```

```
        char key_data;
    } KEY_REC;
```

left_page_num - is the record number of the page to the left of this key.

dbf_rec_num - is the record number in the DBF file where this key originated.

key_data - is the start of the actual key.

Program 12-19 dumps an NDX file, assuming the definitions of NDX_HEADER, NDX_PAGE, and KEY_REC in ndxdump.h.

Program 12-9. Display an NDX File Header

```
/***
* ndxdump.c
*
* 1 - Verify usage (one parameter).
*
* 2 - Open the file.
*
* 3 - Read header.
*
* 4 - Display header.
*
* 5 - dump_page (root).
*
*       5.1 - dump page.
*
*           5.1.1 - Allocate space for page.
*
*           5 1.2 - Seek to it and read it.
*
*           5.1.3 - Print all keys.
*
*           5.1.4 - For each ITEM
*
*               5.1.4.1 - If lower page, dump it (call dump page
*                                   recursively).
*
*           5.1.5 - Release memory.
*/

#include "stdio.h"
#include "stdlib.h"
#include "fcntl.h"
#include "io.h"
#include "malloc.h"
```

```
#include "ndxdump.h"

NDX_HEADER ndx_header;
int ndx_handle;

main(argc, argv)

int argc;
char *argv[];

{
        if (argc != 2)
        {
                printf("usage: ndxdump file.ndx\n\n");
                exit(1);
        }

        ndx_handle = open(argv[1], O_RAW | O_RDONLY);

        if (read(ndx_handle, (char *) &ndx_header, sizeof(NDX_HEADER))
                        != sizeof(NDX_HEADER))
        {
                printf("Error reading %s\n", argv[1]);
                exit(1);
        }

        printf("start key page %lx\n", ndx_header.start_key_page);
        printf("Total pages in file %lx\n", ndx_header.total_pages_in_file);
        printf("Inαex key len %x\n", ndx_header.index_key_len);
        printf("Max keys page %x\n", ndx_header.max_keys_page);
        printf("size key rec %lx\n", ndx_header.size_key_rec);
        printf("key name: '%s'\n", ndx_header.key_name);
        printf("ndx key type %x\n", ndx_header.ndx_key_type);
        printf("Unique %d\n", ndx_header.unique);

        dump_page(ndx_header.start_key_page);
}

/***
* dump_page()
*
*       Page number passed. Display keys, the continue recursively for lower pages.
*/

dump_page(page_num)

long page_num;

{
        char *page;
        KEY_REC *key_rec;
        NDX_PAGE *ndx_page;
```

```
char *ptr;
unsigned i;
double *dptr;

page = (char *) malloc(512);
lseek(ndx_handle, page_num * 512, 0);

if (read(ndx_handle, page, 512) != 512)
{
        printf("Error reading page number %lx\n", page_num);
        exit(1);
}

ndx_page = (NDX_PAGE *) page;
ptr = (char *) &ndx_page ->first_key_rec;

key_rec = (KEY_REC *) ptr;

printf("*************************************************\n");
printf("PAGE NUM %lx\n", page_num);
printf("NUM KEY RECS THIS PAGE %lx\n\n",
                ndx_page -> num_key_recs_this_page);

for (i = 0; i < ndx_page -> num_key_recs_this_page; i++)
{
        printf("         LEFT PAGE %lx\n", key_rec -> left_page_num);
        printf("         dbf rec num %lx\n", key_rec -> dbf_rec_num);

        if (ndx_header.ndx_key_type == 0)        /* char */
                printf("         key: %.10s\n\n", &key_rec -> key_data);
        else
        {
                dptr = (double *) (&key_rec->key_data);
                printf("key: %e\n\n", *dptr);
        }

        ptr += ndx_header.size_key_rec;
        key_rec = (KEY_REC *) ptr;
}

printf("\n        RIGHT PAGE %lx\n", key_rec -> left_page_num);

printf("\n\n");

ptr = (char *) &ndx_page -> first_key_rec;

key_rec = (KEY_REC *) ptr;

for (i = 0; i <= ndx_page -> num_key_recs_this_page; i++)
{
        if (key_rec -> left_page_num)
                dump_page(key_rec -> left_page_num);
```

```
            ptr += ndx_header.size_key_rec;
            key_rec = (KEY_REC *) ptr;
        }
        free(page);
}
```

The dump_page routine takes an NDX record number as a parameter. It converts the number to an offset by multiplying it by the size of the NDX page (512). It then seeks to and reads the page, prints the keys, and processes lower pages by calling itself recursively. Note the checking of the type of the key before printing. The routine prints numeric keys (including dates) with the "e" formatting character.

> **TIP**
>
> Use ndxdump to view index files when you are using Clipper's NDX option.

Hints and Warnings

- Use the stand-alone routines developed in this chapter to dump Clipper files. They are smaller and faster than the equivalent Clipper programs.
- If your files become corrupt, you may be able to use the information in this section to fix them. For example, if you accidentaly ZAP a database, the records are still present, but the last_rec field in the database header is set to 0. Changing this field with DEBUG allows the file to be recovered.
- Remember that C represents longs, unsigneds, and ints in byte-reversed form.
- Use the dbf_create code rather than CREATE and CREATE FROM. The function is faster and easier to use.
- Use the memo file pack routine rather than a database COPY to directly pack your memo files.
- Remember to use the RAW I/O mode in all C code that handles binary files.

Appendix A - Using a Preprocessor with Clipper

Overview

A preprocessor is a program run before a compiler to enhance a language while maintaining source code compatibility. It lets you include features the compiler does not support.

The preprocessor converts its input file, embellished with the unsupported features, into an output file acceptable to the compiler. The compiler never sees the original source file - it sees only the translated version. The extended features supported by a preprocessor usually appears as single line statements. The preprocessor processes them, then replaces them in the output file with blank lines. The programmer can work exclusively with the source file, as the line numbers in the output file are the same.

The PRE/DB preprocessor we will describe is intended specifically for use with the Clipper/dBASE language. It is modeled on the C preprocessor and accepts its commands with some special modifications and additions. Information concerning its publisher and developer appears at the end of this Appendix.

We will show how the preprocessor extends and enhances the Clipper language. We will also give examples of how it can save memory and increase the speed of your applications.

Preprocessors in General

As we said, a preprocessor is a translator. It takes your source code and translates it from an extended dialect to 'plain vanilla code'. It is like a compiler prepass. It takes the input file, processes it, and produces an output file. If you put the preprocessing command in your batch (or make) file, the extra stage is transparent. You always work with the original source file containing the preprocessor commands.

C programmers have long recognized the benefits of a preprocessor. In fact the language definition specifies one.

However, the C preprocessor is not compatible with Clipper code. It does not allow Clipper comments, nor can it handle the TEXT...ENDTEXT construct. The Clipper preprocessor overcomes these and many other problems.

We now describe the features the preprocessor adds to the Clipper language.

True Constants

Throughout this book we have recommended the use of "pseudo-constants" to make code easier to read. For example, the code:

```
ESC=27
IF inkey() = ESC
     •
     •
```

is easier to understand than

```
IF Inkey() = 27
     •
     •
```

The first version is also more portable. If, for example, you decided to use an EBCDIC keyboard where the Escape key was not 27, you would only need to change the definition.

Since Clipper does not allow symbolic constants, we must use memory variables instead. We call them "pseudo-constants," as it is possible to change their values. This can introduce subtle errors. If, for example, some part of the code changed ESC accidentally or used it for some other purpose, we would run into problems that would be difficult to trace.

The preprocessor lets us define true constants. Whenever one is referenced, the preprocessor replaces it with the defined value. The output is thus acceptable to the compiler. The syntax for defining a constant is simple. You follow the preprocessor command #define with the constant's name and value. For example, the following preprocessor command assigns the name ESC to keyboard code 27:

```
#define ESC 27
```

The preprocessor replaces the directive with a blank line and replaces all subsequent occurrences of ESC with 27.

The most common use for constants is as key values. The 'init_consts' routine used throughout the book defined an entire series of key values. The preprocessor lets us define them as true constants with the #define statement. Other uses are for array sizes, screen coordinates, box strings, and flag values.

The fact that no change can occur is not the only benefit of using constant rather than memory variables. Each memory variable requires 22 bytes. By using symbolic names and the preprocessor, we can thus save memory. In addition, unused constants do not increase program size. You could create a file with every key defined by a constant, with no overhead. For example, we could have:

```
#define ESC 27
#define F1 28
#define F2 -1
...etc
```

in all our programs. If we do not use some constants, they are not included. The preprocessor lets you define symbols in terms of other symbols. For example, we could define constants for a window's coordinates with

```
#define WIND_WIDTH 50
#define WIND_HEIGHT 10

#define WIND_TOP_R 10
#define WIND_TOP_C 10
#define WIND_BOT_R (WIND_TOP_R + WIND_HEIGHT)
#define WIND_BOT_C (WIND_TOP_C + WIND_WIDTH)
```

and then use them in

```
* Clear window
Scroll(WIND_TOP_R, WIND_TOP_C, WIND_BOT_R, WIND_BOT_C, 0)
```

The preprocessor converts the scroll statement to

```
Scroll(10, 10, (10 + 10), (10 + 50), 0)
```

If later you decide to place the window higher on the screen, you would only have to change the constant WIND_TOP_R to 5. The window would then start on line 5 and be exactly the same size. Using constants thus makes programs easier to maintain.

Note that the preprocessor replaced WIND_BOT_R with (10 + 10), not 20. This is important. The preprocessor only SUBSTITUTES text, it does not PROCESS it.

The following code shows a common error when using a preprocessor.

```
#define NAME_SIZE 30
#define ADDR_SIZE 60

#define REC_SIZE NAME_SIZE + ADDR_SIZE
#define MAX_RECS 50

? REC_SIZE, " bytes per record"
? MAX_RECS, " records allowed"
? MAX_RECS * REC_SIZE, " total bytes"
```

The code produces the following output when it is preprocessed, compiled, and run:

```
90 bytes per record
50 records allowed 1560 total bytes
```

This is incorrect! We expected 90 * 50 or 4500 total bytes. To understand what went wrong, we must look at the preprocessor output. It appears as follows:

```
<6 blank lines>
? 30+60, " bytes per record"
? 50, " records allowed"
? 50 * 30+60, " total bytes"
```

Clipper evaluates expressions in algebraic order. The expression 50 * 30 + 60 is equivalent to (50 * 30) + 60 or 1560! When using a preprocessor, you must use parentheses to insure the proper order of evaluation. To correct the program, replace:

```
#define REC_SIZE NAMESIZE + ADDRSIZE
```

with

```
#define REC_SIZE (NAMESIZE + ADDRSIZE)
```

As a rule, use parentheses around all expressions in #defines.

Note that we use the C convention of uppercase names for defined constants. There are two reasons for this. One is that it makes constants stand out in your program. The other is that some preprocessors are case sensitive. Thus the identifier ESCAPE is different from Escape. By using only uppercase letters, we can easily differentiate between ordinary variables and constants.

Inline Functions

An inline function is substituted into the code directly instead of being called as a subroutine. We often refer to this as a macro capability. Since Clipper has a runtime macro facility, we will use the term 'inline function' to differentiate the preprocessor facility.

Inline functions can speed execution and increase readability. However, replacing each occurrence of the inline function call with the actual code may make the program larger. This occurs if the function is long and is used often. Generally, the speed increase still makes the use worthwhile.

To show why the inline function is faster, let us look at what the compiler must do to call a function. A general outline is:

Save state variables

Copy arguments and put them in Clipper's stack.

Call the function.

Create space for the function's variables.

Execute the function code.

Put the function's result on the stack.

Restore state variables

Return to the code where we left off.

An inline function avoids all steps except for the actual execution of the code. This can produce significant time savings. If the function is small, it can also save memory.

An example inline function determines whether a specific key has been pressed. We would write it as:

```
FUNCTION key_pressed

PARAM key

RETURN (inkey() = key)
```

We could use the function in the while clause of a batch command, allowing it to be terminated by the user pressing the Escape key. Here is an example involving the REPORT FORM command:

```
ESC = 27
•
•
•
REPORT FORM ... WHILE !key_pressed(ESC)
```

The command executes until it terminates or the user presses the Escape key.

A good optimizing compiler would recognize that a call would take more space and time than the function itself. However, Clipper does not recognize this. Although you could replace the code yourself, it becomes less readable and requires more typing. So we define an inline function. The preprocessor replaces each occurrence with the actual code. We could rewrite the previous example as:

```
#define KEY_PRESSED(key) (Inkey() = key)
```

Later when the key_pressed function appears in our code as:

```
REPORT FORM ... WHILE !KEY_PRESSED(ESC)
```

the preprocessor replaces it with

```
REPORT FORM ... WHILE !(inkey() = 27)
```

This solution is significantly faster and uses much less memory! Since the programmer works only with the preprocessor version, he or she sees only the more readable inline function code.

As you can see, the inline function is basically a #define with parameters. It has the same concept of formal and actual parameter lists as do user defined functions and procedures.

However, there are restrictions on inline functions with Clipper. The function must consist of just one expression. You could not use one to replace a function such as a database lookup, as it requires several lines of code. Also, as we noted previously, inline functions may increase the program's size. If speed is your only concern, however, inline functions are almost always faster.

Conditional Compilation

Conditional compilation lets you include (or exclude) code based on a condition. The usual purpose is to maintain different versions of a program without having separate copies of the source code. One example is a complete version of a program and a simple demonstration version. Another example is a version for dBASE III and one for Clipper.

The preprocessor's conditional commands are much like dBASE/ Clipper conditional statements. The five statements are:

- #if
- #ifdef
- #else
- #endif
- #ifndef

The #if statement evaluates a condition. It can only use variables defined in preprocessor #define statements, since it is evaluated before the program is compiled. The #ifdef and #ifndef statements determine whether a symbol has been defined, or has not been, respectively. The #else and #endif behave just like their Clipper counterparts.

The following code shows the use of conditional compilation to maintain both a demonstration and a real version of a program in the same source file.

```
* Main Menu code

* Remove comment from next line to produce Demo Version
* #define DEMO

#ifdef DEMO
```

```
*******************DEMO VERSION*********************
          count = 0
          DO WHILE count < 10 .and. lastkey() <> ESC
                    count = count + 1
                    DO mainmenu
          ENDDO

          ? "Demo version finished. To order, call...."
          QUIT
#else
          DO WHILE lastkey() <> ESC
           DO mainmenu
          ENDDO
#endif
```

If the symbol DEMO is defined, the preprocessor includes the code between the #ifdef and the #else in the output file. If not, it includes the code between the #else and the #endif. The lines excluded from the output file are replaced with blank lines to maintain numbering.

The preprocessor would produce the following output:

```
* Main Menu code

* Remove comment from next line to produce Demo Version
* #define DEMO

<10 blank lines>
          DO WHILE lastkey() <> ESC
           DO mainmenu
          ENDDO
```

Note that the output does not include code specific to the DEMO version. The compiled program is the same size as it would be if no demonstration code existed.

The following program section shows the use of conditional compilation to maintain dBASE and Clipper versions of a program in the same source file:

```
#ifdef CLIP
          choice = 0
          @ 01, 10 PROMPT "Menu Option 1"
          @ 02, 10 PROMPT "Menu Option 2"
          @ 03, 10 PROMPT "Menu Option 3"
          @ 04, 10 PROMPT "Menu Option 4"
          MENU TO choice
#else
          choice = 0
          @ 01, 10 SAY "Menu Option 1"
          @ 02, 10 SAY "Menu Option 2"
          @ 03, 10 SAY "Menu Option 3"
          @ 04, 10 SAY "Menu Option 4"
```

```
        @ 05, 10 SAY "Enter Choice:" GET choice RANGE 0,4
        Read
    #endif
```

If CLIP is defined, the user will see a bounce bar menu. If not, he or she will see a standard list menu that is dBASE compatible.

Clipper provides a less attractive alternative to conditional compilation. By default, Clipper gives all undefined PUBLIC variables the value .F.. The public variable CLIPPER is an exception. If declared, it is given the value .T.. Since dBASE does not do this, you can enclose Clipper specific code within an IF CLIPPER construct. At run time, this code will be executed if compiled with Clipper. If interpreted under dBASE, however, the ELSE clause will be executed. dBASE will not complain about the Clipper specific code within the IF CLIPPER construct, as it will never see it.

Clipper, on the other hand, generates errors for dBASE commands it does not support. It compiles both sides of the IF statement. It does not know that the ELSE side will not be executed at run time. It will also generate code for valid commands, even though they will never be executed. This makes the EXE file larger than if you had used conditional compilation.

Include Files

One key warning to preprocessor users is that #define's only affect the file in which they are contained. Thus, if we want every PRG file to have access to defined keys, we must include the long #define list in each one. Include files overcome this problem. They allow preprocessor commands to be placed in a separate file. The #include directive directs the preprocessor to include the specified file. The result is the same as if all the definitions had been placed in the actual source file.

For example, we could place all key definitions in one include file and include it in any program that requires it. If the include file is "keys.h", we could do this with:

```
#include "keys.h"
```

Although actual source code can appear in include files, putting it there is not a good practice. The lines of code are included directly in the output file, and the one to one relationship between input and output file is lost. The compiler, run time, and debugger line numbers then no longer refer to the line numbers in the source file.

Examples

The final section of this Appendix contains practical examples. The first inline function assigns a default value to a variable. This is useful in functions that allow default values for parameters not passed.

```
#define P_DEFAULT(x, default) x = IIF(type([x]) = 'U', default, x)
```

You pass the function a parameter and a default value. If the parameter is not defined (its type is "U"), it is assigned the default value. This replaces the Clipper code:

```
IF type('X') = "U"
        X = Default
ENDIF
```

For example, consider a function that returns the maximum value in an array. If no parameters are passed, the search covers the entire array.

```
*Define smallest allowable value
#define MINVAL -9e97

FUNCTION arrmax                    && Find the maximum value in an array

PARAMETER arr, start, end && from element start to element end
PRIVATE mx

        * assign default values if not passed
        P_DEFAULT(Start,1)
        P_DEFAULT(End,Len(Arr))

        mx = MINVAL
        FOR i = start TO end

                mx = max(mx, arr[i])

        NEXT

RETURN mx
```

The parameters are assigned their default values if they are not passed.

A slight variation is a function that assigns the default when the parameter is not the correct type. The following definition shows this:

```
#define PT_DEFAULT(x, typ, def) x = IIF(type([x]) != typ, def, x)
```

You can use this function to pass a variable number of parameters. If you want to omit a parameter from the middle of the list, you must include a dummy. When the function checks the parameters with the PT_DEFAULT inline function, it can check for dummies by comparing the type of the argument with the expected type.

Another example function checks whether a character is a control character.

```
#define ISCTRL(X) (X < 32 .or. X > 255)
```

We can also use inline functions in debugging. To debug a program by generating error conditions, you could define a function that overrides one that is already defined. If you had a function to check for a file error fileerr(), you could define:

```
#define fileerr() .T.
```

to debug the program. Now, instead of checking for a file error, it will generate one automatically. When you finish debugging, just remove this line.

Other useful functions are:

```
*       str() without leading spaces
#define lstr(N, W, D) ltrim(str(N, W, D))

*       Pad a string to width W
#define pad(S, W)   Subs(S + Space(W), 1, W)

*       More meaningful name for file()
#define exists(fl) file(fl)

*       Mathematical FLOOR function
#define floor(x) int(x)

*       Mathematical CEILING function
#define ceiling(x) int(x + .5)

*       Clear window
#define clearwin(x1, y1, x2, y2) scroll(x1, y1, x2, y2, 0)
```

Summary

- A preprocessor translates extensions to a language into normal syntax that is acceptable to the compiler.
- The PRE/DB preprocessor for Clipper lets you define true constants using the #define command.
- The preprocessor allows inline functions that are directly substituted into the program instead of being called.
- The preprocessor lets you compile parts of the program depending on conditions using the #ifdef, #else, and #endif commands.
- The preprocessor lets you include files in your programs by using the #include command.

Distribution

In the U.S.A., PRE/DB, the dBASE language preprocessor (developed by Rick Spence), is available from:

Pinnacle Publishing Inc,
535 Dock St.,
Tacoma,
WA 98402

1-(800)-231-1293

Elsewhere, order from:

Fidelio Software,
Widenmayertrasse 6 / III,
D - 8000,
Munchen 22,
West Germany.

(089) - 291-3361

Appendix B - The SET Functions

Here is the source for the SET functions described in Chapter 11.
The include file libexts.h defines the externals:

```
/***
*       LIBEXTS.H
*/


/* types */
typedef struct
{
        quant key_val;
        char *key_routine;
} KEY_SET;          /* 6 bytes */


/* number of keys that can be set, 32 + help */
#define KEY_SET_COUNT 33

extern KEY_SET _keyset[KEY_SET_COUNT];

extern Boolean _alternate_on;
extern Boolean _alt_open;
extern int _alt_handle;
extern Boolean _bell_on;
extern Boolean _century_on;
extern Boolean _confirm_on;
extern Boolean _console_on;
extern Boolean _curs_on;
extern Boolean _date_mode;
extern Boolean _decimals;
extern char _default_drive;
extern Boolean _deleted_on;
extern Boolean _delimiters_on;
extern unsigned _device_p;
extern Boolean _escape_on;
extern Boolean _exact_on;
extern Boolean _exclu_on;
extern long _fkeys;
extern long _fmt_sym;
extern Boolean _fixed_on;
extern Boolean _intensity_on;
extern Boolean _insert_mode;
extern char _ldelim;
extern char _rdelim;
```

```
extern unsigned _margin;
extern unsigned _message;
extern char _path;
extern Boolean _print_on;
extern char _print;
extern int _p_handle;
extern int _to_print;
extern int _to_handle;
extern int _to_file;
extern Boolean _score_on;
extern Boolean _softseek;
extern unsigned _type;
extern Boolean _unique_on;
extern Boolean _wrap_on;
```

Here is the C code. All functions have the general format described in Chapter 11.

```
/***
*       STATUS.C
*
*               Return states of various sets
*        LOGICALs return 1 when ON, 0 when OFF
*
*        Doesn't handle SET MESSAGE, SET TYPEAHEAD, or SET FUNCTION
*/

#include "nandef.h"
#include "extend.h"
#include "libexts.h"

#include "stdio.h"
#include "stdlib.h"

#include "memory.h"
#include "string.h"

#include "dos.h"

/* maximum depth of stack */
#define STACK_DEPTH  10

char *set_key_stack[STACK_DEPTH];
unsigned sk_ptr = 0;


/***
*  LOGICAL push_keys
*
*          Push the current states of the 'hot' keys
*/
```

```
CLIPPER push_keys()

{
        Boolean ret_val;

        /* If no stack overflow ... */
        if (sk_ptr < STACK_DEPTH)
        {
                if (set_key_stack[sk_ptr] = malloc(sizeof(_keyset)))
                {
                        /* push onto stack by copying and incrementing pointer */
                        memcpy(set_key_stack[sk_ptr], (char *) _keyset, sizeof(_keyset));
                        sk_ptr++;
                        ret_val = TRUE;
                }
                else  /* couldn't allocate memory - complain */
                        ret_val = FALSE;
        }
        else
                /* stack would overflow, so complain */
                ret_val = FALSE;

        _retl(ret_val);
}


/***
*  LOGICAL push_ckeys()
*
*  Push the current states of 'hot' keys, then clear them.
*
*/


CLIPPER push_ckeys()

{
        Boolean ret_val;

        /* if no stack overflow */
        if (sk_ptr < STACK_DEPTH)
        {
                if (set_key_stack[sk_ptr] = malloc(sizeof(_keyset)))
                {
                        /* save them */
                        memcpy(set_key_stack[sk_ptr], (char *) _keyset, sizeof(_keyset));
                        sk_ptr++;

                        /* now clear them */
                        memset((char *) _keyset, 0, sizeof(_keyset));
                        ret_val = TRUE;
                }
```

```
			else	/* memory allocation failed, complain */
				ret_val = FALSE;
		}
		else		/* stack would overflow, complain */
			ret_val = FALSE;

		_retl(ret_val);
}


/***
*  LOGICAL pop_keys()
*
*  Restore keys from top of stack.
*/

CLIPPER pop_keys()

{
		Boolean ret_val;

		/* if stack not empty */
		if (sk_ptr > 0)
		{
			sk_ptr--;
			memcpy((char *) _keyset, set_key_stack[sk_ptr], sizeof(_keyset));

			/* return memory to free pool */
			free(set_key_stack[sk_ptr]);
			ret_val = TRUE;
		}
		else	/* stack was empty so complain */
			ret_val = FALSE;

		_retl(ret_val);
}


/***
*  NUMERIC key_set()
*
*  Get/set state of a function key.  If parameter, set to its
*  value.  Previous value returned.  Value passed must be one returned from
*  this function previously.
*/

CLIPPER key_set()

{
		Boolean ret_val;
		unsigned i, key_look;
```

```
	/* get key under consideration */
	key_look = _parni(1);

	/* search for this key */
	for (i = 0; i < KEY_SET_COUNT && _keyset[i].key_val != key_look; i++)
		;

	if (i < KEY_SET_COUNT)
	{
		/* found, so return its pointer value */
		_retnl((long) _keyset[i].key_routine);
	}
	else
	{
		/* not found, return 0 */
		_retnl(0l);
	}

	/* if this key needs to be set, set it */
	if (PCOUNT == 2)
	{
		/* if we found it before, overwrite the value */
		if (i < KEY_SET_COUNT)
			_keyset[i].key_routine = (char *) _parnl(2);
		else
		{
			/* didn't find it, so look for blank spot, 0 */
			for (i = 0; i < KEY_SET_COUNT &&
						_keyset[i].key_val != 0; i++)
				;

			/* Was blank spot found? */
			if (i < KEY_SET_COUNT)
			{
				/* yes, set new key and pointer */
				_keyset[i].key_val = key_look;
				_keyset[i].key_routine = (char *) _parnl(2);
			}
			/* else can't do anything, table full */
		}
	}
}


/***
*	NUMERIC real_curs()
*
*	Get/set the real cursor from BIOS data area. In a prompt, for example,
*	cursor is off, regardless of the state of SET CURSOR.  If parameter is
*	passed, real cursor is set to its value.  Previous value is returned.
*/
```

```
CLIPPER real_curs()

{
        union REGS inregs;
        union REGS outregs;
        int *cur_ptr;

        /* return state of real cursor */
        /* BIOS keeps two bytes at segment 40, offset 60 */
        cur_ptr = (int *) 0x460;
        _retni(*cur_ptr);

        /* if parameter was passed, set cursor to its value */
        if (PCOUNT)
        {
                /* set to new value */

                /* Registers CH and CL must have start and end lines */
                inregs.x.cx = _parni(1);

                /* Function 01 (AH = 01) */
                inregs.x.ax = 0x0100;

                /* make BIOS call */
                int86(0x10, &inregs, &outregs);
        }
}


/***
*  LOGICAL alt_on()
*
*  Return/set state of SET ALTERNATE ON.  If parameter, set to
*  its value.  Previous state is returned.
*/

CLIPPER alt_on()

{
        _retl(_alternate_on);

        if (PCOUNT)
                _alternate_on = _parl(1);
}


/***
*  NUMERIC alt_hand()
*
*  Get/set the file handle of the ALTERNATE file.  If parameter,
*  set to its value.  Previous state is returned.
*/
```

```
CLIPPER alt_hand()

{
        _retni(_alt_handle);

        if (PCOUNT)
                _alt_handle = _parni(1);
}


/***
* LOGICAL  alt_open()
*
* Get/set the state of SET ALTERNATE TO. If parameter, set to
* its value. Previous state is returned.
*/

CLIPPER alt_open()

{
        _retl(_alt_open);

        if (PCOUNT)
                _alt_open = _parl(1);
}


/***
* LOGICAL bell_on()
*
* Get/set state of SET BELL. If parameter, set to its value.
* Previous value is returned.
*/


CLIPPER bell_on()

{
        _retl(_bell_on);

        if (PCOUNT)
                _bell_on = _parl(1);
}


/***
* LOGICAL cent_on()
*
* Get/set state of SET CENTURY. IF parameter, set to its value.
* Previous value is returned.
*/
```

```
CLIPPER cent_on()

{
        _retl(_century_on);

        if (PCOUNT)
                _century_on = _parl(1);
}


/***
*  LOGICAL conf_on()
*
*  Get/set state of SET CONFIRM. If parameter, set to its value
*  Previous value is returned.
*/


CLIPPER conf_on()

{
        _retl(_confirm_on);

        if (PCOUNT)
                _confirm_on = _parl(1);
}


/***
*  LOGICAL cons_on()
*
*  Get/set state of SET CONSOLE.  If parameter, set to its value.
*  Previous value is returned.
*/

CLIPPER cons_on()

{
        _retl(_console_on);

        if (PCOUNT)
                _console_on = _parl(1);
}


/***
*  LOGICAL curs_on()
*
*  Get/set state of SET CURSOR.  If parameter, set to its value.
*  Previous value is returned.
*/
```

```
CLIPPER curs_on()

{
        _retl(_curs_on);

        if (PCOUNT)
         _curs_on = _parl(1);
}


/***
*       NUMERIC date_mode()
*
*       Get/set state of SET DATE TO.  If parameter, set to its value.
*       Previous value is returned.
*/

CLIPPER date_mode()

{
        _retni(_date_mode);

        if (PCOUNT)
                _date_mode = _parni(1);
}


/***
*       NUMERIC decimals()
*
*       Get/set state of SET DECIMALS TO.  If parameter, set to its value.
*       Previous value is returned.  Value is 2 by default.
*/

CLIPPER decimals()

{
        _retni(_decimals);

        if (PCOUNT)
                _decimals = _parni(1);
}


/***
*       CHARACTER def_drive()
*
*       Get/set current state of SET DEFAULT TO. If parameter, set to its
*       state. Previous value is returned.  The string is null-terminated.
*       Maximum of 64 charcaters including null.
*/
```

```
CLIPPER def_drive()

{
        _retc((char *) &_default_drive);

        if (PCOUNT)
                strcpy((char *) &_default_drive, _parc(1));
}


/***
*       LOGICAL delet_on()
*
*       Get/set state of SET DELETED.  If parameter, set to its value.
*       Return previous state.
*/

CLIPPER delet_on()

{
        _retl(_deleted_on);

        if (PCOUNT)
                _deleted_on = _parl(1);
}


/***
*       LOGICAL delim_on()
*
*       Get/set state of SET DELIMITERS.  If parameter, set to its value.
*       Previous value is returned.
*/

CLIPPER delim_on()

{
        _retl(_delimiters_on);

        if (PCOUNT)
                _delimiters_on = _parl(1);
}



/***
*       NUMERIC device()
*
*       Get/set current state of SET DEVICE TO.  If parameter, set to its
*       value.  Previous state is returned. PRINTER is 1, SCREEN is 0.
*/
```

```
CLIPPER device()

{
        _retni(_device_p);

        if (PCOUNT)
                _device_p = _parni(1);
}


/***
*  LOGICAL escape_on()
*
*  Get/set current state of SET ESCAPE. If parameter, set to its
*  value. Previous value is returned.
*/

CLIPPER escape_on()

{
        _retl(_escape_on);

        if (PCOUNT)
                _escape_on = _parl(1);
}


/***
*  LOGICAL exact_on()
*
*  Get/set current state of EXACT ON. If parameter, set to its
*  value.  Previous value is returned.
*/


CLIPPER exact_on()

{
        _retl(_exact_on);

        if (PCOUNT)
                _exact_on = _parl  (1);
}


/***
*  LOGICAL exclus_on()
*
*  Get/set state of SET EXCLUSIVE. If parameter, set to its
*  value. Current (possibly new) value is returned.
*/
```

```
CLIPPER exclus_on()

{
        _retl(_exclu_on);

        if (PCOUNT)
                _exclu_on = _parni(1);
}


/***
*  NUMERIC fkeys()
*
*  Get/set state of SET FUNCTION TO pointer.  If parameter, set
*  to its value.  Return previous pointer.  The value returned is a
*  pointer, so do not tamper with it.  Set it to 0 to clear all.
*/

CLIPPER fkeys()

{
        _retnl(_fkeys);

        if (PCOUNT)
                _fkeys = _parnl(1);
}


/***
*  NUMERIC fmt_sym()
*
*  Get/set state of SET FORMAT TO.  If parameter, set to its
*  value. Previous value is returned.  The value returned
*  is a pointer, so do not tamper with it.  Set to 0 to clear.
*/

CLIPPER fmt_sym()

{
        _retnl(_fmt_sym);

          (PCOUNT)
                _fmt_sym = _parnl(1);
}


/***
*  LOGICAL fixed_on().
*
*  Get/set state of SET FIXED. If parameter, set to its
*  value. Previous value is returned.
*/
```

```
CLIPPER fixed_on()

{
  _retl(_fixed_on);

        if (PCOUNT)
                _fixed_on = _parl(1);
}


/***
* LOGICAL intens_on()
*
* Get/set current state of SET INTENSITY. If parameter, set to its
* value. Previous value is returned.
*/

CLIPPER intens_on()

{
        _retl(_intensity_on);

        if (PCOUNT)
                _intensity_on = _parl(1);
}


/***
* LOGICAL insert_on()
*
* Get/set state of readinsert flag. If parameter, set to its
* value. Previous value is returned.
*/


CLIPPER insert_on()

{
        _retl(_insert_mode);

        if (PCOUNT)
                _insert_mode = _parl(1);
}


/***
* CHARACTER ldelim()
*
* Get/set state of left delimiter. If parameter, set to its
* value. Previous value is returned.
*/
```

```
CLIPPER ldelim()

{
        /* just return first character */
        _retclen((char *)&_ldelim, 1);

        if (PCOUNT)
                /* just get first character */
                _ldelim = *_parc(1);
}


/***
*  CHARACTER rdelim()
*
*  Get/set state of right delimiter. If parameter, set to its
*  value.  Previous value is returned.
*/

CLIPPER rdelim()

{
        /* just return first character */
        _retclen((char *)&_rdelim, 1);

        if (PCOUNT)
                /* just get first character */
                _rdelim = *_parc(1);
}


/***
*  NUMERIC margin()
*
*  Get/set state of SET MARGIN. If parameter, set to its
*  value.  Previous value is returned.
*/

CLIPPER margin()

{
        _retni(_margin);

        if (PCOUNT)
                _margin = _parni(1);
}


/***
*  CHARACTER gpath()
*
*  Get/set state of current SET PATH. If parameter, set to its
```

```
*  value. Current (possibly new) value is returned.   This string is
*  null terminated.  Maximum length is 64 including a null.
*/

CLIPPER gpath()

{
        _retc(&_path);

        if (PCOUNT)
                strcpy(&_path, _parc(1));
}



/***
*  LOGICAL print_on()
*
*  Get/set state of SET PRINT ON.  If parameter, set to its value.
*  Return previous value.
*/

CLIPPER print_on()

{
        _retl(_print_on);

        if (PCOUNT)
                _print_on = _parl(1);
}


/***
*  NUMERIC printer_to()
*
*  Get/set handle of SET PRINTER TO file.  If parameter, set to its
*  value.  Previous value is returned.
*/

CLIPPER printer_to()

{
        _retni(_p_handle);

        if (PCOUNT)
                _p_handle = _parni(1);
}


/***
*  LOGICAL score()
*
```

```
* Get/set state of SET SCOREBOARD. If parameter, set to its
* value. Previous value is returned.
*/


CLIPPER score()

{
        _retl(_score_on);

        if (PCOUNT)
                _score_on = _score_on;
}


/***
* LOGICAL softseek()
*
* Get/set state of SET SOFTSEEK. If parameter, set to its
* value. Previous value is returned.
*/

CLIPPER softseek()

{
        _retl(_softseek);

        if (PCOUNT)
                _softseek = _parl(1);
}



/***
* LOGICAL to_file()
*
* Get/set state of TO FILE from report/label. If parameter, set
* to its value. Previous value is returned.
*/


CLIPPER to_file()

{
        _retl(_to_file);

        if (PCOUNT)
                _to_file = _parl(1),
}


/***
```

```
*  NUMERIC to_handle()
*
*  Get/set value of TO FILE handle from report/label. If parameter,
*  set to its value.  Previous value is returned.
*/

CLIPPER to_handle()

{
        _retni(_to_handle);

        if (PCOUNT)
                _to_handle = _parni(1);
}


/***
*  LOGICAL to_print()
*
*   Get/set state of TO PRINT from report/label. If parameter, set
*    to its value. Previous value is returned.
*/


CLIPPER to_print()

{
        _retl(_to_print);

        if (PCOUNT)
                _to_print = _parl(1);
}


/***
*  LOGICAL unique()
*
*  Get/set state of SET UNIQUE. If parameter, set to its
*  value. Previous value is returned.
*/


CLIPPER unique()

{
        _retl(_unique_on);

        if (PCOUNT)
                _unique_on = _parl(1);
}
```

```
/***
* LOGICAL wrap()
*
* Get/set state of SET WRAP.  If parameter, set to its
* value. Previous value is returned.
*/

CLIPPER wrap()

{
        _retl(_wrap_on);

        if (PCOUNT)
                _wrap_on = _parl(1);
}
```

Appendix C - Nested READ Code

```
* Nested read code. Allows nested reads to be made from VALID
* functions and from hot key procedures.
*
* Usage:
*
* 1 - Call NREAD_INIT - no parameters required
*
* 2 - Before you build a GET list, call NGET_INIT. Pass it the
*       maximum number of GETs in this GET list.
*
* 3 - For each GET in the list, call NGET. It requires:
*
*               ~ row
*               ~ column
*               ~ say
*               ~ get
*               ~ picture
*               ~ valid
*
* 4 - To do the read, call NREAD.

* The program works by issuing only one GET per READ. This way,
* compatibility and speed are guaranteed. It is Clipper that is
* doing the READ. The code handles the VALID outside the GET.
* It reissues the GET if the VALID expression returns .T., just as
* Clipper does. This way, a function executed from a VALID can
* call a nested GET without harming a pending GET list (no GET
* is currently active).
*
* Detecting the fact that a hot key called a nested read is a bit
* more difficult. Since the nested read issues a READ when it
* returns, the first GET is skipped over. Since we are issuing
* single GET READs, our READ terminates. We detect this by maintaining
* the variable num_nreads. It counts the number of times the
* NREAD function was entered. By saving its value before we issue
* the READ, and checking it after we leave, we can determine whether
* NREAD was called again. If it was, we reissue the READ. The loop
* that does this looks like:
*
*       DO WHILE !ok .OR. last_nread_num != num_nreads
*           last_nread_num = num_nreads
*           @ rows&str_read[cur_get], cols&str_read[cur_get] SAY ;
*               says&str_read[cur_get] GET &cur_name ;
```

```
*                       PICTURE pics&str_read[cur_get]
*                READ
*                .
*                .
*                .
*
* OK is set to the result of the VALID expression. We reissue the READ
* as long as it returns .F., or the nested read was called by a
* hot key.
*


* VOID nread()
*
*       Do the nested read. No parameters - uses GET list built by calls to
* nget

FUNCTION nread

PRIVATE num_gets, cur_get, ok, key, cur_valid, cur_name
PRIVATE key, more_gets, i, str_read, last_nread_num

        num_nreads = num_nreads + 1

        str_read = ltrim(str(read_num))
        num_gets = len(rows&str_read)

        * Clear any pending gets
        CLEAR GETS

        * Place all SAYs and GETs on screen

        draw_gets(num_gets, rows&str_read, cols&str_read, says&str_read, ;
                        vars&str_read, pics&str_read)

        * now clear them
        CLEAR GETS

        * current GET issued
        cur_get = 1

        * All movement keys that do not exit must go through key_handle
        SET KEY DOWN_ARROW TO key_handle
        SET KEY UP_ARROW TO key_handle
        SET KEY CTRL_HOME TO key_handle
        SET KEY CTRL_END TO key_handle

        more_gets = .T.

        DO WHILE more_gets

                CLEAR GETS
                key = 0
```

```
cur_name = vars&str_read[cur_get]

ok = .T.

* This forces loop to enter first time
last_nread_num = num_nreads - 1

DO WHILE !ok .OR. last_nread_num != num_nreads
        last_nread_num = num_nreads
        @ rows&str_read[cur_get], cols&str_read[cur_get] SAY ;
          says&str_read[cur_get] GET &cur_name ;
          PICTURE pics&str_read[cur_get]
        READ

        * save key used to exit
        key = IIF(key = 0, lastkey(), key)

        IF last_nread_num = num_nreads
                * If didn't exit with a HOT key, do valid
                * Remove this IF to allow VALID anyway
                cur_valid = valids&str_read[cur_get]

                IF "" != cur_valid
                        ok = &cur_valid
                ENDIF
        ENDIF
ENDDO

DO CASE
        CASE key = DOWN_ARROW
                IF cur_get != num_gets
                        cur_get = cur_get + 1
                ELSE
                        more_gets = !readexit()
                ENDIF

        CASE key = UP_ARROW
                IF cur_get != 1
                        cur_get = cur_get - 1
                ELSE
                        more_gets = !readexit()
                ENDIF

        CASE key = ENTER
                IF cur_get != num_gets
                        cur_get = cur_get + 1
                ELSE
                        more_gets = .F.
                ENDIF

        CASE key = ESC
                more_gets = .F.
```

```
                    CASE key = CTRL_HOME
                         cur_get = 1

                    CASE key = CTRL_END
                         cur_get = num_gets

                    CASE key = PG_UP
                         more_gets = .F.

                    CASE key = PG_DOWN
                         more_gets = .F.
               ENDCASE
          ENDDO

          RELEASE rows&str_read, cols&str_read, says&str_read
          RELEASE vars&str_read, pics&str_read, valids&str_read

          read_num = read_num - 1

     RETURN .T.

     * VOID draw_gets(num_gets, rows[], cols[], says[], vars[], pics[])
     *
     * A utility function to place GETs on screen. Used to avoid repetitive
     * macro expansion

     FUNCTION draw_gets

     PARAM num_gets, rows, cols, says, vars, pics
     PRIVATE i, cur_name

          FOR i = 1 TO num_gets

               cur_name = vars[i]

               @ rows[i], cols[i] SAY says[i] GET &cur_name ;
                         PICTURE pics[i]

          NEXT

     RETURN .T.

     * VOID nget_init(max_gets)
     *
     *  Call once per nested read before issuing any GETs for it.
     * Pass maximum number of GETs that will be issued for this READ.

     FUNCTION nget_init

     PARAM max_gets

     PRIVATE str_read
```

```
PUBLIC get_num

        read_num = read_num + 1
        str_read = ltrim(str(read_num))
        get_num = 0

        PUBLIC rows&str_read[max_gets], cols&str_read[max_gets]
        PUBLIC says&str_read[max_gets], vars&str_read[max_gets]
        PUBLIC pics&str_read[max_gets], valids&str_read[max_gets]

RETURN .T.

* VOID nget(row_num, col_num, say_str, var_name, pic_str, valid_str)
* Call once per GET to set up GET list

FUNCTION nget

PARAM row_num, col_num, say_str, var_name, pic_str, valid_str
PRIVATE str_read

        get_num = get_num + 1
        str_read = ltrim(str(read_num))

        rows&str_read[get_num] = row_num
        cols&str_read[get_num] = col_num
        says&str_read[get_num] = say_str
        vars&str_read[get_num] = var_name
        pics&str_read[get_num] = pic_str
        valids&str_read[get_num] = valid_str

RETURN .T.

* VOID nread_init
*
*       Call once per PROGRAM, just to set up global read_num for GET
* system

FUNCTION nread_init

PUBLIC read_num, num_nreads

        read_num = 0
        num_nreads = 0

RETURN .T.

* All movement keys that do not force exit go through here so we can
* allow traversal and save value. Sets PRIVATE in nread.

FUNCTION key_handle

        key = lastkey()
        KEYBOARD (chr(ENTER))

RETURN .T.
```

Index

—D—

—E—

—N—

—O—

—R—

—S—

Program Disk Available

All programs listed in Rick Spence's *Clipper Programming Guide* are available on disk. To order send $39.95, plus $3 for shipping and handling, to:

The Data Based Advisor Series
4010 Morena Blvd., Suite 200
San Diego, CA 92117

Or order by phone, (800) 336-6060 or (619) 483-6400 (weekdays 8 a.m. - 5 p.m. Pacific Time).

Visa/MasterCard, check, or money order accepted.

DATA BASED ADVISOR

[illegible]

San Diego, [illegible]

Reader Comments
Clipper® Programming Guide

This book has been edited, the edited material reviewed, and the program matter tested and checked for accuracy; but bugs find their way into books as well as software. Please take a few minutes and tell us if you have found any errors, and give us your general comments regarding the quality of this book. Your time and attention will help us improve this and future products.

Did you find any mistakes? (If so, where?) ______________________

____

____

Is this book complete? (If not, what should be added?) ______________________

____

____

What do you like about this book? ______________________

____

____

What do you not like about this book? ______________________

____

____

What other books would you like to see developed? ______________________

____

____

Other comments: ______________________

____

____

If you would like to be notified of new editions of this book and/or other books that may be of interest to you, please complete the following:

Name: ______________________

Address: ______________________

City/State/Zip: ______________________

Mail to:

Microtrend Books
Slawson Communications, Inc.
165 Vallecitos de Oro
San Marcos, CA 92069-1436